THIRD CANADI

The Family

THIRD CANADIAN EDITION

The Family

J. Ross Eshleman

Wayne State University

Susannah J. Wilson

Ryerson Polytechnic University

Toronto

Canadian Cataloguing in Publication Data

Eshleman, J. Ross
The Family

3rd Canadian ed.
Includes bibliographical references and index.
ISBN 0-205-37151-0

1. Family. 2. Marriage. 3. Family - Canada. I. Wilson, S. J. (Susannah Jane).
II. Title.

HQ515.E75 2001 306.85 C00-931171-8

ISBN 0-205-37151-0

Vice President, Editorial Director: Michael Young
Acquisitions Editor: Jessica Mosher
Marketing Manager: Judith Allen
Development Editor: Lise Creurer
Production Editors: Julia Hubble and Susan Adlam
Copy Editor: Karen Bennett
Production Coordinator: Peggy Brown
Page Layout: Debbie Kumpf
Art Direction: Julia Hall
Interior Design: Julia Hall
Cover Design: Liz Harasymczuk
Cover Image: José Ortega

1 2 3 4 5 05 04 03 02 01

Printed and bound in Canada

CONTENTS

2 MARRIAGE, FAMILY, AND KINSHIP 32

3 MARRIAGE, FAMILY, AND WORK 59

4 *Family income and social class* 90

5 *Establishing intimacy* 118

8 PARENT/CHILD INTERACTION AND SOCIALIZATION 209

9 THE MIDDLE AND LATER YEARS 239

PREFACE

This book represents a unique collaboration. As many readers will know, the third Canadian edition rests on the very sturdy foundation of nine U.S. editions authored by J. Ross Eshleman and two Canadian editions. Like the earlier editions, this one provides a thorough and objective coverage of the basic concepts and ideas in the area of marriage, families, and primary intimate relationships. We have tried to present ideas clearly and intelligibly. The coverage includes specific factual data as well as abstract principles, and empirically supported findings as well as hypotheses for testing. Since this will be the only course on the family that many students take, our goal has been to arouse a curiosity toward and provide tools for an ongoing process of observation, understanding, and analysis of marital and family relationships and organizations.

We believe an introductory family textbook should capture students' interest. The processes and organization of marital and family behaviour should be conveyed to students in a manner that is understandable, readable, and interesting, without being oversimplified. Given this foundation, students should be able to relate personal and familial values and behaviours to differing lifestyles and patterns, both within their own society and in relationship to others. That is, students should be guided to see more clearly their places in the Canadian, North American, and even world pictures.

We have tried to write a text that is comprehensive in its coverage of topics, and that emphasizes the family in Canada and supplements this discussion heavily with historical and cross-cultural references. We have also tried to document extensively in presenting the study of the family as a scholarly discipline and to encourage further thought and reading. Each chapter is documented throughout with endnote citations of sources, and each chapter ends with questions for discussion, an annotated bibliography of further readings, and relevant World Wide Web links. The latest research and census materials have been presented, and boxed-text items have been inserted to illustrate points throughout.

In writing this book, we have attempted to fulfill a number of objectives:

- To present an objective description and analysis of contemporary families within a world perspective
- To apply general theoretical schemes and frames of reference to family issues
- To present basic concepts and descriptive materials clearly and intelligibly
- To suggest questions and supplemental sources to stimulate discussion and reading beyond the text
- To illustrate material with different items of interest
- To cultivate in students an increased awareness of their particular niches in the family and general social orders

PLAN FOR THE TEXT

This third Canadian edition of *The Family* basically follows a sociological and social-psychological approach. Chapter 1 examines approaches to the study of families and theories central to understanding intimate groups, family groups, and systems. Chapter 2 illustrates the boundaries of marital, family, and kinship organization, and Chapter 3 identifies the linkages between the family and other institutions, with a major focus on the institution of paid and unpaid work.

Chapter 4 examines social-class variations in North America, including single parents and the feminization of poverty. Chapter 5 brings structure and process to the creation of a marital and family status by examining partner selection.

The next four chapters consider patterns of interaction throughout the family life course: marriage (Chapter 6), parenthood (Chapter 7), childrearing and socialization (Chapter 8), and the middle and later years, including dying, death, and the postmarital family (Chapter 9).

The next two chapters address contemporary issues in the study of marriage and the family. Chapter 10 examines the nature of family crisis and domestic violence, and Chapter 11 examines divorce and remarriage. The book concludes with a discussion of the family and social policy in Chapter 12.

As a result of an extensive review of the literature and of selected feedback from faculty and students who used previous editions, various changes appear in this edition of *The Family.* This edition is shorter than earlier versions. Many chapters have been considerably reorganized. Extensive new and updated research material will be evident throughout the text, including significant research findings on topics involving intimate relationships beyond traditional marriage/family boundaries.

As in previous editions, selected theories and frames of reference are described and applied throughout the text. Extensive use is made of recent census data and research findings, and boxed texts are provided to supplement and illustrate the basic text. Each chapter ends with several useful study aids: Summary, Key Terms and Topics, Discussion Questions, Further Readings, and Weblinks.

A glossary and name and subject indexes are provided at the end of the book.

It is our hope that students and teachers alike will find the ideas presented in *The Family* stimulating and clearly explained. We hope the book is readable and interesting, that it presents an accurate portrayal of family systems, that it allows flexible use, that it will stimulate thought and discussion, and perhaps most importantly, that it will expand readers' awareness of and sensitivity to self and others.

So that we may continue to update and fine-tune the content and presentation of material in this book, we ask that readers report to us any errors they find as well as any points with which they disagree.

ACKNOWLEDGMENTS

In the ninth U.S. edition of *The Family*, Ross Eshleman wrote:

> It is difficult to know where to begin or end in expressing a deeply felt sense of gratitude and appreciation to many people. First, I want to convey my affection for, and recognize the support received from, my own primary intimates including my wife, Janet; my daughter, Jill; my son, Sid; and his wife, Kristie. Other primary relatives, especially my first (and only) grandchild, Cam, and others—including Robert, Orpha, Effie and Jim, Joyce and Jim, and James and Monica—have been particularly influential in my life and in creating a personal awareness of the significance and importance of family. Close friends—such as John and Ginger Campbell, Millie and the late Milton Cudney, A. M. and Bebe Denton, Ralph and Zeddy Jordan, Joyce and Stewart Rhymer, Harry and Mary Frances Robertson, and John and Chris Turner—are and have been constant sources of encouragement, feedback, and meaningful relationships.
>
> I also wish to acknowledge professional colleagues and students, namely, Kathleen Baltman, Marilyn Daniels, Donald Gelfand, Janet Hankin, Katrina Henry, David Klein, Tamieka Lee, Lionel Matthews, Joe Sloan, Joe Therrien, Mary Jane VanMeter, Leon Warshay, and Leon Wilson who have made specific contributions with library resources, computer applications, editorial assistance, or ideas. And, of course, special thanks go to the persons and couples who agreed to be interviewed and who shared a segment of their personal life experiences: Andrea, Bill, Butch, Dal, David, Dee, Deloris, Effie, Henrietta, James, Jim, Joyce, Larry, Marsha, Mary, Monica, Oscar, Phyllis, Richard, Stewart, Tonya, Yvonne, and others.
>
> To single out others would require a longer list. However, several professionals in the field who used the last edition, as well as the reviewers for this edition, provided valuable reactions, comments, and suggestions: John W. Bedell, California State University–Fullerton; David M. Klein, University of Notre Dame; Pyong Gap Min, Queens College of the City University of New York; Pat Nation, Middle Tennessee State University; and Jay D. Schvaneveldt, Utah State University.
>
> Finally, Karen Hanson and Sarah Kelbaugh at Allyn and Bacon, each fulfilling her professional tasks, were influential in getting this book into its final form. Omegatype provided editorial and production assistance. To each of these individuals I extend my thanks and appreciation.

Sue Wilson is similarly indebted to her mentors and colleagues. She particularly appreciates the support she received from the School of Nutrition at Ryerson Polytechnic University in Toronto. This edition was brought to press through the efforts of Susan Adlam, Peggy Brown, Lise Creurer, Julia Hubble, and Jessica Mosher. Karen Bennett's sensitive editing was an invaluable contribution. Paul, Leslie, and Jay were patient, supportive, and helpful at appropriate moments. Thanks to all of you.

J.R.E. & S.J.W.

CHAPTER

1 MARRIAGE AND FAMILY: DISCIPLINARY AND THEORETICAL APPROACHES

The family? What is *the family?* Does the family consist of one female legally married to one male? Does the family have children, born within wedlock; a husband, employed full-time, serving as the primary provider and ultimate authority; and a wife who is a full-time mother and homemaker? Or is the family a single parent, divorced or never married, raising his or her children? Does the family include a wife who is employed full-time and a husband who chooses to be the primary child-rearer? Is a childless couple a family? Is the family a cohesive, loving, sexually exclusive unit, bound until death do them part? Or is the family sometimes less than cohesive, even conflict-ridden and abusive? Do members of the family always live together?

Sociologically, **the family** is a social group, a social system, and a social institution. As a social group, it is a collection of persons who recognize one another as family members and interact in a sexually bonded, intimate, primary network. As a social system, it has many interdependent components with major differentiations by gender, race, class, age, size, and so forth. As a social institution, the family meets broad societal goals that centre on intimate relationships and the reproduction and socialization of children.

Viewing selected patterns of behaviour as fixed has led a number of scholars to question whether the word *family* is even a meaningful concept, since it implies images of married couples, love, permanence, children, sexual exclusivity, homemakers, legal unions, and intergenerational continuity. Such scholars have questioned whether these images are more than a perceived idealism that is inconsistent with the realities of today's relationships: remarriages, dual careers, childless couples, one-parent households, same-sex unions, gender inequalities, abusive partners, and intergenerational disruptions. Some writers have asked whether it is time to begin thinking differently about the family as a social institution and system and families as pluralistic or diverse units. It is suggested that they be considered less in terms of structure and stability and more in terms of process and change, less in terms of traditional images and standards by which everything else is judged and more in terms of close relationships and sexually bonded primary relationships.[1] The former terms suggest a traditional view held by a select segment of the population, while the latter suggest a broader, comprehensive, more accurate portrayal of the reality of human, close, primary, sexually bonded relationships.

It is difficult to find terms or concepts that differentiate family from nonfamily relationships and experiences. *Family realm* has been suggested as a term that differentiates familial types of human relationships from nonfamilial types such as political, economic, medical, educational, military, and artistic relationships.[2] More recently, the concept of *family transcendence* has been introduced as a unifying theme for family realm characteristics.[3] The transcendent reaches beyond the senses and invites holistic inquiry into connections and dimensions of location and meaning that heretofore have not been seen as appropriate for scientific inquiry. Jan Trost proposes a system of dyadic units to define and conceptualize family.[4] Individuals might define what their own families consist of and may include two men who cohabit, an ex-spouse, parents-in-law, step-parents, siblings, friends, and even pets. Any dyad (two persons) or set of dyads could be considered family.

This book views the family as a social institution and assumes that every society in the world includes a wide range of patterns, structural arrangements, and behaviours that are defined as family or family-like. While the title *The Family* remains, it is with the recognition that the family as a social system includes marriages as well as families that do not fit traditional notions of what marriages and families are or should be. Many relationships (same-sex, cohabitors, fictive kin, unmarried parents, and the like) fulfill responsibilities and functions that are basic to family systems. We will examine a wide range of these family and family-like patterns that exist in Canada and around the world. Current research findings have been incorporated in an effort to understand the similarities as well as the differences among the norms, values, and behaviours that characterize marriage and family-type relationships.

We begin this chapter and text by noting the wide range of disciplines involved in studying and understanding families. The focus then turns to a social science approach and its uses, followed by the major theories that give meaning to research findings and assist in explaining marriage and family processes and organizations.

DISCIPLINES INVOLVED IN FAMILY STUDY

The area of marriage and the family touches on a wide range of topics, lends itself to many types of research, and uses the results of the research in various ways. The orientation used in dealing with families will, in large part, determine the areas to be investigated and then, for each area, the questions to be asked, the research and theoretical approaches to be applied, and the results to be derived. Since no single discipline is able to ask all the questions, obviously none has all the answers.

The problem of disciplinary isolation is strikingly persistent. Anthropologists, who focus on families and family structures, often overlook the emotional dynamics of family life. Psychologists, who focus on child development and personal adjustment, often overlook aspects of cultural variation and social organization. Sociologists, who focus on the social order, often overlook historical and personal developmental factors.

Table 1.1 illustrates the wide range of disciplines that are concerned with families and family-related issues, and the topics associated with each. Clearly, no one discipline or profession dominates the topic of marriage and the family. In fact, the subject itself is highly interdisciplinary.

The new interdisciplinary approaches may lead to closing some of the gaps that separate disciplines and may bring forth new concepts and thus new meanings; yet each discipline will continue to focus attention in a specific direction. The anthropologist will focus on family patterns in a cross-cultural and national context. The counsellor, usually in an applied context, will attempt to assist individuals, couples, and groups in resolving conflicts and modifying attitude or

Table 1.1
Selected disciplines involved in study of the family and family-related issues

Discipline	*Illustrative topics*
Anthropology	Families in developing societies; cross-cultural studies; evolution; kinship
Biology	Human growth; genetics; conception and reproduction
Child development	Infant growth; learning; personality formation
Counselling	Family therapy; interpersonal relationships; vocational guidance
Demography	Marriage, birth, and divorce rates; mobility patterns
Economics	Family finance; consumer behaviour; standards of living
Education	Family life; marriage preparation; child development; sex education
English	Family through literature and mass media
Gerontology	Family life of the elderly; intergenerational links; kin-support systems
History	Family origins, trends and patterns over time
Home economics	Housing; nutrition; ecology; child development
Law	Marriage; divorce; abuse; adoption; welfare; child custody
Psychology	Interpersonal relationships; learning; human development
Public health	Venereal disease; maternal and infant care; preventive medicine
Religion	Morality; marriage vows; love; sex; religious training
Social work	Family, child, maternal, and aging assistance
Sociology	Family systems; interpersonal relationships; social change

behavioural problems. The educator will attempt to convey ideas and elicit thoughts on child development, preparation for marriage, sexual concerns, and parenting. The historian will examine family patterns, events, and changes over time. The politician will formulate policies and enact laws to deal with child care, marriage, and parenting. The social worker will direct knowledge and skills toward assisting families with problems of income, health, and behaviour.

Neither the disciplines described nor the illustrations given in Table 1.1 present an exhaustive listing of approaches to family study. A feminist frame of reference (described at the end of this chapter) alerts the teacher, researcher, and family practitioner to existing values and assumptions in their professions that overlook the perspectives of women. Scholars from the humanities have long been interested in the family realm. For centuries, poets, theologians, philosophers, linguists, artists, musicians, and others have portrayed images of various aspects of intimate relationships and family life. All forms of media—from magazines and newspapers to soap operas and situation comedies on television to dramas in movies—convey values about families and family life.

A sociobiological or biosocial approach to family study is an interdisciplinary perspective that cannot be ignored. Reproductive technologies alone (in vitro fertilization, artificial insemination, freezing embryos, sperm banks, genetic engineering, ovum transfer, cloning, surrogacy) have profound implications for the family.[5] Other scientific advances have similar potential to alter personal well-being and interpersonal interactions in dramatic ways, including the ability to select the sex of an offspring or even manipulate the child's appearance and capacities, the donation and transfer of organs from one person to another, and the availability of mind-altering drugs to treat most pains and illnesses.

The point is that a student could take many family courses and encounter different ideas, approaches, and interests. Some courses would include theories and findings from other disciplines; other courses would not have an interdisciplinary focus. The question becomes less "Which is better or correct?" than "Which fulfills the objectives or purposes desired?" The student interested in how mothers are portrayed in the mass media may not find much satisfaction in a course on child growth and development. Likewise, the student interested in sex education may not care much about insurance plans or budgeting patterns of nineteenth-century English households.

Textbooks, like disciplines and courses, approach the family with a particular focus and orientation. Although this book gives minimal attention to human anatomy, childhood diseases, and family nutrition, these areas are not unimportant. Rather, the frame of reference of this book basically follows that of the social sciences and, more specifically, that of sociology.

SOCIAL SCIENCE APPROACH TO THE FAMILY

The social sciences have a primary interest in the family. Generally, the social sciences include sociology, anthropology, psychology, economics, and political science. Sometimes, history, geography, and linguistics are included in this list. Each discipline examines the same subject matter—namely, the behaviour of human beings—employs the same body of general principles, and shares similar aims and methods. Science is determined by its aims and methods, not by its results.

All phenomena, including social phenomena, have certain regularities and uniformities that operate independently of the researcher or observer. These patterns can be discovered through objective observation. Science is predicated on the assumption that there is a real world, and that things exist and happen naturally and consistently. These things can be demonstrated and verified; thus, they are empirically knowable.

The aims and goals of a social science approach to the family are to establish more or less general relationships. These relationships must be based on empirical observation, and findings must be considered tentative and open to multiple interpretations. Within the social science framework, the following sections examine the sociological approach to the family.

Sociology of the family

Sociology per se is devoted to the study of how society is organized, including its social structures and social processes. The primary units of investigation include human groups, social systems, and institutions.

A sociology of the family seeks to explain the social order and disorder of the family by examining family systems and family groups. A sociology of the family is interested in many related topics: how the family is organized; how the family as a social system is sustained and modified; how family relationships are formed and changed; how the components within the family are interrelated; and how the family as a unit is interdependent with other groups or systems.

A sociological approach to the family differs from both psychological and social psychological approaches to the family. While both of these approaches are primarily concerned with the behaviour of individuals, sociology is interested in the social forms and structures within which this behaviour takes place. The separation of **psychology, social psychology,** and **sociology** is not always distinct, but each of the three branches of social science has a different emphasis. According to Eshleman, Cashion, and Basirico:

> Psychology is concerned with individuals. Social psychology is the study of how an individual influences his or her social interactions with other individuals or with groups, and of how social behavior influences the individual. Sociology deals primarily with groups and social systems.[6]

A sociology of the family does not focus on the motivations and perceptions of individuals. It does not emphasize how each individual is unique or has experiences that are different from those of anyone else. Rather, the sociological focus is on the context in which those individual experiences operate and how individual thinking and behaviour are shaped by social and cultural forces. All people, as social human beings, exist in a larger structural and organizational network that exerts powerful influences on their lives. The language a person speaks, the things that make him or her feel good or guilty, and the way he or she responds to the opposite gender are highly patterned. In their efforts to understand social life, sociologists question the obvious, seek patterns and regularities, and look beyond individuals to social interactions and group processes.

Uses of family sociology

Of what use is a sociological approach to the family, particularly since most people have no intention of becoming either sociologists or family specialists? First of all, family sociology does with *families* what sociologists do with *social life*: It questions the obvious, seeks patterns and regularities, and assesses individual behaviour in the context of a larger society. Thus, family sociology becomes useful in understanding existing behaviours, in presenting new ways of viewing life, and in acquiring knowledge about relationships and families in our society and around the world.

A second important use of family sociology is in applying the knowledge gained within a framework of sound theory and research.

How can this knowledge be gained? One way to acquire knowledge about families is through basic or applied social research done by oneself or others. Here, one might use knowledge of research methods and sampling, interviewing, analytical, and statistical skills to design and carry out a study on single parents, family conflicts, or a similar issue. The results may be:

1. *Descriptive,* presenting how many exist or what the problems are;
2. *Explanatory,* demonstrating why the problems exist;
3. *Evaluative,* recommending what programs or policies are effective.

Most often, however, knowledge is gained by studying the research of others.

How can this knowledge be used? Most important, it can affect one's performance in any profession that deals with people. Some of these professionals focus directly on work with families: counsellors, clergy, social workers, and so forth. Other professionals work with members of families in less direct ways: business- and salespeople, teachers, health care workers, law enforcement personnel, and the like. Anyone associating with people can put to use the knowledge obtained in a course on the family. Would knowledge about Italian-Canadian families, children of divorced parents, or sexual activities of children and adolescents be helpful to a teacher or member of the clergy? Would an understanding of male and female roles or of marital power and decision-making be helpful to a salesperson? Would knowledge about never-married parents or divorced parents be helpful to legislators or politicians who establish policy on welfare or child custody? Would an understanding of nontraditional life-styles help anyone accept and work with people whose values and behaviours differ from his or her own? The answer to each of these questions is clearly yes.

The third and perhaps most important use of family sociology is at a personal level. All people are brought up in a social context (poor, only child, single parent, French-Canadian), which plays a major part in who and what they are and will become. Many people want and have intimate relationships and specific ideas as to what they want and need from parents, partners, and children. While sociology cannot provide answers and solutions to all personal problems, it can provide some assistance and direction in dealing with the complex social world in which people live. How can this be done?

A knowledge of family theories and awareness of research findings can add to one's *critical-thinking* and *problem-solving* skills. Critical-thinking skills include the ability both to analyze a situation or information and to arrive at a careful, precise judgment. Problem-solving skills include the ability to resolve a conflict or difficulty. Family sociology can add to one's *interpersonal* skills, which help in managing everyday life and dealing with others in interactional settings. To understand the values, roles, norms, and behaviours common to people of a particular ethnic group or who practise a nontraditional life-style can improve one's interaction with them. Family sociology can also improve individual *communication* skills. Most assignments in family sociology, written and oral, are concerned not only with giving correct answers but with developing and presenting an argument and getting the point across logically and clearly. The perpetual interplay of ideas provides practical experience in "thinking on your feet" and communicating individual thoughts and ideas to others.

Finally, family sociology can help people *understand* themselves. People are social animals and can only understand themselves by studying the social context in which they live. It is true that knowledge of the social constraints that hinder people can make them feel trapped, frustrated at their inability to control their lives, and angry at the social injustices and inequalities that surround them. But only through understanding the society and the social context in which they exist can people truly understand themselves.

Perhaps reading this book will increase individual knowledge about existing situations, present frameworks for analysis and action, and suggest alternative explanations of family behaviour. After studying the available knowledge and various interpretations of what that knowledge means, the reader will be in a sound position to make his or her own choices and judgments on social policy and social action. Toward that goal, the next section will examine the nature of research and theoretical frames of reference common in literature on the family.

RESEARCH AND THEORY IN FAMILY SOCIOLOGY

Like theorists in most other fields, family scholars try to organize concepts, develop hypotheses and propositions, and interrelate these propositions meaningfully in order to explain particular aspects of marital or family organization and behaviour.

Family theories are ways of looking at and rationally explaining phenomena related to the family. Understanding the most widely used frames of reference can enable the student to study and analyze family behaviour in a way that is organized and logical. Thus, behaviour within the family context becomes patterned, regular, and predictable under certain conditions rather than remaining idiosyncratic and inconsistent.

Concepts and variables, conceptual frameworks, propositions and hypotheses, and theories are important in that they tell scholars where to focus their attention. Each of these topics will be addressed separately.

Concepts and variables

Basic to all theory and to all sociological research tools are **concepts.** A family concept, as in any area, is a miniature *system of meaning*, that is, a symbol, such as a word or phrase, that enables a phenomenon to be perceived in a certain way. Concepts are tools by which one can share meanings. They are unitary (parts of a whole) and thus do not explain, predict, or state relationships. Concepts are abstractions that are used as building blocks for the development of hypotheses, propositions, and theories. In family analysis, concepts are used to identify qualities, attributes, or properties of social behaviour. Examples of concepts within the family area include *nuclear family*, *monogamy*, *roles*, *norms*, *values*, *cohabitation*, *birth order*, *intermarriage*, *sex ratio*, and so on.

Concepts that represent degrees or values are referred to as **variables.** *Husband* is a concept; *years married* is a variable. A variable may be classified as *independent* (the presumed cause) or *dependent* (the presumed effect). The independent variable is antecedent to or simultaneous with the dependent variable. For instance, *family income* (a variable) may be dependent (the presumed effect) on the number of years of education (the presumed cause).

Concepts and variables undergo continuous revision and refinement. Frequently, new concepts must be invented to symbolize new ideas or to identify social properties that have not previously been seen. Thus, *family* may in itself serve as an adequate term for use by laypeople, but the professional differentiates among families of *orientation* or *procreation* and *nuclear*, *conjugal*, *extended*, *consanguine*, *stem*, and *joint* families.

Conceptual frameworks

When a set of concepts is interrelated to describe and classify phenomena—in this case, phenomena relative to the family—the concepts are generally defined as a **conceptual framework.** In the strict sense, a conceptual framework in not a theory. A framework is more frequently descriptive rather than explanatory and is generally employed as a classification scheme or taxonomy.

Considerable changes have occurred in the identification of current conceptual frameworks. In 1957, seven basic frameworks or approaches were defined by Hill and others: institutional-historical, interactional–role analysis, structural-functional, situational–psychological habitat, learning theory–maturational, household economics–home management, and the family-development or family life-cycle approach.[7]

In 1960, in what has become a classic article by Hill and Hansen, the chief conceptual properties and basic underlying assumptions of five frameworks were provided in taxonomic tables.[8] The frameworks delineated included these approaches: interactional, structural-functional, situational, institutional, and developmental.

These two initial works have stimulated a large number of articles and chapters on conceptual frameworks, frames of reference, and theories that are particularly applicable to study of the family but seldom unique to it. These frameworks include conflict, legal, economic, institutional, exchange, evolutionary, biological, psychoanalytic, behaviouristic, balance, game, ecological, and general systems, among others.

Six frameworks are covered in this chapter, namely, structural-functional, social conflict, symbolic-interactional, social exchange, developmental, and feminist. These six tend to appear regularly in the family literature.[9] These frames of reference are not to be substituted for, nor are they to replace an interest in, the creation of hypotheses, propositions, and theories.

Propositions and hypotheses

Conceptual frameworks can be used to generate or establish propositions, hypotheses, and theories. A **proposition** is a statement about the nature of some phenomenon. It generally involves a statement of the relationship between two or more concepts. For example, "Young marriage is related to marital conflict" is a proposition. If this or another proposition were formulated for empirical testing, it would be considered a **hypothesis.** Thus, a testable hypothesis would be "The younger the age at marriage, the higher the rate of divorce."

Hypotheses and propositions are identical, with the exception that hypotheses carry clear implications for testing or measuring the stated relations. Hypotheses serve as an important branch between theory and empirical inquiry. Hypotheses and propositions are formed by combining concepts into statements that set forth meaningful relationships.

Frequently, a proposition states that, if one variable changes in some regular fashion, predictable change will take place in another variable. For example, it has been suggested that "As industrialization increases, extended-family ties decrease." Thus, in this proposition, the two variables, *industrialization* and *the extended family*, are stated as being inversely related (as one increases, the other decreases).

Theories

When it is possible to interrelate logically and systematically a series of propositions that explain some particular process, the result is a **theory.** A good theory should be testable, abstract, and cumulative; have wide application; and give grounds for prediction. Thus, a theory is far more than speculation. It is a set of logically interrelated propositions that explain some process or related phenomena in a *testable* fashion.

It should be clear that theory and research are and need to be closely linked. Lavee and Dollahite suggested that, if the best is to be made of research, researchers must make themselves more familiar with theories about families. These researchers contended that scholars must sensitize themselves and teach their students to "think theory" while doing research and to be clear and explicit about theory when research is reported. It is theory that gives meaning to research findings and enables the development of systematic, consensual explanations.[10]

The application of theory—or perhaps more accurately, *theoretical frames of reference*—is emphasized throughout this book. While no independent chapters exist on theory per se, subsections within chapters use particular frames of reference. For example, the social conflict frame of reference is applied to social class, the marital system, violence, and divorce. The symbolic interaction frame of reference is applied throughout the book to analyses of partnering, sexual relationships, marital interaction, and child rearing (socialization). The developmental framework is applied from Chapters 6 through 8 in viewing marriage over the life cycle. Social exchange theory is applied throughout the book to partnering and the marital system. Likewise, feminist theory is applied to a wide range of issues from inheritance patterns and lineage systems to gender inequality and marital violence.

Other theories (frames of reference) not specifically summarized in this chapter are presented where appropriate throughout the text to offer explanations of particular aspects of the family: an orderly replacement theory of change, a complementary need theory of mate selection, a learning-behaviourist and psychoanalytic theory of socialization, an ABCX model of crisis, and the like. From this list alone, it becomes obvious that many theories exist that explain a variety of processes or sets of phenomena. Those more directly pertinent and widely used in a sociology of the family will be summarized in the section that follows.

Theories and Frames of Reference

Structural-functional frame of reference

The structural-functional frame of reference, sometimes called *functional analysis*, has been a major theoretical orientation in sociology. Within the family area, the scope of this approach is very broad; it provides a framework for dealing with relationships within the family (husband, wife, siblings, etc.) as well as influences on the family from other systems within society (educational, religious, occupational, etc.).

The structural-functional frame of reference stems from the functionalist branch of psychology (especially the gestalt position), from social anthropology, and from sociology (especially as seen by social systems theorists such as Talcott Parsons).[11] A *gestalt* is an organized entity or whole in which the parts, although distinguishable, are interdependent. The gestalt position focuses on the relation between a whole and its parts. Functionalism is identified with the study of interrelationships among the structures of any system. Numerous social anthropologists have stressed the impossibility of studying any particular aspect of life detached from its general setting.

To talk about social structures is to talk about social organizations, social systems, norms, values, and the like. *Cultural structures, social structures, structural interrelations*, and other structure-related terminology refer to the interdependence of parts in a definite pattern of organization. Within this framework, societies (and families) are composed of interdependent parts that are linked together in a boundary-maintaining whole and that are basically in harmony with each other. Since the parts of a system need each other, there is a social bond and high degrees of order, cohesion, stability, and persistence. The implication is that groups, systems and behaviours are not purely random, individualistic, or unpredictable. Family groups and systems and the individuals that make them up, similarly to the other components of a society, are orderly and predictable units that must be viewed in a social context.

The social structure of a family refers to the arrangement of social units, the interrelationship of the parts, and the patterns of organization. These

Families, irrespective of how they are structured, are the most important of all social institutions in fulfilling the function of rearing and nurturing the young. Various theories explain the socialization process; most are based on the necessity of an intimate network of caring adults who serve as caretakers, providers, and role models for children.

patterns differ greatly around the world, but, given a particular type of organization, definite recurrent consequences occur. Linda Bryan and others, for example, found that a family structure consisting of stepparents and stepchildren appeared to lend itself to negative stereotypes. Bryan et al. hypothesized that family structure is a cue by which stereotypes are formed and that stepparents and stepchildren are seen more negatively than married or widowed parents and their children but less negatively than divorced or never-married parents and their children. All hypotheses were supported.[12]

To extend this argument—namely, that structure produces or results in patterned, recurrent consequences—suggests that different outcomes will result if norms or values permit one wife or several, if newlyweds establish a residence with or separate from parents, if the husband makes the basic decisions or both husband and wife share in making them, and if inheritance is given to the oldest child or to all children equally. *Nuclear*, *polyandry*, *patriarchy*, *avunculocal*, *bilineal*, *primogeniture*, *exogamy*, *arranged marriage*, and *consanguine* are all words that define specific structural arrangements of given family systems. Most of these terms will be described and illustrated in Chapter 2.

The concepts of *structure* and *function* can be discussed separately, although they are interrelated and one implies the other. Speaking in circular terms, *social structures* are units of society that carry out or result in one or more basic functions, and *functions* are results or consequences of given social structures.

What specifically is meant by *function*? This term is generally used in one of two related ways. To determine function, one can ask, What does it do? That is, to describe functions of the family in Canada or any given society, one can ask what the family does: Why does it exist? What purposes does it serve? Functions may be *manifest* (that is, intended and recognized) or *latent* (that is, neither intended nor recognized). Functions may be performed for the individual, for a particular social system or social institution, or for the wider society.

It has been suggested that, for individual members, some manifest functions of the family are to provide basic personality formation, basic status ascription, nurturant socialization, and tension management. For the larger society, some manifest functions are to replace members, to socialize the members to the norms and values of the society, and to act as an agent of social control.

More than 45 years ago, Talcott Parsons and Robert Bales suggested that there are two basic and irreducible family functions: (1) the primary socialization of children so that they can truly become members of the society into which they have been born, and (2) the stabilization of the adult personalities of the society.[13] Evidence has shown that these two functions remain basic to the institution of the family today, as well.

Families also perform latent functions for persons and society. While latent functions are real in the sense that they take place, by definition they are neither intended nor recognized. They may include socializing children to be abusive adults or instilling within children negative feelings of self-worth. For the larger society, some latent functions may be to keep women in inferior positions to men or to perpetuate inequality from one generation to the next. Generally, families are not intended to fulfill such functions; nevertheless, such latent functions (some might say *dysfunctions*) exist.

A second way in which the term *function* is used is related to the first way. *Function* may be used to describe consequences or results of activities. Thus, given a certain type of structural pattern—for example, mothers working outside the home—one could ask, What are some of the consequences (results) of the employment of mothers? Are smaller family size, improved levels of mental health, and marital instability consequences of mothers working outside the home? Do families in societies that encourage maternal employment have higher standards of living, closer parent/child relationships, or more egalitarian decision-making patterns? Are the consequences similar, irrespective of cultural context, time, or location?

Three examples, of many that could be cited, illustrate how variations in family structure lead to differing consequences for children. The National Longitudinal Survey of Children and Youth is a comprehensive survey of Canadian children. One of the research concerns it addresses is the effect of family structure on children's problematic behaviour. Children from single-parent families have higher rates of emotional and behaviour problems and more academic and social difficulties. This was true for both boys and girls, although boys have higher rates of problematic behaviour regardless of family type. Part of the explanation is that single-parent families are at greater risk of living in

NEWS ITEM

First annual fathering conference at York University

The first annual conference on fathering was held at York University in May 1997. According to the brochure, the conference "is designed for individuals concerned with the problems of uninvolved or absent fathers and the consequences to children, mothers and fathers." The event is open to professionals and practitioners, including members of PTAs or school advisory councils, public health nurses, pediatricians, sociologists, child psychologists and family counsellors.

According to Wade Horn of the National Fatherhood Initiative, "Many men are psychologically absent from their children's lives because they lack the skills to be good and involved fathers."

Source: Conference brochure, 1997.

low income, and poverty is an additional, independent key to understanding children's problematic behaviour.[14]

Another study examined the relationship between family structure and homicide victimization rates of infants and children in 17 developed nations. Infant homicide rates were higher when rates of births to teenage mothers were high. Child homicide rates were higher under structural arrangements of illegitimacy, teenage motherhood, and divorce.[15]

A third study reinforced the view that child poverty and racial inequality cannot be separated from the issue of changing family structure in the United States. Increases in divorce rates, female headship rates, and nonmarital fertility rates over the past several decades were some of the changes in family structure that fuelled the growing proportion of children living in poverty.[16]

Note some of the implications of these ideas for social policy—that is, if consequences for children (or anyone) vary by type of family structure, conditions can be improved or changed by supporting certain types of structural arrangements rather than focusing only on the individuals who suffer the consequences. In other words, if children's emotional problems occur less frequently when they live with two biological parents, where should the focus be: solely on the children with the problems or also on the types of economic, educational, and community support that can be given to keep parents together? If infant homicide rates are higher among teenage mothers, what can be done to delay parenthood? If childhood poverty increases with female headship and nonmarital fertility rates, how can the number of these types of family structures be decreased?

These arguments should not blind one to the reciprocal and perhaps interfactional nature of *cause*. Consider whether changing family structure is a cause of poverty or whether poverty is a cause of changing family structure. Perhaps both are operative. It is not always easy to answer this type of question, but that does not take away the argument for creating social policies that best support the types of structures that have the most positive consequences.

Today, a major thrust of the structural-functional approach is to explain the parts (structure) of a society and the manner in which these parts interrelate, both within and outside the particular system under study. Each component of society must be seen in relationship to the whole, since each component acts on and reacts to other components. Thus, the task of structural-functional analysis is to explain the parts, the relationship among the parts, the relationship among the parts and the whole, and the functions (both manifest and latent) that are performed by or result from the relationship formed by the parts.[17]

Social conflict frame of reference

Perhaps the most basic assumption of a social conflict frame of reference is that conflict is natural and inevitable in all human interaction. Thus, rather than stressing order, equilibrium, consensus, and system maintenance, as does functionalism, the focus of a social conflict frame of reference is conflict management. Conflict is not viewed as bad and disruptive of social systems and human interaction; instead, conflict is viewed as an assumed and expected part of all systems and interactions.

At a macro level, the conflict may be between the family system and the work/employment/economic system, between sexes (males and females), between social classes, or between age groups. At a micro level, the conflict may be between a husband and wife, a son-in-law and mother-in-law, or two sisters. Since within this frame of reference conflict is quite natural and to be expected, the issue is not how to avoid conflict but how to manage and/or resolve it. In so doing, the conflict, rather than being disruptive or negative, may force change and perhaps make relationships stronger and more meaningful than they were before.

The classical case for social conflict theory stems from Karl Marx, who assumed that economic organization, especially the ownership of property, generates revolutionary class conflict.[18] Marx believed that, as the exploited and oppressed members of the proletariat became aware of their oppression and their true interests, they would revolt and form a revolutionary political organization aimed at overthrowing the dominant, property-holding bourgeoisie.

Basic to Marx and influential in the thinking of contemporary conflict theorists are ideas such as the following: (1) Social relationships are rife with conflicting interests; thus, (2) social systems systematically generate conflict, which (3) is an inevitable and pervasive feature of all social systems and (4) tends to be manifested in the opposition of interests that (5) occurs over the distribution of scarce resources, most notably power and material wealth, which (6) results in change in social systems.[19]

Hypotheses stemming from these assumptions suggest that:

1. The more unequal the distribution of scarce resources, the greater the conflict between the dominant and the subordinate.
2. As the subordinates become aware of their collective interests, they increasingly question the legitimacy of existing patterns.

3. The more the subordinates question inequities, the more likely they are to join in overt conflict against the dominant group.
4. The more overt or violent the conflict, the greater the change and the redistribution of resources that will result.

From this Marxist economic conflict perspective, the family serves to support the capitalistic system that exploits working-class workers by paying them low wages. Similarly, capitalism exploits women, not merely by paying lower wages to those who are employed, but by encouraging them to perform unpaid housework and child care so that husbands can devote their full time to their capitalist employers.

In brief, from a social conflict perspective, the family is not the haven posited by an order perspective such as functionalism (see Table 1.2). Functionalists, who see the family as the primary socialization agent of youth, are seen by conflict theorists as promoting a false consciousness by teaching youth to accept the inequalities between the sexes and classes as natural. Functionalists also see the family as perpetuating the same "life chances" from one generation to another (the rich stay rich and the poor stay poor), whereas conflict theorists feel this perpetuation maintains and promotes inequality based on ascription rather than achievement. Functionalists believe that the isolated nuclear family is consistent with the mobility needs of a capitalist society; conflict theorists believe that mobility is disruptive to individual

Table 1.2
Duality of social life: assumptions of the order and conflict models of society

	Order model	***Conflict model***
Question:	What is the fundamental relationship among the parts of society?	
Answer:	Harmony and cooperation	Competition, conflict, domination, and subordination
Why:	The parts have complementary interests. Basic consensus on societal norms and values.	The things people want are always in short supply. Basic dissensus on societal norms and values.
Degree of integration:	Highly integrated	Loosely integrated. Whatever integration is achieved is the result of force and fraud.
Type of societal change:	Gradual, adjustive, and reforming	Abrupt and revolutionary
Degree of stability:	Stable	Unstable

Source: D. Stanley Eitzen and Maxine Baca Zinn, *In Conflict and Order: Understanding Society,* 7th ed. (Boston: Allyn & Bacon, 1995), 51. Used with permission.

members and their emotional needs. Finally, functionalists, who see the modern family as tranquil, passive, and in a state of equilibrium with other units of society, are seen by conflict theorists as promoting a system fraught with potential and actual conflict. Conflict, which is inevitable in society, in the family, and in interpersonal relationships, leads to change.

Issues related to conflict theory—power, decision-making, marital adjustment, economic factors, and the like—are discussed elsewhere, particularly in Chapters 4 and 6.[20]

Symbolic interaction frame of reference

Symbolic interactionism describes a particular and distinctive approach to studying the group life and personal behaviour of human beings. As a social-psychological frame of reference, symbolic interactionism addresses two issues—socialization and social interaction—both of which are of central concern to the family. The first issue, socialization, focuses on how a newborn becomes social and on how human beings obtain and internalize the behaviour patterns and ways of thinking and feeling of the society and culture in which they live. The second issue, social interaction, is basic to socialization itself and to all aspects of life; it focuses on self in relation to others and on the social interchanges between individuals and groups.

Within social psychology, symbolic interactionism constitutes both a theoretical perspective and a methodological orientation. Its theoretical uniqueness lies in the extent to which covert activity is thought to be a crucial dimension in understanding behaviour and society. Symbolic interactionism includes the observable actions of individuals, and stresses the importance of meanings, definitions of situations, symbols, interpretations, and other internalized processes.

Interaction among socialized human beings is mediated by the use of symbols and by interpreting meanings from the actions of others. Methodologically, the real world is known by any means or set of techniques that offers a likely possibility of ascertaining what is going on: making direct observations, conducting interviews, listening to conversations, securing life history accounts, using letters and diaries, consulting public records, arranging for group discussions, and other allowable procedures that lead to obtaining subjective meanings. Basically, symbolic interactionism involves a *phenomenological* approach, where preferred techniques include use of participant observation, personal documents, and ethnomethodological accounts. The use of quotations from personal interviews is also consistent with this particular frame of reference.

Concepts from the social interaction framework are used extensively throughout this book. For example, the concept *role* is used within both a structural-functional framework and an interactionist framework. However, its use varies significantly. An institutional or structural concept of *role* attaches societal expectations to statuses that people occupy. Certain statuses—such as sex, age, and race—are generally ascribed, whereas marital, occupational, and parental statuses are likely achieved. Each of these statuses or status sets carries

The symbolic interaction approach to families suggests that the human infant at birth is neither social nor antisocial but asocial. He or she learns through interaction with others what is good and bad, acceptable and unacceptable behaviour.

with it expected, appropriate behaviours. These expectations of what is appropriate for men or women, married or single, homosexual or heterosexual, are termed *roles*. *Roles* are culturally defined expectations and exist independently of any given person.

Role, as used within an interactionist framework, does not deny the institutional usage, but, rather than dealing with a package of behavioural expectations wrapped up in a set of rules, it deals with a relationship between what one person does and what others do. The expectations (roles) are developed in interaction. The emphasis here is on process. The interactionist concept of *role* describes the processes of cooperative behaviour and communication. It involves the idea of *role-taking*. Role-taking as a process involves each actor adjusting his or her behaviour and reactions to what he or she thinks the other person is going to do. Perhaps a simple example may clarify the difference in the use of these two schools of thought, functionalism and interactionism.

Suppose there are two students, one male and one female. The fact that they occupy student and gender statuses implies that certain expectations or roles are associated with these statuses. But for the moment, concentrate on the students as male and female. Some of the rules or expectations traditionally associated with the status *male* in relationship to *female* are that he walk on her outside (along the curb), that he open doors and generally permit her to proceed first, that he assist her with a chair, and that he pay the bills. Thus, the institutional concept of *role* emphasizes society's prescribed expectations for behaviour. Whether these rules are actually followed is secondary. The roles (expectations) exist independently of a given individual's fulfillment of them. Failure to conform to the expectations appropriate to status does not eliminate the normative expectations.

In contrast to the institutionalized concept of *role*, the interactionist concept involves the process of determining appropriate behaviour in interaction with others. Now the actor is not the occupant of a position for which there is a standardized set of rules; he or she is a person whose expectations for behaviour are supplied in part by his or her relationship to another person or persons. Since the expectations of the other person can only be inferred and not directly known, there is a continuous process of testing. The clues given by the other person in part determine the expected behaviours (roles) appropriate to that situation.

Getting back to the example male and female, as they interact, the expectations (roles) for appropriate and approved behaviour may vary widely from socially ascribed expectations. The female may quite appropriately pay the bills, open the doors, be the aggressive sexual partner, drive the automobile, and the like. But these roles, too, become patterned and recurrent. This inevitability is what makes behaviour predictable and interaction possible with either strangers or intimate, lifelong friends.

These two conceptions of *role* are not totally independent and separate, for one never escapes the norms or roles established by a given society. At best, however, the expectations associated with a given status offer only generalized guidelines; they do not determine specific behaviour patterns for every situation. Thus, even though the norm prescribes that intercourse is not appropriate on a first date, as the couple interacts, the result may be coitus. The gestures, the clues, the symbols, the verbal communications, and the clarity of shared meanings may lead to intercourse as a highly appropriate role expectation for the dating partners within the interactionist concept of *role*. The behaviour of intercourse on a first date within the institutional concept of *role*, however, is inconsistent with the culturally prescribed rules for unmarried couples.

Other concepts that are key to the understanding of this frame of reference include the *social self*, *significant other*, *reference group*, and *generalized other*. Each will be clarified and illustrated in various chapters throughout the text; a more extensive discussion of the symbolic interaction frame of reference will be presented in Chapter 8. At this point, the family will be recognized as a "unit of interacting personalities"[21] involved in a never-ending, never-completed, or never-fixed process.[22]

Social exchange frame of reference

Seldom does a day pass in which certain social exchanges do not take place. Work, gifts, cards, affection, and ideas are given in hopes of getting something in return. Certain exchanges, such as many economic ones, are institutionalized and predetermined, clarified in precise terms before the exchange. For instance, one can exchange 50 cents for a newspaper or $150 for a membership in the Canadian Association of Sociology and Anthropology. Other exchanges, including the type found in the social exchange frame of reference, leave unspecified the exact nature of the return, although a return—an expectation of reciprocity—does exist. For example, neighbours who lend tools, friends who buy dinner, and politicians who promise lower taxes all expect something in return. That exact something is often unspecified.

Social exchange or social choice theory rests on the belief that human beings try to make choices that they expect will maximize their rewards and/or minimize their costs. Social exchange theory seeks to explain why certain behavioural outcomes occur (marriage, sex, employment) given a set of structural conditions (age, race, gender, class) and interactional potentialities. The following assumptions are made:

- Most types of human gratification originate in the actions of other people (spouse, children, friends, colleagues, fellow workers).
- New associations are entered into because they are expected to be rewarding, and old associations continue because they are rewarding.
- As people receive rewards or benefits from others, they are under an obligation to reciprocate by supplying benefits in return.
- Earning social credit through giving is preferable to building social debt through receiving.

While it may be true that persons exist who selflessly work for others with no thought of reward, such "saints" are rare, and even they seek social or perhaps spiritual approval. Social exchange, or voluntary social actions that are contingent on receiving rewarding reactions from others, cease when the actual or expected reactions are not forthcoming.

Social exchange theory has followed two differing schools of thought, best represented by George Homans[23] and Peter Blau.[24] Homans, the recognized initiator of exchange theory, represented a perspective consistent with that of behavioural psychologists who believe in psychological reductionism and reinforcement theory, where the focus is on actual behaviour that is rewarded or punished by the behaviour of other persons. Humans, like other animals, react to stimuli on the basis of need, reward, and reinforcement. It is expected that, in exchange relationships, the rewards will be proportional to the cost (a notion of distributive justice).

Blau differed considerably with Homans and represented a perspective consistent with that of the symbolic interactionist. That is, not all exchange is explained in terms of actual behaviour of individuals. Exchange is more subjective and interpretative. Exchange, like interaction, is a creative process that occurs between actors. While humans want rewards, the choices and decisions they make are affected by social influences, such as friends or kin. The human mind responds subjectively to stimuli through conceptualizing, defining, valuing, reflecting, and symbolizing. As a result, explaining behavioural outcomes (the goal of social exchange theory) is a function of the actors who interact symbolically, have social selves, and can take roles.

Homans and Blau agreed that what is important is that each party in the exchange receive something perceived as equivalent to that which is given (to Homans—*distributive justice*, to Blau—*fair exchange*). All social exchange involves a mutually held expectation that reciprocation will occur.[25] If resources or exchange criteria are unequal or imbalanced, one person is at a distinct disadvantage and the other has power over the relationship. Specific resources (money, position, physical assets, personality) may be more applicable in one exchange than in another and may have different values in different exchanges. The worth of a resource can only be accurately assessed through participation in actual social markets. Therefore, socialization in exchange and bargaining skills is vital to maximizing the use of available resources.

The family literature is filled with many examples of social exchange. For example, Willard Waller uses the *principle of least interest* to explain the selection of intimate partners. According to Waller, interest is exchanged for control of the relationship in that the person who is least interested in continuing the dating relationship is in a position to dominate. In arranged marriages, for instance, labour, gifts, or a bride price are often exchanged for the right to marry. Robert Winch spoke of complementary needs, involving an exchange of needs that provide maximum gratification. The higher incidence of premarital sexual behaviour by engaged females has been explained as an exchange of sex on the part of the female in return for commitment on the part of the male. Throughout the text, note the value of different types of resources and the exchange processes at work in understanding authority and power, husband/wife interaction, partner selection, kin relationships, sexual patterns, parent/child conflict, and the like.[26]

Developmental frame of reference

Originating in the 1930s, the family development approach to family study attempts to join together various parts of previously delineated theories. Hill and Hansen, who discussed the characteristics of the developmental framework, indicated that this approach is not a precisely unique framework but an attempt to transcend the boundaries of several approaches by incorporating their compatible sections into one unified theme.[27]

> From rural sociologists [the developmental frame of reference] borrowed the concept of stages of the family life cycle. From child psychologists and human development specialists came the concepts of developmental needs and tasks. From the sociologists engaged in work in the professions it incorporated the concept of the family as a convergence of intercontingent careers. From the structure-function and interactional approaches were borrowed the concepts of age and sex roles, plurality patterns, functional prerequisites, and the many concepts associated with the family as a system of interacting actors.[28]

The developmental approach covers a broad area and tends to be both macro- and microanalytic. The peculiar character of this approach lies in its attempt to account for changes in the family system over time as well as changes in patterns of interaction over time. Traditionally, the major conceptual tool among family scholars for this time analysis has been termed the *family life cycle*.[29] Today, frequent reference is made to the term *life course* in dealing with changes and differences over time.

The most systematic, widespread, and long-term use of the family life-cycle idea has been provided by Evelyn Duvall, who attempted to provide a link between life-cycle stages[30] and the developmental-task concept.[31] A *developmental task* is one that arises at or about a certain period in the life of an individual. Successful achievement of the task leads to individual happiness, social approval, and success with later tasks, while failure leads to unhappiness, disapproval, and later difficulties. Developmental tasks have two primary origins: (1) physical maturation and (2) cultural pressures and privileges.[32] The number of developmental tasks an individual faces over a lifetime are innumerable. Many of them are described in human development textbooks.

The developmental theory contends that, like individuals, families also face tasks at given stages in the family life cycle. A family's developmental task is "a growth responsibility that arises at a certain stage in the life of a family, the successful achievement of which leads to present satisfaction, approval and success with later tasks whereas failure leads to unhappiness in the family, disapproval by society, and difficulty with later family developmental tasks."[33] For a family to continue to grow as a unit, they need to satisfy, at a given stage, (1) biological requirements, (2) cultural imperatives, and (3) personal aspirations and values.

Duvall recognized and depicted the family life cycle as consisting of eight stages:

Stage 1	Married couples (without children)
Stage 2	Childbearing families (oldest child, birth–30 months)
Stage 3	Families with preschool children (oldest child, 2 1/2–6 years)
Stage 4	Families with school children (oldest child, 6–13 years)
Stage 5	Families with teenagers (oldest child, 13–20 years)
Stage 6	Families as launching centres (first child gone to last child leaving home)
Stage 7	Middle-age parents ("empty nest" to retirement)
Stage 8	Aging family members (retirement to death of both spouses)[34]

These stages are determined by the age and school placement of the oldest child up to the launching stage (6), after which the situation facing those remaining in the original family is the determinant. This type of scheme explicitly fails to recognize multiple-child families, overlapping stages, the death of a spouse, and many other variations in families, including those of ethnically and racially diverse populations.[35] But this scheme, as most developmental schemes, views stages as distinct periods in the life course of the family group, with certain events (birth of a child, child entering school, etc.) triggering transitions to different stages.

One example of an empirical study using family life-cycle categories can be seen in Chapter 6, which includes a section on marital satisfaction over the family life cycle. Chapters 6 through 9 in general follow a family life-cycle model.[36]

Feminist Frame of Reference

Feminist theories and perspectives assert that gender is basic to all social structures and organizations. The impetus for contemporary feminist theory is a simple question: And what about women?[37] Answers to this question are based on the ideas that the experiences of women are *different* from those of men, are *unequal* (less privileged) to those of men, and are actively *oppressed* (restrained, subordinated, used, and abused) by men.

Related to these ideas are basic assumptions of feminist thought, as discussed in an article in a special issue of *Family Relations* on feminism and family studies:

1. Women—or any group that is defined on the basis of age, class, race, ethnicity, disability, or sexual preference—are oppressed.

FAMILY DIVERSITY

Seven biases in family literature

Canadian family sociologist Margrit Eichler has identified seven biases evident in studies of families. These biases include:

- *Monolithic bias*—"a tendency to treat the family as a monolithic structure by emphasizing uniformity of experience and universality of structure and function over diversity of experiences, structures and functions." Eichler argues that we should look at a well-functioning family regardless of its internal structures.
- *Conservative bias*—a romantic view of the nuclear family in the past which overlooks problematic aspects of family life throughout history.
- *Sexist bias*—"an assumption of a 'natural' division of labour between the sexes."
- *Ageist bias*—familial interactions that are considered mainly from the perspective of the middle-aged adults without considering the perspectives of the children or the elderly.
- *Microstructural bias*—"a tendency to treat families as encapsulated units" rather than taking external factors into account.
- *Racist bias*—a bias which "devalues families of culturally or ethnically non-dominant groups."
- *Heterosexist bias*—a bias that assumes that a heterosexual family is the only "natural" unit.

By identifying these biases we can hope to recognize potential analytic pitfalls and be open to understanding changes in structures and processes of family life.

Source: Margrit Eichler, *Family Shifts: Families, Policies and Gender Equality* (Toronto: Oxford University Press, 1997).

2. The *personal* is *political*. In other words, nothing is exclusive to women's personal lives; everything has social ramifications. The social system imposes a reality on everyday life and is not separate from it. Social structure must be taken into account.
3. Feminists have a double vision of reality: they need to be successful in the current system while working to change oppressive practices and institutions.[38]

Myra Marx Ferree challenged family studies to rethink two notions: (1) that families can be understood separately from the economic, political, and other systems of male power; and (2) that families are unitary wholes in which conflicts of interest between men and women are disregarded.[39] The first notion questions the *separateness* between public and private, where fundamentally different social relations exist in families than in the rest of society. This idea supports the false notion that the family is a private world, where women take centre stage, appear to have unlimited power, and are held responsible for everything—from the quality of the marital relationship to the mental health of the children and even to the prevention of male violence.

The second notion questions the *solidarity* myth, according to which the family is a unitary whole in which everyone shares a standard of living, class position, and set of interests. The reality is that conflicts of interest exist by gender, and feminist thought recognizes this. In the words of Ferree, the feminist perspective "redefines families as arenas of gender and generational struggles, crucibles of caring and conflict, where claims for an identity are rooted, and separateness and solidarity are continually created and contested."[40]

Feminist theorists, while not denying the economic inequalities argued by Marxist theorists, do not blame all male/female inequalities on economic systems. Some feminists have substituted the word *patriarchy* for *bourgeoisie* and even for *sex roles*. *Sex roles*, with its theme of different but equal tasks and power, downplays the structured inequality (male dominance) that is pervasive. Male dominance exists in its own right and cuts across all economic and class lines. In addition, male dominance implies female oppression and sexism. The source of this oppression and sexism is in the home, where women, employed or not, find that housework and home are part of the same system. Until women increase their independence from men and gain resources (power, money, education, job opportunities, etc.) that improve their status, the family will never be an egalitarian institution.

What does a feminist frame of reference suggest for family studies and research? Linda Thompson has argued that a feminist agenda for family studies "includes experience embedded in broader context, the struggle to adapt to the contradictions of family life, a vision of nonoppressive families, diversity among women and families, and rethinking the discipline."[41]

Rethinking the discipline means moving beyond simple refining or revising existing concepts to generating new concepts and theories based on women's work and experiences. It means continually grappling with concepts such as truth, reality, and objectivity. It means believing that science, including family science, is a social activity embedded in a socio-historical context. It means acknowledging that the questions asked (or not asked) about relationships and families are as significant as the answers given (or withheld). It means viewing theory, research, education, and all other aspects of family life from a perspective of social justice, where everyone is treated equally and differences are respected.

APPRAISAL AND EXPANSION OF CONTEMPORARY FAMILY THEORY

The reader should not think that the structural-functional, social conflict, symbolic interaction, social exchange, developmental, and feminist theories are the only frames of reference in family sociology. Udry, for example, suggests that gendered behaviour, fertility, contraception, abortion, nuptiality, occupation choice, and other behaviours will be increasingly influenced by biological choice: a biosocial theory.[42]

The new century may be a time of theoretical synthesis: an integration of macro and micro ideas, a joining of structural and exchange theories into a network theory, or a blurring of distinct theoretical boundary lines, as theories borrow heavily from one another and new or revived ideas come to the fore.

What ideas? Notions of rationality are once again being challenged. Humanists are pressing for the involvement of social scientists in efforts toward achieving social justice and improving social conditions. Many critical and feminist scholars have no desire to subject their theories and ideas to the positivistic (recognizing only matters of proof and fact) principles of science.

Jetse Sprey, who presented an appraisal of current theorizing about the institutions of marriage and the family, raised three concerns that might be labelled "unfinished business."[43] First is the integration of existing conceptual schemes into broader, more flexible vocabularies. Sprey would suggest, for example, that the frames of reference listed in this chapter be viewed not as competitive or unique in their own right but as attempts to incorporate ideas—a conceptual and theoretical integration. The second concern is about modes of explanation. Basically, this involves linking and integrating conceptual vocabularies with appropriate questioning and levels of explanation. Sprey's third concern is the ongoing ambiguous relationship between conceptualization and theory building. Theoretical models, while abstract, can be constructed with "ordinary language or mathematics," either of which may provide a way to think about reality.

Sprey emphasized that theorizing cannot be considered static or unchanging. He proposed three alternatives to current mainstream family theorizing, which he termed hermeneutic, critical, and feminist orientations.[44] **Hermeneutics** refers to the art or theory of interpretation. It goes beyond the methods of science to any mode of experience in which truth is communicated.

Subjectivity is not the opposite of objectivity but an essential human way of interpretative understanding and of managing one's social life. **Critical social science** approaches societies and families in terms of both what exists and what is possible in the future. It questions what types of social change are feasible and desirable as well as how they can be achieved. This orientation links the actual with the possible. **Feminist theorizing** is aimed at recognizing the absence of women in the history of social and political thought. It challenges patriarchal and sexist notions about the family, such as that it is natural or biological or that it is monolithic (having a single structure).

SUMMARY

1. From a social science perspective, the family is a social group, a social system and a social institution. A wide range of disciplines, approaches, and selected frames of reference are used in the study of the family. The marriage and family area is highly interdisciplinary; no single discipline either asks all the questions or provides all the answers. This book uses a social science orientation, with a major concentration focused on a sociology of the family.
2. Of what use is a sociology of the family? It alerts one to question the obvious and assess individual behaviour in the context of the larger society. It enables one to obtain a body of knowledge about persons, relationships, and family structures. It assists one in applying this body of knowledge to work with persons and families. It can be useful personally in improving critical-thinking and problem-solving skills, interpersonal skills, and communication skills. And finally, family sociology helps people understand themselves and the social context in which they live.
3. As the foundation for the entire book, this chapter summarized the nature of conceptual frameworks, frames of reference, and theories in general, and provided an overview of six basic approaches: structural-functional, social conflict, symbolic interaction, social exchange, developmental, and feminist.
4. In this chapter and several that follow, considerable attention is given to concepts and their definitions. Although definitions of concepts seldom make interesting reading, they are important. Concepts are miniature systems of meaning that permit viewing a phenomenon in a certain way and sharing that view with others. In addition, concepts are basic to the development of hypotheses, propositions, and theories.
5. One of the most dominant theories or frames of reference in sociology is the structural-functional theory. This frame of reference uses the social system as the basic autonomous unit of which the family is a subsystem. All systems have interdependent parts (structures) that do certain things for the individual or society and have various social consequences (functions). The basic task of functional analysis is to explain the parts, the relationship among the parts and the whole, and the functions that are performed by or result from the relationship formed by the parts.
6. A second frame of reference that has received increasing attention is that of social conflict. Two significant aspects of this perspective are the view of conflict as (a) natural and inevitable and (b) a major factor that can lead to social change. Conflict theory is particularly applicable to a further understanding of marital relationships, power, the division of labour, and conflict at both macro (societal) and micro (interpersonal) levels.
7. The symbolic interaction frame of reference addresses two basic issues, both of central

concern to the family: socialization and social interaction. The basic premises of this approach are (a) that human beings act toward things based on the meanings things have for them, (b) that these meanings are derived from interaction with others, and (c) that these meanings are modified through an interpretive process. Each human being is unique unto himself or herself, understood only in his or her social context, is neither inherently good nor bad, and responds to self-stimulating or symbolically interpreted stimuli.

8. The social exchange framework helps explain why certain behavioural outcomes occur given a set of structural conditions and interactional potentialities. Two different approaches to exchange were examined in this chapter: one consistent with a behavioural frame of reference and the other with an interactionist frame of reference.
9. The developmental frame of reference has the peculiar characteristic of trying to account for change in the family system and change in patterns of interaction over time with the use of concepts such as the *family life cycle* and *family life course*.
10. A feminist frame of reference recognizes that the experiences of women are different, unequal, and oppressed as compared to those of men. Families cannot be understood apart from other systems of male power, nor are families unitary wholes in which conflicts of interest between men and women can be disregarded. An expansion of contemporary family theory includes integrating conceptual schemes, reinterpreting their meanings, and questioning both what exists and what is possible.
11. Chapter 2 will turn to the family as a social institution, establishing the boundaries of marital, family, and kin groups and systems, and examining selected structural features of this basic institution.

KEY TERMS AND TOPICS

Disciplines involved in family study p. 3
Social science approach to the family p. 5
Psychology, social psychology, and sociology p. 6
Uses of family sociology p. 6
Concepts p. 8
Variables p. 9
Conceptual frameworks p. 9
Propositions p. 10
Hypotheses p. 10
Theories p. 10
Structural-functional frame of reference p. 11
Social conflict frame of reference p. 15
Symbolic interaction frame of reference p. 17
Social exchange frame of reference p. 19
Developmental frame of reference p. 21
Feminist frame of reference p. 23

DISCUSSION QUESTIONS

1. How would you define marriage and families? Must persons be related legally? Biologically? Residentially? Psychologically? Explain.
2. Since no one discipline has all the answers to any family-related question, why isn't all research interdisciplinary? What problems exist in interdisciplinary research?
3. Within the social sciences, compare and contrast how psychology, social psychology, social anthropology, and sociology approach the family as an area of study.
4. Differentiate between terms in the following pairs: concepts and variables; hypotheses and propositions; and conceptual frameworks and theories.
5. Discuss the major functions of the family in Canada. How are these different from the functions of families 30 years ago? What functions

will the family probably perform 30 years from now?

6. Is conflict natural and inevitable in all marriages and families? Is conflict essential for change? Explain.
7. What assumptions and issues are basic to a symbolic interaction frame of reference?
8. Write a paragraph on "Who I am." Begin by listing the statuses you occupy. Take this list of statuses, and write about one or two social expectations appropriate to each status. After reflection, write about the following: Which role expectations do you personally find displeasing? Are there conflicts between different expectations or between your personal preferences and social expectations? How do you handle them?
9. What exchanges can you identify in explaining male/female sexual behaviours, husband/wife spending patterns, and parent/child disciplinary behaviours? What is given and received in each exchange? Can you think of examples where no reciprocity is expected or given in return for a favour or gift? If so, what are they?
10. Identify what stage of the family life cycle your family is currently in (either you and your parents and siblings, or you and your spouse and/or children). Identify the central problems, concerns, and tasks of a family at this particular stage.
11. Describe some basic assumptions of the feminist perspective. What contributions does this approach make to family studies and how people think about families?

FURTHER READINGS

Aldous, Joan. *Family Careers: Rethinking the Development Perspective*. Thousand Oaks, CA: Sage, 1996. A new version of family development that explores couple relations over time, parent-child relations over time, and sibling relations over time.

Baber, Kristine M., and Allen, Katherine R. *Women and Families: Feminist Reconstructions*. New York: Guilford Press, 1992. An examination from a feminist perspective of realms of family life that matter most to women: intimate relationships, sexuality, childbearing, caregiving, and work.

Boss, Pauline G.; Doherty, William J.; LaRossa, Ralph; Schumm, Walter R.; and Steinmetz, Suzanne K. *Sourcebook of Family Theories and Methods: A Contextual Approach*. New York: Plenum Press, 1993. A socio-historical contextual approach to family theories, tracing their origins, assumptions, major concepts, research examples, and application to families.

Collins, Randall. *Four Sociological Traditions*. New York: Oxford University Press, 1994. An expanded edition of his earlier theoretical work, *Three Sociological Traditions* (conflict, Durkheimian, and microinternational), with the addition of a rational/utilitarian tradition.

Collins, Randall, and Coltrane, Scott. *Sociology of Marriage and the Family: Gender, Love, and Property*. 4th ed. Chicago: Nelson-Hall, 1995. A sociology text that incorporates conflict and feminist perspectives into family issues and studies.

Cowan, Philip A.; Field, Dorothy; Hansen, Donald A.; Skolnick, Arlene; and Swanson, Guy E.; eds. *Family, Self, and Society: Toward a New Agenda for Family Research*. Hillsdale, NJ: Lawrence Erlbaum Publishers, 1993. While the title suggests a new agenda for family research, the book includes 21 chapters focusing heavily on conceptual models and family theory that emphasize a contextual approach to the study of family relationships.

Grieve, Norma, and Burns, Ailsa, eds. *Australian Women: Contemporary Feminist Thought*. New York: Oxford University Press, 1994. Twenty-four articles cover the context of Australian feminism, feminist theory, and contesting male power.

Klein, David M., and White, James M. *Family Theories: An Introduction*. Thousand Oaks, CA: Sage, 1996. Six theoretical frameworks from the perspectives of sociology and family studies are presented: exchange, symbolic interaction, family development, systems, and ecological.

Luxton, Meg, ed. *Feminism and Families: Critical Policies and Changing Practices*. Halifax: Fernwood Publishing, 1997. This collection of essays shows how feminism has challenged the traditional model of the family, and identifies the urgent need to develop family politics grounded in feminism.

Mandell, Nancy, ed. *Feminist Issues: Race, Class and Sexuality*, 2nd ed. Scarborough: Allyn and Bacon, 1998. This collection of original chapters by Canadian feminist sociologists begins with three theoretical chapters which frame the sections on women's experience of diversity and the analysis of women's family and work lives.

Rosenblatt, Paul C. *Metaphors of Family Systems Theory: Toward New Constructions*. New York: Guilford Press, 1994. Theoretical metaphors, where one kind of action or idea is used in place of another, are explored as the basis for thinking about family systems and for use in family therapy.

Thorne, Barrie, and Yalom, Marilyn. *Rethinking the Family: Some Feminist Questions*. Boston: Northeastern University Press, 1992. An introduction to feminist thinking on selected issues about the family as it has evolved over the last two decades.

Winton, Chester A. *Frameworks for Studying Families*. Guilford, CT: Dushkin Publishing Group, Inc., 1995. An examination of five theories central to studying families: developmental structural-functional, conflict, social exchange, and symbolic interaction.

WEBLINKS

http://swift.eng.ox.ac.uk/jdr/f_marx.html

Marx's Page: This is part of a larger site that provides a useful, though not definitive, guide to the resources on political theorists that can be found on the Internet.

http://www.runet.edu/~lridener/DSS/INDEX.HTML#marx

This link, from Radford University in Virginia, provides information on Karl Marx. It includes biographical information as well as excerpts from Marx's works and critical commentary on his social theories.

http://www.sociologyonline.net/text/intro/preview/frc11fam.htm

An excellent resource that introduces sociology of the family and offers an overview of theory and issues that are explored more in-depth in this book.

http://teacher.nsrl.rochester.edu/phy_labs/AppendixE/AppendixE.html

This website offers an overview of the scientific method used to study family issues and dynamics and the steps involved in conducting research.

NOTES

1. John Scanzoni, Karen Polonko, Jay Teachman, and Linda Thompson, *The Sexual Bond: Rethinking Families and Close Relationships* (Newbury Park, CA: Sage, 1989). See also: Jaber F. Gubrium and James A. Holstein, *What Is Family?* (Mountain View, CA: Mayfield, 1990); and Jan Trost, "Do We Mean the Same by the Concept of Family?" *Communications Research* 17 (August 1990): 431–443.

2. Ivan F. Beutler, Wesley R. Burr, Kathleen S. Bahr, and Donald A. Herrin, "The Family Realm: Theoretical Contributions for Understanding Its Uniqueness," *Journal of Marriage and the Family* 51 (August 1989): 805–816.

3. Howard M. Bahr and Kathleen Slaugh Bahr, "A Paradigm of Family Transcendence," *Journal of Marriage and the Family* 58 (August 1996): 541–555.

4. Jan Trost, "Family from a Dyadic Perspective," *Journal of Family Issues* 14 (March 1993): 92–104; and Jan Trost, "Family Structure and Relationships: The Dyadic Approach," *Journal of Comparative Family Studies* 27 (Summer 1996): 395–408.
5. See John N. Edwards, "New Conceptions: Biosocial Innovations and the Family," *Journal of Marriage and the Family* 53 (May 1991): 349–360; and Eric E. Filsinger, *Biosocial Perspectives on the Family* (Newbury Park, CA: Sage, 1988).
6. J. Ross Eshleman, Barbara C. Cashion, and Laurence Basirico, *Sociology: An Introduction*, 4th ed. (New York: HarperCollins, 1993), 65–66.
7. Reuben Hill, Alvin M. Katz, and Richard L. Simpson, "An Inventory of Research in Marriage and Family Behavior: A Statement of Objectives and Progress," *Marriage and Family Living* 19 (February 1957): 89–92.
8. Reuben Hill and Donald A. Hansen, "The Identification of Conceptual Frameworks Utilized in Family Study," *Marriage and Family Living* 22 (November 1960): 299–311.
9. For example, five of these frameworks are covered in the book by Chester A. Winton, *Frameworks for Studying Families* (Guilford, CT: Dushkin Publishing Group, Inc., 1995); and five of these can be found in David M. Klein and James M. White, *Family Theories: An Introduction* (Thousand Oaks, CA: Sage, 1996).
10. Yoav Lavee and David C. Dollahite, "The Linkage Between Theory and Research in Family Science," *Journal of Marriage and the Family* 53 (May 1991): 361–373.
11. Talcott Parsons, *The Social System* (Glencoe, IL: Free Press, 1951).
12. Linda R. Bryan, Marilyn Coleman, Lawrence Ganong, and S. Hugh Bryan, "Person Perception: Family Structure as a Cue for Stereotyping," *Journal of Marriage and the Family* 48 (February 1986): 169–174.
13. Talcott Parsons and Robert F. Bales, *Family Socialization and Interaction Process* (New York: Free Press, 1955), 16–17.
14. Ellen Lipman, David Offord and Martin Dooley, "What Do We Know about Children from Single-Mother Families? Questions and Answers from The National Longitudinal Survey of Children and Youth," in *Growing up in Canada*, pp. 83–91. Ottawa:Statistics Canada, 1996. Cat. No. 89-550-MPE, No. 1.
15. Rosemary Gartner, "Family Structure, Welfare Spending, and Child Homicide in Developed Democracies," *Journal of Marriage and the Family* 53 (February 1991): 231–240.
16. David J. Eggebeen and Daniel T. Lichter, "Race, Family Structure, and Changing Poverty Among American Children," *American Sociological Review* 56 (December 1991): 801–817.
17. Key concepts in structural-functional theory in sociology are *social system, social structure, social function, dysfunction, manifest* and *latent functions, functional requisites* and *prerequisites, equilibrium* and *order, status* and *norms.*

    For information on structural-functional theory and the family, examine the following: Pauline G. Boss, William J. Doherty, Ralph LaRossa, Walter R. Schumm, and Suzanne K. Steinmetz, *Sourcebook of Family Theories and Methods: A Contextual Approach* (New York: Plenum Press, 1993); William J. Goode, *The Family*, 2nd ed. (Englewood Cliffs, NJ: Prentice-Hall, Inc., 1982); and Chester A. Winton, *Frameworks for Studying Families* (Guilford, CT: Dushkin Publishing Group, Inc., 1995).
18. Karl Marx, *The Communist Manifesto*, trans. Samuel Moore (Baltimore: Penguin, 1967), originally published in 1849 with Friedrich Engels; C. Wright Mills, *The Marxists* (New York: Harcourt, Brace, 1948); and Rolf Dahrendorf, *Class and Class Conflict in Industrial Society* (Stanford, CA: Stanford University Press, 1959).
19. See Jonathan H. Turner, *The Structure of Sociological Theory*, 4th ed. (Chicago, IL: Dorsey Press, 1986), 135.
20. Key concepts in conflict theory are *conflict, competition, negotiation, patriarchy, resources, scarcity, interests, change, power,* and *class.*

    For information on conflict theory and the family, examine the following: Pauline G. Boss, William J. Doherty, Ralph LaRossa, Walter Schumm, and Suzanne K. Steinmetz, *Sourcebook of Family Theories and Methods: A Contextual Approach* (New York and London: Plenum Press, 1993); Chester A. Winton, *Frameworks for Studying Families* (Guilford, CT: Dushkin Publishing Group, Inc., 1995); Marie Withers Osmond, "Radical-Critical Theories," in *Handbook of Marriage and the Family*, ed. Marvin B. Sussman and Suzanne K. Steinmetz (New York: Plenum Press, 1987), Chapter 5, 103–125; Randall Collins and Scott Coltrane, *Sociology of Marriage and the Family: Gender, Love, and Property*, 4th ed. (Chicago: Nelson-Hall, 1995).
21. Ernest W. Burgess, "The Family as a Unit of Interacting Personalities," *Family* 7 (1926): 3–9.
22. Key concepts in symbolic interaction theory are *symbols, interaction, process, status, role, role-playing, role-taking, role conflict, meaning, reference group, significant other, generalized other, social self, "I," "me," socialization, actor,* and *identity.*

    For information on symbolic interaction theory and the family, examine the following: Pauline G. Boss, William J. Doherty, Ralph LaRossa, Walter Schumm, and Suzanne K. Steinmetz, *Sourcebook of Family Theories and Methods: A Contextual Approach* (New York and London: Plenum Press, 1993); and Chester A. Winton, *Frameworks for Studying Families* (Guilford, CT: Dushkin Publishing Group, Inc., 1995).
23. George C. Homans, *Social Behaviour: Its Elementary Forms* (New York: Harcourt, Brace, 1961); George C.

Homans, "Social Behavior as Exchange," *American Journal of Sociology* 63 (May 1958): 597–606.

24. Peter M. Blau, *Exchange and Power in Social Life* (New York: Wiley, 1964); Peter Blau, "Justice in Social Exchange," *Sociological Inquiry* 34 (Spring 1964): 193–206.

25. Alvin W. Gouldner, "The Norm of Reciprocity," *American Sociological Review* 25 (April 1960): 161–178.

26. Key concepts in social exchange theory are *exchange, reciprocity, negotiation, transaction, resources, cost, distributive justice, fair exchange*, and *power*.

    For information on social exchange theory and the family, examine the following: Pauline G. Boss, William J. Doherty, Ralph LaRossa, Walter Schumm, and Suzanne K. Steinmetz, *Sourcebook of Family Theories and Methods: A Contextual Approach* (New York and London: Plenum Press, 1993); Chester A. Winton, *Frameworks for Studying Families* (Guilford, CT: Dushkin Publishing Group, Inc., 1995); and John Scanzoni, *Sexual Bargaining: Power Politics in the American Marriage*, 2nd ed. (Chicago: University of Chicago Press, 1982).

27. Reuben Hill and Donald Hansen, "The Identification of Conceptual Frameworks Used in Family Study," *Marriage and Family Living* 22 (November 1960): 299–311.

28. Ibid., 307.

29. For a discussion and empirical evaluation of this concept, see Paul C. Glick, "The Family Life Cycle and Social Change," *Family Relations* 38 (April 1989): 123–129; Graham B. Spanier and Paul C. Glick, "The Life Cycle of American Families: An Expanded Analysis," *Journal of Family History* 5 (Spring 1980): 97–111; and Joan Aldous, "Family Development and the Life Course: Two Perspectives on Family Change," *Journal of Marriage and the Family* 52 (August 1990): 571–583.

30. See, for example, Gunhild O. Hagestad, "Demographic Change and the Life Course: Some Emerging Trends in the Family Realm," *Family Relations* 37 (October 1988): 405–410; and Tamara K. Hareven and Kanji Masaoka, "Turning Points and Transitions: Perceptions of the Life Course," *Journal of Family History* 13 (1988): 271–289.

31. Evelyn M. Duvall and Brent C. Miller, *Marriage and Family Development*, 6th ed. (New York: Harper and Row, 1985), Chapter 3.

32. Ibid., 47.

33. Ibid., 61.

34. Ibid., 26.

35. Peggye Dilworth-Anderson and Linda M. Burton, "Rethinking Family Development: Critical Conceptual Issues in the Study of Diverse Groups," *Journal of Social and Personal Relationships*, 13 (August 1996): 325–334.

36. Key concepts in the developmental approach are *life cycle, developmental tasks, family transitions, family stages, family careers, life events, norms, roles*, and *role relationships*.

    For information on the developmental approach and the family, examine the following: Pauline G. Boss, William J. Doherty, Ralph LaRossa, Walter Schumm, and Suzanne K. Steinmetz, *Sourcebook of Family Theories and Methods: A Contextual Approach* (New York and London: Plenum Press, 1993); Chester A. Winton, *Frameworks for Studying Families* (Guilford, CT: Dushkin Publishing Group, Inc., 1995); James M. White, *Dynamics of Family Development: A Theoretical Perspective* (New York: Guilford Press, 1991); Joan Aldous, *Family Careers: Developmental Change in Families* (New York: Wiley, 1978); Evelyn M. Duvall and Brent C. Miller, *Marriage and Family Development*, 6th ed. (New York: Harper and Row, 1985); and Roy H. Rodgers, *Family Interaction and Transaction: The Developmental Approach* (Englewood Cliffs, NJ: Prentice-Hall, Inc., 1973).

37. Patricia Madoo Lengermann and Jill Niebrugge-Brantley, "Contemporary Feminist Theory," in *Contemporary Sociological Theory*, ed. George Ritzer (New York: Alfred A. Knopf, 1988), 282–325.

38. Alexis J. Walker, Sally S. Kees Martin, and Linda Thompson, "Feminist Programs for Families," *Family Relations* 37 (January 1988): 17–22. See also Linda Thompson and Alexis J. Walker, "The Place of Feminism in Family Studies, "*Journal of Marriage and the Family*, 57 (November 1995): 847–865.

39. Myra Marx Ferree, "Beyond Separate Spheres: Feminism and Family Research," *Journal of Marriage and the Family* 52 (November 1990): 866–884.

40. Ibid., 880.

41. Linda Thompson, "Feminist Methodology for Family Studies," *Journal of Marriage and the Family* 54 (February 1992): 3.

42. J. Richard Udry, "Biosocial Models of Low-Fertility Societies," *Population and Development Review* 22 (1996): 325–336.

43. Jetse Sprey, "Current Theorizing on the Family: An Appraisal," *Journal of Marriage and the Family* 50 (November 1988): 881–882. See also Jetse Sprey, ed., *Fashioning Family Theory: New Approaches* (Newbury Park, CA.: Sage, 1990).

44. Sprey, "Current Theorizing," 882–886.

CHAPTER

2 MARRIAGE, FAMILY, AND KINSHIP

Chapter 1 presented a variety of interdisciplinary, social science, and theoretical approaches to family study. Our perspective on family life changes depending on our framework; whether we see families from an interpersonal or institutional point of view; whether we view them as social groups or social systems; or when they are differentiated according to marriage and kin, orientation and procreation, nuclear and extended, and the like. This chapter will note these and other conceptual distinctions in studying and understanding family life.

FAMILIES AS SOCIAL INSTITUTIONS

Frequent reference is made to the family as the most basic of all social institutions. It is most closely linked to the supporting institution of marriage. What do we mean by this?

The concept *institution* refers to specific areas of human social life that have become broadly organized into discernible patterns. *Institution* refers to the organized means whereby the essential tasks of a society are organized, directed, and carried out. In short, it denotes the system or norms that organize human behaviour into stable patterns of activity.

Institution is a noun; *institutionalize* is a verb. The noun *institution* refers to "a system of norms, values, statuses, and roles that develop around a basic social goal."[1] All societies must deal with the social relations established by sexual union as well as the birth and care of dependent children. The institutional norms concerned with these matters constitute familial or kinship institutions.

The verb *institutionalize* means to establish patterned and predictable behaviour; thus, noninstitutionalized behaviour is spontaneous and irregular. Typically, a husband/wife fight is noninstitutionalized behaviour; a professional boxing match is institutionalized. When an activity such as dating, premarital sexual behaviour, or childrearing becomes institutionalized, it becomes accepted by society as a necessary, proper, and predictable activity. At this time, although extramarital intercourse is common in our society, it has not been institutionalized; that is, it has not been accepted as standardized, approved, and a culturally safeguarded behaviour.

Several basic social institutions can be identified in all societies. Familial and kinship, educational, economic, political, and religious institutions have existed in some form in all societies throughout history. Each of these institutions performs certain functions that are basic to the existence of a given society. However, other areas have also become institutionalized. In Canada, marriage, business, communication, medicine, law, science, and recreation have become institutionalized and thus basic to our way of life.

Few institutions have received more recognition and criticism than the family and its central component, marriage. Both have been claimed to be the solution of problems, on the one hand, and the basic cause of problems, on the other. For example, in the late 1990s, a number of professional family scholars claimed that marriage is an institution in decay and basically responsible for the increases in violent crime, child neglect and abuse, the psychological pathology of children and youth, alcohol and drug abuse, poverty, and even declining SAT scores.[2] And if families and marriages are the cause of the problems, their solution resides in the same institution. Marriages are to be made stronger by reclaiming the ideal of marital permanence, declaring that out-of-wedlock childbearing is wrong, having children grow up with two parents, and increasing the time that parents spend raising their children.[3] In brief, stress traditional family values.

Houseknecht and Sastry[4] caution us about accepting at face value such across-the-board deleterious outcomes for child well-being as asserted by Popenoe. In a comparative study of the relationship between family decline and child well-being in four countries (Sweden, United States, the former West Germany, and Italy), the results do not indicate unequivocal support for the thesis that countries ranked higher on family decline will rank lower on child well-being. While, in general, children are better off when they live in a society in which traditional family patterns are strong, there are exceptions. Sweden, for example, which had the highest family decline score, did not demonstrate a high level of negative outcomes for children compared with other countries with lower levels of family decline.

Popenoe has suggested that such textbooks be rewritten to portray marriage, with children, as a desirable social goal and not simply as one of many viable lifestyle alternatives. These writers agree that, at a personal level, such goals and values are of worth. But the intent of this book is not to advocate any particular marital or family value or lifestyle. Rather, the intent is to examine the family as an institution, as well as the diverse nature of family groups and systems.

Families as Groups and Systems

Family and marital **groups and systems** are basic to a sociology of the family and to understanding the family as a social institution. Family systems are used in sociology much as physicists and biologists speak of solar or biological systems. In each instance, the word *system* means a configuration of interdependent parts.

Within the family system are subsystems (marital systems, mate-selection systems, sexual systems, childrearing systems) that are also highly patterned, recurrent, and organized to fulfill selected tasks. Although people are part of the system, it is the statuses, roles, norms, ways of ranking, means of social controls, and values of those people (all abstractions) that are significant in examining social systems.

The basic units of a marital or family system are not persons but the interrelated statuses (positions) and the expectations (roles) that accompany those statuses. The interrelated statuses in the family system include, among others, parent/child, husband/wife, uncle/aunt, grandparent/grandchild, father/mother, and brother/sister. The norms (folkways and mores) and roles, and also the expectations and values that accompany these statuses are of primary concern to the sociologist. In a heterosexual marriage, a married male occupies the status of *husband*. He interacts with a married female who occupies the status of *wife*. These interrelated statuses, *husband* and *wife*, make up a marital system. This system, like the family system or any other system, also has sets of norms and expectations that prescribe appropriate and inappropriate behaviours for the specific persons involved. Thus, systems are abstractions, forms of social organization composed of interrelated statuses.

Family and marital groups, in contrast to systems, are composed of people. These people are physically present and interact with one another in terms of their ascribed or achieved statuses. A person who is married belongs to a two-person marital group. The family group consists of the married partners, children, and any other relatives included in the extended-family context. Marital and family groups are temporary, disbanding when their members depart. The system of which they are a part may continue for centuries, long after the departure or death of any specific member or specific family group.

It is the task of a sociology of the family to examine the nature of marital and family groups within societies and to understand the organizational patterns of marital and family systems that provide order within and among the groups involved.

Primary groups

Sociologists view groups as the core of their attention. They speak of in-groups and out-groups, primary and secondary groups, formal and informal groups, large and small groups, minority and majority groups, open and closed groups, organized and unorganized groups, independent and dependent groups, voluntary and involuntary groups, and others. Some of these ideal-type constructs are more useful to understanding family groups than others. One that appears to be particularly important is that of primary-group relationships.

A **primary group** consists of a small number of people who interact in direct, personal, and intimate ways. Primary-group relationships are facilitated by (1) face-to-face contact, (2) smallness of size, and (3) frequent and intense contact. Most families in the Western world operate under these conditions. Unlike most primary groups, the family is so essential, both to individuals and to society, that its formation is usually legitimized by the community through religious and legal rituals. While most other primary groups can disband voluntarily, the dissolution of the family group is generally accomplished through institutionalized means.

Much of the importance of marital, family, and kin groups lies in their function as primary groups.[5] What functions does a primary group serve?

1. For most individuals, the primary group serves as the basic socializing agent for the acquisition and internalization of beliefs and attitudes.

2. The family, as a primary group, constitutes the chief focus for the realization of personal satisfaction. Perhaps more than any other source, the family provides all members with a general sense of well-being, companionship, ego worth, security, and affection. Most people, when away from home for the first time, experience homesickness, or a nostalgia for the primary group from which their immediate ties have been severed.
3. The family also serves as a basic instrument of social control. The family has an extraordinary capacity to punish deviation and reward conformity, since most people depend on other group members for meeting psychological needs and for realizing meaningful social experiences.

FAMILY DIVERSITY

Extended families in China

The clan system of traditional China was extremely important to the maintenance of ancestral linkages and group solidarity. A clan, sometimes referred to as a *tsu,* included all persons with a common surname who traced descent from a common ancestor. The tsu operated through a council of elders; it often involved several thousand persons—sometimes entire villages.

The significance that this large clan group had for the family can be seen in the functions the clan performed: lending money to members, helping individual families pay for extravagant weddings and funerals, establishing schools, exercising judicial authority, acting as a government agent in collecting taxes, and maintaining ancestral graves and tsu property. The clan performed most of the functions generally associated with government: taxes, law enforcement, schools, welfare, and so on. As one might guess, the tsu came under serious attack when the revolutionary government came into power.

In the contemporary Chinese family, extended family relationships show signs of change. Logan and others say that there have been fundamental changes in family relationships in urban China. Arranged marriages have become less common, women are treated more equitably by their coresiding mothers-in-law than before, and there is greater autonomy for both the parent and child generations. Yet coresidence remains nearly as high in China as in some other East Asian countries and so much higher than in the West.

One state policy that may have deep impacts on the extended family and on intergenerational relations is the one-child family policy. Population control in the 1980s and 1990s has sharply reduced fertility, with an immediate impact on the presence of grandchildren and eventual effects on the number and possibly on the gender of adult children. Clearly the one-child family will force many older people to live alone.

On the other hand, having fewer children, parents and grandparents may invest more in each child and therefore increase the likelihood of reciprocal support in old age. An only child may feel more obligation to parents. Logan et al. say that some data suggest that parents with only one child are more likely to prefer coresidence than those with more than one and that only children are especially likely to live with parents.

See Paul Chao, *Women Under Communism: Family in Russia and China* (Bayside, NY: General Hall, 1977); and John R. Logan, Fuqin Bian, and Yanjie Bian, "Tradition and Change in the Urban Chinese Family: The Case of Living Arrangements," *Social Forces* 76 (March 1998): 851–852.

Secondary groups

The opposite of the primary group is the **secondary group.** Many, if not most, of people's involvements in school, work, and the community are not characterized by the intimate, informal, and personal nature of primary groups but rather by impersonal, segmental, and utilitarian contacts. Secondary groups are basically goal-oriented rather than person-oriented. For instance, the personal life of the bus driver, a classmate in a lecture, or the insurance salesperson is not of major significance in fulfilling the goals established for interactions with these people.

In a society dominated by secondary-group relationships, the family, time and again, provides the primary relationship that is vital to individual health and happiness. Cochran et al., in a book dealing with the social networks of parents and children in several countries, suggested that important social support is given by primary sources such as friends, neighbours, workmates, and organizational/agency contacts. But the *primary* support network—that is, the people who are the most important—consistently is relatives.[6]

An absence or loss of familial networks as primary sources of social support has been linked to a wide range of negative outcomes: school truancy, accidents, suicides, commitment to mental hospitals, pregnancy disorders, coronary disease, and even lack of recovery from all types of illnesses. An argument could be made that, without primary-group relationships or the presence of intimate family bonds, survival itself would be doubtful. This idea has been fairly well substantiated with infants and adults who have no family or close friends.

One possible conclusion to all of this is that, rather than being in a state of decay, losing its significant functions, and becoming obsolete, the Canadian family may be fulfilling a primary-group function that has seldom been more crucial and important in maintaining personal and social stability and well-being.

CHARACTERISTICS OF MARRIAGE, FAMILY, AND KINSHIP GROUPS

Marriage, family, and kinship groups are institutionalized social arrangements in all known societies. However, the nature of the arrangement differs greatly across societies, over time, and even within a given society at a specific time.

Frequently, legal and social norms themselves lack clarity as to what does or does not constitute a marriage, family, or kinship group. For example, is it a marriage if two males live together and recognize each other as spouses, if a male and female live together but are not formally married, or if a man and woman go through a marriage ceremony and then almost immediately separate permanently? Can any group of persons constitute a marriage, a family, or a kinship group? Consider the boundaries of each.

Marriage boundaries

Throughout the world, marriage is an institutional arrangement between persons, generally males and females who recognize each other as husband and wife or intimate partners. Marriage is a social institution that is strictly human and assumes some permanence and conformity to societal norms.

About 35 years ago, William Stephens, an anthropologist, said that marriage is (1) a socially legitimate sexual union, begun with (2) a public announcement, undertaken with (3) some idea of permanence, and assumed with a more or less explicit (4) marriage contract, which spells out reciprocal obligations between spouses and between spouses and their children.[7] For the most part, these same normative conditions exist today, although many marriage-like relationships are not defined by everyone as socially legitimate, are not begun with any type of announcement, are not entered into with the idea of permanence, and do not always have clearly defined contracts (written or unwritten) as to what behaviours are expected. Thus, debate exists as to whether these types of intimate relationships are socially and legally recognized as marriages.

Any definition of marriage or family is, in a certain sense, arbitrary. In fact, many phenomenological, conflict, and feminist theorists call into question the use of labels such as *marriage*, *family*, and *kin*. They suggest that these labels ignore the historic origins and the range of meanings given to marriage and family by persons in their day-to-day lives.

Recognizing the danger of reifying the concept, let us turn our attention to historical and cross-cultural variations in marriage patterns, particularly as related to the number of persons involved.

Marital status

Marital status (single, married, separated, widowed, divorced) and number of spouses (none, one, more than one) are two major components of the boundaries of marriage. With a change in marital status and the number of spouses comes variations in marital interaction patterns; living and sleeping arrangements; exclusivity of sexual interactions; the likelihood of and number of children; patterns of support, decision-making, and authority; and male/female roles, to mention a few.

Obviously, never to have had a spouse is to have a nonmarital status. The never-married single can be expected to share certain characteristics of other single statuses, yet in many ways differs from the widowed or divorced single. The latter two single statuses (widowed and divorced) are discussed in Chapters 9 and 11, respectively.

Single living According to the 1996 Canadian census, there were 3,383,715 single males and 2,811,855 single females over 15 years of age.[8] Since the census definition of single is never married, the proportion of singles in the population is necessarily tied to the marriage rate. During periods when the marriage rate increases, such as in the 1950s and 1960s, the proportion of singles drops. Beginning in 1973 in Canada, there has been an increase in single living, reaching levels in the 1980s and 1990s as high as those of the Great Depression. However,

Definitions and meanings of marriage and intimate relationships are changing. Marriages are no longer defined or labelled as being traditional, singular, or static; rather, they are being defined as nontraditional, pluralistic, and dynamic. Many gay men and lesbian women are forming primary, intimate, long-term relationships and seek the rights and privileges enjoyed by marriages and families.

because the average age of marriage has increased (to 27 for women and 29 for men in 1992),[9] it is difficult to measure life-long singlehood by looking at census data. If marriage patterns remain at 1990 rates, only 631 of every 1,000 Canadian men and 674 of every 1,000 women will marry before age 50. From the 1940s until the early 1970s, more than 900 of every 1,000 men and women married.

If we consider Canadians who are unattached (not currently married or living in a common-law union) instead of never married, there is a sizeable imbalance of women to men. Age is key to understanding these numbers: under 30 there are more men than women; over 30, women outnumber men. Among seniors, the number of women far exceeds the number of men.[10]

> Several factors influence the ratio of unattached men to women. They include the sex ratio at birth; migration; the presence of a military base or prison; the tendency of men to marry younger women; the greater likelihood of men than of women to find another partner when their marriage or common-law union ends; and mortality rates and life expectancy. Thus, in northern towns where occupations attract proportionately more men than women, and in communities where there is a military base or a prison for men, for example, unattached men tend to greatly outnumber women. In contrast, in communities with large senior populations or with nursing homes for seniors, women, who generally live longer than men, predominate.[11]

News Item

Partner selection on the Internet

Reply to ur4me@hotmail.com

SBM, 23. Intelligent, handsome, fit, enjoys hiking and outdoor fun. Seeks SF 18–25 who is intelligent and attractive for good times and possible long-term relationship.

SWF, 35. I know you're there, Mr. Right. Must be nonsmoker. I'm down to earth, open-minded, with good values and morals. I love dogs.

SBF, 31. Voluptuous and sexy. Enjoys movies, walks, cooking, music, dancing. Seeks male who is sensual and caring, honest, open-minded, and loves to be pampered.

SWM, 26. This Bud's for you. You must be very good-looking, physically fit, with great personality. Me? You'll be pleasantly surprised.

GWF, 21. BiCurious in search of an experienced bifemale to have hot fun and explore the world of biactivities. I'm just like honey: sweet, thick, slow, and tasty.

GBM, 39. Corporate professional, emotionally and financially secure with a good sense of humour. I'm attracted to African, Latin, or Italian men who are clean, hard-bodied, masculine bull studs for monogamous safe encounters.

Whether the increased numbers of single (never-married) men and women represents a postponement of first marriage or lifelong singleness is not clear. Some will marry eventually, some will choose singleness, and some will drift into lifelong singleness for various personal reasons. Any stigma that once accompanied single living, which incidentally favoured "bachelors" over "spinsters," has lost its impact. A significant number of Canadians choose singlehood because it has positive outcomes for happiness, career, and social mobility. Take happiness, for example. Studies in the United States have consistently reported considerably higher levels of personal happiness and health for married persons than for persons in any unmarried category (never married, divorced, or widowed). But these married/nonmarried differences in happiness appear to have lessened over the past two decades.[12] The overall change has been due primarily to an increase in the reported happiness of never-married males and a decrease in the reported happiness of married females.

For females, being single is associated with having a number of positive outcomes, including a higher educational level, a higher median income, and a higher occupational status. Such a decrease in single/married differences is not universal, however. For example, in contemporary Japan, it was found that the levels of mortality experienced by single Japanese are staggeringly high in comparison with those of married Japanese.[13] Not only are discrimination and stigma associated with those who do not marry, but unmarried individuals experience relatively high rates of dying and presumably much poorer health. For example, mortality data for the mid-1990s indicate that a 20-year-old Japanese man or woman who remains single can expect to live as much as 15 years less than his or her married counterpart.

This recent finding, while perhaps extreme, supports the many research studies over the past 100 years that have shown that married men and women throughout the world are happier, tend to live longer, and experience better health than do never-married, widowed, and divorced persons.[14] Marriage may serve to improve the financial situation, increase social networks that facilitate access to medical information and services, constrain risk-taking behaviour, and act as a buffering mechanism in stressful situations.

Number of spouses

Monogamy To most of us, the most customary as well as the most usual form of marriage is **monogamy:** one man to one woman (at a time). Throughout the world, this form of marriage is the only one universally recognized and is the predominant form even within societies where other forms exist.

Although Canada is strictly monogamous, it is possible for Canadians to have more than one husband or one wife. Many married people divorce and remarry. This is sometimes called **sequential or serial monogamy.** Thus, in Canada, it is both legally and socially approved to have more than one wife or more than one husband, as long as they occur sequentially and not simultaneously.

Polygamy The suffix *-gamy* refers to marriage or a union for propagation and reproduction. Thus, *monogamy* (single), *bigamy* (two), *polygamy* (several or many), *allogamy* (closely related), *endogamy* (within), and *exogamy* (outside or external) describe the nature of marriage. **Polygamy** refers to marriage to several or many individuals. Theoretically, there could be several or many wives *(polygyny)*, several or many husbands *(polyandry)*, or several or many husbands and wives *(group marriage)*. Each of these is a polygamous marriage, as distinguished from a monogamous (one) or bigamous (two) marriage.

In a classic study using a world sample of 554 societies, polygyny was culturally favoured in 415 (77 percent), whereas polyandry was culturally favoured in only 4 (less than 1 percent): Toda, Marquesas, Nayar, and Tibet.[15] Research over the years has never uncovered a society in which group marriage was clearly the dominant or most frequent form.

Multiple spouses (except in group marriage) are only possible on a large scale when an unbalanced **sex ratio** (number of males per 100 females) exists. Only if the sex ratio is either high or low will polygamy be possible without increasing the number of single persons of one sex.

Second, polygamy, where it exists, is highly regulated and normatively controlled, as are all forms of marriage. Rarely does it involve a strictly personal or psychological motive. Rather, polygamy is likely to be supported by the attitudes and values of both genders and linked closely to the sex ratio, economic conditions, and belief systems.

Third, polygamy itself has many forms and variations of normative structure that determine who the spouse should be. For example, in some cases, all the multiple husbands are considered brothers *(fraternal polyandry)* or all the multiple wives are sisters *(sororal polygyny)*. A levirate and sororate arrangement existed in the ancient Hebrew family. The **levirate** was a situation (technically, sequential monogamy) in which the wife married the brother of her deceased husband, whereas the **sororate** was a situation in which the preferred mate for a husband was the sister of his deceased wife.

- **Polygyny**—the marriage of one man to more than one woman at the same time—is the most frequent form of polygamy. It appears to be a privilege of the wealthy. Having more than one wife is a mark of prestige, distinction, and high status.

Most people who have been socialized in the Western world and frequently in the Judeo-Christian tradition (including readers of this text) would probably not favour polygyny as a personal choice. They would suspect jealousy, competition, and conflict as disruptive factors among the multiple wives. In contrast, a study from Ibadan, Nigeria, where polygyny is common, indicated that co-wives get along fairly well. When wives were asked how they would feel if their husbands took another wife, some 60 percent said they would be pleased to share the housework, husband care, and childrearing, and to have someone to talk and "play" with.[16]

Jealousy among co-wives, however, does seem to be considerably more frequent than jealousy among co-husbands, for several reasons. The greater likelihood of jealousy among co-wives may stem from the fact that women are more frequently *chosen*, whereas men more likely *choose* to have co-spouses. Understandably, having less choice in the matter of being married may contribute to much greater potential for jealousy. In addition, it has been suggested that co-husbands are more likely to be brothers than co-wives are likely to be sisters. If this is the case, it is possible that jealousy would be less among siblings than among nonsiblings.

Anthropologists have observed that, if co-wives are sisters, they usually live in the same house; if co-wives are not sisters, they usually live in separate houses. Thus, for some reason, it seems that siblings can better tolerate, suppress, and live with a situation of sexual rivalry than can nonsiblings.

What about polygyny in North America today?[17] The most frequently cited sources of polygyny are those of certain Mormon fundamentalists living in "underground" family units in Utah and neighbouring states. The number of these marriages is unknown.

- **Polyandry**—the marriage of one woman to more than one man at the same time—appears to be quite rare. Stephens has made several generalizations about polyandry. First, polyandry and group marriage tend to go together; where one is found, the other will likely be found.[18]

Second, co-husbanding is fraternal. In the few cases in which the husbands are not brothers, they are clan brothers; that is, they belong to the same clan and are of the same generation. Among the Todas, a non-Hindu tribe in India, it is understood that when a woman marries a man, she becomes the wife of his brothers at the same time. Among the Yanomama Indians living in northern Brazil, a wife may have other recognized sexual unions with the

Polygyny has been illegal in the United States since 1878, when the U.S. Supreme Court ruled that religious freedom did not extend to having multiple wives. Yet, today, a number of dissident Mormons (not recognized as Mormon by the mainstream Church of Jesus Christ of Latter Day Saints) continue to practise polygyny. Shown here is a Utah husband with his nine wives and several of his many children.

consent of her husband. The most frequent union is with the husband's younger brother, who, until he acquires his own wife, has a quasi-right to his older brother's wife. The husband may also consent to share his wife with other males, kin or nonkin, who may be recognized as secondary husbands throughout their lives.[19]

Third, an economic inducement is often mentioned. A man tries to recruit co-husbands so they will work for him. In other instances, co-husbandry is practised for economic security or as an answer to a land shortage. When several men marry one woman, the fragmentation of holdings, especially land, is avoided. Cassidy and Lee argued that economic factors are the key to understanding the very existence of polyandry.[20] The two most important antecedents to polyandry appear to be (1) extreme societal poverty with harsh environmental conditions and (2) limited roles for women in the productive economy.

Where polyandry does exist, female infanticide is frequently mentioned. It is a curious anomaly that male infanticide is rarely, if ever, mentioned in the literature. Female infanticide eliminates the wife surplus among polyandrous families; however, male infanticide does not seem to be used to eliminate the husband surplus in polygynous societies.

- **Group marriage**—exists when several males and several females are married simultaneously to each other. Except experimentally, this is an extremely rare occurrence and may never have existed as a viable form of marriage for any society in the world.

The Oneida Community of upstate New York has been frequently cited as an example of a group marriage experiment (see the "Oneida Today" box). In the mid-1800s, the Oneida practised economic and sexual sharing based on spiritual and religious principles. The group was an experimental religious community and not representative of American society at the time. In addition, similarly to most group marriages on record, the time span of this experiment was limited. Rarely do such arrangements endure beyond one or two generations.

Group marriage has various difficulties that include, among others, getting all members to accept each other as spouses; avoiding jealousy over status, privileges, affection, and sex; and problems related to housing, income, children, privacy, and division of labour in general. What's more, when group marriage does exist, the strong negative reactions of outside persons who are aware of it force anonymity and secrecy. It seems reasonable to assume that group marriage will never become very common.

Family boundaries

The family signifies a set of statuses and roles acquired through marriage, procreation, adoption, or a recognition and inclusion of certain persons as family members. The primary relatives, such as parents and children, tend to share a residence but it may include many other persons as well. Generally, the members assume reciprocal rights and obligations to one another.

One key function of families that appears to be a cultural universal is the socialization of children.

It could be said that all marriages are families but not all families are marriages. And certain functions expected in the marital relationship (sexual relationships) are taboo among certain family members (between brothers and sisters). As marriages differ structurally in the number of spouses, so do families differ structurally in size and composition.

Typology of family structures

One controversy in the family literature has focused on the extent to which families, particularly in North America, are small, isolated, independent units as opposed to large, interdependent networks. The extremes are usually represented by a nuclear/extended dichotomy, with modified nuclear and modified extended as intermediate positions. The major characteristics of these family types are outlined in Table 2.1.

Nuclear and conjugal families **Nuclear and conjugal families** both characterize the family unit in its smallest form. Generally, this form includes the husband, the wife, and their immediate children. The terms *nuclear* and

Family Diversity

Oneida today

The Oneida Community began in New York in 1848 with approximately 25 members. The leader, John Humphrey Noyes, gave up law to enter the ministry. He preached that human beings were capable of living sinless lives based on a spiritual equality of all persons: materially, socially, and sexually. Monogamy was a sign of selfish possessiveness.

Under the charismatic leadership of this man, the group grew and prospered. The emphasis was on *we* rather than on *I*. Economically, there was self-sufficiency and equal ownership of property. The Oneida made traps, marketed crops in cans and glass jars, did silk spinning, and manufactured silverware. To eliminate feelings of discrimination and sexual inequality, jobs were rotated.

The group differed from most other communal groups in their *group marriage*, or pantogamous (marriage for all), relationship. It was felt that romantic love made spiritual love impossible to attain and gave rise to jealousy, hate, and the like; therefore, everyone should literally love everyone else. Requests for sexual relationships were made to a central committee. A go-between, usually an older woman, would get the consent of the requested female (women rarely made requests), and, if agreed upon, the couple would go to the woman's bedroom.

Any discord or problem among the Oneida was handled daily in a practice known as *mutual criticism*, where the followers would subject themselves to criticism by the rest of the group. The criticized member would sit quietly while the others listed his or her good and bad points. The result was said to be a catharsis, a spiritual cleansing, with remarkably successful outcomes.

When Noyes left the group for Canada in 1879, for whatever reason (outside pressures, age, health, intracommune strife), the group marriage practice came to an end. However, the economically successful venture continued.

On November 20, 1880, the group incorporated as Oneida Community, Ltd., to succeed Oneida Community. The present title, Oneida Ltd., was adopted in 1935.

Today, Oneida Ltd. is listed on the New York Stock Exchange. A recent chairman of the board was Peter T. Noyes, a grandson of John Humphrey Noyes, founder of the Oneida Community. The company makes flatware, silver-plated and pewter holloware, jewelry, and gift items. It also markets tableware products and makes cookware and industrial wire products. This international corporation has plants in Arkansas, New York (three), Massachusetts, Kansas, England (three), Canada, and Northern Ireland. In early 1999, the stock was selling at $15 per share, paid a forty-cent dividend per share, and had yearly sales of over $800 million.

Thus, Mr. Noyes would be proud. His children and grandchildren have prospered well. While group marriage is out, profits are in.

conjugal are at times used interchangeably; however, they are not true synonyms. A conjugal family must include a husband and wife. A nuclear family may or may not include the marriage partners but consists of any two or more persons related to one another by blood, marriage, or adoption, assuming they are of the same or adjoining generations. Thus, a brother and sister or a single parent and child are both nuclear families but would not, technically speaking, be conjugal families.

Table 2.1
Typology of family structures

Nuclear-conjugal	***Modified-nuclear and modified-extended***	***Extended***
Small size	Intermediate size	Many kin
Geographic isolation	Kin within easy visiting distance	Geographic proximity
Minimal kin contact	Regular contact	Daily contact
Family autonomy	Family autonomy with kin influences in decision-making	Intergenerational authority
Self-sufficient economically	Considerable exchange of goods and services	Economic interdependence
Nonkin models of socialization	Kin, friendship, nonkin models of socialization	Kinship network as model for socialization
Emotional support and protection from nonkin	Emotional support and protection from kin and nonkin	Kinship completed source of emotional support and protection

Since most persons marry, it is likely that during their lifetime they will be members of two different but overlapping nuclear families. The nuclear family into which someone is born and reared (consisting of self, brothers and sisters, and parents) is termed the **family of orientation.** This is the family unit where the first and most basic socialization processes occur. When an individual marries, he or she forms a new nuclear (and conjugal) family: a **family of procreation.** This family is composed of self, spouse, and children.

The controversy over whether the family system in Canada and the United States is nuclear centres on questions related to geographical isolation, economic independence, and social autonomy. Do families live separately from kin? Do other relatives outside the nuclear unit provide financial assistance or aid in times of need? Do kin provide significant emotional support, visiting patterns, and social activities? And if the nuclear family is isolated, independent, and autonomous, does this lead to high divorce rates; to the need for more public assistance programs for people who are aged, for single parents, or for families in poverty; and to an increase in personal instability (alcoholism, suicide, mental illness, and the like)? Whatever the actual state of the family, questions such as these seem highly relevant to individual health as well as societal functioning.

In Canada, according to the 1996 census, three-generation households represented less than 3 percent of all family households.[21] Although proportinately this is a small group, the numbers of three-generation households increased during the 10-year period between the 1986 census and the 1996 census. In 1996, almost half of these three-generation households were headed by immigrants, the majority of whom were Asian. Thus the increase in nonnuclear households is explained by immigration patterns and cultural tradition. Most Asian immigrants are recent arrivals and thus more likely to follow the family patterns of their country of origin than immigrants who have been in Canada for longer periods. Interestingly, grandparents played a significant financial role in contributing substantially to shelter costs.[22]

Modified-nuclear and modified-extended families A number of writers have suggested that the isolated nuclear family is largely fictitious. That is, families of procreation as well as never-married single, widowed, and divorced persons actually function within a network of other nuclear families and social networks, offering services and gifts, and maintaining close contact.[23] Thus, the idea of a modified form of nuclear or extended family has developed.

In a **modified-nuclear** or **modified-extended** family structure, the nuclear family retains considerable autonomy, yet maintains a coalition with other nuclear families with whom they exchange contacts, goods, and services. Modified-nuclear and modified-extended families take intermediate positions between the isolated, independent, small nuclear unit and the interdependent kin network of the extended family (see Table 2.1).

Glick and others[24] suggest that the long-term downward trend in the percentage of extended family households in the United States came to a halt during the 1980s. One key factor in this change is immigration. Changes in national origin of the immigrant population have influenced increased rates of extended family living among all immigrants since 1970. Immigrants from countries that are both closer to the United States and more likely to send labour migrants (Mexico and Latin America) have contributed significantly to the increase in extended households. But increases in immigration from Asian countries have also made significant contributions to increasing family households. The result is a widening gap between immigrants and natives in the proportion of the U.S. population residing in extended family households.

Extended families The term **extended family** refers to family structures that extend beyond the nuclear family. As stated, there may be a multiple number of nuclear family groupings within the extended family. Sometimes the terms *consanguine families* and *joint families* are used interchangeably with *extended families*.

The term **joint family** is not used as frequently today as in times past. The term has most often been used to describe large families in India, where at least two brothers, with their own wives and children, lived together in the same household. The joint family was consanguine in that the brothers were related by blood and extended in that the wives of the brothers (sisters-in-law) and their children (nephews, nieces, and cousins) lived together. The family was joint in that there existed a common treasury, common kitchen and dining room, and common deities. This Indian form of joint family was usually patrilineal and patrilocal and emphasized filial and fraternal solidarity.

The smallest variety of extended family is the **stem family.** Normally, a stem family consists of two families in adjacent generations, joined by economic

FAMILY DIVERSITY

Living with relatives

While most Canadians live with members of their nuclear family, nearly a million people live with other relatives. This arrangement is defined as an economic family by Statistics Canada. Interestingly, the proportion of people living in economic families has remained stable for the last two decades. The majority of people living in economic families are older women. This seems predictable, given women's greater longevity. Aboriginal women and immigrant women are more likely than nonaboriginals and Canadian-born women to live with relatives.

Seniors who live with family members might be expected to benefit financially, but it is a reciprocal relationship. In 1991, 40 percent of people living with relatives contributed financially to the household, and this group tended to be older, rather than younger. It seems likely that people live together in order to pool resources.

Source: Nancy Z. Ghalam, "Living with Relatives," *Canadian Social Trends* (Autumn 1996), 20–24.

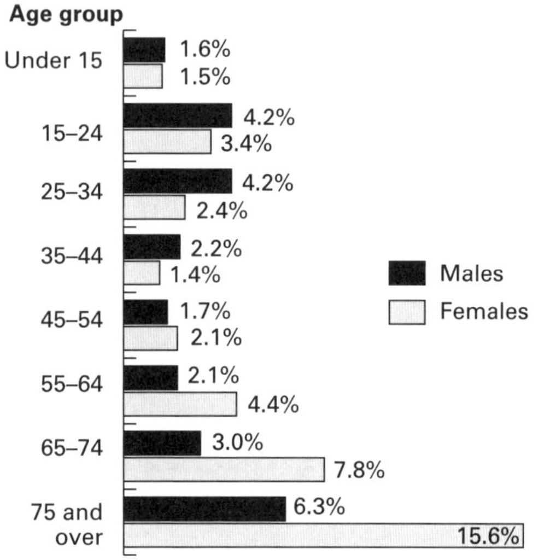

Source: Statistics Canada, *1991 Census of Canada.*

and blood ties. This type of family is quite common in Japan where, despite rapid urbanization, approximately 25 percent of middle-aged married couples live with one spouse's parents.[25] These stem families are most common if the marriage was arranged, the husband was the oldest son, and/or the wife was the oldest daughter and had no brothers.

Another example of the stem family is found in rural Ireland, where the family consists, for example, of a father and mother living in the same household with a married son, his wife, and their children. This type of family is a common device for maintaining the family estate. In contrast to the joint family, in the stem family, the male members of the original family do not pool their resources. Rather, the estate belongs only to the son to whom it is given by the father. The father continues to live in the place, contribute his labour, and derive his living from it. The other sons are given cash settlements in lieu of their shares of the land, and they then leave the family place.

Irrespective of the specific structure of the extended family, kin have both instrumental and psychological value. Close emotional relationships, especially

Extended-family networks exist in all societies. Even in Canada, the transmission of property, the proximity of residence, and the formal and informal contacts made through calls, visits, and gifts demonstrate the presence and importance of extended-kin networks. Some families even have regular reunions to bring old and new members together.

between grandparents and grandchildren, can be quite important and can serve to relieve parents from being the sole sources of affection, general socialization, and care. Economically, the advantages of living in an extended household or family include having a number of active members share the work and costs as well as the resources. Older kin can provide experiences of historical continuity and awareness of important aspects of the life cycle. Extended kin are also important for stable transmission of ideologies and value systems.

Given the importance of these extended relationships, it is logical that, as ties with extended kin weaken or disappear, people will increasingly experiment with new family forms that incorporate extended-kin features. These forms may include communes, with common ownership of goods and sharing of tasks; family networks, where three or four nuclear families join together to share problems and exchange services; and affiliated families, where a nuclear family accepts (socially adopts) one or more unrelated older persons and recognizes them as part of the kin network.

The following section will look more closely at the boundaries of the kinship network and the major importance it holds for most people today.

Boundaries of kinship

The kinship system, like marital and family systems and groups, involves special ties, bonds, and linkages among its members. However, family groups and systems are units upon which kinship systems are built. Kinship systems are regulated by patterns of social norms. These norms vary widely from one society to another; thus, it is impossible to categorize all of them. However, certain norms exist universally among kinship relationships.

The most widely used example of a universal norm is a taboo on incest. All societies forbid sexual relations between persons in certain kinship positions, particularly those within and closest to the nuclear family: father and daughter, mother and son, brother and sister, stepfather and stepdaughter, and the like. Violations of these norms arouse strong feelings among the kinship group as well as in the larger society.

It is unsettling to imagine the confusion of statuses and role expectations that would result if fathers and daughters or mothers and sons had offspring. Consider, for example, a female child born to a mother–son relationship. The child would be a daughter to her brother, a sister to her father, a granddaughter to her own mother, a stepdaughter to her grandfather, and so forth. Should her father, who is also her brother, discipline her as a parent or treat her as a sibling? Could she marry her stepfather, who is her grandfather, if he divorced her mother?

In North America, sexual incest occurs in all social classes and in urban as well as rural environments. The most frequent target is a daughter, and the most frequent perpetrator is a biological father; often, however, a stepfather or foster father or even a boyfriend or lover of the mother may be the perpetrator.

Interestingly, an analysis of narrative accounts of incest perpetrators revealed that almost all of them defined incest as love and care and their behaviour as considerate and fair.[26] Some even described their experience as mutual romantic love. These professed notions of love and care, however, were contradictory in many ways, including their refusal to stop when children wanted them to. Another account, focusing on the meaning surrounding incestuous relationships, reported that both fathers and daughters saw the sexual activity growing out of already existing family interactions such as backrubs, wrestling, reading before bed, or watching TV.[27] Few verbal interactions occurred, leaving the children to rely on their interpretations of what was happening. Many distrusted what they felt, and if they felt it was wrong, blamed themselves.

As might be expected, the thoughts of the fathers and daughters differed. The fathers' thoughts were dominated by themes of sexual gratification and/or curiosity. More than half of the men reported thinking that the child enjoyed what was happening. None of the children concurred, and spoke instead of disbelief, confusion, guilt, and anger. Many saw no way to end the situation. Only as the children reached adolescence did many of them tell a friend or their mother.

In interviews with a random sample of more than 900 adult women in San Francisco, Diana Russell found that, although the most frequent incest perpetrators were biological fathers (since, as girls, most women lived with and were accessible to biological fathers), the next largest group of perpetrators was stepfathers.[28] The likelihood of incestuous abuse was far greater if a stepfather was the principal figure in the woman's childhood years (17 percent, or one out of approximately every six women) than if a father was the principal figure (2 percent, or one out of approximately fifty women). And perhaps more significantly, when stepfathers sexually abused their stepdaughters, they were much more likely than any other relative to abuse the girls seriously, namely, performing forced penile/vaginal penetration, oral/vaginal/penile sex, or anal intercourse. In contrast, other less serious experiences involved digital penetration of the vagina; touching of breasts, buttocks, thighs, and legs; forced kissing; and so forth.

Russell explained these differences by suggesting that stepfathers, who are not biologically related to stepdaughters, may feel less bound by the normative taboo on incest. Another explanation is that the bonding that commonly occurs between biological fathers and daughters may often be absent between stepfathers and stepdaughters. A third explanation is that the daughter, often feeling betrayed by her mother who remarried, may compete with the mother for the attention of the stepfather. Whatever the explanation, the far greater prevalence and seriousness of stepfather–stepdaughter incest over biological father–daughter incest suggests that daughters in parental remarriages face substantial risks of incestuous abuse.

In addition to kinship sexual restrictions, all societies also forbid intermarriage between certain kinship group members. The circle of prohibited relatives for marriage does, however, vary widely in different societies. One extreme, in ancient Egypt, permitted brother–sister and father–daughter marriages. The other extreme may be represented by the traditional clan system of China and by certain extended families in India, where the prohibition extended to a very wide group of relatives, including cousins to the sixth degree.

In areas other than incest, within kinship groups women are accorded lower status than men in most societies. The eldest male or the eldest son may be accorded greater prestige, power, and responsibility than younger men. In general, status positions in the kinship network are differentiated by rights, privileges, and obligations; by inheritance; and by general social expectations.

In some societies, kinship is such an integral part of all aspects of the society that it is difficult to differentiate it from other nonkinship institutions and relationships. Particularly in peasant societies, the political, educational, religious, economic, and property systems are so interlinked and meshed with the kinship system that it becomes impossible to separate kinship networks from nonkinship networks. That is, other institutions are part of the kinship system itself. In contrast are the kinship systems known in most Western societies, where kinship is separate and clearly distinguished from other institutions and relationships. The economic system, while not totally independent of kinship networks or influences, exists separate from and is distinguishable from the kinship system. This differentiation is also true for other institutionalized patterns of norms and activity.

Functions of kinship systems

Kinship groups tend to fulfill certain functions even when the kinship network is indistinguishable from other institutions. These functions include:

1. Property holding and inheritance
2. Housing and residential proximity
3. Obligation, to help in time of need, keeping in touch and gift-giving
4. Affection, emotional ties and primary relationships

Each of these four basic characteristics of kinship groups will be discussed in a following section.

Property holding and inheritance The holding, ownership, and control of property and the transmission of this property from one owner to another is an issue of central concern to family sociologists and anthropologists, in general, and to conflict theorists and feminists, in particular. Property tends to indicate wealth and power. Inheritance tends to indicate how wealth and power are transmitted. Within family systems, this transference is directly linked to inheritance and the rules of descent.

At birth, each person inherits two separate bloodlines; thus, a key issue in most societies (less so in North America) is whose bloodline, the mother's or the father's, is the most important. If the descent pattern is *unilineal*—as is true in most societies in Asia, India, and Africa—the name, property, authority, and marriage controls are traced through one line, usually that of the father and his bloodline. This pattern is **patrilineal.** A **matrilineal** pattern, a unilineal system that traces the lineage through the female line, is found much less frequently. The system of descent most prevalent in Western families is the **bilateral** system, under which power and property are transferred through both the mother's and the father's line to both males and females.

One key exception to this pattern is name; both genders tend to assume the surname of their fathers, and wives often take their husbands' family names upon marriage. This too may be changing, albeit slowly. Female college students were found to be far more accepting of nontraditional name choices and more tolerant of choices made by others than males.[29] Even so, more than 80 percent of females said that if they marry, they plan to change their last name to that of their husband. Women planning to marry at a later age and expected nontraditional work roles were less likely than other women to want to change their last name to that of their husband.

Patterns of descent take on special significance to many feminists and conflict theorists for several reasons. First of all, most family systems throughout the world tend to perpetuate power and wealth through successive generations—that is, the rich stay rich and the poor stay poor. Also, most family systems differentiate this power and wealth between the genders, with males receiving preferential treatment. The result is that class and sexual inequalities are built into most family systems, such that the inequalities come to be viewed as natural and legitimate. In other words, some families have the right to be wealthier than others, males are expected to be dominant, and females are supposed to submit to their male counterparts.

Housing and residential proximity All family systems have rules of residence that establish who lives where and with whom. Since husbands and wives come from different families and most spouses choose to share the same residence, to achieve this, one or both individuals must move.

The most common residential pattern is **patrilocal,** in which the bride changes residence and lives with the parents of the groom. In the **matrilocal** pattern, which is much less frequently found, the newlywed couple lives with the parents of the bride. In Western families, far more common than either of the preceding are the **bilocal** system, in which the couple lives near the parents of either spouse, and the **neolocal** system, in which the couple lives in a home of their own that may be located apart from both sets of parents.

The pattern of residence takes on a special significance as one looks at the third and fourth aspects of kinship, namely, obligation and emotional ties among kin. Helping patterns and showing affection to grandparents, parents, and siblings take on a different character when the people involved share the same building, live in the same neighbourhood or community, or reside hundreds of miles apart.

Keeping in touch and gift-giving Around the world it is expected that kin communicate or keep in touch, particularly with parents, to a lesser extent with siblings, and even less so with other relatives such as aunts, uncles, and cousins. Many extended families have a person who could be considered a "kinkeeper," usually a female, who works at keeping the family members in touch with one another.[30] Often it is expected that services or gifts be shared as gestures of goodwill and kindness. Gift-giving, whether with friends or family, tends to cement social relationships. The gifts may be material or nonmaterial: presents of food (having guests for dinner), lodging (offering guests a place to stay in one's home), and care or help. Data from the Netherlands that examined gift-giving in Western societies revealed that gifts are given approximately to the same extent to extended kin and to friends, but gifts to friends seem to be given more out of affection than out of obligation.[31] Gift-giving to extended kin is more obligatory, but at the same time it is more enduring than giving to friends. Family ties have a relatively high degree of stability in contrast to friendships, which have a greater risk of change.

Affection and primary relationships Affection and primary relationships are the emotional dimensions of visits, calls, and letters. *Affection* means being emotionally close to kin. Women seem to be the "specialists" in affectionate kin relationships. In Middletown, as elsewhere, women expressed more affection than men did for every category of relative. The distribution of affection was highest for mothers, next highest for fathers and near siblings, and lowest for best-known cousins. The affection dimension between children and parents seems to increase with age but weaken with kin such as cousins.

Family boundary ambiguity

This chapter first focused on the family as a social institution and as a group or system. It then explored the boundaries of marriage, family, and kin. The reader who desires to segment and isolate these three interrelated components is likely to face many difficulties, for the boundaries of each are seldom precise and distinct. This is true both conceptually and in real life.

Pauline Boss and Jan Greenberg, for example, wrote about **family boundary ambiguity** as a new variable in understanding family stress.[32] They defined *boundary ambiguity* as not knowing who is in and out of the family system. New and old spouses, stepparents and stepchildren, in-laws, distant relatives, and others may or may not be fully recognized as part of a particular family network. Lynn White, using two waves of data from a large national sample of adults, asked the simple question "How many siblings do you have?" Over 16 percent reported fewer siblings at time two than time one.[33] The discrepancies were greatest among, but not limited to, those with complex family structures. In other words, is a stepsibling a sibling if all share the same residence? If your mother and stepfather divorce, are his children no longer your siblings? Is a nonresident child of a stepfather a brother or a sister?

While families' perceptions of boundaries will differ from one cultural context to another, the central notion of Boss and Greenberg is that a high degree of boundary ambiguity over time will lead to a high level of stress in the family system. Determining who is in and who is out of the family becomes a major issue in determining task performance and inheritance as well as visiting, communicating, and helping responsibilities. With the growing complexity of families and kin groups, it is likely that it will become increasingly difficult to determine just who is kin.

SUMMARY

1. The family, as a social institution, is an organized, formal, and regular system of carrying out certain essential tasks in society. The family is defined by a wide system of norms that organize family units into stable and ongoing social systems. This chapter presented numerous ways in which marital, family, and kin groups and systems are organized to fulfill certain tasks.
2. The family system is an abstract network of interrelated statuses and the social expectations that accompany them. The family group is a concrete set of persons who interact with one another. The primary family group, which is small in size and has frequent and intense contact among members, is distinguished from the secondary group, which is more formal and involves the impersonal contacts that characterize much of an individual's life.
3. The boundaries of marriage are not always precise and clearly defined. Generally, marriage includes a heterosexual union of at least one male and one female. It grants legitimacy to children and approval to sexual relationships. Marriage is usually a public affair and establishes reciprocal rights and obligations between the spouses. Finally, marriage is usually a binding relationship that assumes some permanence.
4. The variations in marriage and number of spouses include singlehood, monogamy, and polygamy (polygyny, polyandry, and group marriage). The number of Canadians who remain single has risen over the past two decades.
5. Polygyny and polyandry, two forms of polygamy, occur in a wide range of contexts and take numerous forms. The plural spouses may be brothers or sisters, may marry simulta-

neously or sequentially, and may perform various functions. Polygyny is common, but polyandry is quite rare. Group marriage, as well, occurs extremely infrequently and may never have existed as a viable and lasting form of marriage for any society in the world.
6. As do those of marriage, the boundaries of the family vary considerably. Usually, a family results from marriage and includes people united by marriage, blood, and adoption. The members, some of whom share a residence, have reciprocal rights and obligations to one another. This institutionalized pattern fulfills certain basic functions for society, particularly as related to socialization and primary relationships.
7. One typology of family structures differentiates the nuclear/conjugal unit from a variety of extended units. Some of these include families of orientation and procreation; modified-nuclear and modified-extended families; and consanguine, joint, and stem families.
8. The boundaries of kinship serve as an extension of those of the marital and family units. The kinship system also involves special ties, bonds, and links among its members. This system tends to have key functions and characteristics that include property holding and inheritance; housing and maintenance of residential proximity; obligation or helping in time of need; and affection and emotional ties.
9. Kinship systems have key functions and characteristics that include property holding and inheritance, housing and maintenance of residential proximity, obligation or helping in time of need, and affection and emotional ties.
10. The next chapter will address how the marital, family, and kin systems are interrelated with other major systems, particularly the economic, employment, and work-related system. The employment of none, one, or both spouses is a key factor in better understanding the functioning of marital, family, and kin networks.

KEY TERMS AND TOPICS

Families as social institutions p. 33
Groups and systems p. 34
Primary group p. 35
Secondary group p. 37
Marriage, family, and kinship groups p. 37
Marriage boundaries p. 38
Single living p. 38
Monogamy p. 41
Sequential or serial monogamy p. 41
Polygamy p. 41
Sex ratio p. 41
Polygyny p. 42
Polyandry p. 42
Group marriage p. 44
Family boundaries p. 44
Nuclear and conjugal families p. 44
Family of orientation p. 46
Family of procreation p. 46
Modified-nuclear family structure p. 47
Modified-extended family structure p. 47
Extended family p. 47
Joint family p. 47
Stem family p. 47
Boundaries of kinship p. 50
Patrilocal p. 53
Matrilocal p. 53
Bilocal p. 53
Neolocal p. 53
Family boundary ambiguity p. 54

DISCUSSION QUESTIONS

1. What is meant by the phrase *family as a social institution*? Are factors such as homosexuality, illegitimacy, and child support part of this institution?
2. Differentiate *family groups* from *family systems*. Since systems are abstractions, of what relevance are family systems to understanding the family?

3. Describe what would probably happen to a person who was removed from all primary-group relationships. Why are such relationships so crucial?
4. Define the terms *marriage* and *family* in a way that would be comprehensive enough to include marriages and families in most societies in the world. How are the two terms similar and different? How do marriage and family differ from other groups and relationships? Should gay men and lesbians be able to marry, divorce, adopt children, and be families? Why?
5. Is it likely that the trend of an increasing percentage of people choosing to remain single will continue? Is this trend the same for males and females? Explain.
6. Why is monogamy so strongly stressed in Canada? What advantages or disadvantages do polygyny, polyandry, and group marriage have?
7. In societies where polygamy is culturally approved, polygyny appears to be far more common than polyandry. Why? What factors explain the exceptions that occur?
8. Think of your own kin group. How many persons in it do you know (uncles, cousins, and so on)? With how many kin do you interact regularly (say, at least yearly)? What differentiations do you make between kin on your mother's side and kin on your father's side?
9. What arguments will feminists and conflict theorists probably make about traditional unilineal descent and inheritance systems?
10. List all the relatives that you actually know and can identify. Which ones do you visit, maintain contact with, and feel obligated toward? How much is geographical proximity a factor in your visits, contacts, and feelings? How many commitments extend beyond parents and siblings?

FURTHER READINGS

Gillis, John R. *A World of Their Own Making: Myth, Ritual, and the Quest for Family Values.* New York: Basic Books, 1996. A reconstruction of the history of the myths, rituals, and other cultural practices of the Western family from the late Middle Ages to the present.

Goode, William J. *World Revolution and Family Patterns.* Glencoe, IL: The Free Press, 1963. A description and interpretation of the main changes in family patterns that have occurred over the past half-century in various cultures.

Hansen, Karen V., and Garey, Anita Ilta., eds. *Families in the U.S.: Kinship and Domestic Politics.* Philadelphia: Temple University Press, 1998. Sixty-two essays that reveal the complexity of families when viewed within their economic, political, and cultural contexts.

Jacobs, Janet Liebman. *Victimized Daughters: Incest and the Development of the Female Self.* New York: Routledge, 1994. A study of white, African American, and Latina incest survivors with a focus on the identification with the incestuous father and its impact on the identity formation.

Kephart, William M., and Zellner, William W. *Extraordinary Groups: An Examination of Unconventional Life-Styles.* 5th ed. New York: St. Martin's Press, 1994. A look at eight different cultural groups and lifestyles that exist in the United States: the old-order Amish, the Oneida Community, the gypsies, the Church of Christ—Scientist, the Hasidim, the Father Divine Movement, the Mormons, and the Jehovah's Witnesses.

Marsiglio, William, and Scanzoni, John H. *Families and Friendships: Applying the Sociological Imagination.* New York: HarperCollins, 1995. A focus on primary relationships, with a particular emphasis on families and friendships.

Murdock, George P. *Social Structure.* New York: Free Press, 1965. Although recommended reading for a general and excellent cross-cultural perspective on family structure, the book also extensively analyzes sexual patterns and incest.

Ottenheimer, Martin. *Forbidden Relatives: The American Myth of Cousin Marriage.* Urbana: University of Illinois Press, 1996. An exploration of why 31 states in the United States prohibit first-cousin marriages, the development of this myth, and an argument for legislation to revive marital laws.

Rochelle, Anne R. *No More Kin: Exploring Race, Class, and Gender in Family Networks.* Thousand Oaks, CA: Sage, 1997. An analysis of how race, class, and gender affect minority family structures and relationships.

Smith, Raymond T. *The Matrifocal Family: Power, Pluralism, and Politics.* New York: Routledge, 1996. Eleven essays written by the author that focus on matrifocal families in the West Indies and most specifically in Guyana and Jamaica.

Westerlund, Elaine. *Women's Sexuality After Childhood Incest.* Scranton, PA: W. W. Norton, 1992. A study of the sexual attitudes and practices of women with incest histories, including both statistical and anecdotal findings.

WEBLINKS

http://gozips.uakron.edu/~dje/HOMOLINK.HTM

Homosexuality/Sexuality Issues Links: Has sections "Gay Marriages" and "Gay Families."

http://www.oneida.com/theoneid.htm

The Oneida Community, Oneida Ltd. Home Page. This gives a capsule history of the Community, answering the questions: What was the original Oneida Community? What was its relation to Oneida Ltd. today?

http:// emuseum.mankato.msus.edu/cultural/kinship/index.shtml

This site explores the different forms of kinship recognition and marriages. It includes terms, explanations and a tutorial.

http://www.ffef.ca/

The Foundation for Equal Families homepage offers up-to-date developments on issues relating to gay and lesbian unions, including challenges and changes to existing legal definitions of marriage in Canada.

http://www.polygamy.com

This website offers an interesting overview of polygamy, providing concrete examples of this marital, familial and kinship structure.

NOTES

1. J. Ross Eshleman, Barbara G. Cashion, and Lawrence Basirico, *Sociology: An Introduction*, 4th ed. (New York: HarperCollins, 1993), 109.
2. David Popenoe, Jean Bethke Elshtain, and David Blankenhorn, *Promises to Keep: Decline and Renewal of Marriage in America* (Lanham, MD: Rowman and Littlefield Publishers, Inc., 1996).
3. Ibid., 308.
4. Sharon K. Houseknecht and Jaya Sastry, "Family 'Decline' and Child Well-Being: A Comparative Assessment," *Journal of Marriage and the Family* 58 (August 1996): 726–739.
5. Note in particular William Marsiglio and John H. Scanzoni, *Families and Friendships: Applying the Sociological Imagination* (New York: HarperCollins, 1995).
6. Moncrieff Cochran, Mary Larner, David Riley, Lars Gunnarsson, and Charles R. Henderson, Jr., *Extending Families: The Social Networks of Parents and Their Children* (Cambridge: Cambridge University Press, 1990).
7. William N. Stephens, *The Family in Cross Cultural Perspective* (New York: Holt, Rinehart, and Winston, 1963), 7.
8. *Population 15 Years and Over by Marital Status. Showing Selected Age Groups and Sex for Canada, Provinces and Territories, 1996 Census—100% Data*, Statistics Canada Catalogue No. 93F0022XDB96005.

9. The numbers in this paragraph are taken from Jillian Oderkirk, "Marriage in Canada: Changing Beliefs and Behaviours, 1600–1990," *Canadian Social Trends*, Statistics Canada Catalogue 11-008E (Summer 1994): 1–7.

10. Robert Riordan, "Two by Two? Sex Ratios of Unattached Canadians," *Canadian Social Trends*, Statistics Canada Catalogue 11-008E (Spring 1994): 26–29.

11. Ibid., 27.

12. Norval Glenn and Charles N. Weaver, "The Changing Relationship of Marital Status to Reported Happiness," *Journal of Marriage and the Family* 50 (May 1988): 317–324.

13. Noreen Goldman, "The Perils of Single Life in Contemporary Japan," *Journal of Marriage and the Family* 55 (February 1993): 191–204.

14. Steven Stack and J. Ross Eshleman, "Marital Status and Happiness: A 17-Nation Study," *Journal of Marriage and the Family* 60 (May 1998): 527–536.

15. George P. Murdock, "World Ethnographic Sample," *American Anthropologist* 59 (August 1957): 686.

16. Helen Ware, "Polygyny: Women's Views in a Traditional Society, Nigeria 1975," *Journal of Marriage and the Family* 41 (February 1979): 188.

17. See Irwin Altman and Joseph Ginat, *Polygamous Families in Contemporary Society* (New York: Cambridge University Press, 1996).

18. Stephens, *The Family in Cross Cultural Perspective*, 39–49.

19. John D. Early and John F. Peters, *The Population Dynamics of the Mucajai Yanomama* (New York: Academic Press, 1990), 40.

20. Margaret L. Cassidy and Gary R. Lee, "The Study of Polyandry: A Critique and Synthesis," *Journal of Comparative Family Studies* 20 (Spring 1989): 1–11.

21. Janet Che-Alford and Brian Hamm, "Under One Roof: Three Generations Living Together," *Canadian Social Trends*, Statistics Canada Catalogue 11-008E (Summer 1999): 6–9.

22. Ibid.

23. Eugene Litwak and Stephen Kulis, "Technology, Proximity and Measures of Kin Support," *Journal of Marriage and the Family* 49 (August 1987): 649–661; and Naomi Gerstel, "Divorce and Kin Ties: The Importance of Gender," *Journal of Marriage and the Family* 50 (February 1988): 209–219. See also the classic article on this topic by Marvin B. Sussman, "The Isolated Nuclear Family: Fact or Fiction," *Social Problems* 6 (Spring 1959): 333–340.

24. Jennifer E. Glick, Frank D. Bean, and Jennifer V. W. Van Hook, "Immigration and Changing Patterns of Extended Family Household Structure in the United States," *Journal of Marriage and the Family* 59 (February 1997): 177–191.

25. Yoshinori Kamo, "Husbands and Wives Living in Nuclear and Stem Family Households in Japan," *Sociological Perspectives* 33 (1990): 397–417.

26. Jane F. Gilgun, "We Shared Something Special: The Moral Discourse of Incest Perpetrators," *Journal of Marriage and the Family* 57 (May 1995): 265–281.

27. Patricia Phelan, "Incest and Its Meaning: The Perspectives of Fathers and Daughters," *Child Abuse and Neglect* 19 (1994): 7–24.

28. Diana E. H. Russell, "The Prevalence and Seriousness of Incestuous Abuse: Step-fathers vs. Biological Fathers," *Child Abuse and Neglect* 8 (1984): 15–22.

29. Laurie K. Scheuble and David R. Johnson, "Marital Name Change: Plans and Attitudes of College Students," *Journal of Marriage and the Family* 55 (August 1993): 747–754. Note also David R. Johnson and Laurie K. Scheuble, "Women's Marital Naming in Two Generations: A National Study," *Journal of Marriage and the Family* 57 (August 1995): 724–732.

30. Carolyn J. Rosenthal, "Kinkeeping in the Familial Division of Labor," *Journal of Marriage and the Family* 47 (November 1985): 965–974.

31. Aafke Komter and Wilma Vollebergh, "Gift Giving and the Emotional Significance of Family and Friends," *Journal of Marriage and the Family* 59 (August 1997): 747–757.

32. Pauline Boss and Jan Greenberg, "Family Boundary Ambiguity: A New Variable in Family Stress Theory," *Family Process* 23 (1984): 535–546.

33. Lynn White, "Who's Counting? Quasi-Facts and Stepfamilies in Reports of Number of Siblings," *Journal of Marriage and the Family* 60 (August 1998): 725–733.

CHAPTER

3 MARRIAGE, FAMILY, AND WORK

Chapter 2 discussed how marriage, family, and kin groups and systems are organized, showing variation in the number of spouses, presenting a typology of family structures, and noting some of the basic functions of kinship networks. In most societies, family/kin networks are such an integral part of society that it is difficult to separate and differentiate the family system from other major institutions.

Although this chapter will focus primarily on linking marriages and families to work and the economic system, religion, politics, and education affect and are affected by the family. These influences are briefly outlined in the first part of the chapter, and many will be reemphasized throughout the text, as in discussions of economics and social class (Chapter 4), interfaith marriage (Chapter 5), the significance of formal education (Chapters 4, 7, and 11), and government policies (Chapter 12).

RELATIONS BETWEEN THE FAMILY AND OTHER SYSTEMS

It appears obvious that linkages exist between family systems and other systems. As the economy changes, so do employment rates and family spending patterns. As wars affect international relations, so do they affect divorce rates. As political decisions determine policies related to health and welfare, so do they affect attitudes toward one-parent families and child-support responsibilities. And as education, employment, and the advancement of fertility-control methods modify the opportunities and options available to women and men, so do these changes affect male/female, husband/wife, and parent/child interactions and expectations.

Mass media and the family

Today, the mass media can be considered an emerging social system and social institution. The mass media includes newspapers, magazines, television, radio, films, and most recently the Internet. On the one hand, the media that is presented to a widely dispersed public (the mass) is a source of information. On the other hand, it is far more, in that it influences our attitudes toward marital and family structures—such as single parenthood or same-sex marriages, marital and family behaviours such as parenting and human sexuality, and even our definitions of self.

Television seems to draw the most attention, since it is the primary media source immediately accessible to children and adults alike on a day-to-day basis. Television is one media that varies little in use by gender, race, or household income. It is a potent agent of socialization and, unlike movies, does not require that viewers leave the privacy of their home. Television is free (except for cable subscribers), requires no special skills (even literacy), and broadcasts the same pictures and words into people's homes regardless of whether the viewers are adults or children, wealthy or poor, and even living in congested urban areas or isolated rural ones.

Many families use television as an electronic baby-sitter. Volti says that children in the United States spend more time in front of a television set than they do in school.[1] Since they are exposed to so much, of particular concern is its impact on them. Looking at something such as violence alone, Volti indicates that by the age of 18, the average adolescent has watched about 18,000 people being strangled, smothered, stabbed, shot, poisoned, blown up, drowned, run over, or beaten to death. It is possible that they view 10 times as many armed robberies and assaults. Perhaps it should not be totally surprising that in the late 1990s, several media reports included teenagers shooting their classmates, rapes and beatings on college campuses, and the use of violence as an acceptable solution to personal or social problems in dating, the home, or elsewhere.

Feminist theorists and scholars in particular have expressed concern over how the mass media serves as a powerful force in reinforcing cultural expectations of males and females and of gender stereotyping. **Stereotypes** are widely held beliefs about the character and behaviour of all members of a group that seldom correspond to the facts. They are usually oversimplified summary descriptions.

Gender stereotypes are not always consistent but in general let us know that males and females are not only different but are unequal. Advertising frequently portrays men as dominant and women as sex objects. The rugged Marlboro man and the use of female models to sell automobiles come to mind as cases in point. Magazines directed at adolescent girls feature articles and ads focused on being beautiful, thin, and popular, while those directed at males feature being muscular and successful in sports. Music frequently portrays males as aggressive and domineering, females as dependent and nurturing. Some even argue that music not merely stereotypes popular gender images but focuses exclusively on men, with females as irrelevant or as background displays for men. Television too, features far more males than females and frequently portrays the wife as dependent upon and submissive to her authoritative, decision-making husband.

These recurring images make the mass media a powerful force in shaping our ideas of gender and interpersonal relationships. Ideas are conveyed that men are more important than and superior to women, that the elderly who are underrepresented on television and in advertisements are of little consequence and can be ignored, and that women should do the housework, raise the children, and not disturb the husband while he is watching sport events.

You may argue that these stereotypes are simple media portrayals and in "real life" people don't believe them. But research suggests that recipients of the media are influenced by what is presented. This may be best illustrated by the effects of advertising on sales of products or the influence of spending millions of dollars in campaigns to generate votes. Research on the effects of violence has arrived at similar conclusions. It should be noted that people rarely imitate exactly what they see in films or on television. Yet what they see does socialize them to become desensitized to violence and makes it more acceptable for husbands to dominate wives and parents to hit their children.

This section is not meant to support the idea that the media only conveys violence and negative stereotypes. That, too, would be stereotyping. The media, including television, can have a positive influence on people's behaviour, in or out of marriage. For better or worse, the media has a powerful influence on marriages and families and what happens in them.

Religion and the family

Cross-culturally as well as historically, the relationship between the religious system and the family system has been reciprocal.[2] In most societies, many family celebrations are religious in nature. Religious norms also influence speech patterns, nonmarital as well as marital sexuality, male and female roles, husband/wife and parent/child relations, and so forth. Marriage contracts and birth and death rituals frequently involve the clergy and religious organizations.

Today, differences between those who attend religious services and those who do not are more pronounced than those between people of particular religious groups, such as Protestants and Catholics. Churchgoers, for example, are more likely to have stable marriages; to have more children; to be more conservative on issues relating to sexuality, such as abortion, homosexuality, and premarital sex, and to stress traditional gender roles. People who attend church regularly in Canada place more importance on a lasting relationship, being married and having at least one child than Canadians who do not attend.[3] Regular attenders hold more traditional family values and are more likely to support women's nurturing role within the family. Interestingly, regular attenders also say that they have happier and less stressful lives and happier relationships with their partners than Canadians who do not attend regularly.

Canadian sociologist Reginald Bibby has tracked changing religious trends in Canada for decades. His research shows that attendance at religious services dropped sharply in the 1970s and has continued to decline since. The greatest declines are for Catholics in Quebec. In the mid-1990s, only one-quarter of Quebec Catholics were weekly attenders, in contrast to 40 percent in the rest of Canada.[4] For the last decade, weekly attendance figures for Canada have remained lower than U.S. rates.[5] Generally, attendance by young people is low, so congregations tend to be getting older. More recent data from the National Longitudinal Survey of Children and Youth found that slightly less than one-quarter (23 percent) of Canadian children aged 12 and under attend religious services weekly.[6] Highest attendance was reported by Jehovah's Witnesses and lowest by Anglican and United Church children. Children in Atlantic Canada were the highest regular attenders and children in Quebec the lowest. Most children attend church with a parent, typically their mother.

The decline in attendance at traditional churches is partly offset by interest in spirituality and by private observance, so we should not necessarily conclude that Canadians are less religious now. Despite low attendance, most Canadians believe in God and identify with a religion. Only 3.4 percent of Canadians reported "no religious affiliation" in 1996.[7]

Politics and the family

The study of politics and the family examines the relationship between the family and the state (or government). The *state* is defined by civil laws and policies created by legislators whom the citizenry has elected; these laws and policies are enforced by agents of local, provincial, and federal governments. The state (that is, the political system) influences families through laws that regulate and support families.

For instance, families are regulated through laws that govern marriage, including the choice of spouse, the number of spouses permitted, the age at which marriage is permissible, the necessity of a blood test, the acceptance or nonacceptance of common-law marriages, the prohibition or acceptance of same-sex marriages, what relationships are seen as incestuous, and the soundness of the mental condition. Families are also regulated through laws that specify the rights and duties of parenthood, such as those that relate to contraception, pregnancy, and abortion; legitimacy; custody of children; and abuse. Other regulations of families include laws on divorce and separation, as well as economic factors, such as the distribution of property. Some of these laws are general and establish guidelines or boundaries of permissible behaviour; others are precise and specific, and carry legal and civil sanctions.

The state not only regulates families; it supports them as well. The extent to which the state has this responsibility is an ongoing controversy. For example, is the government responsible for guaranteeing adequate housing for everyone or should it simply serve as a "safety net," a last resort when all else fails? Do welfare programs generate a positive response from people who believe that government is fulfilling its responsibility to the poor, or do such programs generate feelings of anger from people who feel that tax dollars are being distributed to those who have not contributed their fair share in work or money? A variety of government programs provide support for families: family benefits, old age security, disability insurance, provincial medical coverage, student loans, energy allowances, and tax breaks for children and the elderly. Granted, all sorts of regulations specify conditions of eligibility for these programs; nonetheless, the focus is on the assistance (support) of families and family members in need. How this support is given, who gets it, and how much is enough are topics of debate in every election. Issues of social policy are addressed more explicitly in Chapter 12.

Education and the family

Just as family structures and processes affect educational achievement, so too do schools and the education system affect the lives of families and their members.[8] Schools affect socialization, employment, and vacations. Schools group students according to their ages and sometimes their abilities. Family life changes when young children enter school, become active in school endeavours, and move through the system. Schools take children through an established curriculum of academic subjects, yet schools focus heavily on the so-called *hidden curriculum*, teaching civic and moral responsibility, obedience to rules, respect for authority, punctuality, success through competition, conscientiousness, and other areas traditionally believed to be in the family domain. The extent of social literacy and social competence are clearly linked to the education system.

Family and education systems tend to supplement one another in teaching selected cultural values, norms, and skills. One intended function of education is to supplement family socialization. The schools use experts (teachers) to teach children knowledge, values, and selected skills that parents frequently are incapable of teaching and that are necessary for individuals to function successfully in a changing world. The close relation between the family and education systems appears in many studies that show educational training in the home to be directly linked to the success of training in the school. Why, then, do we spend so much time in schools?

Participation in the education system from early childhood through late adolescence is expected to increase the individual's level of knowledge, and mental and interpersonal skills. Ideally, having these skills will improve the individual's marital and parental performance in addition to employment performance. Sometimes, the training given adolescents in schools is at odds with parents' values or perhaps exceeds the level of training that parents have had. Thus, the authority of the family may be undermined or the skills of the parents may be less than those of the child. In such instances, parental authoritarianism may give way to more egalitarian parent/child relations or may set the stage for emancipation from the household. Again, the linkages between the education and family systems are evident.

The economy and the family

Perhaps more than any other institution, the economic system influences family organization and interaction. The economy is the component of society concerned with the creation, distribution, and consumption of goods and services. The family contributes labour and skills, and in turn receives wages or other forms of compensation (prestige, insurance, services, etc). Managing work and family responsibilities is stressful for everyone, but particularly so for poorer families. And financial stress, in turn, has pernicious consequences for both adults and children.[9] Poor mental health, erosion of self-image, increased risk of suicide, alcohol-related disease, divorce, and child abuse are a few of the negative consequences for adults. Children have also been found to exhibit a range of emotional and behavioural problems.

At a macro level of analysis, the economic system includes issues ranging from rates of employment and unemployment to indices of depression and inflation. Economic restructuring, for example, affects all families but has a worse impact on those people least often employed, or on fixed or low incomes: female heads of families; children; people who are retired, elderly, or disabled; and so forth.[10]

According to conflict theorists, the economic system is the key to understanding inequality within or outside the family system. More than 100 years ago, Karl Marx's co-writer, Friedrich Engels, argued that marriage represents a class antagonism in which the well-being and development of one group are attained through the misery and repression of the other.[11] In marriage, as in the economy, the dominance of husbands and the suppression of wives is self-reinforcing.

This dominance/suppression issue is at the heart of gender inequality discussions. There is still strong cultural support for a gendered domestic division of labour, despite dramatic changes in the labour force. Universally, housework is not highly valued, nor is much consideration given to the physical and emotional demands of housework. The phrase *working wives* usually describes wives who are employed outside the home; work typically does not refer to domestic work and child care done by women at home. Before turning to an analysis of housework we will describe the dynamics of women's paid work in Canada.

TRENDS IN WOMEN'S PAID WORK

Since the beginning of the century, female labour force participation rates have increased in Canada, as in most other Western countries. Over the same period, male rates have decreased as more men over 15 stay in school, return to school, retire, or leave the labour force for other reasons during their working lives. In 1911, nine out of ten Canadian men were in the labour force. Now it is three out of four. The change for women has been far more dramatic. In 1911, 16.2 percent of Canadian women over 15 were employed. Now the number is almost 60 percent. The greatest change for women occurred since the 1960s, when, for the first time, large numbers of married women, including mothers, entered the paid labour force.

When clerical and other service jobs first became available to women, the typical pattern was to work until marriage. During the Second World War, when there was a need for women's work, more and more married women joined the labour force. But beginning in the 1960s the employment of married women has steadily increased. The gap in participation rates for married and single women has narrowed considerably, even for mothers of young children.

As Table 3.1 shows, participation rates for single and married women 25 and over are very similar, and young (15–24 years) married women have *higher* participation rates than young single women. Married couples, with or without children, have come to depend on the earnings of both partners. The labour force participation of women with school-age and pre-school-age children has dramatically increased over the last two decades. Having young children remains a slight deterrent to women's labour force participation, but only minimally so in contrast to 30 years ago.

Table 3.1
Female employment by marital status and age, Canada, 1997

	Marital Status % Employed			
Age	**Single**	**Married**	**Separated/Divorced**	**Widowed**
15–24	47.7%	60.1%	45.5%	—
25–44	72.7%	72.1%	67.0%	63.9%
45+	41.5%	40.9%	49.1%	8.3%
Total	54.8%	57.1%	57.2%	9.6%

Source: Statistics Canada Catalogue 71F0004-XCB, www.statcan.ca/english/Pgdb/People/Labour/labor24c.htm.

In 1967, husbands were the only income earners in 58 percent of husband-wife families. By 1991, this figure had dropped to 19 percent, and 61 percent of husband-wife families were dual-earner.[12] Some (15 percent) of the remaining families had no earners; in 5 percent of families, wives were the only earners. Typically husband-only earner families were older, or younger families with two or more young children. Wives' earnings relative to husbands' have also increased since the 1960s. One of the consequences of this shift is an increase in the number of families in which wives earn more than their husbands. In 1967, in 11 percent of households, wives earned more than husbands. In 1993, during a severe economic downturn, this figure was 25 percent.[13] The fact that these numbers accelerated during the recessionary years 1990–92 supports the idea that some wives may have become main breadwinners. Indeed, in approximately one-third of families in which wives earned more, husbands had been unemployed at some point during the year. Almost half of those husbands had been unemployed 26 weeks or more.

In 1997 only 31 percent of husband-wife families with at least one child under 16 were single-earner, compared to 59 percent in 1976. In an increasing number of these single-earner families, it is wives who are breadwinners. While they represent a small proportion of all families, the numbers are increasing dramatically.[14] We do not know how many families choose to have a "stay-at-home dad." Part of the increase is presumably due to job loss, limited employment opportunities and underemployment. Katherine Marshall found that, "Among the stay-at-home parents who have worked in the past year, 67% of fathers and 43% of mothers said they had lost their last job."[15]

How do children affect the work patterns of parents? A Canadian study of dual-earner couples found that children have a significant impact on work scheduling for mothers and no impact on fathers' schedules.[16] This study focused on couples with wives in the childrearing stage (age 25–44). Mothers' work patterns were greatly affected by the presence and ages of children. Compared to mothers with older children, mothers with preschoolers were more likely to work part-time and more likely to work an irregular schedule that involved evening and weekend work. Ninety percent of women aged 25–44 with no children under 25 at home were gainfully employed in 1991. This participation rate drops to 84 percent for mothers of older children and to 68 percent for mothers of preschoolers. Children also affect the likelihood that women will work part-time. Only 9 percent of women with no children work part-time, while 31 percent of mothers of preschoolers do. These modified work patterns occur regardless of occupation.

Jenny Blain asked a sample of Canadian parents how they deal with changed work routines occasioned by a sick child.[17] All parents in this group agreed that if the child is very sick, mothers will stay home. Mothers and fathers attribute needed positive characteristics to mothers, and some identified negative characteristics of fathers that would be detrimental. If the child's illness is not particularly serious, more pragmatic considerations such as which parent can take time off work without penalty come into play. These decisions are based in large part on what reaction the parents expect from employers or co-workers.

While Canadian women continue to experience greater work discontinuity than men, women today have fewer and shorter interruptions now than women in the past. Women today have fewer children and return to work within months of giving birth.[18] Recent analysis of Canadian employment data found that about 60 percent of women return to work within six months of giving birth. Ninety percent return within a year. Self-employed women and women who did not receive maternity benefits were more likely to return to work within a few weeks, suggesting that these decisions are economically driven.[19] In sum, mothers who contribute all or much of the total family income are more likely to remain employed, exit from employment more slowly, and return to employment more quickly after childbirth.

Attitudes have changed to reflect changing labour force patterns. Younger Canadian women (83 percent) and men (91 percent) are more inclined to feel that being able to work for pay is important or very important to their personal happiness. Among those over 65, 75 percent of men but only 37 percent of women thought this. Another sign that Canadians accept the inevitability of women's employment is the general agreement with the statement "men and women should contribute to household income." According to the 1995 General Social Survey, 68 percent of men and 73 percent of women agreed with this statement.[20]

These trends have implications for both the economic system and the family system. The Canadian economy is highly dependent on work done by women, and family life has changed dramatically with the employment of married women. This change has affected child care, elder care, and the management of household work. Both the increased number of dual-earner families where wives earn more than husbands and the increased number of husband-wife families where wives are the only breadwinners predict shifting family dynamics. In some families this change may lead to tension and conflict. In others it may mean increasingly blurred distinctions in the division of labour.

HOUSEWORK AND FAMILY WORK

The rest of this chapter focuses on the often-conflicting demands of work and family for all family members. We begin with a discussion of housework.

Housework in the past

Although it is customary to describe the role of homemaker as women's traditional role, this is a misperception. For only a short period of time, from about 1920 to 1960, is it accurate to say that most married women were or wanted to be full-time housewives. During this period, most homes had some labour-saving appliances, such as refrigerators, washing machines, and so on. Prepared food, including canned food, was generally available, saving many hours of preparation time. For the first time in history, women could devote time to child care and household management. It was in this context that the idea of housework as nonwork developed. This situation changed quickly in the 1960s when large numbers of married women, including mothers of young children, entered the labour force, ending the cultural expectation of full-time housework as a lifetime expectation for married women.[21]

NEWS ITEM

Wives, "submit graciously" to your husbands

The New York Times (June 10, 1998) reported that the Southern Baptist Convention amended its essential statement of belief to include a declaration that a woman should "submit herself graciously" to her husband's leadership and that a husband should "provide for, protect, and lead his family."

The amendment, a 250-word declaration on family life, was adopted at the Baptists' annual meeting in Salt Lake City as an addition to the denomination's basic theological statement of beliefs and the Baptist Faith and Message. Because the Southern Baptist Convention is a creedless organization, no Baptist is required to agree with the Faith and Message statement. But the statement is nonetheless important. It stands as a central theological proclamation for the denomination, and Southern Baptist ministers are expected to agree with it.

Not all clergy or church members agree, however. For example, *The Charlotte Observer* (September 25, 1998) noted that after 153 years, Raleigh, North Carolina's, oldest Baptist church broke away from the Southern Baptist Convention in part because of this "submitting graciously" call. Churchgoers said they would no longer tolerate "authoritarian trends" within the 15.6-million-member denomination. This followed earlier grievances with the conservative convention such as a resolution against the ordination of women and a 1997 measure calling for a boycott of the Walt Disney Company.

Historically housework was physically demanding and time-consuming. In the early years of the nineteenth century, most families in Canada lived in rural areas and depended on farming or a combination of farming and paid employment (typically lumbering or mining) for a livelihood. Family members had a strong sense of economic interdependence. Women cared for domestic animals, grew and preserved food, and made clothes for the family. Child care was part of the daily routine. Daughters began to help with household tasks as soon as they were capable, and sons helped fathers with their work from an early age. Farm labour was physically demanding and relentless, bearing little resemblance to what we now call housework. Indeed, the word *housework* did not become accepted terminology until the middle of the nineteenth century.[22]

As Canada became more and more industrialized and people were drawn off the farms and into the cities, women continued the time-consuming and physically demanding work of feeding, clothing, and caring for family members. While these jobs had been shared (albeit according to a strict division of labour) on farms, in urban settings, with men away from home all day, household jobs became more women's responsibilities. Housework and housewife became synonymous. At the same time cultural justifications developed concerning women's natural propensity for motherhood and domesticity. These jobs became thought of as part of what women *were*, not what they *did*. It was not until the 1960s, influenced by the women's movement, that social scientists began to analyze housework from the point of view of those who did it—women. Before then, housework was given little academic attention.

Housework today

Housework is an umbrella concept that includes a huge number of tasks both physically demanding (washing outside windows) and menial (cleaning toilets), and emotionally wrenching (taking an injured child to hospital) and rewarding (reading bedtime stories). Several different conceptualizations have been suggested to try to capture this diversity—for example, by separating physical and emotional work, housework and motherwork, or identifying the tasks of household management. Anthropologist Micaela di Leonardo argues that a neglected aspect is kin work, by which she means "the conception, maintenance, and ritual celebration of cross-household kin ties, including visits, letters, telephone calls, presents and cards to kin; the organization of holiday gatherings; the creation and maintenance of quasi-kin relations; ... the mental work of reflection about all these activities," and so on.[23]

Household work is usually measured by time and task. One method of measurement is to ask family members to indicate how much time they spend performing each of a list of tasks. Another approach is to ask family members to keep time diaries of their daily activities. However, these measurement techniques see housework in instrumental terms and do not take into consideration the emotional aspects of child care and household management. Hochschild's study of housework, *The Second Shift*, divided family work into housework, parenting, and management of domestic labour.[24]

FAMILY DIVERSITY

Stay-at-home dads and housework

Katherine Marshall analyzed the Canadian Labour Force Survey to find out about the number and characteristics of stay-at-home dads. Over the last two decades, the number of single-earner, two-parent families with young children has decreased with the increased employment of married women. However, an increased proportion of the single-earners are mothers, not fathers. In other words, there has been a small but increasing number of stay-at-home dads. While the proportions are small (6 percent of stay-at-home parents are dads), the numbers are increasing (from 41,000 in 1976 to 77,000 in 1997).

Marshall used the 1992 General Social Survey, which included questions on time use to compare the amount of time stay-at-home moms and dads spend doing housework. Stay-at-home moms spent over two hours a day more than stay-at-home dads doing unpaid child care and housework, meal preparation, meal clean-up, indoor cleaning, laundry and other related work, shopping and volunteer work. Single-earner mothers did 4.3 hours of unpaid work daily—in addition to their paid work. Single-earner fathers did 3.2 additional hours of unpaid work.

Source: Katherine Marshall, "Stay-at-home Dads," *Perspectives* (Spring 1998): 9–15.

Economists have devised a number of ways of estimating the societal value of household work. In 1992, household work in Canada was valued at between 31 percent and 46 percent of gross domestic product. Household work is defined as follows: "those economic services produced in the household and outside the market, but which could be produced by a third person hired on the market without changing their utility to members of the household."[25] The three broad groups of activities measured are domestic work, caregiving for household members, and shopping. The three ways of measuring the value of this work are gross opportunity costs, net opportunity costs, and replacement cost. **Opportunity cost** is what homemakers would earn if they were employed for money—that is, what work does or would the homemaker do if gainfully employed? Gross opportunity costs are before tax; net opportunity costs are after tax. Both are calculated as hourly earnings and by province and sex. **Replacement cost** is the hourly earnings of someone who does similar work in the labour market. In other words, what would it cost to hire someone to babysit, clean the house, buy and prepare food, do errands, garden, repair things, organize a birthday party, send cards, and so on?

Table 3.2 summarizes the findings of the three estimates. Not surprisingly, all three methods found that women do a disproportionate share of household work. Gross opportunity cost is the highest estimate of housework at 46.3 percent of gross domestic product. This figure implies that almost half of the productive work done in Canada is done in private households.

Table 3.2
Estimates of the value of household work in Canada, 1992

	Net Opportunity Cost Estimate	*Gross Opportunity Cost Estimate*	*Replacement Cost Estimate*
Estimate of value ($ millions)	$210,773	$318,779	$284,862
Percentage of gross domestic product	30.6	46.3	41.4
Annual average—men	$7,730	$12,920	$9,960
Annual average—women	$11,920	$16,860	$16,580
Female share of household work	61.7%	57.6%	63.4%

Source: Figures taken from William Chandler, "The Value of Household Work in Canada," *National Income and Expenditure Accounts, Fourth Quarter, 1993,* Statistics Canada Catalogue 13-001, Vol. 41, No. 4 (March 1994): xxxix.

These measures are problematic. For one thing, both measures reinforce existing labour force inequities and pay differentials. In other words, the replacement costs for women's work is less than the replacement cost for men's work because babysitters earn less than carpenters. The same inequity applies to opportunity costs. Women typically earn about 60 percent of what men earn, so their opportunity costs are lower. More fundamentally, professional women will have higher opportunity costs than service workers, although they will not work any harder at housework. Furthermore, valuing housework by including it in the GDP has little more than symbolic benefit. Homemakers will not be relieved of their unequal burden by the gesture.

FAMILY DIVERSITY

Family businesses in China

A study by Entwisle and others examined the role of gender in family businesses in rural China. They revealed that men are about three times more likely than women to work in the household business and women are more than twice as likely as men to work exclusively in agriculture. Part of this difference is explained by women having considerably less schooling than men, which puts them at a disadvantage in their ability to bargain well. The difference is explained as well by the patrilocal and exogamous character of marriage in rural China: Rural women typically become "outsiders" when they marry.

See Barbara Entwisle, Gail E. Henderson, Susan E. Short, Jill Bouma, and Zhai Fengying, "Gender and Family Business in Rural China," *American Sociological Review* 60 (February 1995): 36–57.

THE DOUBLE DAY

The double day, or the second shift, refers to the combination of paid and unpaid work most women do. It appears that women in all countries, even when employed, do most of the housework.[26] Women also do more child care than men. Women who are employed spend somewhat less time doing household work than homemakers do. Husbands spend little if any additional amount of time doing housework when their wives work outside the home.

Arlie Hochschild, whose study of household work was mentioned in the previous section, described a "leisure gap" between men and women at home not unlike the wage gap in the workplace.[27] It seems that while women have adjusted their lives to the demands of paid work, men have not made the parallel adjustment by contributing proportionately to household work and child care. Certainly, more men do more housework than was the case in the past, and younger, better educated men do the most housework. However, the distribution of domestic work is far from equitable, and the "leisure gap" is great.

Household division of labour

The performance of housework and child care are less balanced than is paid work. Universally, husbands do far less housework or child care than wives, even if both are employed full-time. This even holds true when wives are employed and husbands unemployed. A study of Israeli couples found that, although unemployed husbands did more than their employed counterparts, they did far less child care and meal preparation than their employed spouses.[28]

Statistics Canada has collected survey data regarding the distribution of household work in Canada. It defines housework as meal preparation and clean-up, indoor and outdoor cleaning, laundry, home repairs and maintenance, gardening, pet care, bill paying, and travel to and from these household chores. Child care is not included on the list. According to the 1986 General Social Survey, adult Canadians did an average of 1.75 hours of housework a day. Women did most of it, spending an average of 2.5 hours on housework a day, in contrast to one hour for men.[29] In most households, women did most of the housework, including meal preparation, meal clean-up, cleaning, and laundry.

The 1990 General Social Survey (GSS) found some shifting of household responsibilities, although the division of labour is far from equal.[30] Figure 3.1 shows that more than half of wives with full-time employment do all of the housework. Women still typically do meal preparation, meal clean-up, cleaning, and laundry. Men tend to be responsible for repairs, maintenance, and outside work. The majority of wives, including 72 percent of wives with full-time employment, were solely responsible for meal preparation.

Ten percent of dual-earner couples shared housework, and in 10 percent of the cases husbands did all or most of it. Dual-earner couples employed full-time are most likely to share responsibility for housework. Sharing is most common among young, well-educated couples with few children who are

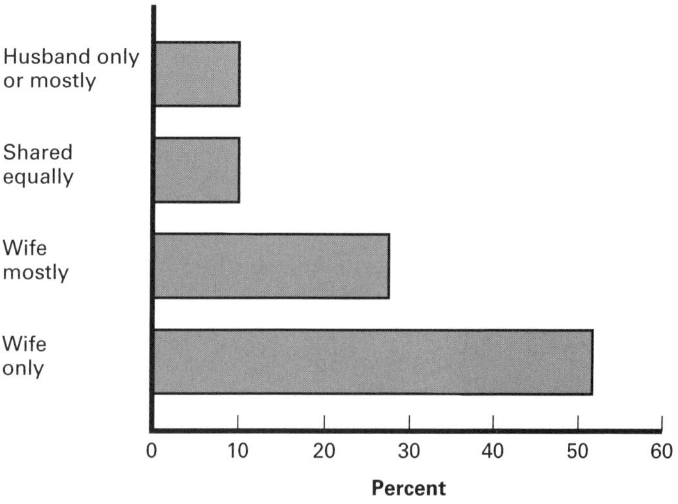

Figure 3.1
Division of housework

Source: Katherine Marshall, "Employed Parents and the Division of Housework," *Perspectives,* (Autumn 1993): 26.

FAMILY DIVERSITY

Measuring perceived time stress

The General Social Survey (GSS), conducted annually since 1985, gathers data on social trends and policy issues of current or emerging interest. Each cycle of the GSS covers one of five subject areas—health and social support, time use, personal risk, education and work, and family—each of which is repeated every fifth cycle.

Respondents to the 1992 GSS were asked a set of 10 questions intended to measure their perceptions of time stress. The number of positive responses to these questions represents an overall measure of time stress, with scores ranging from zero (no positive responses) to ten (positive responses to all of the questions). Scores of seven or higher are considered to indicate "high" perceived time stress.

1. Do you plan to slow down in the coming year?
2. Do you consider yourself a workaholic?
3. When you need more time, do you tend to cut back on your sleep?
4. At the end of the day, do you often feel that you have not accomplished what you had set out to do?
5. Do you worry that you don't spend enough time with your family or friends?
6. Do you feel that you're constantly under stress to accomplish more than you can handle?
7. Do you feel trapped in a daily routine?
8. Do you feel that you just don't have time for fun any more?
9. Do you often feel under stress when you don't have enough time?
10. Would you like to spend more time alone?

Source: Adapted from Janet Fast and Judith Frederick, "Working Arrangements and Time Stress," *Canadian Social Trends* (Winter 1996): 15.

satisfied with their lives. The likelihood of sharing rises with the wife's income, but the higher the husband's income the greater the likelihood that the wife will do all of the housework. As we would expect, spouses in households where housework was shared reported greater satisfaction than those who did all of the housework, although overall satisfaction was high for all couples.

According to the 1992 GSS, Canadian women spent 78 percent more time on unpaid work than men did.[31] If time spent at both unpaid and paid work is combined, men and women work the same number of hours a week. Figure 3.2 shows time use of Canadians as measured by the 1992 GSS. On average, one-eighth (14 percent) of our time is spent on unpaid work. Most (95 percent) of unpaid work is household work. The rest is volunteer work and helping others. The most time-consuming household tasks are meal preparation and clean-up, which take up 23 percent of the time.

Table 3.3 documents how often household and child-care tasks are performed by men and women, based on findings from a survey done in the United States and a study done in Australia. In both countries, the breakdown of duties was fairly traditional: women more often performed housework and

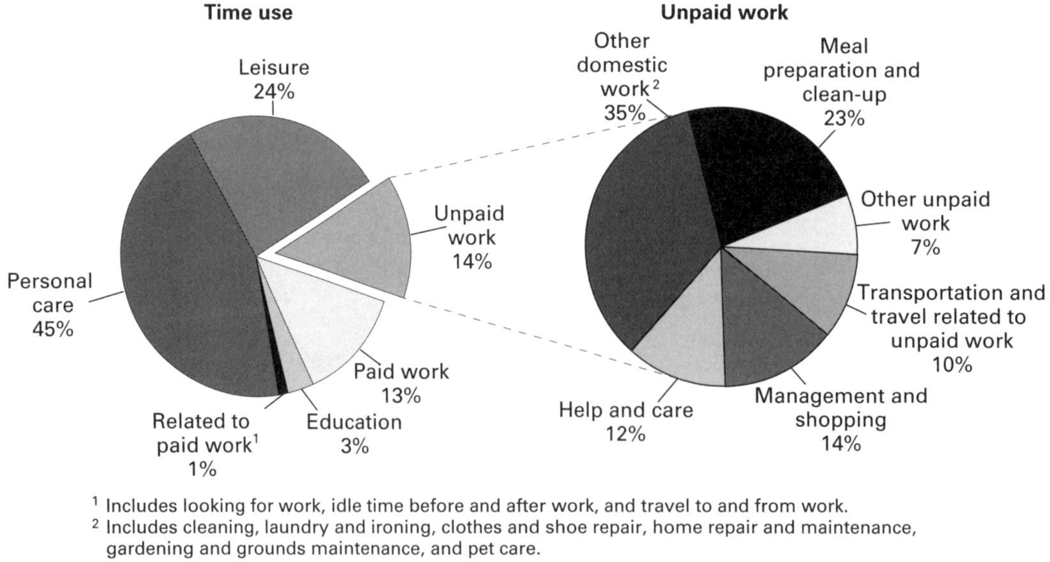

[1] Includes looking for work, idle time before and after work, and travel to and from work.
[2] Includes cleaning, laundry and ironing, clothes and shoe repair, home repair and maintenance, gardening and grounds maintenance, and pet care.

Source: Statistics Canada, *1992 General Social Survey.*

Figure 3.2
Time spent by Canadians on unpaid and paid work, 1992
Source: Chris Jackson, "Measuring and Valuing Households' Unpaid Work," *Canadian Social Trends* (Autumn 1996): 26.

Table 3.3
Who performs all or most of selected household and child-care chores? A comparison of men and women in the United States and Australia (in percentages)

	United States		Australia		
	Women	Men	Wife more	Husband more	About equally
Doing laundry	79%	27%	88%	3%	9%
Preparing meals	78	26	81	6	13
Grocery shopping	72	26	73	5	22
Cleaning house/vacuuming	69	22	78	7	15
Washing dishes	68	31	63	9	28
Caring for children (U.S.)/taking	72	12	—	—	—
them to activities (Aust.)	—	—	60	5	35
Disciplining/punishing children	42	28	23	9	68
Working in the yard	21	63	9	74	17
Making minor home repairs	16	74	7	81	12

Source: U.S. data were selected from *The Gallup Poll Monthly* 293 (February 1990): 31; Australian data were selected from Helen Glezer, "Juggling Work and Family Commitments," *Family Matters* 28 (April 1991): 3.

child-care tasks, whereas men more often did yard work and home repairs. Interestingly, in both countries, disciplining and punishing children was the task for which men's and women's performance levels were most comparable.

American men show a similar reluctance to do housework.[32] For example, the mean number of hours devoted by the average husband to the five tasks of cooking, dishes, cleaning, shopping, and laundry was 8.6 per week. Of the husbands in the survey, about half contributed less than 6 hours of housework per week, and fewer than one in ten (8.4 percent) performed 20 or more hours. In contrast, eight of ten wives (82.9 percent) performed 20 or more hours of housework per week, with one-third devoting 40 or more hours to these tasks. These tremendous husband-wife differences appear to exist not only in North America or Australia but throughout the world, including Scandinavian countries, which are perceived to have greater gender equality. As reported by women, the percentage contributed to total housework by their husbands was 24.7 percent in Sweden, 19.3 percent in Norway, 20.5 percent in Canada, and 22.6 percent in Australia.[33] Men reported figures about 5 percent higher than did women in each of these countries. The results, whether reported by wives or husbands, suggest that from 75 to 80 percent of the housework is done by women.

Factors that increased the husband's proportionate contribution to housework are the wife having greater resources, the wife having less traditional values, the husband having greater time availability, the wife having less time availability, and an increase in child-care demand. In other words, the average woman does most of everything, but the average husband's involvement is influenced by time availability, relative resources, and ideology.[34]

The role of children in the performance of household tasks should not be overlooked. In particular, children have been found to do increasing amounts of housework with age. Daughters do more than sons, and children in one-parent households do more than in two-parent households. As might be expected, children do more housework when a parent is in poor health.[35]

Catherine Ross and others also found that the household division of labour is shaped by the husband's values and the relative power of husband and wife.[36] Well-educated husbands and husbands with less traditional gender-role beliefs are more likely to participate in household tasks. Ross also found that the smaller the gap between the husband's and the wife's earnings, the greater the husband's relative contribution. In other words, the more the husband's earnings exceed the wife's, the less housework he does.

Why do women appear to accept such an inequitable division of labour? Several studies suggest that women holding traditional gender attitudes do not perceive the difference as unjust.[37] Nontraditional women, on the other hand, were more likely to perceive such inequalities as inequitable. Feminists see the division of household labour as a prime example of an unequal division of labour between men and women that generates tension, conflict, and change. Women's housework augments men's power, particularly in the case of full-time homemakers. The family remains a primary area in which men exercise power. One could also analyze this dynamic using the idea of relative deprivation. Relative deprivation theory suggests that gender ideology functions as a moderator variable between objective inequality and perceived inequality. In brief, wives' perceptions of the fairness of the division of labour are better predictors of marital conflict than the actual extent of inequality.

Now the question becomes, why do some women perceive such an objectively unfair division of labour as fair? Thompson and others[38] encouraged family scholars to apply the framework of distributive justice (note exchange theory in Chapter 1) to understand this situation. The distributive justice framework suggests that wives will perceive the allocation of family work as unfair if they lack (1) some valued outcomes (feeling appreciated, serving loved ones, confirming their sense of proper gender roles), (2) a comparison referent (comparing their husbands' involvement to that of other men rather than to themselves, comparing the value of their unpaid and invisible work to that of paid work), and (3) a justification (a mutually agreed-upon decision of how things will be done, excuses such as men are incompetent at domestic labour or wives have a greater need for a clean house than men).

Some aspects of housework can be rewarding, and some women are housewives by choice. As suggested by Ahlander and Bahr, perhaps the time has come to conceptualize housework and family work less in terms of technical, economic, or political dimensions and more in terms of a moral context that encourages attention to the cultural and personal meanings of activity, interaction, and sentiment.[39] They propose reappropriating the image of family work as a calling that is essential to the physical, mental, and spiritual maintenance of a family group. Among the products of this fundamental and inescapable work are strong bonds of kinship, linking of persons to one another, and transmitting the aspirations and skills that make up human cultures.

Stresses and strains of the double day

The fact that most Canadian families rely on the earnings of both husbands and wives creates time pressures for all family members. Family time is obviously reduced when both spouses are in the labour force. There is less time for leisure activities or relaxing together. Mealtime is typically rushed and more family members "eat on the run." Many dual-earning couples work very long hours; about 20 percent of them work over 90 hours a week.[40] The tendency to work such long hours is affected by the number and age of children and by education. However, whether or not they have children, wives with university degrees work longer hours. For a small but growing number of dual-earner families, one or both spouses work at two jobs.[41] The families most apt to moonlight are young and childless, although rates are increasing among parents of all ages.

Not surprisingly, people who juggle work and family responsibilities experience time pressures. The 1992 GSS asked Canadians a number of questions about time stress—see the Family Diversity box on page 73. As we might expect, employed parents report more stress than couples without children, and women report more stress than men.[42]

Alternative working arrangements are assumed to ease the burden of working parents, but as the GSS discovered, some do and some do not. Part-time work has the advantage of less time stress, but the disadvantages of low pay and few benefits. Flextime reduces perceived time stress, particularly for women, but employees who work a compressed work week (longer hours for fewer days) feel more time pressures than employees who work a regular day.

How do Canadians cope with their pressured lives? Many Canadians (about 44 percent) say they cut back on sleep in order to manage their commitments.[43] Does that suggest we are a nation suffering from sleep deprivation? Not at all. Indeed, only 4 percent of us are chronically short of sleep, according to the 1991 GSS.[44]

In most Canadian families, both parents work outside the home. The following section looks at the effect of children on maternal employment and the effect of maternal employment on children.

Maternal employment and children

In the past, it was assumed that maternal employment had many effects on a child—all bad. People generally have less apprehension today, although in a January 1993 Canadian Gallup Poll over half of the respondents (53 percent) thought that the increased employment of married women had a harmful effect on family life.[45] This was an increase of 5 percent since 1988. Sixty-three percent of Canadians in 1995 thought that an employed mother can establish just as warm and secure a relationship with her children as a mother who does not work in the paid labour force. At the same time, 55 percent of Canadians thought that a pre-school-age child will suffer if both parents are employed.[46] More highly educated Canadians were less likely to worry about harmful effects, perhaps because this is the group most likely to be employed. Few recent studies have reported meaningful differences between the children of employed mothers and the children of mothers at home. What differences do exist are often explained less by the mother's employment status than by other factors: social class, part- or full-time employment, age of the child, mother's attitude toward employment, and other social and psychological factors.

Various positive outcomes of maternal employment are found in the research literature. For example, mothers' holding high-status jobs leads to positive effects on children's schooling.[47] Both sons and daughters are more likely to do better in school, complete high school, enter college, and complete a degree. It was found as well that occupational complexities and the resources that employed mothers bring to the home and family environment lead to positive outcomes for children.[48]

The resources that accrue from employment and opportunities for workplace autonomy that benefit parenting skills appear to outweigh any disadvantages that stem from decreased time that working mothers have to spend with their children when compared to nonworking mothers. And while mothers who spent more time in work outside the home shared less traditionally defined child-care time, it was determined that parent–child shared housework and shared leisure time increased.[49] Personal resources that employed mothers bring to child rearing—such as high levels of self-esteem, educational attainment, the delay of childbearing, and older age and maturity—also have positive effects on their children's home environments.

Jay Belsky, who has done extensive research on parental and nonmaternal child care and the socioemotional development of young children, found that children whose mothers were employed full-time, beginning in the first or second year of the child's life, scored more poorly on a compliance component of adjustment than did children whose mothers were not employed.[50] *Compliance* referred to items such as whether the child would eat the food given, protest going to bed, or turn off the television when told. However, other areas of adjustment (behaviour problems, insecurity, sociability, inhibition) showed no negative effects of maternal employment.

Belsky's review of the effects of employed mothers on children's socioemotional development has suggested that maternal employment per se is less important than the degree to which child care (by parents or nonparents) is sensitive and responsive. Childrearing that is sensitive and responsive seems to promote security in the infant and toddler, and cooperation, compliance, and even achievement in the older child. Conversely, inconsistent, unsupportive, and unresponsive care fosters uncooperative and problematic behaviour, irrespective of the employment of the mother.

The increasing employment of mothers has created a need for day care beyond what can be provided by spouses, grandparents, in-laws, and other family members. Many corporate, university, community, and private centres have been established to help fill this gap, but costs and the availability of competent staff are still major concerns.

In brief, maternal employment is too endemic to produce major distinctions in effects on children. Now, young men and women have very similar labour force participation rates. The differences in employment patterns are far smaller than differences in expectations regarding children and child care. While the role of fathers has attracted increased research attention, the emphasis is far from equivalent to the consideration of women's maternal roles. It is interesting that sociologists have not considered the effect of fathers' employment on children to be an important research question. However, the number of employed women and mothers does focus attention on other areas, such as the need for day-care services. For most parents, child care is a great concern. It is costly and the number of regulated spaces is limited. According to a Toronto *Globe and Mail* article, "Almost two million Canadian children are cared for regularly by someone other than their parents. But only one in five receive care in a regulated setting like a daycare centre or after-school program."[51] Ironically, middle-income families are less likely to have children in licensed child care than are low-income families. Quite simply, they cannot afford the cost of unsubsidized regulated child care.[52]

What about children too old for day care? **Latchkey** ("self-care") **children** come home after school to an empty house, let themselves in with a "latch key," and remain home alone until a working parent gets home. We do not know how many Canadian children are in this situation, nor their family situations.

WORK AND FAMILY: FINDING A BALANCE

It is difficult for parents to make equally strong commitments to work and family life. Parents whose greatest commitment is to the family will inevitably sacrifice some career advancement, income security, and so on. It is less clear what parents—particularly mothers who focus on careers—give up. Indeed, women in professional and management positions are far more likely than comparable men to be single, married with no children, or divorced as a consequence of their career involvement. Perhaps Harold Benenson is correct in arguing that assumptions about dual careers, while widely believed, are fundamentally flawed and run counter to certain basic realities.[53] For example, in spite of recent gains, married women professionals remain a numerically insignificant group among married women as a whole.

More typically, as the data described in the section above show, employed mothers more than employed fathers will back away from employment commitments by working fewer hours or working nontraditional schedules. What are the long-term costs of these decisions to women's employment? Peter Li and Dawn Currie used longitudinal data from the Canadian Labour Force Survey to measure the effects.[54] The authors found that women were much less likely than men to return to employment after a job interruption, and those who returned to the labour force were more likely to work part-time—even after an extended period of time. Female part-time workers were less likely than full-time workers to return to paid employment. Women's job discontinuity is directly related to childrearing responsibilities and increases with the number of children. Male discontinuity is unrelated to family size. This data supports the conclusion that labour force inequality is closely tied to the unequal responsibilities for domestic labour and child care.

Men face a different dilemma. Social expectations continue to push men in the direction of career commitment as the most appropriate way to fulfill commitments to family. We do not question why men work and what effects paternal employment have on marriage and family life. We do not do research to investigate ways young children are affected by their fathers' employment. We do not encourage boys to think of fatherhood in the same way we encourage girls to think of motherhood. Despite almost equal numbers of men and women in the labour force, paid employment and parenthood have different connotations for men and women. Work, to men, is generally defined in terms of labour force employment, not in terms of housework and child care. One consequence of this distinction is that unemployment is emotionally harder on men than women.

Studies of the Depression in the 1930s found that the husband's unemployment had a negative effect on his self-esteem, personal functioning, and marital and family relationships. Similar results have appeared in studies since then. Jeffry Larson, looking at blue-collar families, reported that the unemployment of husbands corresponded to significantly lower marital adjustment, poorer marital communication, and lower satisfaction and harmony in family relations.[55] Men who were unemployed spent less on entertainment, food, gasoline, and home energy consumption, all of which might affect marital/family relationships.

Stress on the job also has negative effects on family members. Research found that the job stress experienced by husbands detracted from the psychological health of their wives.[56] It was suggested that the wives' response to their husbands' job problems may be rooted in the nature of their emotional involvement with their husbands. That is, concern for a loved one may increase one's own vulnerability to emotional stress. Or it may be that the time and energy expended in support of someone else tends to jeopardize one's own well-being.

Men, like women, work for financial reasons. But the emphases on having a job, getting ahead, and gaining prestige or achieving power are stressed in socialization more for men than for women.

Traditionally, husbands and fathers did not accept responsibility for any substantial amount of housework and child care. The husband's responsibility to the family was to provide economic support through paid employment. In terms of *role differentiation,* the male held primary responsibility for relationships and needs external to the family; the female held responsibility for relationships and needs internal to the family. In terms of *exchange,* the husband exchanged his work and economic services for the wife's companionship and household services. In terms of *resources* (see Chapter 6) relative to housework and child care, the wife/mother supposedly had time for these activities whereas the full-time employed husband/father did not.

How much have these traditional ideas changed? The evidence suggests that change has not been dramatic. Indeed, women have adjusted their lives to the demands of paid work with far greater ease than men have adjusted to the demands of parenting and household management. Some have suggested that male avoidance of housework and child care is a deliberate strategy to maintain power over women. Studies reported earlier in this chapter revealed that (1) husbands generally do very little housework and, more significantly, (2) husbands of employed wives do not spend much more time doing housework than husbands of nonemployed wives. (That is, employed wives do less housework than nonemployed wives, but husbands do about the same amount, irrespective of the employment status of the wife.) The burden of the double day is great for most married women, and the lag between the slower rate of change in men's participation in housework and the more rapid rate of change in women's paid employment is substantial.

Some evidence for greater change is seen in subgroups such as single-parent fathers, fathers deliberately holding part-time jobs, single adoptive fathers,

While there are few stay-at-home dads in Canada, men have proven to be effective parents and housekeepers. Relatively few men, married or single, give up employment to serve as full-time homemakers, as women have traditionally done, but men appear to be assuming more responsibility for the care of their children.

and full-time male homemakers; in these situations, men assume major household and child-care duties. An American study of Hispanic male homemakers, for example, revealed that their homemaker role was brought about by external economic circumstances and viewed as a temporary status.[57] They did, however, report greater involvement in family life, increased insight into their spouses' experiences, and as a result, closer relations with their spouses and children.

While there is no question that wives continue to hold the primary responsibility for housework and child care and that the pace of change may seem both slow and minimal, in fact, men's behaviour appears to be changing. Young men in dual-income households are more likely to do housework and child care. Significantly, couples in these marriages say they are happier than couples in marriages where housework is not shared.[58]

Commuter marriages

One way some couples adapt to the demands of two careers is to live separately for periods of time. The pattern of one spouse leaving home temporarily is nothing new: politicians, professional athletes, and salespersons routinely spend time apart from their spouses. In addition, military service, imprisonment, and seasonal work in selected occupations force the separation of husbands and wives.

As the number of married women with strong employment commitments increases, the potential for periodic episodes of commuting also increases. Several studies of the quality of life of commuting couples compared to single-residence, dual-career couples revealed both benefits and costs of both types of arrangements.[59] Commuters were more satisfied with their life work and the time they had for themselves. They reported significantly less overload and a less stressful life than did their single-residence counterparts. Commuters listed as benefits increased independence, greater self-sufficiency, and enhanced appreciation for spouse and family. On the other hand, commuters were more dissatisfied with family life and with the lack of emotional support and companionship from their partners. Most saw commuting as a temporary life-style.

An earlier study by Harriet Gross examined dual-career marriages in which the spouses lived apart for at least four days at a time for several months or more.[60] About half the husbands and wives saw each other weekly, about 10 percent saw each other once a week to once a month, and about 40 percent saw each other less than once a month. The couple's decision to live apart typically rested on advantages such as the freedom it granted to each spouse's work; for example, one spouse could work long and uninterrupted hours without planning on meals, sleep, or recreation with the other.

In Gross's study, wives tended to miss the emotional protection they expected from their husbands and sensed that this was a cost of their gain in independence. Wives also recognized that responsibilities for household and car repairs were theirs to manage singlehandedly. Husbands expressed loneliness and some guilt for being unable to provide the emotional protection they sensed their wives needed.

What became evident to couples living apart was the difficulty of transition from the older, traditional marital roles to the newly emerging roles that accompany two-resident living. A summary of Gross's findings suggested that older couples, couples who had been married longer, couples in which at least one spouse had an established career, and couples without childrearing responsibilities found their separated life-style less stressful.

For many commuter couples, the telephone and e-mail become means of regular contact. Time together becomes well planned and is not spent in meaningless socializing with uninterested others. A number of factors appear to make the separation easier: strong career commitment by both parties, having adequate financial resources to meet the expense of maintaining two residences, making phone calls, travelling to see one another, living short distances apart, and maintaining established patterns of interaction.

SUMMARY

1. This chapter began by briefly looking at selected linkages between the family and other institutions. Cross-culturally as well as historically, major connections have existed at a macro level between basic systems within all societies. Families are linked to religion not only at weddings and funerals but also in terms of sex roles, sexual behaviours, and family size. Families are linked to politics in terms of social policy and legislation, ranging from taxation deductions for dependents to providing income for people who are elderly through Old Age Security. Families are linked to education in terms of learning social norms, skills, and mobility patterns.
2. The focus of the chapter was the link between work and family systems. Conflict theorists view the economic system as the key to understanding inequality within or outside the family; inequality in the labour force is reinforced by and reinforces inequality in household work.
3. Most Canadian women are employed, but still assume most responsibility for housework. While housework is time-consuming, some aspects of it are satisfying for many women. Generally, attitude surveys find that women are not unhappy doing housework, although they typically do an unequal share.
4. The number and proportion of wives and mothers in the paid labour force has increased yearly for over 20 years. Women work for many of the same reasons men work, especially income. Most Canadian households now rely on the earnings of more than one breadwinner.
5. The proportion of men working relative to the total male population has decreased over time. Because there is widespread agreement on the expectation that men should be employed, work is a key source of identity and self-worth for men.
6. There is some evidence of change in the amount of time and frequency with which men engage in household tasks, but the rate of change is slow.
7. The increasing employment of women combined with the constant high employment of men has resulted in a large number of dual-employed marriages. This arrangement creates both rewards and costs, and is stressful for both men and women.
8. A significant issue for most parents is child care. For some parents, shift work is a possibility, but for single parents and many two-parent households, it is not. Day care for children is a major need in Canada. Group care is limited in availability, and costs for all types of care are often high.
9. Some couples deal with the demands of dual careers by living separately, in a commuter marriage. For some, this type of living arrangement serves as the compromise between giving up the marriage or the career.
10. Chapters 1 through 3 have provided an introduction to marriage and the family: namely, family issues and change; disciplinary and theoretical approaches to the family; marital, family, and kinship organization; and the linkages among marriage, family, and work. Chapter 4 focuses on social-class variations in family life.

KEY TERMS AND TOPICS

DISCUSSION QUESTIONS

1. Discuss linkages among the family system and other systems, such as religion, politics, and education. What does each system contribute to and receive from the other?
2. Discuss the statement, "Differences between those who attend religious services and those who do not are more pronounced than differences between denominations or particular religious groups."
3. Why is the assumption made that *housework* is not really work when wives and mothers are asked, "Do you work?" What arguments can be made linking housework to male/female roles and gender inequality?
4. Will men and women eventually share paid and unpaid work equally? Why or why not?
5. Explain reasons for the increase in female paid employment. What factors most influence the nature of married women's paid employment?
6. What strains may occur in dual-career marriages that are less likely to occur in one-career marriages? What rewards exist in each type of marriage?
7. What is kin work? Why do men not do kin work?
8. What are the effects of children on maternal employment? What are the effects of maternal employment on children?
9. What solutions do you feel might best address the unequal burden of housework, referred to as the double day? Is this a private or a public matter?
10. Discuss the pros and cons of commuter marriage. What conditions might increase or decrease the strain living apart has on a couple's relationship?

FURTHER READINGS

Chaykowski, R. and Powell, L., eds. *Women and Work.* Montreal and Kingston: McGill-Queen's University Press, 1999. The papers in this collection address key issues in Canadian women's labour force participation, including training and education, income security programs, school-to-work transitions, and collective bargaining. Many of the papers report original research.

Duffy, Ann; Glenday, D.; and Pupo, Norene, eds. *Good Jobs, Bad Jobs, No Jobs: The Transformation of Work in the 21st Century.* Toronto: Harcourt Brace, 1997. This collection of papers looks at labour market dislocation in manufacturing and service industries in Canada, the impact of technology on work and the impact of job loss creating high levels of unemployment and underemployment. Two chapters focus specifically on the dilemmas of combining paid and unpaid work.

Duffy, Ann; Mandell, Nancy; and Pupo, Norene. *Few Choices: Women, Work and Family.* Toronto: Garamond Press, 1989. A study of how Canadian women manage employment, child care, and domestic responsibilities.

Evans, Patricia M. and Wekerle, Gerda R. *Women and the Canadian Welfare State.* Toronto: University of Toronto Press, 1997. This collection of articles by leading Canadian feminists addresses key aspects of women's paid and unpaid work.

Frankel, Judith, ed. *Families of Employed Mothers: An International Perspective.* New York: Garland, 1997. Ten chapters consider employed mothers and their families in Britain, Germany, India, Israel, Mexico, Nigeria, the Philippines, Puerto Rico, Taiwan, and the United States.

Gerson, Kathleen. *No Man's Land: Men's Changing Commitments to Family and Work.* New York: Basic Books, 1993. A look at how and why men's lives are changing, the differences among men, and the varied ways men are reassessing their commitments to family and work.

Giles, Wenona and Arat-Koc, Sedef. *Maid in the Market: Women's Paid Domestic Labour.* Halifax, NS: Fernwood, 1994. The papers in this book focus on three kinds of paid domestic work: commodified housework, service work performed in commercial settings, and service work that is marketed and sold in familistic terms.

Higginbotham, Elizabeth, and Romero, Mary, eds. *Women and Work: Exploring Race, Ethnicity, and Class.* Thousand Oaks, CA: Sage, 1997. A collection of 10 original research articles that explore how race, etchnicity, and social class have shaped the work lives of women.

Hochschild, Arlie. *The Second Shift*. New York: Avon Books, 1989. An insightful and detailed classic study of the dynamics of sorting out domestic responsibilities in two-income families.

Hochschild, Arlie. *Time Bind.* New York: Henry Holt and Company, 1997. The author of the widely read study *The Second Shift* has taken another look at the conflicting demands of work and family. Hochschild documents the cost to parents, children and family life of the time squeeze felt by working families.

Kauppinen, Kaisa, and Gordon, Tuula, eds. *Unresolved Dilemmas: Women, Work, and the Family in the United States, Europe, and the former Soviet Union.* Brookfield, VT: Ashgate Pub. Co., 1997. An exploration of both theoretical themes and empirical issues relating to the unresolved dilemmas of women and the tightrope between home and work.

Luxton, Meg. *More Than a Labour of Love.* Toronto: The Women's Press, 1980. This is a classic study of housewives in Flin Flon, Alberta.

Rubin, Rose M. and Riney, Bobye J. *Working Wives and Dual-Earner Families.* Westport, CT: Praeger, 1994. Descriptive and empirical research is presented on the economics of dual-earner families and their central role in the economy and society.

Waring, Marilyn. *Counting for Nothing: What Men Value and What Women are Worth*, 2nd ed. Toronto: University of Toronto Press, 1999. This book addresses the issue of the invisibility of women's work internationally. Waring suggests alternate ways of attributing value to work not tied to profit motives.

Wilson, Susannah J. *Women, Families and Work.* Toronto: McGraw-Hill Ryerson, 1996. A short, readable analysis of women's paid and unpaid work in Canada and the political struggle for equality. The book contains chapters on the historical roots of the household division of labour and labour market segregation.

WEBLINKS

http://www.trinity.edu/~mkearl/family.html

A guide to family relations as the most basic and fundamental building block for any society, and families as the key shock-absorbers of social change.

http://www.uoguelph.ca/cfww/

Based at the University of Guelph, The Centre for Families, Work and Well-Being is a valuable resource, offering findings in research and analysis of social policy relating to families and work in Canada.

http://www.dol.gov/dol/wb/

After accessing the Women's Bureau, click 20 Facts on Women Workers to find information on women's economic well-being including labour-force participation rates, earnings comparisons with men, and facts about female-headed households.

NOTES

1. Rudi Volti, *Society and Technological Change* (New York: St. Martin's Press, 1995): 196.

2. See, for example, Arland Thornton, "Reciprocal Influences of Family and Religion in a Changing World," *Journal of Marriage and the Family* 47 (May 1985): 381–394; and Darwin L. Thomas and Marie Cornwall, "Religion and Family in the 1980s: Discovery and Development," *Journal of Marriage and the Family* 52 (November 1990): 983–992.

3. Warren Clark, "Religious Observance, Marriage and Family," *Canadian Social Trends* (Autumn 1998): 2–7.

4. Reginald W. Bibby, *The Bibby Report: Social Trends Canadian Style* (Toronto: Stoddart, 1995), 123–138.

5. Clark, "Religious Observance, Marriage and Family," 7.

6. Frank Jones, "Are Children Going to Religious Services?" *Canadian Social Trends* (Autumn 1999): 13–16.

7. Clark, "Religious Observance, Marriage and Family," 7.

8. William J. Weston, ed., *Education and the American Family: A Research Synthesis* (New York: New York University Press, 1989).

9. Patricia Voydanoff, "Economic Distress and Family Relations: A Review of the Eighties," *Journal of Marriage and the Family* 52 (November 1990): 1099–1115; and David T. Takeuchi, David R. Williams, and Russell K. Adair, "Economic Stress in the Family and Children's Emotional and Behavioral Problems," *Journal of Marriage and the Family* 53 (November 1991): 1031–1041.

10. See, for example, Joan Aldous, Rodney Ganey, Scott Trees, and Lawrence C. Marsh, "Families and Inflation: Who Was Hurt in the Last High-Inflation Period?" *Journal of Marriage and the Family* 53 (February 1991): 123–134.

11. Friedrich Engels, *The Origin of the Family, Private Property and the State* (New York: International, 1942) (originally published in 1884).

12. Jillian Oderkirk, Cynthia Silver, and Marc Prud'homme, "Traditional Earner Families," *Canadian Social Trends*, Statistics Canada Catalogue 11-008E (Spring 1994): 22–29.

13. Susan Crompton and Leslie Geran, "Women as Main Wage-Earners," *Perspectives* (Winter 1995): 26–29.

14. Katherine Marshall, "Stay-at-home Dads," *Perspectives* (Spring 1998): 9–15.

15. Ibid, 14.

16. Katherine Marshall, "Balancing Work and Family Responsibilities," *Perspectives* (Spring 1994): 26-30.

17. Jenny Blair, "I Can't Come in Today, the Baby has Chicken Pox: Gender and Class Processes in How Parents in the Labour Force Deal with the Problem of Sick Children," *Canadian Journal of Sociology* 18(4) (1993): 405–429.

18. Janet Fast and Moren Da Pont, "Changes in Work Continuity," *Canadian Social Trends* (Autumn 1997): 2–7.

19. Katherine Marshall, "Employment after Childbirth," *Perspectives* (Autumn 1999): 18–25 .

20. Nancy Z. Ghalam, "Attitudes Toward Women, Work and Family," *Canadian Social Trends* (Autumn 1997): 13–17.

21. See Susannah Wilson, *Women, Families and Work*, 4th ed. (Toronto: McGraw-Hill Ryerson, 1996) for a detailed discussion of these changes.

22. Ruth Schwartz Cowan, "Women's Work, Housework and History: The Historical Roots of Inequality in Work-Force Participation," in Naomi Gerstel and Harriet Gross, eds., *Families and Work* (Philadelphia: Temple University Press, 1987), 164–177.

23. Micaela di Leonardo, "The Female World of Cards and Holidays: Women, Families and the Work of Kinship," in Barrie Thorne and Marilyn Yalom, eds., *Rethinking the Family*, rev. ed. (Boston: Northeastern University Press, 1992), 246–261.

24. Arlie Hochschild, *The Second Shift* (New York: Avon Books, 1989).

25. William Chandler, "The Value of Household Work in Canada, 1992," *National Income and Expenditure Accounts, Fourth Quarter, 1993*, Statistics Canada Catalogue 13-001: xxxv–xlviii.

26. Arne L. Kalleberg and Rachel A. Rosenfeld, "Work in the Family and in the Labor Market: A Cross-National, Reciprocal Analysis," *Journal of Marriage and the Family* 52 (May 1990): 331–346; and April A. Bayfield, "Employment Resources and Housework in Canada," *Journal of Marriage and the Family* 54 (February 1992): 19–30.

27. Arlie Hochschild, *The Second Shift*.

28. Boas Shamir, "Unemployment and Household Division of Labor," *Journal of Marriage and the Family*, 48 (February 1, 1986): 195–206.

29. Katherine Marshall, "Household Chores," *Canadian Social Trends*, Statistics Canada Catalogue 11-008E (Spring 1990): 19–20.

30. Katherine Marshall, "Balancing Work and Family Responsibilities," *Perspectives* (Spring 1994): 26–30.

31. Chris Jackson, "Measuring and Valuing Households' Unpaid Work," *Canadian Social Trends* (Autumn 1996): 25–29.

32. Scott Coltrane and Masako Ishii-Kuntz, "Men's Housework: A Life Course Perspective," *Journal of Marriage and the Family* 54 (February 1992): 43–57. Note also Beth Manke, Brenda Seery, Ann Crouter, and Susan McHale, "The Three Corners of Domestic Labour: Mothers', Fathers' and Children's Weekday and Weekend Housework," *Journal of Marriage and the Family* 56 (August 1994): 657–668.

33. Janeen Baxter, "Gender Equality and Participation in Housework: A Cross-National Perspective," *Journal of Comparative Family Studies* 28 (Autumn 1997): 220–247.

34. Harriet B. Presser, "Employment Schedules Among Dual-Earner Spouses and the Division of Household Labor by Gender," *American Sociological Review* (June 1994): 348–364; and April Bayfield, "Juggling Jobs and Kids: The Impact of Employment Schedules on Father's Caring for Children," *Journal of Marriage and the Family* 57 (May 1995): 321–332.

35. Glenna Spitze and Russell Ward, "Household Labor in Intergenerational Households," *Journal of Marriage and the Family* 57 (May 1995): 355–361.

36. Catherine E. Ross, "The Division of Labor at Home," *Social Forces* 65 (March 1987): 816–833; and Yoshinori Kamo, "Determinants of Household Division of Labor," *Journal of Family Issues* 9 (June 1988): 177–200.

37. Theodore N. Greenstein, "Gender Ideology and Perceptions of the Fairness of the Division of Household Labor: Effects on Marital Quality," *Social Forces* 74 (March 1996): 1029–1042; and Alfred DeMaris and Monica A. Longmore, "Ideology, Power and Equity: Testing Competing Explanations for the Perceptions of Fairness in Household Labor," *Social Forces* 74 (March 1996): 1043–1071.

38. Linda Thompson, "Family Work: Women's Sense of Fairness," *Journal of Family Issues* 12 (November 1991): 181–196; and Alan J. Hawkins, Christina M. Marshall and Kathryn M. Meiners, "Exploring Wives' Sense of Fairness about Family Work," *Journal of Family Issues* 16 (November 1995): 693–721.

39. Nancy R. Ahlander and Kathleen S. Bahr, "Beyond Drudgery, Power and Equity: Toward an Expanded Discourse on the Moral Dimensions of Housework in Families," *Journal of Marriage and the Family* 57 (February 1995); 54–68. Note also John P. Robinson and Melissa A. Milkie, "Back to Basics: Trends in and Role Determinants of Women's Attitudes Toward Housework," *Journal of Marriage and the Family* 60 (February 1998): 205–218.

40. Dan Charrette, "Hours of Working Couples," *Perspectives* (Summer 1995): 9–11.

41. Henry Pold, "Families and Moonlighting," *Perspectives* (Summer 1995): 7–8.

42. Janet Fast and Judith Frederick, "Working Arrangements and Time Stress," *Canadian Social Trends* (Winter 1996): 14–19.

43. Judith Frederick, "Tempus Fugit ... Are You Time Crunched?" *Canadian Social Trends* (Winter 1993): 6–9.

44. Sue Crompton, "Tired Workers," *Perspectives* (Summer 1995): 28–31.

45. Canadian Gallup Poll, "Canadians Split Over the Effects of Working Moms," January 24, 1993.

46. Nancy Z. Ghalam, "Attitudes Toward Women, Work and Family," *Canadian Social Trends* (Autumn 1997):16.

47. Matthijs Kalmijn, "Mother's Occupational Status and Children's Schooling," *American Sociological Review* 59 (April 1994): 257–275.

48. Elizabeth G. Menaghan and Toby L. Percel, "Determining Children's Home Environments: The Impact of Maternal Characteristics and Current Occupational and Family Conditions," *Journal of Marriage and the Family* 53 (May 1991): 417–431.

49. W. Keith Bryant and Cathleen D. Zick, "An Examination of Parent-Child Shared Time," *Journal of Marriage and the Family* 58 (February 1996): 227–237.

50. Jay Belsky and David Eggebeen, "Early and Extensive Maternal Employment and Young Children's Socioemotional Development: Children of the National Longitudinal Survey of Youth," *Journal of Marriage and the Family* 53 (November 1991): 1083–1110; and Jay Belsky, "Parental and Nonparental Child Care and Children's Socioemotional Development: A Decade in Review," *Journal of Marriage and the Family* 52 (November 1990): 885–903.

51. Andre Picard, "Good Childcare Harder to Find: Study," *Globe and Mail* (January 25, 2000): A1.

52. Anne McIlroy, "Middle Class Families Can't Afford Best Daycare," *Globe and Mail* (January 24, 2000): A1, A5.

53. Harold Benenson, "Women's Occupational and Family Achievement in the U.S. Class System: A Critique of the Dual-Career Family Analysis," *The British Journal of Sociology* 35 (March 1984): 19–41.

54. Peter Li and Dawn Currie, "Gender Differences in Work Interruptions as Unequal Effects of Marriage and Childrearing: Findings from a National Survey," *Journal of Comparative Family Studies* XXIII(2) (Summer 1992): 217–229.

55. Jeffry H. Larson, "The Effect of Husbands' Unemployment on Marital and Family Relations in Blue-Collar Families," *Family Relations* 33 (October 1984): 503–511.

56. Karen Rook, David Dooley, and Ralph Catalano, "Stress Transmission: The Effects of Husbands' Job Stress on the Emotional Health of Their Wives," *Journal of Marriage and the Family* 53 (February 1991): 165–177.

57. Sharon Kantorowski Davis and Virginia Chavez, "Hispanic Househusbands," *Hispanic Journal of Behavioral Sciences* 7 (1985): 317–332.

58. Katherine Marshall, "Balancing Work and Family Responsibilities," *Perspectives* (Spring 1994): 26–30.

59. Barbara B. Bunker, Josephine M. Zubek, Virginia J. Vanderslice, and Robert W. Rice, "Quality of Life in Dual-Career Families: Commuting Versus Single-Residence Couples," *Journal of Marriage and the Family* 54 (May 1992): 399–407; and Melissa M. Groves and Diane M. Horm-Wingerd, "Commuter Marriages: Personal, Family and Career Issues," *Sociology and Social Research* 75 (July 1991): 212–217.

60. Harriet Engel Gross, "Dual Career Couples Who Live Apart: Two Types," *Journal of Marriage and the Family* 42 (August 1980): 567–576.

CHAPTER

4 FAMILY INCOME AND SOCIAL CLASS

One of the most significant changes in Canadian families in the second half of the twentieth century is the increased labour force participation of married women. Women's employment has consequences for women's lives, for the organization of family life, and for the economic well-being of families. In this chapter we focus on some of the ways differing access to economic resources affects families.

FAMILY INCOME AND FAMILY ECONOMIC SECURITY

From 1950 until the 1970s, the Canadian economy was buoyant, and women were pulled into the labour force by expanding opportunities. Real family income rose dramatically in the 1960s and continued to increase in the 1970s. The picture in the last 20 years, following a recession in the early 1980s and a second in the early 1990s, has been far more bleak. In this period, real incomes have declined and the labour market has become less stable. Jobs for both men and women are less secure, and more jobs are part-time or temporary. Median family income was $58 945 in 1990, dropping to $57 546 in 1996.[1]

The recession of the early 1990s, government cutbacks and the erosion of the safety net created a period of deeply felt economic insecurity for Canadian families. Unemployment levels were higher during the recessions of the early 1980s and 1990s than for any time since the Depression. In 1989 Canada's unemployment rate was 7.5 percent. Three years later, in November 1992, unemployment reached a high of 11.9 percent. By June 1999 the rate had dropped again to 7.6 percent.[2] To the extent that family incomes have risen, it is because more wives are employed—and more employed wives work full-time.

While all families feel some degree of economic insecurity, two-income families will be buffered and single-parent and poor families most disadvantaged. In the face of declining male employment rates and a stagnation of men's real earnings over the past 20 years, women's paid work has become an increasingly important part of family economic survival. As we saw in Chapter 3, families increasingly rely on women's incomes. There has also been an increase in the number of families where wives earn more than husbands and an increase in the number of families where wives are the *only* breadwinner. Both of these trends reflect male unemployment. In the face of declining real wages the number of people living in poverty has increased, as have the numbers in the highly compensated group, while the middle is shrinking.[3] The average income of Canadian families in the lowest quintile (the poorest one-fifth of the population) declined during the 1990s. Over the same period the average income of the wealthiest Canadian families increased marginally, although these families too experienced some income erosion in 1993 and 1994.

Factors affecting family economic well-being

Immigration, race, and ethnicity

Canada's population is small compared to our American neighbours, but it is increasingly diverse. British and French are still the largest ethnic groups, but

Family Diversity

Projections of visible minority groups, 1991–2016

Recent projections by Statistics Canada estimate that the proportion of the population who are members of visible minority groups will double between 1991 and 2016. In 1991 an estimated 2.7 million Canadians, or 10% of the population, were visible minorities. These figures are expected to rise to 7.1 million, or 20% of the population, by 2016. Currently more than half of Canada's visible minority population lives in Ontario, and this is expected to increase.

Visible minorities identified by the Canadian Employment Equity Act include blacks, South Asians or Indo-Pakistanis, Chinese, Koreans, Japanese, Southeast Asians, Filipinos, other Pacific Islanders, West Asians, Arabs, and Latin Americans.

Source: "Projections of Visible Minority Groups, 1991 to 2016," *Canadian Social Trends* (Summer 1996), 3.

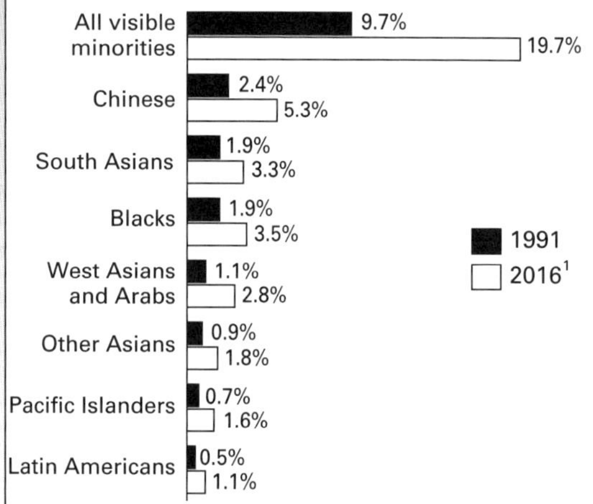

[1]Projections based on medium growth scenario.
Source: Statistics Canada Catalogue 91-541-XPE.

the proportion of Canadians who are neither British nor French is increasing. (Ethnicity as measured by the census refers to the ethnic or cultural group to which an individual's ancestors belonged. It does not mean place of birth or nationality. Canadians can report more than one ethnic origin, and they can report their origin as Canadian.) In 1996 over 30 percent of Canadians gave their ethnicity as "Canadian."

The number of people who identified themselves as visible minorities increased from 9.4 percent in 1991 to 11.2 percent in 1996.[4] Visible minorities make up a larger and larger share of immigrants. Before 1961, only 3 percent of immigrants were visible minorities.[5] Table 4.1 shows the distribution of visible minority Canadians by population group as determined by the 1996 census. Most visible minority immigrants settle in Toronto, Vancouver and Montreal. Visible minorities make up over 30 percent of the population of Toronto and Vancouver. Recent immigrants and visible minorities face a higher risk of low income than native-born Canadians or immigrants who have been in Canada a number of years.

Marital status

Most Canadians marry at least once, and most families (77 percent) are headed by married couples, although this proportion has been decreasing. The proportion of common-law couples and lone-parent families is increasing. In 1971 there were

Table 4.1
Visible minority population by group, 1996

Chinese	26.9%
South Asian	21.0%
Black	17.9%
Arab/West Asian	7.7%
Filipino	7.3%
Latin American	5.5%
Southeast Asian	5.4%
Japanese	2.1%
Korean	2.0%
Other	4.1%
Total Visible Minority Population	100.0%
	N=3 197 480

Source: Statistics Canada, "1996 Census: Ethnic Origin, Visible Minorities," *The Daily* (February 17, 1998).

478 000 lone-parent families in Canada. By 1996 there were 1 137 505. The vast majority of these families are headed by women. While most of these women are separated or divorced, there has been an increase in the number of young (25–34-year-old) never-married women raising children on their own.

According to the 1996 census, average disposable income (income + transfers – tax) was $60 300 for families with two full-time earners and $13 800 for lone parents without earnings (see Figure 4.1).[6] Figure 4.1 shows the real disposable income of Canadian families by family structure and number of income earners. The disadvantage of lone parents is evident. Single mothers face a very high risk of poverty. In 1996, 61.4 percent of single mothers under 65 with children under 18 were poor. Over 90 percent of single mothers under 25 were poor.[7]

Although single-parent families are at far greater risk of poverty than two-parent families, there are more poor children living with two parents than one. Is child poverty more affected by changes in the labour market or by family structure changes? A recent study of Canadian children moving into and out of low income found that for individual children, marriage, separation and divorce have greater impact on children's economic well-being than parental job change. However, changes in family status are infrequent compared to job changes, so in the aggregate, the effect of the two factors is almost equal.[8]

SOCIAL CLASS AND FAMILY LIFE

Social class refers to an aggregate of individuals who occupy a broadly similar position on a scale of wealth, prestige and power. Typically, in social science research, class identification is determined by indicators like occupation,

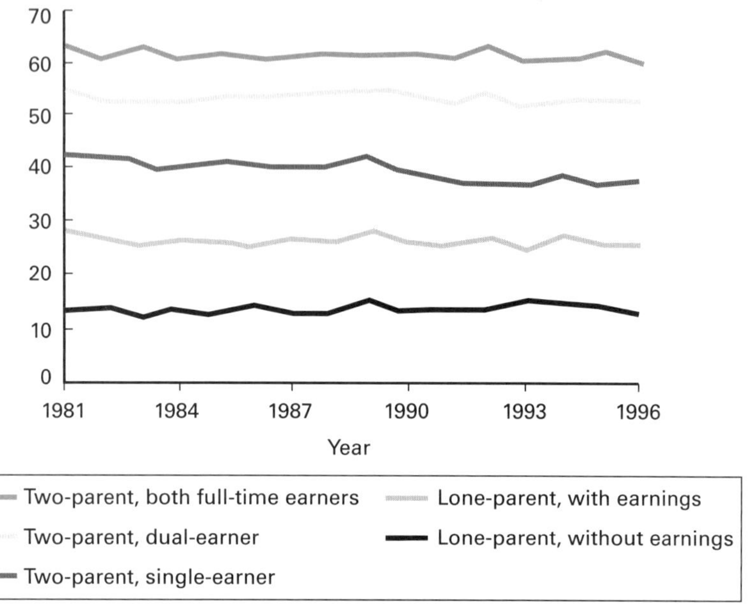

Figure 4.1
Family status and real disposable income ($000)
Source: "Key Labour and Income Facts," *Perspectives* (Autumn 1999), Statistics Canada Catalogue 75-001-XPE: 75.

income, education or wealth. However, the real significance of class stems from some of its consequences. In addition to influencing one's chances to live (including the likelihood of being born in the first place), to live through the first year, and to reach retirement, social class influences early socialization, role expectations and role projections, values, standards of appropriate behaviour, and likelihood of mental illness. In addition, class affects educational opportunities (type of education available, the motivation to get it, the likelihood of doing so) and outcomes (the ends for which education is meant). Dropout rates, scores on intelligence tests, grades, occupational/vocational aspirations, and almost all other factors related to education are also related to class. Most significantly, social class both determines and results in important differences in influence, power, and opportunities.

Similar consequences of class hold true for marriages and families. Social class affects the age at which one is likely to marry, the success of the marriage, the meanings attached to sexual behaviour, the size of family, the recreation engaged in, the type of food eaten, the discipline and care given to children, sleeping arrangements, and contraceptive use.

Although it is true that no sharply defined boundaries separate one class from another, many life experiences vary with social class. For example, in North

America, the divorce rate is higher for the upper and working class than for the middle class. The birth rate increases as the social-class level drops. Young people of the upper class have less freedom of choice of partners than young working-class people. In the Western world, particularly, the age of men at marriage rises with class position. If class lines are crossed in marriage, women are more likely to be upwardly mobile (hypergamy).

One could continue with a list of family variables that are related to class position. The key point is that, within a culture as well as between cultures, significant regularities occur between a family's attitude and behaviour patterns and the class position that family occupies.

Wealthy families

Compared to other income levels, sociologists know relatively little about wealthy families. One of the privileges of wealth is privacy—including privacy from the inquisitive eyes of sociologists. This group of families possesses enormous economic and social resources. Families are obviously the units within which wealth is accumulated and transmitted.

Using information from the 1991 census, Rashid[9] analyzed selected characteristics of Canada's richest families. As is clear from Figure 4.2, this is a small but extremely wealthy group. Families in the top 5 percent income group had

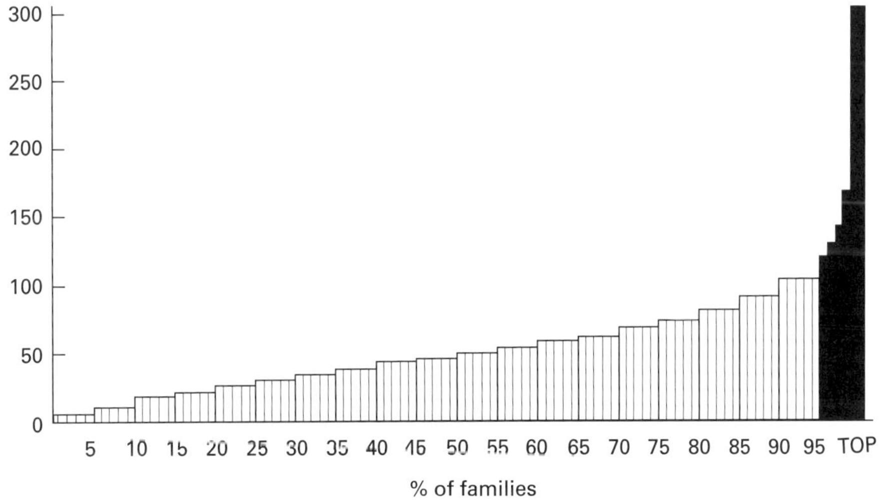

Figure 4.2
1990 average family income ($000)
Sources: Census of Canada, 1991; Abdul Rashid, "High Income Families," *Perspectives* (Winter 1994): 48.

an average income of $164 400, in contrast to an average income of $6 000 for the lowest 5 percent income group.

The high-income families examined by Rashid were those in the top percentile of income. These 73 600 families had an average income of $295 300 in 1990. Wives were important sources of income in these families. Almost one-fifth (18 percent) of wives had incomes over $100 000. Wealthy families are older than average, and members tend to work beyond typical retirement age. Fifty-nine percent of men and 24 percent of women *over 70* worked. Not surprisingly, this is also a highly educated group, with 58 percent of the men and 36 percent of the women holding a university degree.

Women in the wealthy class serve as "gatekeepers" of many of the institutions of the very rich. They launch children, serve as board members at private schools, run social and service clubs, and facilitate marriage pools through events such as debuts and charity functions. Susan Ostrander conducted interviews with 36 upper-class American women and found that they held a clear preference for being with people like themselves (such as through private and exclusive clubs, by invitation only), felt a sense of being better than other people (materially, morally, and in terms of volunteer work and contributions to the community), and conveyed an awareness that people define and judge them by who they are rather than by what they do.[10]

Ostrander noted that these wives, like traditional wives in other social classes, held a subordinate position to their husbands, had an unequal voice in family decisions, and maintained sole responsibility for home and family. But at this class level, women did not perform the nitty-gritty tasks of housework and child care. Women of other races and classes did such work for them. At this class level, women did not need—economically, personally, or socially—to seek paid work outside the home. Instead, women's accommodative and supportive function to their husbands enabled the men to manage the economic and political affairs of society and to perpetuate the dominance of the upper class.

Without doubt, the upper class is gender-segregated. Interestingly, this gender separation is an accepted fact, virtually unchallenged by upper-class women. Why? Ostrander suggested that perhaps the gains of *gender* equality are not enough to balance the losses of *class* equality.

By any measure, this category of wealthy persons is the smallest numerically of all social classes but has the highest influence. Members maintain their positions by preserving symbols of status, such as genealogies, biographies of ancestors, heirlooms, and records of ancestral achievement. The wealthy also maintain their position by carefully controlling the marriage choices of their children.

Middle-class families

When asked to what class they belong, most North Americans will probably respond "middle." Relatively few people can honestly respond "wealthy," and few people are comfortable saying they live with low income. A response of "middle class" generally carries positive connotations.

Middle-class families are likely to receive salaries rather than hourly wages, which are more prevalent among working-class families. This more stable income resource base appears to be one key factor in differentiating the middle class from the working class. With this stable resource base is likely to come a range of amenities that lessen the shock of unanticipated crisis events: pension and retirement plans, bank credit, investment income, and the like. Higher levels of income and greater job security also allow for some discretionary spending and leisure activities.

Given these opportunities for a stable resource base, high levels of education, and professional careers, value systems are promoted among the middle class that emphasize personal autonomy and the ability to develop and carry out rational plans. This ability to control and logically plan one's own life seems to be highly characteristic of the middle class and may partially explain the belief of many members that people of all classes should be able to do likewise.

Beliefs in self-determination and autonomy may also explain why employed professional women in the middle class give work a high priority in their lives.[11] In both the workplace and the home, these women have structural advantages, such as greater job flexibility and available child care. In contrast, working-class women experience more structural disadvantages (limited family income, inadequate child care, inflexible jobs), such that family roles must be given higher priority. Working-class women are more likely to give family roles higher priority than work roles.

The nuclear family of the middle class espouses the ideal of equality between husband and wife and seems to be an important indicator of marital conflict if not shared. In contrast, for working-class wives, a more consistent indicator of frequency of marital conflicts is not equity but the division of feminine tasks. In other words, for a working-class wife, conflict is avoided when she does "the women's work," whereas for a middle-class wife conflict arises when her husband is not taking on, in her view, his "fair share" of family work.[12]

A widely studied area that shows differences between the middle class and the working class is parent/child relations and childrearing practices. Nearly 40 years ago, Melvin Kohn suggested that, in terms of discipline, middle-class parents were more likely to use reason, verbal threats, or withdrawal of rewards to punish a child or solicit the child's compliance.[13] In contrast, working-class parents were more likely to rely on physical punishment. Kohn's reasoning was that, by virtue of experiencing different conditions of life, members of different social classes come to see the world differently and to develop different conceptions of social reality and desirable personality characteristics as well as different aspirations. The middle class (white-collar occupations), in contrast with the working class (blue-collar occupations), requires the individual (1) to deal more with the manipulation of ideas, symbols, and interpersonal relations; (2) to be involved in work that is more complex and requires great flexibility, thought, and judgment; and (3) to be less closely supervised. From these occupational differences come different values, which are reflected in patterns of discipline. Middle-class values are likely to include self-direction, freedom, individualism, initiative, creativity, and self-actualization.

Thus, parents encourage in their children *internal* standards, such as consideration, curiosity, and self-control. Discipline is based on the parents' interpretation of a child's motive for a particular act.[14]

Kohn's ideas in regard to parent/child interaction by social class have received widespread attention, and attempts have been made at extension and replication. Most studies have found that, since Kohn's original survey in the early 1960s, clear trends have existed in self-direction values among middle-class parents and that social class is a primary differentiation in childrearing values. Studies done in Germany and the Netherlands confirm the effect of social class on childhood socialization; the middle-class tendency is to use psychological rather than physical approaches to discipline.[15] This class effect appears to be due largely to the higher level of educational attainment of middle-class parents.

Working-class families

Blue-collar, or working-class, families are employed in processing and machining, product fabrication, construction, transport, farming, fishing, and forestry. Service jobs are generally also classified as blue-collar occupations. Most women are employed in the service sector.

Randall Collins argued that most women are either white-collar working class or blue-collar working class because, in terms of the power of the position, women are order takers, not order givers.[16] Women in paid employment as secretaries, clerks, retail sales personnel, operators of machines, and the like are order takers. Even nurses, Collins claimed, in spite of their professional classification, tend to be assistants (order takers) to physicians (order givers). Ironically, women married to middle-class men, who are assumed to take their husbands' class positions, still provide the services of cooking, cleaning, and emotional support for men and children.

The job of a blue-collar worker generally requires some sort of manual skill. The "elite" of the blue-collar workers—usually, male electricians, plumbers, and highly skilled operators—frequently earn more than members of the middle class. For example, social workers, generally assigned to the middle class, are likely to earn less than certain blue-collar workers.

Formal education beyond high school or trade school is not generally required to learn the manual skills necessary for members of the working class. Physical health is quite crucial to blue-collar workers, since many jobs depend on the ability to perform physical labour. Blue-collar groups are often represented by trade unions. A great amount of faith is placed in the union to protect workers from those above them in the hierarchy, to provide help with long-term medical expenses, and to prevent dismissal.

Working-class families are more dependent on the swings of the business cycle, and less likely to enjoy economic stability than the middle class. Working-class jobs are less secure than managerial and professional jobs.

Members of the blue-collar family, more than any other, conform to the traditional roles of husband and wife. The husband's role is to be a good

Working-class families, when compared to families in other social classes, tend to conform closely to traditional images of husband and wife roles—for example, that the husband is the principal provider and final authority. Because the need for blue-collar work is highly influenced by swings in the business climate, these families often suffer the greatest hardship during economic downturns.

provider, and as the primary wage earner, he is the final authority and disciplinarian. The wife's role is expected to centre on home and family, although she is typically gainfully employed.

The strains associated with life's uncertainties for members of the working class lead to a higher degree of family instability. Divorce occurs with greater frequency among this class group than among any of the higher-income, education, or occupational groups.

Working-class children are more likely to be treated as subordinates than middle-class children. Unlike middle-class parents, who stress that children stay in school and who make major sacrifices to keep them there (including college and university), working-class parents are more likely to expect that children will leave school after fulfilling the minimum legal requirements or, at most, after completing high school. Boys and girls are taught to be self-sufficient, to be tough-minded, and to be able to compete for personal rights and privileges. In the United States, working-class boys have heterosexual experiences earlier and have intercourse more frequently than do boys from middle-class families. Working-class girls often marry early.

Low-income families

As we said in the introductory section of the chapter, real income (taking into account the effects of inflation) in Canada remained quite stable during the 1980s. It rose only 3 percent in the 1980s, in contrast to 26 percent in the 1970s and 46 percent in the 1960s.[17] The lack of increase in the 1980s was primarily a result of the recessions of the early 1980s and early 1990s (see Figure 4.3). During the 1980s, for the first time in history, the real wages of Canadian men declined. While the drop was small—less than half a percentage point—it was a significant reversal of past trends. Women's wages increased during the 1980s, but the increases in average family income are primarily due to the wages of additional earners, including children.

Statistics Canada measures low income by the amount spent on necessities (food, shelter, and clothing).[18] The percentage of gross income spent by the average Canadian family is calculated, and low income is this proportion plus 20 percent. Currently, the low-income cut-off is defined as families or individuals who spend 56.2 percent or more of their gross income on necessities. The average Canadian family spends 36.2 percent of gross income on the necessities of food, shelter, and clothing. Low-income cut-offs vary by size of family and area of residence. For example, in 1996, the low-income cut-off for a family of five living in a large urban area (a population over 500 000) was $35 373. The comparable number for a family of three living in a rural area was $19 143 (see Table 4.2).

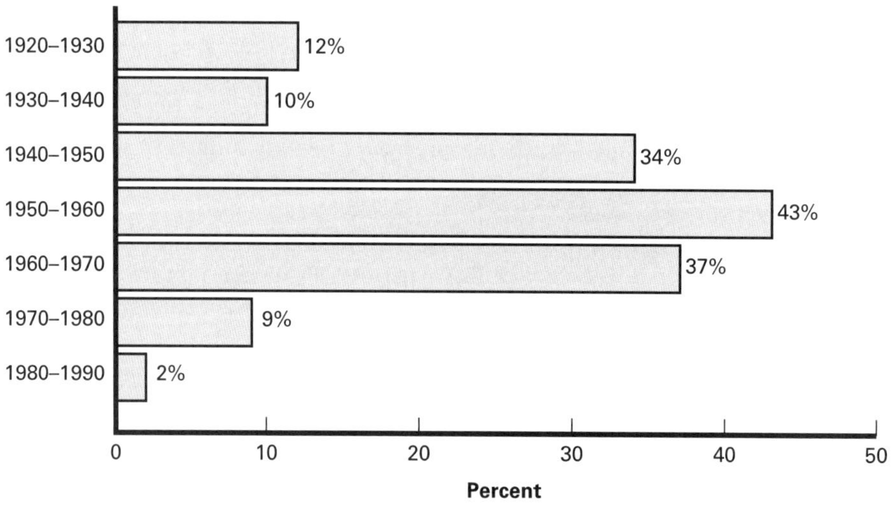

Figure 4.3
Real average annual wage increases, 1920–90
Source: Abdul Rashid, "Changes in Real Wages," *Canadian Social Trends,* Statistics Canada Catalogue 11-008E (Spring 1994): 18.

Table 4.2
Statistics Canada's low-income cut-offs (1986 base) for 1997

	Community size				
Family size	***500 000+***	***100,000–499 999***	***30,000–99 999***	***Less than 30 000***	***Rural areas***
1	$16 320	$14 335	$14 004	$12 766	$11 110
2	22 121	19 432	18 982	17 302	15 062
3	28 119	24 700	24 128	21 994	19 143
4	32 377	28 434	27 780	25 325	22 040
5	35 373	31 068	30 351	27 668	24 082
6	38 397	33 721	32 944	30 031	26 140
7+	41 297	36 273	35 435	32 303	28 115

Source: National Council of Welfare, *Poverty Profile, 1996* (Ottawa: Minister of Supply and Services, 1998), Catalogue H67-1/4-1995E: 93.

Other factors besides family and community size that affect poverty are age, sex, family type, province of residence, education, and employment status.

According to the most recent Canadian estimates, one in six Canadians—about 17.6 percent of the population—is living in poverty (see Figure 4.4). Unattached individuals have far higher poverty rates (37.0 percent in 1996) than people who live in families (14.8 percent in 1996). By province, poverty is highest in Newfoundland and Quebec—where poverty rates are over 20 percent. However, there is considerable variation when one controls for family type. Everywhere, single-parent mother-headed families have the highest rates of poverty.

Although there has been some fluctuation in the numbers of poor Canadians and the rates of poverty, the overall trend has been increasing. In 1980, there were over 3.6 million poor Canadians. By 1996, there were over 5 million. In the intervening years, poverty rates and numbers increased in the early 1980s, declined, and increased again in the 1990s.

Feminization of poverty

The "feminization of poverty" is the term used to describe the increased numbers of divorced, widowed, and elderly women who live in poverty. Without the economic support of a partner's income or pension, these women have to rely on their own incomes or on social assistance to support themselves and their children. Labour force inequities and the unequal responsibility for child care make this task difficult.

A look at sex differences in poverty has provided strong evidence of the feminization of poverty. In a study of the gender poverty gap in eight industrialized countries, only Sweden revealed poverty rates of men to be higher than those of women. The key to the low gender poverty ratio in Sweden is employment

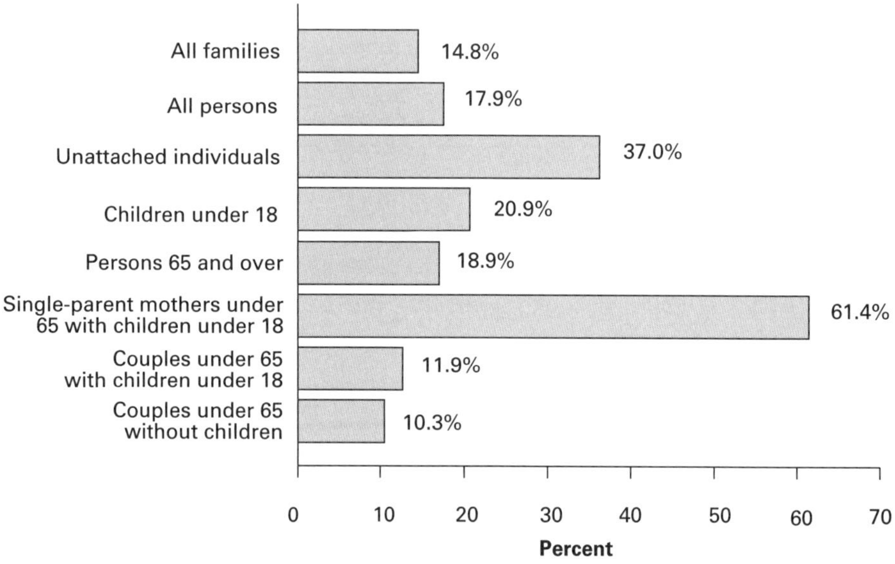

Figure 4.4
Poverty rates for persons and families with selected characteristics
Source: Data taken from National Council of Welfare, *Poverty Profile, 1996* (Ottawa: Minister of Supply and Services Canada, 1998), Catalogue H67-1/4-1995E: 11, 12, 14, 16, 18.

where men and women have very similar rates of labour force participation. Gender differences were slight in Italy, with high rates of marriage being the key, and in the Netherlands, where a generous welfare system appears to be the key. The United States led all eight countries in both the rate of poverty and the male-female difference. In all countries with large gender poverty differences, employment and parenthood (including single-parenthood) were the most important factors.[19]

As suggested by this research, a number of interwoven demographic and socioeconomic trends contribute to the feminization of poverty. First is the increased numbers of female-headed families with dependent children. Second, income inequality, although improving, has not reached the point where women earn enough to support themselves and their children. A third trend is the inadequate level of personal and child support available from absent husbands and from social assistance and other programs. Since female lone parents have low labour force participation rates compared to other women, it is not surprising that many lone parents depend on a combination of alimony or child support and social assistance. As we would expect, lone-parent families not receiving alimony or child support are more dependent on social assistance.

To what extent has dependency on welfare or social assistance added to the feminization of poverty? The absence of supports, such as child care for employed mothers, coupled with the availability of welfare and government programs make living in poverty a probable option for many lone mothers. Does welfare exacerbate the situation of lone-parent mothers and create a self-fulfilling prophecy of poverty? Strong evidence suggests not. Kathryn Edin contended that the welfare system in the United States actually prohibits dependence by paying too little to make this possible.[20] The "welfare trap" is less one of behavioural dependency than one of economic survival. In Edin's words:

> In a society where single mothers must provide financially for their children, where women are economically marginalized into unreliable jobs that pay little more than the minimum wage, where child-support is inadequate or nonexistent, and where day-care costs and health insurance (usually not provided by employers) are unaffordable for most, it should surprise no one that half the mothers supporting children on their own choose welfare over reported work.[21]

Are government benefits a net or a trap? Is welfare a disincentive to employment? Is it an incentive to having children? The idea that women receiving government assistance have a high fertility rate is often implicitly accepted by social and policy analysts. Such beliefs are simply not supported. In fact, Mark Rank found that women on welfare have a rate of fertility considerably below that of women in the general population.[22] Furthermore, the longer a woman remains on welfare, the less likely she is to give birth. The women themselves suggested that the financial and social situation they find themselves in is not conducive to having more children. The economic, social, and psychological costs of becoming pregnant and having a child are perceived as clearly outweighing the benefits.

Nor is welfare enough of a disincentive to work to explain declines in employment income. "Studies examining the effects of transfer payments in Canada and elsewhere, conclude that changes in the system of taxation and social transfers have only modest effects on labour supply."[23]

Child poverty

The number of poor children in Canada and the poverty rates for children rose predictably following the recession of 1981–82, fell during the recovery, and rose again during the recession of the early 1990s. In 1984, over 1.2 million children under 18 were living in poverty, and the poverty rate was 19.6 percent. The number of poor children in 1988 and 1989 dropped to under a million. By 1996, the numbers were close to 1.5 million and poverty rates were over 20 percent.[24] The lowest child poverty rates are in Prince Edward Island, the highest in Manitoba and Quebec.

Fluctuations in child poverty rates over the past two decades can be attributed to changes in the business cycle.[25] The overall picture suggests relative stability in rates, which is not what would be expected in the face of declines in real income. One reason that poverty rates have not climbed in this period is

FAMILY DIVERSITY

National Longitudinal Survey of Children and Youth

Conducted by Statistics Canada on behalf of Human Resources Development Canada, the purpose of the National Longitudinal Survey of Children and Youth (NLSCY) is to derive a clearer understanding of the way children grow and develop. Over the years, the survey will help researchers to identify specific factors that contribute to a child's development, how they contribute, and if these factors can be moderated to ensure a more positive outcome for the child.

The NLSCY collected information on over 22 500 children from newborn to 11 years. New infants will be added to the survey sample in the second, third and fourth cycles (1996, 1998 and 2000). The same panel of children will be interviewed every two years until they reach adulthood. Information is gathered about the children and their families in an interview with the "person most knowledgeable" about the child; teachers and principals are asked for their evaluation of the child's development, and 10- and 11-year-olds are also asked about their experiences with friends, family and school.

The complete findings of the first cycle of the NLSCY (1994) are being released in two publications. This series of articles is based on the first Statistics Canada report, *Growing Up in Canada*, released in November 1996. The report covers topics such as child temperament, behaviour and school readiness; basic sociodemographic characteristics of children and their families; and data on how well those families are functioning.

The second report will present results of the questionnaire completed by teachers and principals as well as complete findings of the interview with 10- and 11-year-olds. It will also cover such topics as child health, literacy, activities, and the family and custody history of children.

Source: "Canadian Children in the 1990s," *Canadian Social Trends* (Spring 1997): 4.

that poor families rely more on transfer payments (including social assistance) now than in the past. Another reason that poverty rates for children have not increased in the face of declining wages is that family structure has changed. Families are smaller, and children are more apt to be born to older women who typically are employed. As the safety net is eroded by government cutbacks, we may see children in the future bear a greater burden of poverty.

The most important determinant of the risk of poverty is family type. At greatest risk are lone-parent mother-headed families with children under 18. For the country as a whole, the rate of poverty for this group is 61.4 percent. However, as Figure 4.5 shows, there are more poor children in two-parent families than in single-parent families—although the gap between the two is shrinking. Table 4.3 shows the poverty rates and numbers of children at risk by family type and province. Children in lone-parent families fare better in Prince Edward Island and British Columbia.

Children are poor because their parents are poor, and a key reason for poverty among parents is the lack of a good job.[26] When employment is irregular, income is irregular. Thus, a considerable amount of insecurity exists in regard to food, clothing, shelter, transportation, and other essential items. Children may be forced or encouraged to contribute to the financial needs of the

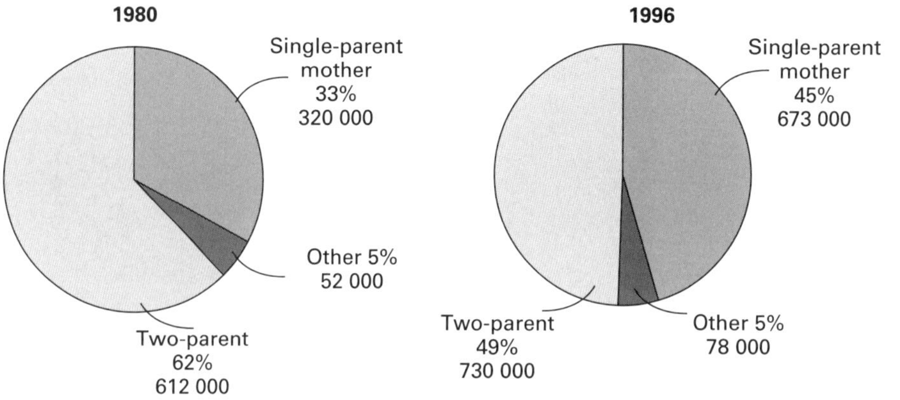

Figure 4.5
Poor children by family type, 1980 and 1996

Source: National Council of Welfare, *Poverty Profile, 1996* (Ottawa: Minister of Supply and Services Canada, 1998), Catalogue H67-1/4-1995E: 79.

Table 4.3
Children under 18 living in poverty, 1996

	Poor children in all family types		***Poor children of two-parent families under 65***		***Poor children of single-parent mothers under 65***	
	Number of children	*Poverty rate*	*Number of children*	*Poverty rate*	*Number of children*	*Poverty rate*
Newfoundland	27 000	20.0%	15 000	12.7%	11 000	72.1%
Prince Edward Island	5 000	14.8	2 000	8.3	2 000	45.3
Nova Scotia	51 000	23.7	25 000	14.7	24 000	70.5
New Brunswick	34 000	19.6	16 000	11.4	17 000	67.6
Quebec	372 000	22.2	184 000	13.7	167 000	62.4
Ontario	538 000	19.9	271 000	12.2	245 000	66.2
Manitoba	69 000	25.4	37 000	16.9	28 000	71.6
Saskatchewan	55 000	20.9	24 000	11.3	29 000	68.7
Alberta	148 000	20.3	69 000	11.5	72 000	70.7
British Columbia	180 000	20.3	86 000	12.0	78 000	59.8
Canada	1 481 000	20.9	730 000	12.6	673 000	65.3

Source: National Council of Welfare, *Poverty Profile, 1996* (Ottawa: Minister of Supply and Services Canada, 1998), Catalogue H67-1/4-1995E: 77.

News Item

Homeless youth

A World Health Organization (WHO) study entitled "A One Way Street?" estimates that approximately 100 million children worldwide are homeless. The same study guesses that the number of street kids in Metro Toronto is about 10 000. It is difficult to imagine a positive future for children who have lived on the street for any length of time. Drug and alcohol abuse are universal problems for homeless youth. The WHO study found that almost all Toronto street children used drugs. Basic needs, such as having a place to sleep or bathe, are difficult to meet; needs for education and medical attention may be impossible to meet.

Lisa Priest, "Down and Out and Very Young in Metro," *The Toronto Star* (April 13, 1993): A1.

family, and few remain in school beyond the minimum legal age. These conditions contribute to and are highly related to other concerns. For example, in the United States, families in poverty have the highest rates of divorce, psychoses, and physical disabilities; the least amount of dental and health care; the largest proportion of people on public welfare; the highest crime rate; the largest number of children; the highest rate of venereal disease; the most unemployment; and, as perceived by many middle-class persons, "the most of the worst."

The majority of persons and families who live below the level of poverty typically do so for intermittent periods. Researchers at the Survey Research Center at the University of Michigan found that, over a 15-year period, American children had frequent transitions in and out of poverty.[27] Although about one-third of the children in the United States actually fell below the official poverty line, nearly half found themselves in a vulnerable economic position at least once during their childhood. The researchers claimed that the average black child could expect to spend more than five years in poverty before reaching the age of fifteen; the comparable average for white children was about nine months.

Single parents and poverty

The vast majority of single-parent families are economically disadvantaged. Survey studies have consistently revealed that, psychologically, single parents are more depressed, are more anxious, have poorer self-images, and are less satisfied with their lives. In short, single parents constitute a group with pressing social and economic needs.

How many children in Canada live in single-parent families? In 1996, there were over one million single-parent families in Canada, 14.5 percent of all families.[28] Most of these result from separations or divorces, although a significant number (22 percent) are never-married men or women raising children on their own. For most Canadians living with low income, the experience is a temporary one. Low-income families headed by women are an exception to this rule. As Table 4.4 shows, the chances of exiting or re-entering a low-income spell depends primarily on family status.

As could be expected, most literature on single-parent households has dealt with the mother/child unit. What is more, rather than consider the mother

Table 4.4
The probability of exiting or re-entering a low-income spell

	Exit rate after		*Re-entry rate after*	
	1 year	*4 years*	*1 year*	*4 years*
Married, two incomes, no children				
Male	69%	42%	12%	4%
Female	71	45	10	3
Married, two incomes, 2 children				
Male	74	48	9	3
Female	75	41	9	3
Married, one income, no children				
Male	46	22	28	10
Female	49	24	25	9
Married, one income, 2 children				
Male	52	26	23	8
Female	54	28	22	8
Lone-parent, divorced, 1 child				
Male	54	27	21	8
Female	40	18	30	12
Lone-parent, divorced, 2 children				
Male	49	24	23	9
Female	37	16	31	12
Lone-parent, single, 1 child				
Male	55	29	21	8
Female	38	17	26	9
Lone-parent, divorced, 2 children				
Male	51	25	24	9
Female	35	15	27	10
Non-family person, single				
Male	46	21	26	10
Female	38	17	25	9
Non-family person, widowed				
Male	46	22	29	11
Female	43	20	26	10

Source: Mireille Laroche, "In and Out of Low Income," *Canadian Social Trends* (Autumn 1998), Statistics Canada Catalogue 11-008-XPE.

who is present, this literature has considered the father who is absent. Thus, it seems the real topic has been the fatherless family. The following sections will consider both the mother/child family (the father-absent family) and the father/child family (the mother-absent family).

Mothers as single parents Most (83 percent) of lone parents in Canada are women. We have said that these women (not only in Canada, but in all Western countries) face a great risk of poverty. Indeed, 61.4 percent of single-parent mothers under 65 with children under 18 are poor.

Lone mothers also tend to be younger, to have less education, and to be raising younger children than lone fathers.[29] What are the impacts of growing up in a mother-headed family? Sara McLanahan and Karen Booth studied problems, prospects, and politics in mother-only families.[30] When compared with two-parent families, the authors found that mother-only families were much more likely to be poor, to have higher levels of stress, and to have lower levels of social integration. Economic insecurity, the authors suggested, was high in mother-only families because of low earning capacity, lack of child support from nonresidential parents, and meager public benefits. The authors also found evidence of negative intergenerational consequences. Children living in mother-only families were more likely to be poor in adulthood than children who lived with both parents. Children living with single mothers were also more likely to become single parents themselves.

Researchers have found that children who grow up in single-parent families are less likely to complete high school and attend college or university,[31] and more likely to smoke cigarettes, use drugs, and have sexual intercourse.[32] Children from the two groups also differ in many other dimensions. What are the findings when factors such as socioeconomic status are controlled for? That is, are the differences among children due more to *family structure* (one parent or two) or to *social class* (level of poverty)?

Barbara Cashion reviewed the social-psychological research pertaining to female-headed families published over a decade and concluded that children in mother-only families are likely to have good emotional adjustment, high levels of self-esteem (except when they are stigmatized), intellectual development comparable to that of others in the same socioeconomic status, and a rate of juvenile delinquency comparable to that of others in the same socioeconomic status.[33] Major problems in mother-only families stem from *poverty* and *stigma*. Poverty, as a general social problem, may be associated with juvenile delinquency and the child's problems in school as well as with the mother's poor attitude about her own situation and her sense of not being in control. The stigma of being without a father causes lowered self-esteem in children; they may also be labelled or defined problematic even in situations where problems are minimal or nonexistent. Overall, Cashion concluded that the majority of single-female-headed families, when not plagued by poverty, raise children comparable to those from two-parent families.

The National Longitudinal Survey of Children and Youth (NLSCY) confirms that socioeconomic status and family structure are two important determinants in a Canadian child's life. (For details regarding the survey see the Family Diversity box on page 104.) It is difficult to separate the effects of poverty from the effects of family structure; however, initial analysis suggests that lone-mother status is *more problematic* for children. Children in lone-parent, mother-headed families, regardless of family income, face a greater risk of having one or more emotional or behavioural problems than children in two-parent families. It is important to keep in mind that both marital and income status are likely to change, so that *length of time* in a high-risk situation will also be an important risk factor.[34]

Fathers as single parents The father/child family, like the mother/child family, is the result of widowhood, divorce, separation, nonmarriage, and, more recently, single-parent adoption. Seventeen percent of lone-parent families in Canada are father-headed. Very few of these men (5 percent) have never been married. As we might expect, after reading the male/female income differentials in Chapter 3, single-parent fathers are far less likely to live in poverty than are single-parent mothers. Only about 20 percent of single-parent fathers live in poverty.[35] Typically, single-parent fathers are older and more highly educated than single mothers. They are also far more likely to be in the labour force. The number of single-parent fathers is likely to increase as more divorced fathers seek custody of their children. Canadian courts tend to award custody of younger children to mothers, but give older children a say in the decision, with the result that more older children are placed with fathers.[36] Research on fathers as single parents has been relatively infrequent and generally limited to small nonprobability samples. Yet father/child studies may prove to be more insightful than mother/child studies in the light of the extreme importance placed upon the mother as the key agent of socialization. Can men "mother"?

This question was posed by Barbara Risman, who surveyed fathers about their experiences as homemakers, the nature of the father/child relationship, and their overall role satisfaction.[37] Risman's major finding was that most men felt comfortable and competent as single parents, regardless of the reason for custody or their financial status. This was true even though four out of five single fathers had no outside housekeeping help, either paid or volunteer. These men felt very close to and very affectionate toward their children, were glad to be fathers, and had little trouble fulfilling either the instrumental or expressive functions of single-parenthood. Clearly, successful mothering is not an exclusively female skill. Men *can* "mother."

Similar support for men as single parents came from a study that examined whether significant differences exist between children reared in single-mother and single-father families. Factors examined included self-perception, self-esteem, social competencies, and the frequency and severity of reported behavioural problems. The historical assumption that single mothers are more effective parents than single fathers was not supported.[38] In a number of ways, fathers who maintain families alone are better situated than their female counterparts. Single-parent fathers typically have higher levels of education, are in the labour force, and, as shown earlier, are well situated economically.

Do males do better in single-father households and females better in single-mother households? That is, are there advantages to living with the same-sex parent in single-parent households? Apparently not. In a national study of several thousand eighth-graders living in mother-only and father-only homes, of 35 social psychological and educational outcomes, not even one revealed significant benefits from living with the same-sex parent as contrasted with the opposite-sex parent.[39] This research casts doubt on the advocacy of same-sex custody determinations.

Overview of single-parenthood Can any conclusions be drawn from the data available? It does seem clear that, just as growing up in a two-parent family does not guarantee happy, well-adjusted, and well-behaved children, growing up in a one-parent family does not predict the opposite. But neither can the findings be understood to imply that the absence of a father or mother has no effect whatsoever. There are definite limitations on the time and energy parents have to do various tasks. Children in single-parent families are assumed to have more responsibility than children in two-parent families. In two-parent families, parental expectations may be more traditional regarding gender-stereotyped chores and activities for children. Single parents may serve to model more nontraditional and flexible gender-role values and behaviours for their children.[40]

Parent-absent families

What about parent-absent families, those 2.9 percent of Canadian children under age 15 who do not live with a parent? Apparently, most of these children live with relatives, especially grandparents. As the children get older, they are more likely to live in families with brothers or sisters or with other relatives. The conditions that result in children living separately from their parents, the effects of parent absence on the children, and the existing support services for these children are questions in need of research.

SOCIAL MOBILITY

Although the "American Dream" of upward social mobility for all is largely a dream, family economic well-being is not static. Some families will experience severe economic hardship, including the death or desertion of the main breadwinner; many families will be touched by unemployment; and many will experience some relief from economic constraints when additional family members enter the labour force. **Social mobility** can be either upward or downward. Although Canadians have a stronger collective sense than Americans,[41] we nonetheless generally believe in the merits of hard work, perseverance, and motivation. Given the extent of organizational restructuring that occurred in Canada over the last decade, the high unemployment we have experienced, and the fact that male wages have declined rather than increased, as was always the case before, upward mobility becomes increasingly illusory. Indeed, downward mobility is a more real possibility. Katherine Newman, in her

FAMILY DIVERSITY

The Kerala factor

In wealth, the Indian state of Kerala falls below the average for India as a whole. In social progress it is considerably more advanced. Along with Kerala's long history of progressive social policies, two of the most powerful factors are a tradition of participatory democracy and a strong commitment to female education. Almost all girls complete secondary as well as primary education.

Sources: Government data, chiefly from sample registration system and 1991 census; UNICEF, *The State of the World's Children, 1995* (Oxford University Press, 1995): 49.

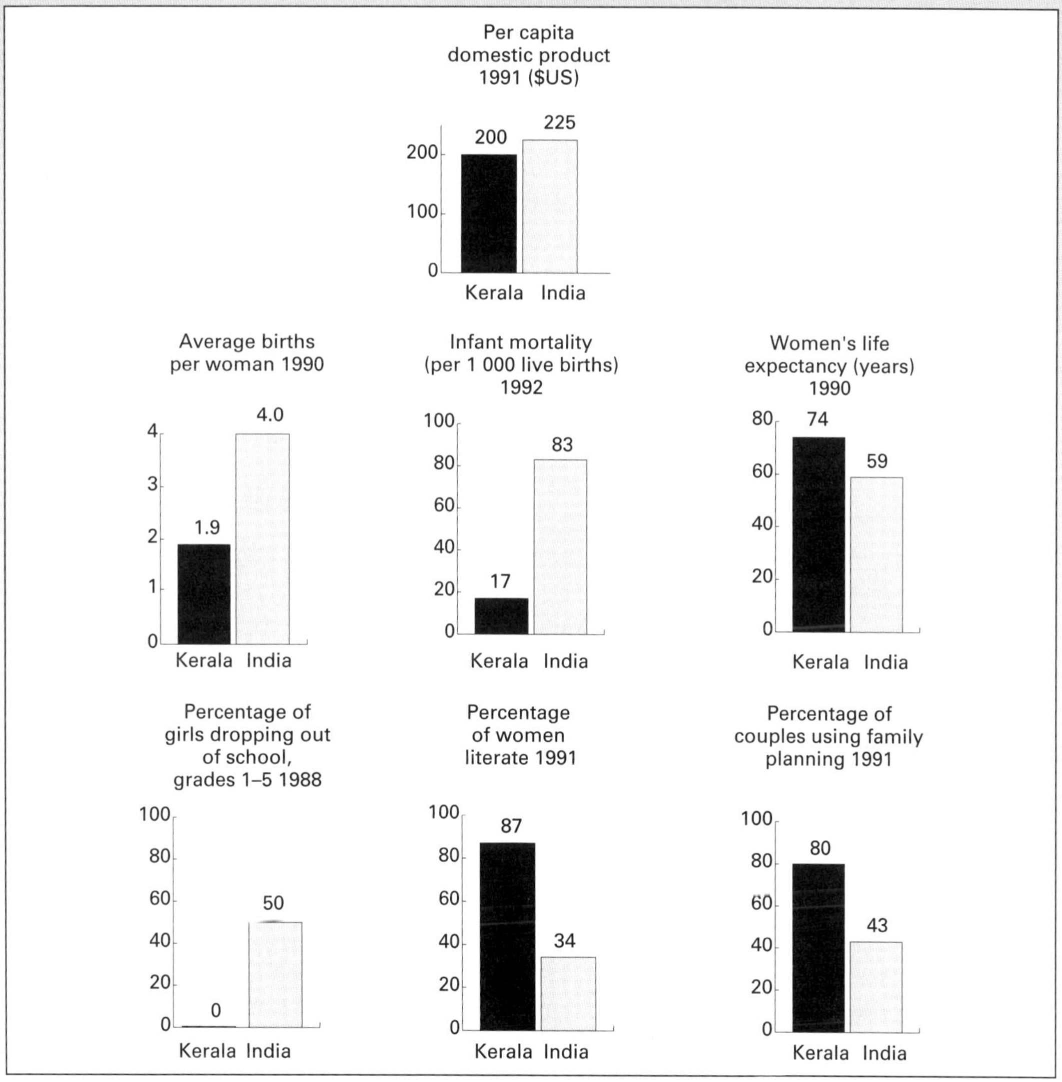

book on the experience of downward mobility in the American middle class, claimed it is a widespread and serious problem for families at all levels of the class structure.[42]

Patricia Smith, in two articles (one with the subtitle "Sinking Boats in a Rising Tide"), notes that over two separate three-year periods, in spite of a growing economy, a substantial minority of Americans (5 to 20 percent) experienced downward income mobility.[43] A large share of the downward mobility came from the middle and lower classes. Women who separated or divorced faced the highest risk of downward mobility. The factors that increased the odds of downward mobility included male headship, minority headship, family dissolution, nest leaving, and having a household head who works in mining, construction, manufacturing, transportation, trade, or farming. The factors that lowered the odds included having a college-educated head of household, retaining the same household heads, and having them working in a professional, technical, or operative occupation or in the finance, insurance, or real estate industry.

Downward mobility involves more than a loss of job and drop in income. It includes a loss of occupational prestige and demotion from one's place in society as well. Marriage, child rearing, divorce, widowhood, and employment of wives all affect families and the status they hold. As will be shown in Chapter 11, divorce, in particular, is a traumatic event, leading to the downward mobility of women. Most victims of downward mobility, male or female, express feelings of anger, dismay, and injustice.

Empirical studies of social mobility have suggested several general conclusions:

1. Most children will ultimately live at approximately the same class level as their parents.
2. A substantial proportion of sons and daughters will experience some mobility.
3. Short-distance mobility is more common than long-distance mobility.

Few people are immune to the possibility of downward social mobility, and many would probably embrace the opportunity for upward social mobility. With this opportunity comes a better job, a higher income, a more luxurious home, a more prestigious neighbourhood, opportunities to travel, better clothes, a new car, freedom from debt—in short, a more luxurious and refined life-style. Many, if not most, people believe that education is one means to obtain these rewards. In Canada, with its fairly open class system and its increasing requirements for specialized and highly trained technicians and experts, "brain power" frequently means higher status. But not all consequences of upward mobility are positive.

Students may discover that their increased education (a potential contribution to upward social mobility) has some disruptive effects. The most obvious is likely to be an increasingly estranged relationship with parents. Many students find that, as they become more educated, their beliefs and values change in ways that may conflict with those of their parents. The paradox of this situation is that these parents may have made major sacrifices to provide college or university education for their children. The painful consequence is that their children become socially distant from them.

In some instances, marriage itself may be threatened by upward social mobility. The wife who works to assist her husband in completing his education may find that his value system and life-style changes while hers remains static. Success in business may encourage certain husbands to seek the friendship of more sophisticated or like-minded females. Career-oriented wives may discover that, with increased economic and social opportunities, they can be self-sufficient and independent, perhaps eliminating the need or desire for a husband. Women with a career may discover men whose values and behaviour patterns are more to their liking than those of their husbands. These and many other examples of upward social mobility illustrate how this supposedly desirable phenomenon may disrupt husband/wife relationships.

Obviously, not all social mobility has negative consequences. In a relatively open class system, a high rate of social mobility may tend to stabilize the social order by providing outlets for change to persons with particular skills or talents. The question is not so much whether social mobility is good or bad but rather what consequences to individuals and families result within societies that have closed or open class systems.

SUMMARY

1. The term *social class* refers to an aggregate of individuals who occupy a similar position on a scale of wealth, prestige, and power.
2. The determination of social-class position varies widely, from examining who owns, manages, and controls production to noting differential rankings of occupational prestige, income, and education. Four general social categories of families were described: wealthy, middle-class, and working-class families, and low-income families.
3. Because one of the key capabilities wealth brings is the ability to protect one's privacy, sociologists have not generally had access to the intimacies of family life among the wealthy.
4. The middle class are professionals and white-collar bureaucrats. At this class level, married couples tend toward the ideal of equality between the spouses but, in reality, perform highly segregated roles. In child rearing, middle-class parents use reason, verbal threats, and withdrawal of rewards to punish their children, instilling belief in self-determination.
5. Working-class families do not have the economic stability found in middle-class families because the working class is more highly dependent on the swings of the business cycle. Marriages are more unstable than among the higher social groups, husband/wife roles are highly traditional, and children are subordinate to parents. Early marriage and parenthood are frequent.
6. Nearly one in six Canadians live in poverty, including about 14.8 percent of all families. The families at greatest risk of poverty are lone-parent mother-headed. The insecurity faced by these families is a consequence of increased divorce, an increase in unmarried parenting, income inequality and labour force segregation, and inadequate alimony and child support. Public assistance does not keep families out of poverty.
7. What are the chances for and consequences of family social mobility, upward or downward? Upward social mobility has probably never been as widespread as has been widely believed, and it seems now to be decreasing.

8. The next two chapters will examine structures and processes that deal primarily with partner selection. In a general sense, the next several chapters follow the marital and family life-cycle, from the point of selecting a partner or spouse through cohabitation or marriage, parenthood, the middle years, and, finally, the later years. A variety of frames of reference, or theoretical approaches (structural-functional, exchange, conflict, psychoanalytic, behaviourist, symbolic-interactional, feminist, and others), are used in examining organizational and process patterns at various stages of the life-cycle.

KEY TERMS AND TOPICS

Economic insecurity p. 91
Social class p. 93
Wealthy families p. 95
Middle-class families p. 96
Working-class families p. 98
Low-income families p. 100
Feminization of poverty p. 101
Child poverty p. 103
Single parents and poverty p. 106
Mothers as single parents p. 108
Fathers as single parents p. 109
Parent-absent families p. 110
Social mobility p. 110

DISCUSSION QUESTIONS

1. What is meant by *social class*? How many social classes are there in Canada? in the United States?
2. What evidence do you see in Canada of class conflict? (Strikes are one example.) Where does the middle class fit into this scheme?
3. Observe the outward signs of class membership in your community. Are there class differences in where people in different classes live, work, play, and worship? Are there differences in family size, attitudes toward child-rearing, and the like? Outline the style of living that characterizes each class. Examine your description for middle-class biases.
4. Using the media as a resource, discover what you can about the family and work lives of the Canadian elite. How are these families identified? Are there consistent patterns in what information is published about the elite?
5. Discuss these two statements: "When a university student from a middle-class family takes a job in a factory, he or she becomes a member of the working class," and "When the same student becomes unemployed, he or she enters the poverty level." Are these ideas valid? Why or why not?
6. What kinds of programs or policies may be effective in helping families escape from poverty? Should subsidized housing, welfare programs, and the like be cut or eliminated? Why or why not?
7. What factors explain the increase in the number of one-parent families? Why is this increase of concern to policy-makers and to the general public?
8. What differences exist between one- and two-parent families? What differences exist between single-father and single-mother families? Why?
9. What factors foster upward social mobility? Downward social mobility? Why are many consequences of upward social mobility disruptive to kin and community ties?

FURTHER READINGS

Bane, Mary Jo, and Ellwood, David T. *Welfare Realities: From Rhetoric to Reform*. Cambridge, MA: Harvard University Press, 1994. Five chapters that examine welfare, its recipients, its providers, and policy proposals.

Danziger, Sheldon H.; Sandefur, Gary D.; and Weinberg, Daniel H., eds. *Confronting Poverty: Prescriptions for Change*. Cambridge, MA: Harvard University Press, 1994. A work that documents trends in poverty and income inequality, reviews government programs, and analyzes the public's attitudes toward these policies.

Evans, Pat and Wekerle, Gerda, eds. *Women and the Canadian Welfare State.* Toronto: University of Toronto Press, 1997. This collection of papers looks at the effects of government cutbacks on women's work and family lives and the subsequent impacts on family economic security.

Goldberg, Gertrude Schaffner, and Kremen, Eleanor. *The Feminization of Poverty: Only in America?* New York: Praeger, 1990. Eight chapters on the feminization of poverty in seven industrialized nations: the United States, Canada, Japan, France, Sweden, Russia, and Poland.

Hanson, Shirley M. H.; Heims, Marsha C.; Julian, Doris J.; and Sussman, Marvin B., eds. "Single Parent Families: Diversity, Myths and Realities," *Marriage and Family Review* 20 (1995): 1–55.

Hurtig, Mel. *Pay the Rent or Feed the Children.* Toronto: McClelland and Stewart, 1999. This book examines the causes of Canada's poverty crisis and presents realistic solutions to alleviate the economic insecurity that threatens an increasing number of Canadian children.

Luxton, Meg. *More Than a Labour of Love: Three Generations of Women's Work in the Home.* Toronto: The Women's Press, 1980. An insightful study of the lives of working-class housewives in Flin Flon, Alberta.

McLanahan, Sara, and Sandefur, Gary D. *Growing Up with a Single Parent: What Hurts, What Helps?* Cambridge, MA: Harvard University Press, 1994. Drawing on four national surveys and a decade of research, the authors show how race, gender, and class influence children's chances for well-being.

National Council of Welfare. *Poverty Profile, 1996*. Ottawa: Ministry of Supply and Services, 1998. This is available free of charge from the Council. It includes the most current figures on family and individual poverty in Canada.

Ostrander, Susan A. *Women of the Upper Class*. Philadelphia: Temple University Press, 1984. Interviews with 36 upper-class women about their lives as wives, mothers, club members, and volunteers.

Rubin, Lillian B. *Families on the Fault Line: America's Working Class Speaks About the Family, the Economy, Race, and Ethnicity*. New York: HarperCollins, 1994. An insightful, very readable book about what Rubin refers to as invisible Americans: working-class families in a contracting economy.

Stacey, Judith. *Brave New Families*. New York: Basic Books, 1991. A readable analysis of working-class families in Silicon Valley caught in the economic upheavals of the 1980s. Stacey argues that it is the working class, not the middle class, who are the true innovators in postmodern families.

Yalnizyan, Armine. *The Growing Gap.* Toronto: The Centre for Social Justice, 1998. The Growing Gap is the first major project of the Centre for Social Justice. It documents the increasing disparities of income and wealth in Canada and offers policy alternatives to existing approaches that try to moderate inequities.

WEBLINKS

http://homebrew.cs.ubc.ca:8900/SCRIPT/soc121_pub/scripts/student/serve_page?838801357+UNIT2.HTM

This site is an interesting and informative resource that explores family and class in contemporary society from an ideological perspective. To access this site, you must login with name: "Guest" and the password: "Friendly."

http://www.cfc-efc.ca//docs/00000467.htm

This site addresses the question, "To what extent do individuals inherit their economic status?" and whether the children of the wealthy are most likely to become wealthy adults, while very poor children are most likely to grow up to be poor.

http://www.epn.org/

A family's social class and its position in the economic order affect the relationship between parents and their children. One important economic trend is polarization, an ongoing process by which the people in the U.S. are being divided into two broad social classes: the "haves" and the "have-nots." This website documents this phenomenon by analyzing wage, income, and wealth trends in the U.S.

http://www.nfb.ca/FMT/E/seri/F/TheFeminofPover.html

The Feminization of Poverty (Series), National Film Board: Currently there are four films in this series. The National Film Board of Canada (NFB), created in 1939, is a public agency that produces and distributes films and other audiovisual works which reflect Canada to Canadians and the rest of the world. Since its beginnings the NFB has played a crucial role in Canadian and international film-making. NFB videos are available in many public libraries and stores.

http://www.hrdc-drhc.gc.ca/hrdc/corp/stratpol/arbsite/publish/backgr_e.html

Growing Up in Canada: A Detailed Portrait of Children and Young People: The full text of the report is available at this site.

http://www.keral.com/

Kerala Connection: Gateway to All Kerala Cyber Resources: Here you get information on all aspects of the Indian state of Kerala; has search capability.

NOTES

1. Statistics Canada, "Social Indicators," *Canadian Social Trends* (Spring 1999): 27.
2. Statistics Canada, *Labour Force Update* (Summer 1999): 8.
3. Armine Yalnizyan, *The Growing Gap* (Toronto: The Centre for Social Justice, 1998).
4. Jennifer Chard and Viviane Renaud, "Visible Minorities in Toronto, Vancouver and Montreal," *Canadian Social Trends* (Autumn 1999): 20–25.
5. Ibid, 23.
6. Statistics Canada, *Key Labour and Income Facts* (1999): 75.
7. National Council of Welfare, *Poverty Profile, 1996* (Ottawa: Minister of Supply and Services, 1998): 35; and Mireille Laroche, "In and Out of Low Income," *Canadian Social Trends* (Autumn 1998): 20–24.
8. G. Picot, M. Zyblock and W. Pyper, *Why Do Children Move Into and Out of Low Income: Changing Labour Market Conditions or Marriage and Divorce?* Statistics Canada, Analytic Studies Branch, No. 132, 1999.
9. Abdul Rashid, "High Income Families," *Perspectives* (Winter 1994): 46–57.
10. Susan A. Ostrander, *Women of the Upper Class* (Philadelphia: Temple University Press, 1984).
11. Beverly H. Burris, "Employed Mothers: The Impact of Class and Marital Status on the Prioritizing of Family and Work," *Social Science Quarterly* 72 (March 1991): 50–66.
12. Maureen Perry-Jenkins and Karen Folk, "Class, Couples, and Conflict: Effects of the Division of Labor on Assessments of Marriage in Dual-Earner Families," *Journal of Marriage and the Family* 56 (February 1994): 165–180.
13. Melvin Kohn, "Social Class and Parent-Child Relationships: An Interpretation," *American Journal of Sociology* 68 (January 1963): 471–480; and Melvin Kohn, *Class and Conformity* (Homewood, IL: Dorsey Press, 1969).
14. In contrast, lower-class or blue-collar workers deal more with the manipulation of physical objects, require less interpersonal skill, have more standardization of

work, and are more closely supervised. This leads to values of conformity to external standards, such as orderliness, neatness, and obedience. Discipline is based on the consequences of the child's behaviour rather than on the interpretation of motive for the behaviour.

15. Robert C. Williamson, "A Partial Replication of the Kohn-Gecas Nye Thesis in a German Sample," *Journal of Marriage and the Family* 46 (November 1984): 971–979; and Maja Dekovic and Jan R.M. Gerris, "Parental Reasoning Complexity, Social Class, and Child-Rearing Behaviors," *Journal of Marriage and the Family* 54 (August 1992): 675–685.
16. Randall Collins, "Women and Men in the Class Structure," *Journal of Family Issues* 9 (March 1988): 27–50.
17. Pina La Novara, "A Portrait of Families in Canada," *Canadian Social Trends*, Statistics Canada Catalogue 89-523E (November 1993): 33.
18. Ibid. The National Council of Welfare regards low-income cut-offs as poverty lines. Statistics Canada takes pains to avoid references to poverty, claiming that low-income cut-offs have no official status as poverty lines.
19. Lynn M. Casper, Sara S. McLanahan, and Irwin Garfinkel, "The Gender-Poverty Gap: What We Can Learn from Other Countries," *American Sociological Review* 59 (August 1994): 594–605; and Marjorie E. Starrels, Sally Bould, and Leon J. Nichols, "The Feminization of Poverty in the United States: Gender, Race, Ethnicity, and Family Factors," *Journal of Family Issues* (December 1994): 590–607.
20. Kathryn Edin, "Surveying the Welfare System: How AFDC Recipients Make Ends Meet in Chicago," *Social Problems* 38 (November 1991): 462–474 (quotation, 472).
21. Ibid.
22. Mark P. Rank, "Fertility Among Women on Welfare: Incidence and Determinants," *American Sociological Review* 54 (April 1989): 296–304.
23. Garnett Picot and John Myles, "Children in Low-Income Families," *Canadian Social Trends* (Autumn 1996): 19.
24. National Council of Welfare, *Poverty Profile, 1996* (Ottawa: Minister of Supply and Services, 1998).
25. Garnett Picot and John Myles, "Children in Low-Income Families," *Canadian Social Trends* (Autumn 1996): 15–19; Sue Crompton, "Transfer Payments to Families with Children," *Perspectives* (Autumn 1996): 42–48.
26. National Council of Welfare, *Poverty Profile, 1995* (Ottawa: Minister of Supply and Services, 1997).
27. Greg J. Duncan and Willard L. Rodgers, "Longitudinal Aspects of Childhood Poverty," *Journal of Marriage and the Family* 50 (November 1988): 1007–1021.
28. Statistics Canada, *The Daily* (October 14, 1997).
29. Jillian Oderkirk and Clarence Lochhead, "Lone Parenthood: Gender Differences," *Canadian Social Trends* (Winter 1992): 16–19.
30. Sara McLanahan and Karen Booth, "Mother-Only Families: Problems, Prospects, and Politics," *Journal of Marriage and the Family* 51 (August 1989): 557–580.
31. Nan Marie Astone and Sara S. McLanahan, "Family Structure, Parental Practices and High School Completion," *American Sociological Review* 56 (June 1991): 309–320.
32. Robert L. Flewelling and Karl E. Bauman, "Family Structure as a Predictor of Initial Substance Use and Sexual Intercourse in Early Adolescence," *Journal of Marriage and the Family* 52 (February 1990): 171–181.
33. Barbara G. Cashion, "Female-Headed Families: Effects on Children and Clinical Implications," *Journal of Marital and Family Therapy* (April 1982): 77–85.
34. Ellen Lipman, David Offord, and Martin Dooley, "Problems of Children in Lone-Mother Families," *Canadian Social Trends* (Spring 1997): 7–8.
35. Jillian Oderkirk and Clarence Lochhead, "Lone Parenthood: Gender Differences," *Canadian Social Trends* (Winter 1992).
36. Ibid.
37. Barbara J. Risman, "Can Men 'Mother'? Life as a Single Father," *Family Relations* 35 (January 1986): 95–102. Note also Barbara J. Risman and Kyung Park, "Just the Two of Us: Parent-Child Relationships in Single Parent Homes," *Journal of Marriage and the Family* 50 (November 1988): 1049–1062.
38. A. Reuben Schnayer and R. Robert Orr, "A Comparison of Children Living in Single Mother and Single Father Families," *Journal of Divorce* 12 (1989): 171–184.
39. Douglas B. Downey and Brian Powell, "Do Children in Single-Parent Households Fare Better Than Living with Same-Sex Parents?" *Journal of Marriage and the Family* 55 (February 1993): 55–71.
40. Marie Richmond-Abbott, "Sex-Role Attitudes of Mothers and Children in Divorced, Single-Parent Families," *Journal of Divorce* 8 (Fall 1984): 61–81.
41. Seymour Lipset, *Continental Divide* (New York: Routledge, 1990).
42. Katherine S. Newman, *Falling from Grace: The Experience of Downward Mobility in the American Middle Class* (New York: Free Press, 1988).
43. Patricia K. Smith, "Recent Patterns in Downward Income Mobility: Sinking Boats in a Rising Tide," *Social Indictors Research* 31 (1994): 277–303; and Patricia K. Smith, "Downward Mobility: Is It a Growing Problem?" *American Journal of Economics and Sociology* 53 (January 1994): 57–72.

CHAPTER

5 ESTABLISHING INTIMACY

With this chapter, the discussion shifts from family institutions and variations in family living to structures and processes in selecting intimate partners and creating marriages. The chapter begins by examining five normative structures in partner selection: age, residence, class, religion, and race/ethnicity. Next we will look at some of the processes involved in developing intimacy, and some of the theories to explain these processes. The final section of the chapter looks at the relationship between sexuality and intimacy. This and the following three chapters follow families through the life-cycle stages of partnering and parenting.

HOMOGAMY AND ENDOGAMY IN INTIMATE RELATIONSHIPS

People choose partners like themselves more often than could be due to chance. The terms generally used to describe the selection of a primary intimate partner from among those who share similar characteristics are **homogamy** and **endogamy.** *Homogamy* denotes likenesses or similarities among couples. *Endogamy* describes marriages and relationships within specific groups of almost any kind. While we might feel free to marry anyone we choose, free choice is only "free" within selected socially appropriate categories. And no society in the world leaves the selection of an intimate or marriage partner unregulated. The consequence is that throughout the world there are high rates of racial/ethnic, religious, class, educational, and age homogamy. Whether the choice is made by the persons themselves, by parents, by relatives, by delegated persons or groups, or by specific social agencies, it is always subject to regulation by social and cultural controls.

The most universal of all norms regarding marriage and sexual relationships—the incest taboo—is an exogamous norm. **Exogamy** requires that members of a society choose their partners from outside their kin group. Thus, all marriages are exogamous in that they do not occur between members of the same nuclear-family unit. The terms *exogamy* and **heterogamy** are often used interchangeably. However, technically speaking, exogamy *requires* differences whereas heterogamy *denotes* differences. A relationship could conceivably be endogamous in regard to race/ethnicity, exogamous in regard to kin, heterogamous in regard to religion, and homogamous in regard to values and personality traits. At what point does any difference or characteristic determine homogamy or heterogamy, endogamy or exogamy?

SOCIAL/STRUCTURAL CHARACTERISTICS

The discussion that follows will examine selected social/structural characteristics that affect interpersonal relations and the selection of a marriage partner. These characteristics include age, residence, social class, religion, and race/ethnicity. Discussion of these characteristics will clearly demonstrate the extent to which endogamous marriages predominate.

Age at marriage

The age at which people marry is an important social/structural characteristic in most countries. It influences family/kin networks, birth rates, and educational advancement, and, in turn, is influenced by social class, women's roles, occupational and educational opportunities, and countless other factors. The general trend in age at marriage around the world—in countries such as Ireland, Japan, Australia, Canada, and the United States—seems to be upward: a delay in or shift away from marriage. What about the homogamy, or age similarity, factor?

Age homogamy

Most couples are relatively homogamous in terms of the age at which they marry. Although in many countries a person is free to marry someone considerably older or younger, most often a single person selects someone from a closely related age group. In Canada, in 1997, the average age at first marriage was 29.5 for men and 27.4 for women.[1]

Figure 5.1 shows the average age at first marriage for Canadian men and women since 1921. Historical data show a gradual increase in the age of marriage until the 1860s, a slight drop at the end of the nineteenth century, followed by a three-decade decline following the Second World War, and a subsequent rise since 1971. Before 1740, the average age of marriage in New France was 21.8 years for women and for men 27.3 years—a gap of 5.5 years.

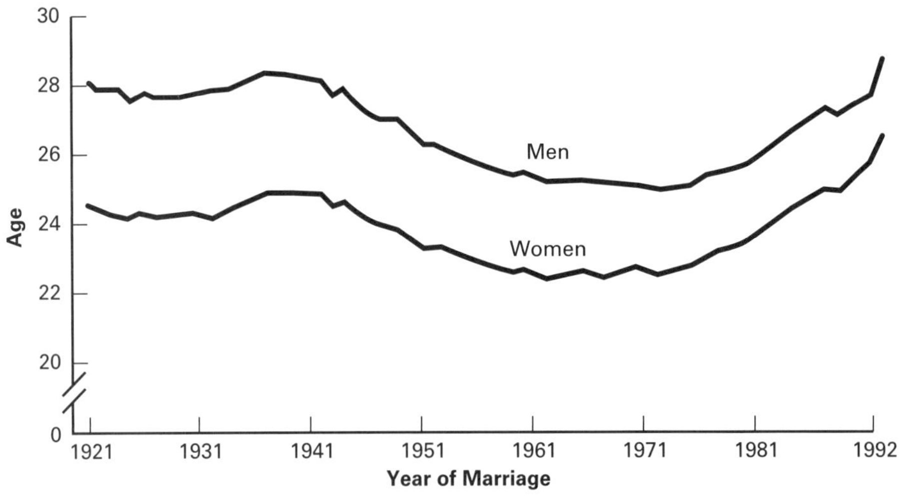

Figure 5.1
Average age at first marriage, 1921–92
Source: Jill Oderkirk, "Marriage in Canada: Changing Beliefs and Behaviours, 1900–1990," *Canadian Social Trends,* Statistics Canada Catalogue 11-008E (Summer 1994): 4.

Most marriages are relatively age homogamous, which means that the partners are very similar in age. In Canada, when marriages are exogamous, the most common pattern is for an older male to marry a younger female.

Estimates for the nineteenth century suggest that women were between 23 and 26 when they married and men between 26 and 29 years. The age differences were between 2 1/2 and 3 1/2 years throughout the century. Late marriage was typical of most Western countries, and necessary if couples were to establish an independent household at marriage. As Figure 5.1 shows, the age gap has narrowed to a fairly constant difference of two years. During the post–Second World War period, when age of marriage dropped for both men and women, the proportion remaining single also dropped. Only 5 percent of Canadians in these generations did not marry.

What explains this increase in age of marriage in such a short time period? Are people delaying marriage because they are spending more time in school? Is the delay due to increased job opportunities or the lack of them? Do people delay marriage until they attain income security? Or are delays in marriage, as suggested by other writers, due to macro-level factors, such as labour market fluctuations that people experience over their life course?[2] Does an increase in cohabitation cause a delay in or replacement of marriage? Or might the "marriage squeeze," relating to a shortage of marital partners, be a contributing factor? (The "marriage squeeze" is described in the next section.)

Canadian wives are younger than husbands in 73 percent of couples, older in 17 percent, and the same age in the rest. Though age differences range from the wives being 78 years older to the husbands being 67 years older, these are obviously extremes; age differences in the majority of marriages are far smaller. Age at marriage is a strong predictor of age differences between spouses. Young people tend to marry someone close in age. As age of marriage increases, so does the age gap between spouses. Figure 5.2 shows that men over 45 typically marry women 10 years younger.[3]

Why the overwhelming likelihood that males will be older than females? Several explanations have been offered, including the husband's slower physiological and psychological maturity compared to that of his wife, the traditional responsibility of the husband to be the major breadwinner (which requires more preparation time), the slight excess of males through the early twenties, the "mating gradient" (described later in this chapter), and status differences between men and women. This last gender argument is consistent with the proposition that female/male marital age differences narrow as societies become more egalitarian.

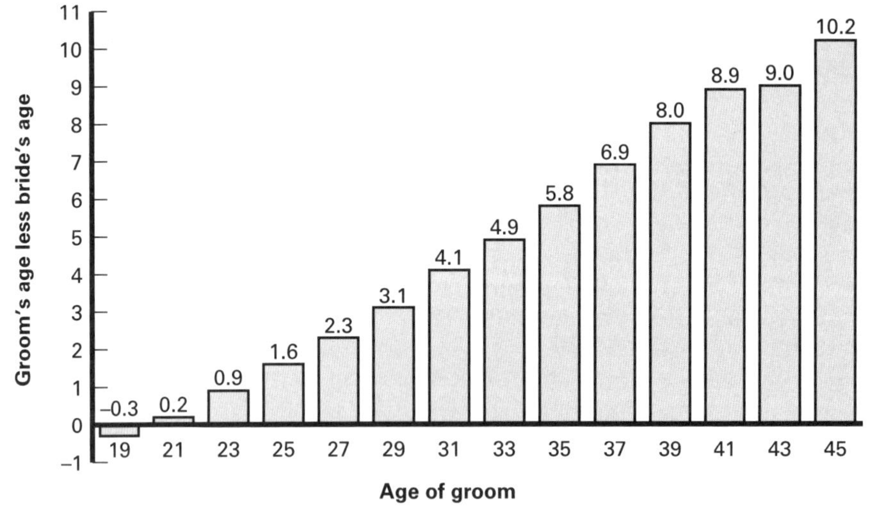

Figure 5.2
Age difference between spouses, by age of groom at marriage,* 1987
*Includes only marriages between two single people.
Source: Jill Oderkirk, "Marriage in Canada: Changing Beliefs and Behaviours, 1900-1990," *Canadian Social Trends*, Statistics Canada Catalogue 11-008E (Summer 1994): 4.

NEWS ITEM

Young and beautiful marries old and wealthy

On June 27, 1994, Anna Nicole Smith, age 26, married J. Howard Marshall II, age 89. Smith is a six-foot-tall, former Guess Jeans model, 1993 Playboy Playmate of the Year, *Naked Gun 33 1/3* actress, and former waitress and topless dancer. Marshall was an ailing, wheelchair-bound Houston oilman believed to be worth about $500 million. Following a courtship that began several years ago, Smith entered her second marriage and Marshall his third.

On August 4, 1995, J. Howard Marshall II, at the age of 90, died of pneumonia. This raised the question as to who would inherit his fortune as his son, E. Pierce Marshall, had held the power of attorney over his father's wealth.

The split between his wife and his son became obvious immediately with separate funeral arrangements. Pierce, the son, held a dignified private funeral. Anna Nicole, the wife, held a showy memorial service at a Houston funeral home. She appeared wearing a white dress with a plunging neckline and her wedding veil. Her son wore a white tuxedo and held a small black dog.

Another immediate fight developed over Marshall's remains. This ended in a settlement in which he was cremated and his ashes divided between the two sides. The battle over who gets what and how much of the estate is under way.

Age differences in marriage are smallest at young ages and increase with age (see Figure 5.2). Although the usual pattern is for men to choose women younger than themselves, the difference in their ages increases with the age at first marriage for the male. In other words, as men get older, they marry increasingly younger women.

One study found that age differences in marriage affected how long women live. One analysis showed that women married to younger men tended to live longer than expected, while women married to older men tended to die sooner than expected.[4] These results can be explained in two ways. One explanation suggests a mate-selection factor. That is, healthy and active women select or are selected by younger men and will live longer whomever they marry. The second explanation bases women's longevity on the biology, psychology, and sociology of marital interaction. Combinations of genetic factors, interpersonal interactions, and social norms lead partners to develop similar activities, interests, appearances, emotional states, and so forth. The causal factor of age difference in marriage and longevity may be related to the literal chemistry that people create in close relationships.

A final question dealing with age homogamy is whether age differences affect the quality of marriage. Are "May/December marriages," as they are referred to in the popular literature, problem-ridden and unstable? Evidence has suggested that they are not. An analysis of two public-use data sets yielded no significant differences in marital quality among couples from various age-dissimilar categories.[5] This finding, a dramatic contradiction of conventional wisdom, might suggest that age is becoming a less compelling determinant of adult attitudes and behaviour.

In the Canadian study of age differences in marriage and divorce referred to earlier, Gentleman and Park[6] found that couples with large age differences are more likely to divorce than couples with small age differences. This is particularly true for couples with wives older than husbands. However, the authors note that the marriage of a couple with an extremely large age difference is much more likely to end with the death of one spouse than in divorce.

The "marriage squeeze"

The term **marriage squeeze** is used to describe the effects of an imbalance in the sex ratio, or the number of males and females available for marriage. Any shortage of marriageable males (a low sex ratio) or shortage of females (a high sex ratio), for whatever reason, will produce a "marriage squeeze."

The squeeze (a low supply of either sex) may be due to wealth, power, status, level of education, age, or other factors. As will be noted in the discussion of the *mating gradient* later in this chapter, women at the top and men at the bottom of a class or professional hierarchy have lower marriage rates. This type of squeeze exists in most countries. High-caste women in India are a good illustration of this trend.[7]

Age is the characteristic considered most often in examining the marriage squeeze. Consider the hypothetical population, where males age 26 typically marry females age 23. If the annual number of births decreases each year, 26-year-old males will be looking for brides among the smaller cohort (an age-specific group) of females born three years later. The males will be caught in a marriage squeeze because they will encounter a shortage of females. Conversely, if a population experiences a substantial increase in the annual number of births, the same process will operate, but the females will be caught in the marriage squeeze. (That is, the male population born three years earlier will be smaller than the female population born three years later.)

The marriage squeeze phenomenon is a significant factor in marriage behaviour. In the 1950s, men faced a shortage of women. The situation reversed in the 1980s, when women faced a shortage of men. It will reverse again in the 1990s and at the turn of the century, when there will be a shortage of women. How are these imbalances and shifts explained?

Basically, the 1950s marriage squeeze was the result of a decline in the absolute number of births each year during the late 1920s and early 1930s, combined with the fact that men tended to marry women two or three years younger than themselves. Because there were more men born in 1930 than women born in 1932 and 1933, the pool of women two or three years younger from whom to choose was smaller. Thus, a male marriage squeeze existed. A reverse female marriage squeeze resulted in the 1970s and early 1980s due to the increased number of births during the post–Second World War "baby boom" of the 1950s. And finally, given the sharp decline in the birth rate in the 1960s and 1970s, we faced a return to the male marriage squeeze in the 1990s. Assuming a two- or three-year difference between men and women in marriage age, the smaller female population born several years later than the larger male population will have a larger pool from which to select.

Law and age at marriage

British common law required that males should be at least 14 years old and females 12 to marry. All provinces have raised the minimum age for marriage for both men and women. In most provinces, young men and women who are 18 can marry without parental consent. In Nova Scotia, the Northwest Territories, Nunavut and the Yukon Territory, the minimum age is 19. If parents consent to the marriage, the minimum age is 16 or earlier if the young woman is either pregnant or the mother of a living child.

Legislation reflects the social concern for young marriages. The consequences of teenage marriages are fairly well known: high incidence of dropping out of school,[8] high unemployment rates, higher-than-average fertility rates (the consequences of young parenthood are discussed in Chapter 7), lower-than-average lifetime earnings, and a high divorce rate (from two to four times that for persons who marry after age 20).

Certainly, all of these consequences are serious and have negative long-range effects.[9] Some support was found for the idea that people who marry young are unprepared for marriage, experience relatively low marital satisfaction as a result, and therefore appear disproportionately in divorce statistics.[10]

Residential propinquity

Well established in the literature on sociology of the family is the idea that mate selection involves a *propinquity factor*. (*Propinquity* means "proximity.") A lengthy list of studies has established the general conclusion that urban persons tend to marry people who live within fairly limited distances of their homes. Evidence to support this idea usually takes the form of a frequency distribution or cumulative percentage of marriages in some community, classified by the distance separating the bride's residence from the groom's residence just before marriage.

Since most propinquity studies were completed two or three decades ago, it is difficult to determine whether place of residence is as significant a factor in mate selection today. One might also expect considerable variations among different groups, such as rural dwellers, college and university students, and people who are elderly. However, it seems that people tend to marry those who live near them.

How can one account for the propinquity factor in mate selection? An obvious explanation is that people meet and interact with others who live nearby and attend the same schools, religious institutions, and social events. While the pool of potential mates increases dramatically with increasing distance, proximity facilitates contact. People are less likely to meet and get to know intimately those who do not live near them. And obviously, people are not likely to fall in love with or marry people they do not meet.

Another explanation for propinquity has been called the **norm-segregation theory,** which suggests that people marry others who adhere to similar cultural norms and that these people reside in segregated clusters. People of similar normative categories of race/ethnicity, class, religion, and educational level tend to cluster together residentially. Neighbourhoods and

FAMILY DIVERSITY

Looking for a mate? Where should you go in Canada?

Canada has more "unattached" women than men, although the sex ratio reverses for men and women under 30. Imagine that you want to play matchmaker and introduce some of these singles to each other. How could you help them meet Mr. or Ms. Right? Women anxious to meet dating partners will find the sex ratio in their favour in Montreal, Ottawa-Hull, Edmonton, and Vancouver. Some women may want to avoid cities and search out rural areas, and smaller western and northern communities.

The opposite is true for males. The best community of all for males is Joliette, Quebec, where the sex ratio is 72 men per 100 women. Better inquire about the age structure before you go!

Source: Robert Riordan. "Two by Two? Sex Ratios of Unattached Canadians," *Canadian Social Trends* (Spring 1994): 26–29.

communities often tend to be characterized by norm-homogamous groupings. Thus, the combination of norm similarity and geographical proximity provides an additional explanation of residential propinquity in mate selection.

In a highly mobile society, one might expect nearness of residence to be less relevant in mate selection. For certain groups and persons, this is probably true. Higher-status groups may be less propinquitous than lower-status groups because money and time may be more readily accessible. Higher-status individuals may also be willing to travel farther. Propinquity differences among class and occupational groups can be ascribed to differences in time and resources.

One final point is that *propinquity* does not mean *nonmobility*. As an individual moves about for college or university, employment, or whatever, he or she becomes increasingly likely to marry someone currently living close by. Past ties will likely be broken. The individual who spent his or her childhood and adolescent years in Manitoba but goes to school and takes a job in Vancouver may well marry someone from Vancouver. In short, time and cost factors affect residential propinquity.

Social status

Class endogamy seems to be a desirable social norm in most societies, although this may be so only for higher-status parents in regard to their children. Whether mates are selected by the individuals themselves, by parents, or by someone else, many social conditions support class endogamy. Irrespective of the desired or preferred circumstances, most marriages are class-endogamous.

Class endogamy

Numerous studies in the past 50 years have found that both men and women marry persons within their own classes with greater consistency than could be expected simply by chance. As early as 1918, an analysis of marriages in

Philadelphia showed that intermarriage between men and women in the same industry was distinctly more common than chance expectancy, revealing something of an endogamous trend.[11]

Like occupational endogamy, educationally endogamous or homogamous marriages occur more often than could be expected by chance. What's more, educational endogamy has been found (1) to be more important than social-class origins and (2) to have increased between the 1930s and the present.[12] Educational endogamy is common among all groups but particularly for highly educated persons and for those who marry shortly after leaving school. This intraclass pattern is often viewed by exchange theorists as a process in which individuals attempt to achieve the best possible bargain for themselves and their children by weighing marital resources and alternatives. If this is true, it would be highly surprising if the class-origin/occupation/education endogamy pattern were not the most prevalent. It is at similar class levels where marital resources will most likely be similar.

If this is the case, what does a person of lower social class have to "trade" with someone of higher social status? The following discussion will examine some patterns of marriage across class lines.

Mésalliance

Marriage with a person of a lower social position has been termed **mésalliance.** Special cases of mésalliance are **hypergamy,** denoting the pattern whereby the female marries into a higher social class, and **hypogamy,** whereby the female marries into a lower social class.

With particular reference to the United States and Canada, a number of writers have concluded that hypergamy is more prevalent than hypogamy; that is, women marry men of higher status more frequently than men marry women of higher status. On the basis of the exchange theory argument, the social advantages of hypergamy seem to exist primarily for low-status women. For equity to occur, this type of exchange would require that the woman be exceptional in those qualities defined as desirable by the culture into which she marries. Depending on the society, qualities in women that determine status might include skin shade, facial and morphological features, and relative age.

Mating gradient

If, as stated, when persons marry outside their social class, men tend to marry down and women tend to marry up, then it can be assumed the same patterns occur before marriage. Thus, when men and women date or engage in intimate personal interaction, women seek men of similar or higher status and men seek women of similar or lower status. This tendency has been called the **mating gradient.** It is rooted in the notion that men at the top have a wider range of mate choice than do men at the bottom, with the reverse being true for women; namely, women at the top have a more narrow range of choice than those at the bottom.

One interesting consequence of these choices is an excess number of unmarried men at the bottom of the socioeconomic ladder and an excess number of unmarried women at the top. Lower-status men must compete against other lower-status men as well as against higher-status men for the lower-status woman. Conversely, the higher-status women compete against other higher-status women as well as those below them for the higher-status man. Thus, unmarried men are likely to be disproportionately of lower status and unmarried women are likely to be disproportionately of higher status. However, higher-status or professional women who are more economically independent increasingly choose not to marry (or remain married) in spite of the smaller pool of eligible men.

The mating gradient also seems to operate in campus dating. For example, first-year men and graduating-year women have the smallest choice of probable dating partners. The first-year woman may date men from any year, whereas most first-year men will date first-year women. Among students in their graduating year, the situation is reversed: men can date women from any year, whereas most women will date men their age or older—a smaller group on most campuses.

Religion

Although church attendance has declined over the past 40 years, most Canadians still think of themselves as having a religious faith. And Canada remains an overwhelmingly Christian country: 82 percent of the population identified themselves as Catholic or Protestant in 1991 (the most recent census to ask religion). Only 12 percent said they had no religious affiliation, and 3 percent claimed affiliation with an Eastern non-Christian religion such as Islam, Buddhism, Hinduism, or Sikhism. Less than 30,000 Canadians identified themselves as members of parareligous groups such as Scientology, New Age, Pagan, Theosophical, and so on.[13]

Religious endogamy is very strong in Canada. The number of people who marry within their own religion is far greater than chance occurrence can explain. According to the 1991 census, a full 85 percent of couples (including common-law couples) said they had the same religious identification. (Couples who both reported "no religion" were included in this percentage.)[14] The remaining 15 percent were defined as interfaith unions. The largest numbers of intermarriages are between Protestants and Catholics.

The general opposition to interfaith marriages stems from the widespread belief that they are highly unstable and create a multitude of problems that intrafaith marriages do not. Some empirical evidence has supported this belief. Tim Heaton and Edith Pratt suggested that interreligious marriages are less satisfying than religiously homogamous ones.[15] Couples of the same denomination as well as those who attend a religious institution frequently are more likely to have happy, stable marriages than those whose religions are different. Nevertheless, the negative consequences often assumed of interfaith marriages regarding the success of the marriage and the secularization of the children do not have much empirical support.

Race/ethnicity

Of all the norms involving intermarriage, few are more widely held or rigorously enforced than those pertaining to race and ethnic origins. Despite scientific findings and removal of legal barriers, the restrictions concerning interracial marriage still remain the most inflexible of all mate-selection boundaries.

In the United States, racial intermarriage was legally restricted until 1967 when the U.S. Supreme Court struck down as unconstitutional a 1924 Virginia law forbidding marriage between persons of different races. According to the Court, laws of this type violate rights guaranteed to all persons under the Fourteenth Amendment to the Constitution, which extended citizenship rights to freed black slaves. Irrespective of the Supreme Court's decision declaring such laws unconstitutional, the social mores and the disfavour placed on interracial marriage by all major racial, religious, and ethnic groups are so strong in most areas that relatively few interracial marriages take place.

Dumas and Peron used country of origin as a measure of the extent of ethnic intermarriage in Canada.[16] Although country of origin is a rough indicator of ethnic intermarriage, the data give some indication of its extent. According to this estimate, three-quarters (76.9 percent) of the 932 810 marriages in the 1981–85 period were between Canadian-born partners. The remaining 215 889 marriages included 82 376 between two foreign-born persons: 78 050 immigrant women who married Canadian-born men and 55 457 male immigrants who married Canadian-born women. Of course, many of these marriages may be between an immigrant and the Canadian-born son or daughter of an immigrant.

Black/white intermarriages, while increasing, still make up a small proportion of all marriages in North America. When they do occur, a disproportionately large number of couples include a black male and a white female.

If we use country of origin to represent ethnicity, women show a greater tendency to marry within their ethnic group. Immigrants from certain countries, such as China, India and Japan, have a much higher tendency to marry people from their native country than immigrants from Greece, Italy, Africa, or France.

Do interracial and interethnic marriages face unique difficulties? Obviously the success or failure of an interracial or interethnic marriage does not depend solely on the fact that it is mixed; as with other marriages, success is influenced by age, religious beliefs, educational level, residence location, first marriage or remarriage, and many other factors. Research findings would certainly lead one to seriously question the negative aspects of interracial/interethnic marriage.

Whether dealing with husband/wife, parent/child, or employer/employee relationships, the success of the relationship depends on the total situation and not merely on the fact that the partners have different skin colours or ethnic heritages. Interpersonal relationships of any sort are clearly affected by external forces: the reactions of parents, kin, neighbours, teachers, politicians, and society in general. Success is relative to the social/cultural context, extending far beyond the boundaries of any two persons—whether their skin colour is alike or different.

The selection of an intimate partner is not only a matter of preference or choice. Despite the increases in freedom and opportunities available to people both young and old to marry whom they please, many factors limit the number of Canadians who actually meet and socialize together. Restrictions placed on age, sex, marital status, class, religion, and race/ethnicity in most societies considerably narrow the "field of eligibles."

ARRANGED MARRIAGE VERSUS FREE CHOICE OF PARTNER

All societies have systems of norms, rules and controls about who may marry whom and how marriage partners are selected. These norms are likely to vary from one culture to another and to differ for a first marriage and a remarriage, for males and females, for wealthy and poor people, and so forth.

On an ideal-type continuum, these norms may vary from totally arranged marriages at one extreme to totally free choice of partner at the other. Where marriages are arranged, the couple has nothing to say about the matter. The selection is usually, but not always, made by parents or kin. The other extreme, totally free choice where parents and kin are not consulted and may not even be aware of the marriage, is rare.

Between these two extremes are various combinations of arranged/free-choice possibilities. Parents may arrange a marriage and give their son or daughter veto power. The son or daughter may make his or her own selection and give the parents veto power. One of the persons to be married, usually the son, may select the bride with his parents. Regardless of the method of partnering, every society has a set of norms to prescribe the appropriate procedure.

Where selection of a partner is arranged, marriage is a means of providing for the continuity and stability of the existing family. Arranged marriage has the effect (function) of providing elders with control over younger family members. The elders also control which outsiders become part of the family unit. In addition, arranged marriage preserves family property, furthers political linkages, protects economic and status concerns, and keeps the family intact from one generation to another.

As a result, almost without exception, chosen partners in an arranged marriage share similar group identities. Racial/ethnic, religious, and particularly economic statuses must be similar. Arranged marriage is not based on criteria such as romantic love, desire for children, loneliness, and sexual desire; rather, it will probably be based on factors such as a dowry or the size of the bride's price, the reputation of the potential spouse's kin group, levirate and sororate obligations, and traditions of prescribed marriage arrangements.

A contemporary example of arranged marriage comes from Japan, where about 25 to 30 percent of all marriages are arranged.[17] A "marriage drought" makes it very difficult for young people to find desirable partners. As a result, professional "go-between services," modelled after the more traditional type of arranged marriage, have arisen.

Free choice of a marriage partner implies that the couple can ignore the wishes of parents and kin. As well, free choice implies that instrumental considerations such as money, power, social rank, occupation, education, age, incest, family ties, and even sex are not major considerations in the choice. But in fact, parents' wishes as well as instrumental considerations are part of most decisions to marry, though personal needs and values also are significant.

The social construction of love

Love is an elusive concept. We all talk about it, some experienced it at first sight, and others claim they fell in it, made it, have it, or would like to find it. But what is this thing called love? The dictionary gives definitions such as: an intensive affection for another person based on familial or personal ties; an attachment based on shared experiences or interests; and an intense attraction to another person based largely on sexual desire. Love is also defined as a zero score in tennis, but it may be difficult to link this specifically to partner selection.

However love is defined, it is something that takes on different meanings, importance, and behaviours according to the context in which it is used. To love pizza and baseball, our parents and children, money and vacations, or intimacy and sex elicit different meanings and corresponding behaviours. In short, it is socially constructed. This construction varies not only from one culture to another but within a given culture and social context within that culture. As a result, males and females learn different meanings of love, attach greater or lesser importance to it, and behave differently in response to it. It varies from one context to another: dating, selecting a marriage or live-in partner, or in marriage itself. Even demographic variables such as age, income, and occupation play an important role in love relationships. In American society, women seem to be socialized to more easily "fall in love" with a man who is wealthy or holds a prestigious position, while men seem to be socialized to more easily love a woman with physical features the culture defines as attractive.

Patricia Noller from Australia writes of the love that supports marriage and family. She reviews the literature that explores the emotional, cognitive, and behavioural aspects of both mature and immature love. In her words,

> Given the evidence that love is socially constructed, however, and that love relationships occur in a social and cultural context, the cognitive aspect of love may be the most important determinant of the love experienced by those in love relationships. It seems that the emotional and behavioural aspects of love are both strongly affected by the ideas about love that have been accepted by the individuals concerned.[18]

In the context of partner selection, love has different meanings in arranged marriages than where the choice is made by the persons themselves. It is socially constructed.

INDIVIDUALISTIC EXPLANATIONS OF PARTNERING

With a decrease in kinship control over mate selection, particularly in Western societies, has come a freedom that has brought about an enormously complex process. This process clearly begins long before the first meeting. And for many, the selection process never ends, since in North America it is possible to have many relationships and several marriages. Most psychological and other individualistic theories explaining the choice of mate are based on a wide range of experiences, along with a variety of subconscious drives and needs.

Instinctive and biological theories

One of the oldest and perhaps most radical explanations of partner selection suggests that what guides a man to a woman (rarely is it thought to be the other way around) is *instinct*. Instinct is established by heredity and deals with unlearned behaviour. Related to the instinct theory is that of genetic similarity. The idea is that genetically similar others, be they strangers or kin, have a tendency to seek each other and provide supportive environments. In contrast, genetically dissimilar others have a tendency to form natural antipathies and provide mutually hostile environments. Assortive mating in both animals and humans is based on genetic similarity.

As far as is known, no one has ever discovered any instinctive, unconscious, or purely biological determinant for mate selection. Of course, the fact that such motivations are unconscious or innate makes them difficult if not impossible to discover. In short, to attribute selecting a mate to the unconscious adds little more to understanding basic processes involved in mate choice than does attributing it to spirits, fairies, or supernatural powers.

Parental image theory

Sigmund Freud and other psychoanalysts suggest that a person tends to fall in love with and marry a person similar to his or her opposite-sex parent. In other words, mate selection is rooted in the unconscious.

According to Freud's **Oedipus complex,** early in a boy's life, his mother becomes his first love object. But the presence of his father prohibits him from fulfilling his incestuous desire. As a result, the male infant develops an antagonism toward his father for taking his love object from him. This, in turn, results in an unconscious desire to kill his father and marry his mother. The male infant's desire for his mother and fear of his father becomes so great that he develops a fear of castration, or, as Freud called it, *castration anxiety*—a fear that his father wants to emasculate him by removing his penis and testes. But since the father is also protective and helpful and respected by the mother, the son experiences a great amount of ambivalence, which is resolved only by a primary type of identification with his father. The Oedipus complex is thus temporarily resolved for the male, but the repressed love for his mother remains. By adolescence, when the male is free to fall in love, he selects a love object that possesses the qualities of his mother.

The opposite but parallel result occurs for the female. At an early age, the girl becomes aware that she does not have a male sexual organ and develops *penis envy*. Feeling castrated, her feelings are transformed into the desire to possess a penis, especially her father's. These feelings for the forbidden object remain repressed throughout childhood, but her love for her father, known as the **Electra complex,** culminates in marriage when she selects a mate with the qualities of her father.

Although it seems reasonable to believe that young people in selecting partners would be keenly aware of the qualities of their parents and the nature of their marriage, no clear evidence has supported the hypothesis that the boy seeks someone like his mother and that the girl seeks someone like her father. In some instances, close resemblances seem to exist between a man's wife and his mother or between a woman's husband and her father. Davor Jedlicka argued that this occurrence is more frequent than could be expected by chance; however, whether the explanation is rooted in Oedipus or Electra complexes is subject to question.[19]

Complementary needs theory

The theory of complementary needs in mate selection was developed and enhanced by Robert F. Winch about 45 years ago. It was his belief that, although mate selection is homogamous with respect to numerous social characteristics—age, race/ethnicity, religion, residential propinquity, socioeconomic status, education, and previous marital status—when it comes to psychological needs and individual motivation, mate selection tends to be complementary rather than homogamous. The idea grew out of a modified and simplified version of a need-scheme theory of motivation, but the needs tend to be complementary rather than similar.

To test his hypothesis of mate selection, Winch subjected to intensive study 25 husbands and their wives. In each of three early papers, Winch claimed that the bulk of the evidence from these couples supported the hypothesis that mates tend to select each other on the basis of complementary needs.[20] Conversely, Winch claimed that support is not available for the conflicting hypothesis that spouses tend to be motivationally similar.

Several years later, Winch published his book on mate selection.[21] For mate selection to take place on the basis of love—that is, due to complementary needs—it is understood that both man and woman must have some choice in the matter. The theory would not be operative in settings where marriages are arranged (by parents, marriage brokers, or others). Thus, love will likely be an important criterion only under cultural conditions where (1) the choice of mates is voluntary, (2) the culture encourages premarital interaction between men and women, and (3) the marital friendship is culturally defined as a rich potential source of gratification. Since love is defined in terms of needs, the general hypothesis is that, when people marry for love, their needs will be complementary.

Reports by Winch and his colleagues led to a constant flow of articles trying to retest the complementary needs hypothesis. The results were basically negative, failing to provide empirical support for the idea that people tend to choose mates whose needs complement their own.

Various interpretations have been presented to explain why the complementary needs theory refutes popular opinion and fails to gain research support. Perhaps there are problems in the measurement of needs. Perhaps the basic theoretical considerations of the complementary needs theory are incorrect. Perhaps, like the findings of endogamous factors presented in the previous chapter, needs also are more homogamous than heterogamous, more similar than different. Perhaps "likes do marry likes" rather than "opposites attract."

Any or all of these reasons may be correct. What is clear is that relatively little empirical support exists for the theory of complementary needs as originally formulated. In fact, most of the research that has tried to explain mate selection on the basis of personality traits—whether similar, different, complementary, or some combination thereof—seems to have bogged down into a morass of conflicting results. Most findings have suggested the probable futility of further pursuits of personality matching. Perhaps instincts, drives, needs, complexes (including Oedipus ones), and personality traits all fail to find empirical support because they are based within persons rather than resulting from interactions. The cultural contexts and social situations in which these needs, drives, and traits are expressed are not considered.

In spite of the research, unsupported theories—whether instinctive, parental image, complementary needs, or personality traits—die hard. Further research on these ideas is sure to follow.

Sociocultural Explanations of Partnering

Age, residential propinquity, class, religion, and race/ethnicity are sociocultural factors that influence mate selection. Any factor in which social norms and endogamous factors play a part in who marries whom falls into this category. Values and roles, although basic to norms of endogamy, can also be viewed as interaction processes that explain the choice of a mate.

Value theory

A value theory of partner selection suggests that interpersonal attraction is facilitated when persons share or perceive themselves as sharing similar value orientations. Values define what is good, beautiful, moral, or worthwhile. They are the criteria or conceptions used in evaluating things (including objects, ideas, acts, feelings, and events) as to their goodness, desirability, or merit. Values are not concrete goals of action but criteria by which goals are chosen.

A value theory suggests that when persons share similar values, this in effect validates each person, thus promoting emotional satisfaction and enhancing the means of communication. When a value is directly attacked or is ignored under circumstances that normally call it to attention, those who hold the value are resentful. Because of this emotional aspect, it seems reasonable to expect that persons will seek informal social relations with others who uncritically accept their basic values and thus provide emotional security. Such compatible companions are most likely to be those who feel the same way about important things (those who possess similar values). This accounts for the tendency to marry homogamously and explains why friendships (homophily) and marriages involve people with similar social backgrounds.

In brief, the theory posits that:

1. Persons with similar backgrounds learn similar values.
2. The interaction of persons with similar values is rewarding, resulting in effective communication and a minimum of tension.
3. Rewards leave each person with a feeling of satisfaction with his or her partner and thus a desire to continue the relationship.

The inverse is equally true. Persons from different backgrounds learn different values; interactions among such persons are less rewarding and will likely result in feelings of tension and dissatisfaction and little desire to continue the relationship. Suppose, for example, a woman places a high value on heterosexual dating, marriage, and sexual activity. Holding this value, would she accept as a dating or marriage partner someone who is known to have engaged in homosexual activities? Value theory suggests (predicts) that she would not, and research has strongly supported this very example.[22]

Value theory helps explain findings about homogamy, endogamy, propinquity, parental image, and ideal-mate conception. Sharing values brings people together, both spatially and psychologically. A person may want to marry a member of the same religious denomination, for example, because this might be an important value in and of itself. Persons who share similar social backgrounds have probably been socialized under similar conditions and consequently have developed similar value systems.

Partner selection and the quality of family life are greatly influenced by sharing common values. Amish families preserve a life-style that is distinct from the ways of the larger North American society. They do not use electricity or drive automobiles, and they dress in simple clothing. They have a strong sense of values which includes avoiding conflict; hence, they refuse to participate in wars.

The same holds true for other explanations, such as parental image. Since parents are the major socializing agents for most children, it can be expected that one's personal values, those of his or her parents, as well as those desired in a mate will all be similar or related. Thus, it is perhaps not parent image that influences marital choice but rather parent-image influence via the internalization of a set of values.

Role theory

Role theory, like value theory, appears to be conceptually more justifiable as an overall explanation of marital choice than any of the previous individualistic explanations. All social humans—or, more specifically, all marriageable persons—have expectations regarding their own behaviour and also that of their respective mates. One perception of *role* (as described in Chapter 1) refers to a set of social expectations appropriate to a given status: husband, wife, male, female, single, and the like. These expectations, implicit or explicit, have been internalized and serve to direct and influence personal behaviour as well as the behaviour desired in a prospective marriage partner. Basically, people tend to desire (internalize) the roles defined by the society, subculture, and family in which they live.

Roles and personality needs differ in an important respect. With roles, the focus of attention is on behaviours and attitudes appropriate to situations, irrespective of the individual, whereas with personality needs, the focus is on behaviours and attitudes that are characteristic of the individual, irrespective of the situation. The difference is crucial. Roles focus on definitions, meanings, and social expectations. In regard to mate selection, individuals select one another on the basis of role consensus (compatibility) or on the basis of courtship, marital, and family-role agreement.

Role consensus, widely used as an indicator of marital success or adjustment, has been applied relatively infrequently to mate selection. However, similar processes are probably operative before marriage in mate selection as they are during marriage. When role discrepancies exist, marriage is unlikely to occur in the first place. Would a man who expects a wife to care for children, cook meals, and clean the house marry a woman who despises these activities? Or reciprocally, would this woman want to marry this man if that is what he expects of her?

Disparity in role agreement can be obtained by listing a series of expectations associated with various statuses and comparing the responses of the couple. The expectations of the couple of any given dimension can be used: decision-making, recreation, sex, religious attendance, care of children, employment, and the like. A given role expectation is less crucial than the agreement of the persons involved. For example, if one spouse expects to sleep in on the Sabbath, believing this is more important than religious attendance, no conflict will exist if the other spouse holds a similar expectation or attaches little importance to the expectation. The role itself is not as important as the consensus of the partners in regard to the role. Also, the role expectation itself may change as the situation changes. Maybe one spouse thinks the other should attend a religious institution on the Sabbath but does not expect him or her to do so when out of town or on vacation.

In brief, the couple likely to marry is the male and female who share similar role definitions and expectations. This assumes, of course, that other forces—such as an existing marriage, age, parents, money, schooling, or other sociocultural factors—do not hinder or prevent the marriage.

Exchange theory

Exchange theory was described briefly in Chapter 1. As mentioned in several places in the previous and current chapters, the idea of some type of exchange is basic to the mate-selection process. Whether it is an exchange of athletic prowess for beauty or an exchange of sex for money, the central idea is that some type of transaction and bargaining is involved in mate selection.

Before 1940, a major contribution of Willard Waller's treatise on the family was his analysis of courtship conduct as bargaining and/or exploiting behaviour. In his words, "When one marries he makes a number of different bargains. Everyone knows this and this knowledge affects the sentiment of love and the process of falling in love."[23]

Today, it is doubtful that only *he* makes bargains or that "everyone knows this." But it is well established that bargaining or some type of social exchange takes place in mate selection and affects the process of falling in love. The difference between *bargaining* and *exchange* is that bargaining implies a certain purposive awareness of the exchange of awards. Bargaining entails knowing what one has to offer and what the other person can get, whereas in a simple exchange, this awareness is not always readily apparent. What is apparent is that few people get something for nothing; thus, articles tend to support mate selection as a process of social exchange.[24]

Exchange theorists argue that the behaviour of socialized persons is purposive, or goal-oriented, and not random. Implicitly, this suggests that people repeat behaviours that are rewarded and avoid those that go unrewarded. As well, each party in a transaction will attempt to maximize gains and minimize costs. Over the long run, however, in view of the principle of reciprocity, actual exchanges tend to become equalized. If reciprocity does not exist—that is, nothing is given in return—the relationship will likely terminate. A key factor in exchange theory that may deter or delay termination of an inequitable exchange is the lack of an alternative to the current relationship. But if an alternative to the current relationship is perceived as superior to the present relationship, one of the partners will terminate the present relationship in favour of pursuing the more attractive alternative.

In perhaps few areas does social exchange appear more evident than in research on dating and mate selection. In dating, for example, the male may consider sexual intercourse as a desired goal and a highly valued reward. To achieve this reward, he may have to offer in exchange flattery ("My, how beautiful you look tonight"), commitment ("You are the only one I love"), goods ("I thought you might enjoy these flowers"), and services ("Let me get you a drink").

The social exchange approach to partner selection neither explains how interaction arises nor describes the larger social environment. Rather, it seeks to explain why certain behavioural outcomes take place.

Sequential theories

Up to this point, it is evident that, although single factors were stressed as significant in the process of selecting an intimate partner, most explanations take into account factors implied in other explanations. Several writers have consciously and intentionally combined or placed in sequence selected single factors: roles, values, needs, exchanges, and the like. An example of this is seen in the SVR idea of Bernard Murstein.[25]

Murstein described dyadic pairing as a three-stage sequence, involving *stimulus-value-role (SVR)*. These three stages denote the chronological sequence in the development of a relationship. Social exchange theory is used within each stage to explain dynamics of interaction and attraction.

SVR theory holds that, in a relatively free-choice situation, most couples pass through three stages before deciding to marry. In the *stimulus* stage, an individual may be drawn to another on the basis of the perception of his or her own qualities that might be attractive to the other person (intellect, physical attributes, voice, dress, reputation, social standing). Because initial movement is due primarily to noninteractional cues not dependent on interpersonal interaction, these are categorized as stimulus values.

If mutual stimulus attraction occurs between a man and a woman and they are both satisfied, they enter the second stage, *value comparison*. This stage involves the appraisal of value compatibility through verbal interaction. The couple may compare their attitudes toward life, politics, religion, abortion, nuclear energy, or the roles of men and women in society and in marriage. If, as they discuss these and other areas, the couple find that they have similar value orientations, their feelings for one another are likely to develop. Murstein suggested that couples may decide to marry on the basis of stimulus attraction and verbalized value similarity. But for most persons, it is important to be able to function in compatible roles, an ability that is not as readily observable as verbalized expressions of views on religion, politics, and the like. For this reason, Murstein placed the role stage last in the sequence leading to marital choice.

The *role* stage requires the fulfillment of many tasks before the couple is ready to move into marriage. It is not enough to have similar vales if each partner is dissatisfied with how the other is perceived in such roles as lover, companion, parent, and housekeeper. The partners must increasingly confide in each other and become more aware of each other's behaviour. They must measure their own personal inadequacies and those of their partner. If the partners navigate the three stages successfully, they are likely to become a permanent pair (marry or cohabit), subject to such influences as parents, friends, job transfers, competition from more attractive partners, and so forth.

Other sequential theories exist. For example, Bert N. Adams established a series of propositions in summarizing mate selection that includes:

1. Conditions or barriers, such as proximity;
2. Early attractions, such as physical qualities, similar interests, disclosure, and rapport;
3. Deeper attractions, such as the development of consensus, personality similarity, lack of unfavourable parental intrusion, empathy, and role compatibility;
4. A final series of escalators or perpetuators that move the persons toward marriage—that is, defining the other as "right" or "the best I can get."[26]

All sequential theories of relationship development or partner selection tend to view the movement toward marriage as a series of changing criteria, stages, or patterned regularities. However, the progression to marriage may not be quite so orderly or simple. Many alternative pathways to marriage exist that involve other partners, getting into and out of a relationship with the same partner several times, or factors totally separate from the personal and interactional exchanges that are generally part of relationship developmental processes. Factors external to the person or couple (family/kin influence, socioeconomic conditions, community heterogeneity, technological changes) are likely, from a sociological perspective at least, to be important factors or dimensions in understanding the process of changing one's status from single to married.

PROCESSES OF STATUS CHANGE: SINGLE TO PARTNERED

All human societies have some socially approved and structured procedures to follow in getting married, particularly for the first time. Remarriage, an increasingly common event in industrialized societies, involves less established norms and procedures for partner selection, and what norms exist may or may not parallel those of first marriage. A selection process that involves the individuals themselves only exists where there is some degree of personal choice in marital partners. As described earlier, where marriages are arranged, the process generally occurs between kin groups. In any case, it is rare for mate-selection processes to exist independently of other institutions, such as schools, churches, and businesses.

In North America, the partner-selection process encompasses a wide range of social relationships before marriage that involve increasing degrees of commitment. Writers have used different terminology to describe this process, but, generally, it entails stages that may include group activities, casual dating, going steady, cohabiting, being engaged, or some other process toward a more binding relationship. The flexibility of the process provides that it can be followed once or many times before marriage, covering a time span of days to years and including or omitting one or several stages.

Dating

Dating has been called a curious institution.[27] Where it is practised, in North America, Great Britain, Germany, Australia, and New Zealand, dating is a relatively new way for young people to meet. It seems to have emerged first in the United States after the First World War. Before then, courting behaviour consisted of more formal visits between young men and women, with parental knowledge and often in the presence of parents. Daughters in particular were supervised and protected. The practice of dating evolved as it became more and more socially accepted that marriage should be based on love and sexual attraction, and that young people should select their own spouse.

From the point of view of the larger society, dating is a mechanism that enables individuals to develop intimacy and to go through a process of anticipatory socialization for the marital role. Dating provides an opportunity to get to know what is expected of oneself and others. Steady dating, or "going with someone," fills the gap between recreational or dalliance dating and engagement or marriage.

Today, dating may occur at several stages throughout life, from adolescence to old age. Young people have many opportunities to interact with other adolescents without adult supervision.[28] Because there are now many pathways to commitment, the sense of progression involving increased intimacy and increased commitment may no longer be evident for many. Some may follow the traditional route, others will cohabit soon after meeting, still others will choose lifelong singlehood. One consequence of the older age at marriage has been the emergence of new forms of partner selection for dating, including computer matchups, videotape selections, singles clubs and groups, newspaper advertisements, singles bars, and other informal opportunities for meeting.[29] Women often initiate dates and share dating expenses.

Engagement

Engagement, in some form, has existed in almost every society in the world. Since marriage is seldom taken lightly, most societies have provided some social structure to instill an awareness in the couple and the community that the relationship is serious and that marriage will likely occur. In many societies, engagement is considered extremely important and much more binding than it is in much of the Western world today. Since engagement implies the final transition in the process of changing status from single to married, various rituals are conducted and gifts are given to implant in the minds of the couple and the public the importance of the relationship.

Engagement serves a variety of functions for both the couple and society. For the couple, it provides a clear indication that marriage is about to occur. Engagement provides the final opportunity before the legal union for each person to understand himself or herself in relation to the other. It is likely that many couples view an engagement as a kind of trial marriage, including total sexual intimacy, the sharing of certain financial obligations, and, in some instances, living together.

An engagement ring, like a public announcement, serves the purpose of enabling the female to publicly and continuously display her symbol of commitment. The ring, which involves a financial commitment, symbolizes the seriousness of the relationship and the intent of a forthcoming marriage.

SEXUALITY AND INTIMACY

Few topics draw as much widespread attention and occupy as much thought as matters relating to sex, as both a social and a personal phenomenon. The significance of sex in modern life is evidenced by the recent controversies centring on AIDS, abortion, gays in particular professions, pornography, distribution of contraceptives to adolescents, and general concern over gender identity and male/female roles.

All societies have social norms that grant approval to certain sexual behaviours and disapproval to others. Perhaps the most universal *taboo* on sexual behaviour relates to incest; the most universal *approval* is granted to sexual behaviour in marriage. Clearly, no society grants unrestricted sexual liberties; all societies control sexuality.

Sexual expression is regulated and controlled through social norms, social statuses and roles, and social sanctions. Sexual expectations, as well as rights and privileges, differ for males and females; in public and private places; for married people and single ones; for grandparents and grandchildren; or for heterosexuals and homosexuals. Laws may be established that punish the prostitute, the distributor of child pornography, or the rapist. Violators of approved behaviour may face public shame, ridicule, fines, imprisonment, physical and/or mental torture, and even death. In brief, sexual expression is highly regulated in a variety of ways in every society in the world.

SEXUALIZATION AND SEXUAL SCRIPTS

Sexualization, that is, sexual socialization, is the process by which persons learn and internalize their sexual self-concepts, values, attitudes, and behaviours. It is a process that begins at birth and continues into adulthood and old age. Details of the socialization process, with regard to sexuality, gender, violence, and other factors, are described in Chapter 8. At this point, attention will focus specifically on the learning and development of sexual knowledge, attitudes, and values. These aspects of sexualization appear to be vital to understanding sexual behaviour.

Symbolic interaction theory posits that people become sexual beings through social interaction. Even though there is an important biological and hormonal basis to sexual development, simply having female or male genitals does not guarantee that one's gender identity or preferences will follow anatomical makeup. This is evidenced in transvestism (dressing in the clothing of the opposite sex), transsexualism (feeling trapped in the body of the wrong sex), and homosexuality (preference for same-sex relationships).

Symbolic interaction theory posits as well that sexual behaviour can only be understood in terms of internalized symbolic meanings. This suggests that the definition of the situation and the meaning given to a certain behaviour are basic to understanding that behaviour or lack of behaviour. If premarital coitus is defined as sinful, if masturbation is believed to cause insanity, and if homosexuality is perceived as perverted, these meanings will have a major but not absolute influence on whether the behaviour occurs and also how. That is, definitions, attitudes, meanings, values, and other internalized mental processes predispose behaviour.

These ideas, basic to a symbolic interaction frame of reference, parallel the ideas of William Simon and John Gagnon. They conceptualized the outcome of what is here termed *sexualization* in terms of **sexual scripts.**[30] Like a script for a play or movie, a sexual script provides an overall blueprint of what sexuality is and how it is practised. The sexual script designates the *who, what, where, when,* and *why* of sexuality.

Scripts are the plans that people have in their heads. The sexual script defines *whom* one has sex with. Sex is not allowed with certain categories of people, but others are fantasized about and are on the "approved" list. The script defines *what* sexual behaviours are right or wrong, appropriate or inappropriate. While kissing or masturbation may be on the approved list, intercourse or oral sex may not. The script includes the *when* and *where* of sex. Is it appropriate only at night in a bedroom? Is it also appropriate at noon in an automobile? And finally, the script includes the *why* issue. Is sex acceptable for fun, intimacy, reducing tension, procreation, or some other reason?

One's sexual script is the internalized notions of these who, what, when, where, and why questions. It is learned in interaction with others and contains notions of the society, subculture, reference groups, and significant others in which one is a member and with whom one interacts. In interaction with others, an individual builds his or her script, that cognitive scheme that affects his or her actual conduct.

Simon and Gagnon argued that, for behaviour to occur, something resembling scripting must occur on three distinct levels: cultural scenarios, interpersonal scripts, and intrapsychic scripts.[31]

Cultural scenarios are the instructional guides that exist at the level of collective life. The enactment of virtually any role reflects the institutions, groups, and social context in which one was born and raised and currently functions. *Interpersonal scripts* transform the person trained in cultural scenarios and general social roles to context-specific behaviour. What one does is influenced by the responses of others. These cultural scenarios and interpersonal scripts result in *intrapsychic scripting*, an internal dialogue, a world of fantasy, or in interaction terms, a personal self that is in reality a social self. The private world of individual wishes and desires is bound to social life. All sexual behaviour includes all three levels of scripting.

Sexual scripting, like the general process of sexual socialization, follows the life cycle. Until recently, infancy, childhood, and old age were periods in which sex-seeking behaviour was viewed as deviant; these people were either too young or too old to be capable of comprehending or experiencing the full meaning of sexual behaviour. In the context of this and most family texts, sexual life cycles tend to be subsumed under headings of *premarital, marital, extramarital*, and *postmarital* experiences. Each label carries specific requirements and meanings for appropriate sexual behaviour. Thus, a traditional premarital sexual script says that "nice girls don't" whereas a marital sexual script says that "nice girls do."

Consistency between attitudes and behaviour

Sexual scripts include both attitudinal and behavioural components. How consistent are sexual beliefs, values, and attitudes with sexual behaviour?

One could assume that, for the most part, attitudes and behaviour are highly related. That is, people tend to behave, for the most part, in ways consistent with their beliefs. Research over the years has provided strong evidence that where sexual norms are restrictive (such as with certain religious groups such as the Amish or Mormons), conservative behaviour will result. Where sexual norms are more permissive (such as in Scandinavian countries or among certain college groups in the United States), behaviours will be more free and less restrictive. The result is a high correlation between beliefs and behaviours. On the other hand, many people experience interests, desires, and fantasies that may greatly exceed any possibility (or opportunity) of carrying them out. Here beliefs will be more permissive than actual behaviours.

Cross-culturally, it appears that most societies permit or even encourage premarital sexual relationships, particularly for males. The taboo that falls primarily on females is more a precaution against childbearing than a moral sanction. Using a global perspective, the crucial question, particularly for females, may not be whether premarital intercourse is permitted but whether unmarried motherhood is allowed. It is likely that a female's commitment to norms of chastity lessens as a separation of premarital intercourse from pregnancy becomes possible. Thus, if contraceptives, sterilization, abortion, and other social arrangements exist to prevent or terminate a pregnancy, premarital **sexual permissiveness** will increase.

The occurrence of premarital sex can be viewed in a number of ways. One way is to look at the **incidence**—that is, the occurrence or nonoccurrence of an experience. Generally, one has or has not had intercourse, is or is not a virgin, has or has not experienced orgasm. Since few people have sex only once, another way to view frequency is to deal with **prevalence**—that is, how often the experience has occurred or occurs. Premarital intercourse may have occurred once or a thousand times; it may occur infrequently or regularly. Thus, the *incidence* of premarital sex (number who have or have not) differs considerably from the *prevalence* (frequency). Both incidence and prevalence appear to have increased significantly over the past several decades.

Many social forces have led to behavioural changes regarding premarital coitus and have the potential for producing further changes. In the 1960s, the birth control pill became available. Sexual candour became increasingly legitimized in the mass media, even by one of the most conservative media: television. Social forces such as these have led to increased rejection of many traditional values, resulting in changes in the sexual behaviour of never-married people.

Canadian Gallup polls have periodically questioned Canadians about premarital sexual activity. In 1970, 57 percent of Canadians said they thought premarital sexual activity was wrong. This proportion decreased with each poll. By 1992, only 22 percent of Canadians felt this way. People on the Prairies are more conservative about premarital sexuality, and, as we might expect, older Canadians are also more conservative. However, older people changed their attitudes in the same direction and as extensively as young people when the surveys are compared over time.[32]

The so-called sexual revolution was real, but it was restricted to premarital heterosexual relations. Attitudes toward extramarital and homosexual relations and, as noted above, promiscuity, have remained distinctly restrictive.

In the 1980s, a new and serious health epidemic involving a sexually transmitted disease now widely known as AIDS first appeared. One would expect that apprehension about AIDS would restrict the sexual activities of people of all ages. Has the risk of acquiring an STD and AIDS in particular restricted sexual expression?

FAMILY DIVERSITY

Sexual behaviour in China

In China, the norms concerning the sexual behaviour of teenagers suggest that premarital intercourse is politically and culturally wrong. Kaufman and others note, however, that both teenage fertility and abortion rates are quite high, suggesting that the actual prevalence of premarital sexual behaviour may be quite at variance with the norm. They report one study that revealed that 8 percent of college students said they had experienced vaginal intercourse and over 55 percent said they did not disapprove of couples who did.

Their own data from over 5 000 students in grades 7 to 12 revealed that teenage sexual attitudes about self-conduct are fairly conservative but much more permissive with regard to their views about respecting others who have engaged in premarital sex.

A study by Renaud and others of married Chinese men and women living in Beijing and Shanghai indicated that most couples reported moderate frequencies of affectionate and sexual behaviour of between two or three time a month to once or twice a week. About 15 percent said they rarely or never engaged in physically affectionate or sexual activity. The men and women differed little in their reports of sexual satisfaction.

See Gayle Kaufman, Dudley L. Poston, Jr., Thomas A. Hirschi, and J. Mayone Stycos, "Teenage Sexual Attitudes in China," *Social Biology* 43 (1996): 141–154; and Cheryl Renaud, E. Sandra Byers, and Suiming Pan, "Sexual and Relationship Satisfaction in Mainland China," *The Journal of Sex Research* 34 (1997): 399–410.

However, few Canadians have changed their behaviour as a result of their concern. In a national survey, 13 percent of Canadians said they had changed their behaviour and another 4 percent were thinking of changing, leaving 83 percent who saw no need to change.[33] In a survey conducted in Alberta, even Albertans who participated in high-risk activities such as unprotected sexual contact or intravenous drug use did not feel they were particularly at risk. Those at risk were not more likely to use condoms during sexual intercourse.[34]

Despite the risks, young people continue to engage in **high-risk sexual behaviour.** High-risk behaviour is basically sex with multiple partners and a failure to protect oneself or one's partner against STDs and/or unwanted pregnancies. Over one-third of a sample of American students from a Midwestern university had, on at least one or more occasions, used no form of protection from STDs and no method of contraception for pregnancy protection.[35] These high levels of sexual activity, the tendency toward multiple partners, and the nonuse or inconsistent use of condoms and contraception are well-documented antecedents to unplanned pregnancy and contraction of STDs.

Why do young people engage in these high-risk behaviours? Susan Moore and Doreen Rosenthal, after studying 1,000 nonvirgin adolescents in Australia, found that youth justified not using condoms by many reasons, including that they defined their current relationships as monogamous with promises to be long-term.[36] Risk among youth with both regular and multiple partners was

News Item

Please reply in confidence

North Vancouver Suburbs—Happily marrieds, 26 and 33, white, would like to hear from social-minded married for fun evenings and good times. Phone and photo please.

Banff-Area Marrieds—Attractive, would like to hear from other similar-minded adults for dining, nights out, and games. Not necessarily in that order.

Hamilton Marrieds—Late 30s, attractive, Oriental, would like to hear from other Oriental or white marrieds for adult fun and friendship. Answer all. Phone and photo please.

Quebec City Marrieds—Liberal-minded, affectionate, attractive, late 20s, would like to hear from other, similar qualified marrieds. We can travel. Phone, photo, and address, if possible.

Halifax Marrieds—White, 29 and 30, happily married, discreet and liberal-minded. Would like to hear from other liberal-minded marrieds who enjoy photography and correspondence. Age and race no barrier. Photo please with phone will bring prompt reply.

Vancouver Island Marrieds—Attractive, white, liberal-minded. Would like to hear from other marrieds for adult fun. Discretion assured. Will answer all who include phone and photo.

Southern Ontario Area—Attractive and happily marrieds, 28 and 25, white, would like to hear from other liberal-minded marrieds. Phone and photo and must be discreet.

linked to negative attitudes toward taking precautions: "Condoms are a nuisance," "Precautions are a hassle," and so forth. Many youth denied the existence of risk: "None of my friends are the kind of people who would be AIDS carriers," or "Self-control is the answer, not condoms." Abrogation of responsibility was another key reason for high-risk behaviour: "If I talk about AIDS with a sex partner, they might be insulted," or "My partner should be responsible for initiating the use of condoms." The authors termed a fourth and final reason for not using condoms *fatalism*: "Life is full of risks, and AIDS is just one example," "It's hard to know what to think about AIDS—even the experts don't agree," or "There's a chance I could get AIDS, I suppose, but that's life."

What kinds of external factors are associated with sexual risk-taking among adolescents? A sample of several thousand Midwestern sexually active teenagers comparing high-risk-takers (multiple partners with rare or no use of contraception) with low-risk-takers (one partner and regular use of contraceptives) revealed significant differences between the two groups. For females and males, the high-risk-takers had lower GPAs, more frequent alcohol consumption, lower levels of parental monitoring, a lack of communication with mothers about birth control, more frequent contemplation of suicide, a much greater history of sexual and physical abuse, and more troubled relationships with their parents.[37]

Much research is underway in areas such as AIDS education, adolescent sexual behaviour, condom use, and so forth. It is clear that changes are taking place but often not as dramatically as one might think.

SUMMARY

1. The terms *homogamy* and *endogamy* refer to the extent of intermarriage among people who share similar characteristics. This chapter examined the nature of intermarriage and five normative structures surrounding the selection of intimate partners: age, proximity of residence, social status, religion, and race/ethnicity. The choice of a partner along these and other structural dimensions has significant consequences for society, the marriage, and the persons involved.
2. Most couples in Canada are relatively homogamous in the age at which they marry. The term "marriage squeeze" is used to describe the effects of an imbalance in the sex ratio, or the number of males and females available for marriage. On the basis of age alone, this squeeze resulted in a shortage of women in the 1950s and a shortage of men in the 1980s, and will predictably result in a shortage of women early in this century.
3. Marriages are highly endogamous by social class, more so than could be expected to occur simply by chance. When marriage occurs with someone from a lower social position (mésalliance), it may denote hypergamy or hypogamy. The general tendency for men to date and marry downward more frequently than upward has been termed the *mating gradient*. The literature on social-class heterogamy and marital success has revealed highly inconsistent findings.
4. Religious endogamy is less rigid than racial/ethnic endogamy. There seems to be consensus that people who are religiously devout marry endogamously in greater frequency than those who are religiously less devout, and that endogamous marriages have higher levels of happiness and slightly lower rates of divorce than interfaith marriages.
5. The processes followed in partner or mate selection vary widely from one society to another, ranging from arranged marriages to freedom of choice. The difference lies in who makes the choice of partner.
6. A range of explanations addresses who selects whom and why. At one extreme are individualistic explanations, which are rooted in drives, parental images, and complementary needs. In contrast are sociocultural explanations, which are rooted in norms, values, roles, and social exchanges.
7. Sociocultural explanations operate at a more conscious level, are more readily testable, and have greater research support than individualistic explanations. Sociocultural theories are not fully adequate to explain partner selection, but they are more useful than individualistic theories. One sociocultural theory suggests that interpersonal attraction is facilitated when persons share or perceive themselves as sharing similar value orientations. This sharing of values, in effect, validates oneself and thus promotes emotional satisfaction and enhances the means of communication.
8. Related to sharing values is sharing roles—the internalized, learned, social expectations as to what attitudes and behaviours are appropriate or inappropriate in the selection of a partner. In brief, the couple likely to cohabit or marry is the male and female who share similar role definitions and expectations.
9. Exchange theorists view partner selection as a bargaining or social exchange process. Even though it does not explain how interaction occurs, the theory does explain behavioural outcomes. The choice of partner is based on the selection of persons who share equivalent resources; each has something to offer that is desired by the other. A relationship characterized by an unequal exchange may continue if no better alternative to that relationship is perceived.
10. Some researchers see the selection of a partner as the result of several of the above processes operating simultaneously or sequentially. One explanation involves a three-stage chronological sequence of stimulus, value, and role (SVR).
11. Human sexuality is regulated through social institutions, social norms, and a wide range of social sanctions.
12. This chapter examined normative structures in partner selection, theories of intimacy, and sexuality and intimacy. Continuing within a partner selection and marital life course sequence, attention is directed in the next chapter to marital structures and processes.

KEY TERMS AND TOPICS

Homogamy p. 119
Endogamy p. 119
Exogamy p. 119
Heterogamy p. 119
Age homogamy p. 120
"Marriage squeeze" p. 124
Law and age at marriage p. 125
Residential propinquity p. 125
Social status and class endogamy p. 126
Mésalliance p. 127
Hypergamy p. 127
Hypogamy p. 127
Mating gradient p. 127
Arranged marriage versus free choice p. 130
Complementary needs theory p. 133
Value theory p. 135
Role theory p. 136
Exchange theory p. 137
Sequential theories p. 138
Sexualization p. 142
Sexual scripts p. 142
Consistency between attitudes and behaviour p. 143
High-risk sexual behaviour p. 145

DISCUSSION QUESTIONS

1. Differentiate between terms in the following pairs: *endogamy/exogamy* and *homogamy/heterogamy*. What constitutes *intermarriage* or *mixed marriage*?
2. What trends are probable regarding age at marriage, place of residence, social class, religion and race/ethnicity? Why?
3. Describe the "marriage squeeze." What factors account for a shift from a shortage of women to a shortage of men and vice versa?
4. Discuss *hypergamy* and *hypogamy*—how likely each is to occur, why it occurs, and what consequences result from its occurrence.
5. Although the theory of complementary needs seems logical, it has little empirical support. Why do you think this is the case?
6. What values are most important to you? Could you marry someone who did not share these values? Why?
7. Discuss with someone a generation older than you the ways in which dating has changed over time. What predictions can you make about the future of dating?
8. All societies control sexual activities. Why? How?
9. Consider your own sexual script—with whom, what, where, when, why, and so forth. What factors are most influential in your script?

FURTHER READINGS

Buchanan, David and Cernada, George, eds. *Progress in Preventing AIDS? Dogma, Dissent and Innovation: Global Perspectives*. Amityville, NY: Baywood, 1998. An edited volume on global AIDS prevention in nine countries covering the voices of dissent as well as innovation in field practice.

Buss, David M. *The Evolution of Desire: Strategies of Human Mating*. New York: Basic Books, 1994. An evolutionary psychological approach to understanding why conflict, competition, and manipulation pervade human mating.

Cate, Rodney M. and Lloyd, Sally A. *Courtship*. Newbury Park, CA: Sage, 1992. An exploration of courtship, including its importance, history, interpersonal models, and future perspectives.

Douglas, Jack D. and Atwell, Freda Cruse. *Love, Intimacy and Sex*. Newbury Park, CA: Sage,

1988. An effort at establishing a systematic, scientific model of love, including its major dimensions and their interdependencies.

Hendrick, Susan S. and Hendrick, Clyde. *Romantic Love*. Newbury Park, CA: Sage, 1992. An interdisciplinary overview of the complexity and the elusiveness of love.

Minow, Martha, ed. *Family Matters: Readings on Family Lives and the Law.* New York: The Free Press, 1993. Approximately 60 readings covering a broad range of topics of concern to family law—defining who is in or out of a family, who may marry, custody, divorce, violence, the courts, etc.

Richard, Madelaine A. *Ethnic Groups and Marital Choices.* Vancouver: University of British Columbia Press, 1991. A comparison of ethnic intermarriage in Canada in 1871 and 1971.

Rosenblatt. Paul C.; Karis, Terri-A.; and Powell, Richard D. *Multiracial Couples: Black and White Voices.* Thousand Oaks, CA: Sage Publications, 1995. Using a qualitative research design, the authors explore the interpersonal dynamics of 21 interracial couples in committed relationships.

Schwartz, Pepper and Rutter, Virginia. *The Gender of Sexuality*. Thousand Oaks, CA: Pine Forge Press, 1998. A concise, well-written paperback presenting a sociological analysis that combines the topics of gender and sexuality.

Segal, Lynn, ed. *New Sexual Agendas.* New York: New York University Press, 1997. An edited volume of 19 writings under sections entitled "Historical Roots, New Shoots"; "Medicine and Morality"; and "Sexual Subjectives, Social Conflict."

Surra, Catherine A. "Research and Theory on Mate Selection and Premarital Relationships in the 1980s," *Journal of Marriage and the Family* 52 (November 1990): 884–895. A decade-review article of major research and theory about mate selection and relationship development.

WEBLINKS

http://www.socialpsychology.org/

This page contains research studies related to social interaction that are currently being conducted online by professors and college students. There are studies investigating interpersonal relations and social perceptions including facial attractiveness, romantic relationships, mate choice, forgiveness, and reconciliation.

http://purelove.org/oldplasite/statistics/sex_in_america.html

The most comprehensive study to date on expressions of sexuality and intimate relationships is E. O. Laumann's *Sex In America*. This website presents a statistical summary of Laumann's findings.

http://www.aamft.org/families/index.htm

The American Association for Marriage and Family Therapists offers "information on topics important to the health and well-being" of families. Topics covered are intimacy and depression, after an affair, male sexual problems, female sexual problems, depression, and alcohol problems.

NOTES

1. Statistics Canada, "Marriages," *The Daily* (October 28, 1999).
2. Teresa M. Cooney and Dennis P. Hogan, "Marriage in an Institutionalized Life Course: First Marriage Among American Men in the Twentieth Century," *Journal of Marriage and the Family* 53 (February 1991): 178–190.
3. Jane F. Gentleman and Evelyn Park, "Age Differences of Married and Divorcing Couples," *Health Reports, 1994* 6(4): 225–239.
4. Laurel Klinger-Vartabedian and Lauren Wispe, "Age Differences in Marriage and Female Longevity," *Journal of Marriage and the Family* 51 (February 1989): 195–202.
5. Herman Vera, Donna H. Berardo, and Felix M. Berardo, "Age Heterogamy in Marriage," *Journal of Marriage and the Family* 49 (August 1985): 553–566.
6. Gentleman and Park, "Age Differences of Married and Divorcing Couples," 237–238.
7. Michael S. Billig, "The Marriage Squeeze on High-Caste Rajasthani Women," *The Journal of Asian Studies* 50 (May 1991): 341–360.
8. George D. Lowe, D. Lin Hughes, and David D. Witt, "Changes in the Influence of Early Marriage on the Educational Attainment of Men and Women," *Sociological Spectrum* 9 (1989): 163–173.
9. Douglas M. Teti and Michael Lamb, "Socioeconomic and Marital Outcomes of Adolescent Marriage, Adolescent Childbirth, and Their Co-occurrence," *Journal of Marriage and the Family* 51 (February 1989): 203–212.
10. Alan Booth and John N. Edwards, "Age at Marriage and Marital Stability," *Journal of Marriage and the Family* 47 (February 1985): 67–75.
11. D. M. Marvin, "Occupational Propinquity as a Factor in Mate Selection," *Publications of the American Statistical Association* 16 (1918–19): 131–150.
12. Matthijs Kalmijn, "Status Homogamy in the United States," *American Journal of Sociology* 97 (September 1991): 496–523.
13. Reginald W. Bibby, "The Persistence of Christian Religious Identification in Canada," *Canadian Social Trends* (Spring 1997): 24–28.
14. Ibid.
15. Tim B. Heaton and Edith L. Pratt, "The Effects of Religious Homogamy on Marital Satisfaction and Stability," *Journal of Family Issues* 11 (June 1990): 191–207.
16. Jean Dumas and Yves Peron, *Marriage and Conjugal Life in Canada*, Statistics Canada Catalogue 91-534E (March 1992): 78–82.
17. Kalman D. Applbaum, "Marriage with the Proper Stranger: Arranged Marriage in Metropolitan Japan," *Ethnology* 34 (Winter 1995): 37–51.
18. Patricia Noller, "What is This Thing Called Love? Defining Love That Supports Marriage and Family," *Personal Relationships* 3 (1996): 111–112.
19. Davor Jedlicka, "Indirect Parental Influence on Mate Choice: A Test of the Psychoanalytic Theory," *Journal of Marriage and the Family* 46 (February 1984): 65–70.
20. Robert F. Winch, Thomas Ktsanes, and Virginia Ktsanes, "The Theory of Complementary Needs in Mate Selection: An Analytic and Descriptive Study," *American Sociological Review* 19 (June 1954): 241–249; Robert F. Winch, "The Theory of Complementary Needs in Mate Selection: A Test of One Kind of Complementariness," *American Sociological Review* 20 (February 1955): 52–56; and Robert F. Winch, "The Theory of Complementary Needs in Mate Selection: Final Results on the Test of the General Hypothesis," *American Sociological Review* 20 (October 1955): 552–555.
21. Robert F. Winch, *Mate Selection* (New York: Harper, 1958).
22. John D. Williams and Arthur P. Jacoby, "The Effects of Premarital Heterosexual and Homosexual Experience on Dating and Marriage Desirability," *Journal of Marriage and the Family* 51 (May 1989): 489–497.
23. Willard Waller, *The Family: A Dynamic Interpretation* (New York: Cordon, 1938), 239.
24. James W. Michaels, Alan C. Acock, and John N. Edwards, "Social Exchange and Equity Determinants of Relationship Commitment," *Journal of Social and Personal Relationships* 3 (1986): 161–175; and Rodney M. Cate, Sally A. Lloyd, and Edgar Long, "The Role of Rewards and Fairness in Developing Marital Relationships," *Journal of Marriage and the Family* 50 (May 1988): 443–452.
25. Bernard I. Murstein, "A Clarification and Extension of the SVR Theory of Dyadic Pairing," *Journal of Marriage and the Family* 49 (November 1987): 929–933.
26. Bert N. Adams, "Mate Selection in the United States: A Theoretical Summarization," in *Contemporary Theories About the Family,* Vol. 1, ed. Wesley R. Burr et al. (New York: Free Press, 1979), 259–267.
27. Martin King Whyte, "Choosing Mates—The American Way," *Society* 29 (March/April 1992): 71–77.
28. Note, for example, Bruce Roscoe, Mark S. Diana, and Richard H. Brooks II, "Early, Middle, and Late Adolescents' Views on Dating and Factors Influencing Partner Selection," *Adolescence* 22 (Spring 1987): 59–68.
29. Note, for example, Aaron C. Ahuvia and Mara B. Adelman, "Formal Intermediaries in the Marriage Market: A Typology and Review," *Journal of Marriage and the Family* 54 (May 1992): 452–463; and Stanley B. Woll and Peter Young, "Looking for Mr. or Ms. Right: Self-Presentation in Videodating," *Journal of Marriage and the Family* 51 (May 1989): 483–488.

30. William Simon and John H. Gagnon, "Sexual Scripts: Permanence and Change," *Archives of Sexual Behavior* 15 (1986): 97–120. For a more detailed discussion of sexual scripts, see William Simon and John H. Gagnon, "A Sexual Script Approach," in James H. Geer and William T. O'Donohue, eds., *Theories of Human Sexuality* (New York: Plenum Press, 1987): 363–383.
31. Simon and Gagnon, "Sexual Scripts," 98–104.
32. Canadian Gallup Poll, "Only 24% Believe Premarital Sex Is Wrong" (February 12, 1990).
33. Allison L. McKinnon, "AIDS: Knowledge, Attitudes, and Behaviours in Alberta," *Canadian Social Trends* (Toronto: Thompson Educational Publishing, Inc., 1994), 113; Canadian Gallup Poll, "Public Increasingly Fearful of AIDS Epidemic" (August 13, 1990).
34. Ibid.
35. June M. Reinisch, Stephanie A. Sanders, Craig A. Hill, and Mary Ziemba Davis, "High-Risk Sexual Behavior Among Heterosexual Undergraduates at a Midwestern University," *Family Planning Perspectives* 24 (May/June 1992): 116–121.
36. Susan M. Moore and Doreen A. Rosenthal, "Condoms and Coitus: Adolescents' Attitudes to AIDS and Safe Sex Behavior," *Journal of Adolescence* 14 (1991): 211–227.
37. Tom Lesser and Stephen Small, "Factors Associated with Sexual Risk-Taking Behaviors Among Adolescents," *Journal of Marriage and the Family* 56 (August 1994): 622–632.

CHAPTER

6 ESTABLISHING COMMITMENT

This chapter concentrates on cohabitation and marriage. In Chapter 2 we differentiated marriages from families and presented a wide range of alternative marital patterns, including those with multiple spouses. Chapters 4 and 5 provided information on social-class differences, interfaith and interracial situations, structures and processes in partner selection, and sexual relationships in marital contexts. This chapter will consider the social institution of marriage, cohabitation, and marriage rates and trends, conjugal power, and factors associated with marital quality.

MARRIAGE AS A SOCIAL INSTITUTION

Marriage remains a strong cultural expectation for Canadians. Although marriage no longer has the sense of permanence it had in the past as divorce has become relatively common and cohabitation and childbirth outside of marriage have become more socially accepted, most Canadians marry at least once.

When examined cross-culturally, the reasons for and consequences of marriage differ as the structure of marriage differs. For example, when marriage is specifically an extension of the kinship and extended-family systems, then procreation, passing on the family name, and continuation of property become basic functions. Consequently, not having a child (or more specifically, not having a male child) is sufficient reason to replace a present wife or add a new wife. In Canada, even though most children are born to married couples (and most married couples want children), not having children is rarely sufficient reason to divorce and remarry. Conversely, not wanting or being unable to have children—an issue faced by women who are career-focused, infertile, or older—is not sufficient reason for not marrying.

Marriages, and marriage-like relationships, fulfill many functions attributed to the family in general. These include basic personality formation, status ascription, nurturant socialization, tension management, replacement of members, economic cooperation, reproduction, and the like. Even though many of these functions do not require marriage or sexual exclusivity to be fulfilled, they are enhanced by the marital system. Note, for example, the impact that marriage has on personal well-being.

Marital status and well-being

Robert Coombs, in reviewing more than 130 empirical studies on a number of well-being indices, found that married men and women are generally happier and less stressed than unmarried men and women.[1] The pattern was highly consistent. Studies of alcoholism, suicide, mortality (death) and morbidity (disease or poor health), schizophrenia and other psychiatric problems, and self-reported happiness have supported the hypothesis that married individuals experience fewer or less serious emotional and health problems than their unmarried counterparts.

Family Diversity

Marital status and mortality in developing countries

Two researchers at the Office of Population Research at Princeton University reported on several consistent and striking patterns that emerged from an exploration of marital status differentials in mortality across 16 developing countries. They found that:

1. In all countries, the excess mortality of unmarried men relative to married men greatly exceeded that of unmarried women.
2. In most countries, divorced men had the highest rates of mortality among the three unmarried groups (single, divorced, widowed). This finding also held true for females in more than half of the countries.
3. Age-specific effects indicated that widowed and divorced persons in their twenties and early thirties experienced the highest mortality risks, sometimes 10 times as high as those for married persons of the same age. Among single persons, the highest risks were associated with men and women between the late twenties and early forties.
4. In the majority of countries, the relative mortality ratios of the three unmarried groups increased over the past two to three decades.

This consistency of findings across countries strengthened previous speculations about the importance of marriage in maintaining health and reducing the risk of dying and also about the increased stresses associated with both single and formerly married life-styles.

Source: Yuanreng Hu and Noreen Goldman, "Mortality Differentials by Marital Status: An International Comparison," *Demography* 27 (May 1990): 233–250.

It has been suggested that marital partners provide companionship, interpersonal closeness, emotional gratification, and support that serves to buffer individuals against physical and emotional pathology (a **protection hypothesis**). Married individuals are more likely to abstain from smoking, drink moderately, avoid risk-taking behaviour, and lead more stable, secure, and scheduled life-styles. Married people also tend to live longer than the unmarried.

One explanation why married women are healthier than single women (including those separated, divorced, or widowed) is greater economic resources.[2] This economic "safety net" provides access to better housing, food, and services than they would have otherwise, resulting in a lower level of stress and a higher level of health. For both men and women, income was found to have a mediating effect on the mortality rate. For example, nonmarried individuals with high incomes experienced lower mortality than married ones with low incomes. The higher mortality was experienced by those who were both poor and single.[3]

Interestingly, men, more than women, receive mental health benefits from marriage. Women, more than men, provide emotional aid and other support in marriage. American public opinion polls support the conclusion that more married men are satisfied with their marriages than are women. When asked, "Would you say that your marriage is very happy, pretty happy, or not too happy?"

about two-thirds of the men and 57 percent of the women said "very happy."[4] Very few said "not too happy" (1 percent of men and 4 percent of women), but these figures must be considered carefully. Perhaps many of those people who would respond "not too happy" have been divorced, ending an unhappy situation.

The differences among married and unmarried people have not been stable over time. Norval Glenn, using American survey data, demonstrated a substantial decline in marital stability and quality, and Glenn and Weaver showed a rather steady decline in the positive relationship between being married and marital happiness.[5] The changes occurred primarily through an increase in the reported happiness of never-married males and a decrease in the reported happiness of married females.

Glenn and Weaver suggested that these changes may relate to the increasingly similar circumstances of being married and unmarried. A substantial proportion of unmarried persons, for example, have regular sexual relations without stigma. As well, given the ease with which divorce can be obtained by either spouse, marriage no longer provides the security it once did, financial or otherwise. In other words, the functions that marriage has traditionally fulfilled may be increasingly found in contexts other than marriage. When marriage is based on free choice, individualistic forces are accorded greater significance. The greater the extent to which the perceived needs of marriage are met and the fewer the alternatives to replacing unmet needs, the greater the likelihood of marriage and the continuation of marriage.

CANADIAN MARRIAGE AND COHABITATION TRENDS

Marriage rates (the proportion of people who marry) vary from society to society and over time within a society. For example, an investigation of 111 countries showed that high sex ratios (a relative undersupply of women) were positively associated with the proportion of women who married and inversely associated with women's average age at marriage.[6] That is, the fewer the number of women relative to men, the higher the proportion who marry and the younger the age at which they do so.

The number and proportion of people who marry are influenced by other factors as well. Economic recessions and depressions generally have had an inhibiting effect on marriage, as have shifts in the age distribution. Marriage rates in Canada declined during the Great Depression, rose during and after the Second World War and declined again over the last two decades. During wartime, anticipating conscription, many single men may have married in the hope that they could postpone being called to service.[7]

Marriage rates continued to rise in the postwar period until 1973 when the trend reversed, and they began to drop significantly. From 1939 to 1972, total first marriage rates remained above 900 of every 1000 men and women. Between 1970 and 1980, total first-marriage rates dropped to under 700. But by 1997, only 505 of every 1000 men and 539 of every 1000 women in Canada were married by age 50.[8]

Family Diversity

Cohabitation in Sweden

In a dramatic contrast to China, Swedish partners are selected on the basis of love relationships with only minimal parental involvement in couple decision-making. And an acceptable norm is to engage in nonmarital cohabitation. Nonmarital cohabitation is the lifestyle of couples who form consensual unions, or who live together but are not legally or officially married. In Sweden, these people are classified as living in "marriage-like relationships." It is estimated that, today, about one in four, or 25 percent, of Swedish couples live in this type of arrangement, and it is generally recognized that virtually all Swedes now cohabit before marriage. Trost notes that very few couples are against marriage and many view it as something to come eventually. But marriage is not necessary for a couple to live together, nor is it necessary for a "respectable" woman to have a child. For cohabitants, marriage is something they can switch over to whenever they want, if they ever do want.

Trost notes as well that increasing in incidence is the phenomenon of LAT (living apart together). This means that two persons constitute a couple under marriage-like conditions but they keep separate housing units. They may stay overnight for weekends or for other periods of time in either one's household. They see themselves as a married couple and might also be considered so by their social environment. He suggests that LAT will probably soon be regarded as a social institution.

See Jan Trost, "Family Studies in Sweden," *Marriage and Family Review* 23 (1996): 723–743.

The variation from province to province is dramatic. Newfoundland and Saskatchewan have the highest marriage rates. In Saskatchewan in 1997, 633 of every 1000 men and 655 of every 1000 women were expected to marry at least once by age 50. The comparable numbers for men and women in Quebec in 1997 were 329 and 362. In the Northwest Territories, where legal unions among Aboriginal Canadians have always been less common, only 260 per 1000 men and 310 per 1000 women will marry before age 50.[9]

A number of recent changes in family life have been attributed to declines and delays in marriage:

- Increases in nonmarital sexual activity
- Increases in the independence of young people
- A reduction in fertility
- A temporary shortage of eligible males in the marriage market (a "marriage squeeze")
- An increase in divorce
- An increase in nonmarital cohabitation

Although these represent dramatic changes from the past that could suggest further declines in marriage, people in Canada continue to value marriage and intimacy. In the following section we will look at the dramatic increases in cohabitation in Canada.

Nonmarital cohabitation

While most Canadians—and most people everywhere—marry at least once, an increasing number cohabit. Common-law unions may begin with little ceremony and dissolve without legal ruling—although many will be as enduring as a marriage.

The number of couples living in common-law unions has increased in most Western countries as marriage rates have declined. This transition was first evident in Sweden, then in the other Scandinavian countries, followed by Germany, Britain, and France, and then Canada and the United States. In Sweden, it is uncommon for couples to marry without first cohabiting. For some, common-law relationships are a prelude to marriage, for others an interim between divorce and remarriage. Some live together to save money by sharing expenses or for the tax advantages.

In 1996 one couple in seven was living common-law, compared to one couple in nine in 1991. Almost half of these families included children. Indeed the number of children living in common-law couple families increased dramatically from 1991 to 1996.[10] Of course, some of these children would have been born to previous unions. Table 6.1 shows the proportion of common-law unions by age. Younger couples are far more likely to cohabit than marry. Indeed, the majority of couples under 25 were cohabiting rather than married.

In Canada, Quebec is unique in its marriage and cohabitation patterns (see Figures 6.1 and 6.2). Cohabitation is much more common in Quebec than in any other province, although the percentages for Yukon Territory, the Northwest Territories and Nunavut are the highest in Canada. One-quarter of Quebec

Table 6.1
Common-law unions by age group, Canada 1986–1996 censuses (100% data)

Age group	*Common-law as a percentage of all couples*		
	1986	***1991***	***1996***
Total	8.27	11.33	13.53
15–19	59.53	75.41	76.69
20–24	32.83	46.80	55.74
25–29	16.60	24.57	32.17
30–34	10.26	15.28	20.48
35–39	7.37	11.10	15.19
40–44	5.92	8.73	11.82
45–49	4.52	7.42	9.46
50–54	3.46	5.62	7.87
55–59	2.61	4.12	5.70
60–64	2.06	3.03	4.02
65+	1.47	1.98	2.30

Source: Age, Sex, Marital Status and Common-law Status, Statistics Canada Catalogue 92-353-XPB: 34.

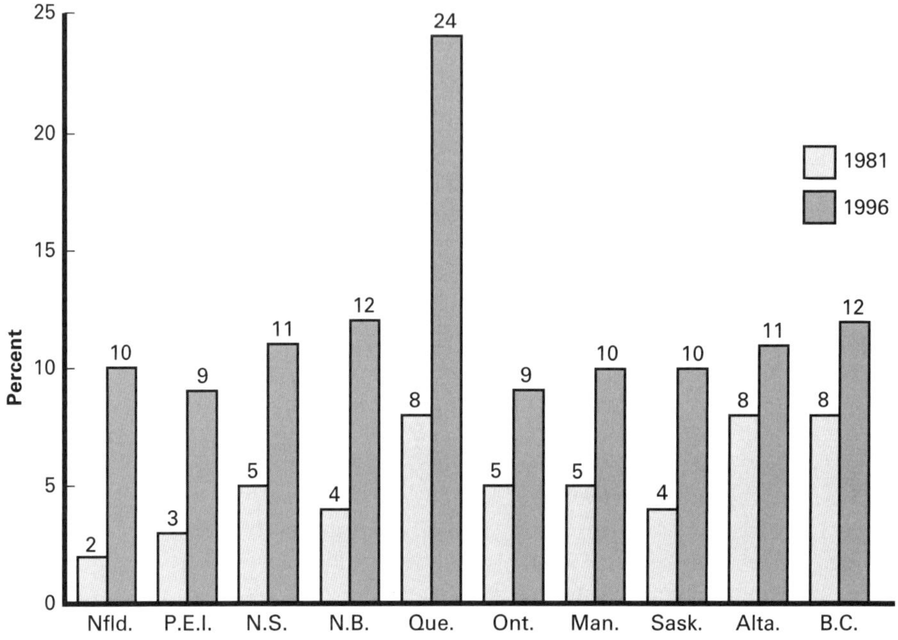

Figure 6.1
Proportion of all couples* living common-law, by province, 1981 and 1996
*Includes married and common-law couples with and without children.
Source: Jo-anne Belliveau, Jillian Oderkirk, and Cynthia Silver, "Common-Law Unions: The Quebec Difference," *Canadian Social Trends,* Statistics Canada Catalogue 11-008E (Summer 1994): 9; and *Age, Sex, Marital Status and Common-law Status,* Statistics Canada Catalogue 92-353-XPB: 34.

couples live common-law. Furthermore, cohabiting couples in Quebec do not fit the profile of cohabiters in the other provinces, who tend to be young and childless. In Quebec, common-law unions are increasing among older couples and couples with children. For young couples (where the woman is under 35), the difference between Quebec and the other provinces is dramatic. Sixty-one percent of these couples without children and 25 percent of young couples with children cohabit. Interestingly, within Quebec, francophones are twice as likely to cohabit as anglophones.[11]

Cohabitation and marital stability

Does establishing an unmarried-couple household provide a basis for a successful long-term relationship or even make for a better marriage? Does cohabitation increase, decrease, or have no effect on marital stability? Data from the National Survey of Families and Households (U.S.) showed that couples who cohabited before marriage reported lower-quality marriages, lower commitment

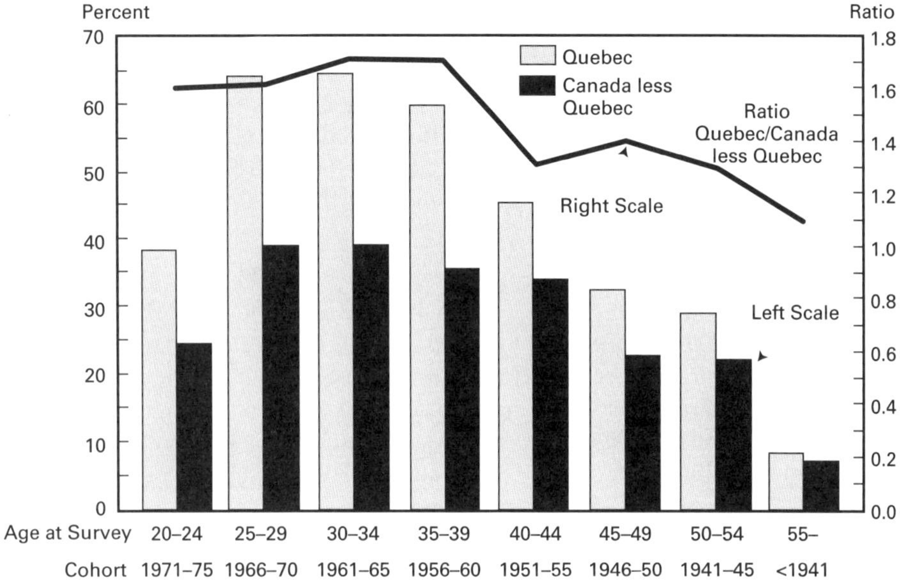

Figure 6.2
Proportion of the population having ever lived in a common-law union by cohort, Quebec, and Canada less Quebec, 1995
Source: Jean Dumas and Alain Bélanger, "Common-Law Unions in Canada at the End of the 20th Century," *Report on the Demographic Situation in Canada, 1996* (Ottawa: Minister of Industry, March 1997): 138.

to the institution of marriage, more individualistic views of marriage, and greater likelihood of divorce than couples who did not cohabit.[12]

Similar results came from other studies of national samples in the United States, Canada, and Sweden. Alan Booth and David Johnson, in a national sample of over 2000 married persons in the United States, rejected the idea that cohabitation improves partner selection and marital training.[13] They concluded that cohabitation is negatively related to marital interaction and positively related to marital disagreement and proneness to divorce. Support was found for the notion that some people who cohabit are poorer risks before they marry.

In Sweden a national sample of nearly 5000 women found that those who cohabited premaritally had almost 80 percent higher marital dissolution rates than those who did not.[14] Women who cohabited for over three years had over 50 percent higher dissolution rates than those who cohabited for shorter periods. With an increase in marital duration came a decrease in the difference in dissolution rates between cohabiters and noncohabiters, with no differences found among those whose marriages remained intact for eight years. The conclusion strongly suggests a weaker commitment to the institution of marriage on the part of those who cohabit premaritally.

Robert Schoen[15] noted that the association between cohabitation and marital dissolution may largely disappear as cohabitation becomes more common. When comparing earlier cohabiters to more recent cohabiters (rather than to noncohabiters), Schoen found the earlier cohabiters were at a greater risk of marriage dissolution. Thus, as the probability of cohabiting increases and becomes more acceptable, so may the negative aspects associated with cohabitation decrease.

Why is cohabitation related to less marital stability and higher rates of marital dissolution? Explanations vary widely, but Thompson and Colella provided three major ones:

1. Those who cohabit rather than marry perceive themselves or the relationship as a poor risk in terms of long-term happiness and commitment.
2. Cohabiters are less committed to the institution of marriage than noncohabiters and therefore more likely to dissolve a problematic marriage.
3. Cohabiters define marriage in more individual than in couple terms, so that cohabiters view marital quality as more central to the relationship's stability than noncohabiters.[16]

In sum, although most Canadians marry, an increasing number of couples (with and without children) cohabit. The 1996 census found that the proportion of Canadians living in a couple was declining.[17] Existing data do not support the contentions that cohabitation serves as an effective training ground for marriage or that it results in improved marital quality or stability.

Variations in marriage rates

In the past, wedding dates were determined to some extent by religion and seasonal work schedules. Different religions have different optimal (and restricted) times for couples to marry. Free time is needed for the couple and their guests to plan for the wedding or to travel to attend. Dumas and Peron measured changes in marriage seasonality over time using Canadian data from 1926, 1939, and every 10 years beginning in 1945.[18] Until 1965, there were two peaks in the frequency of weddings: June and September/October. Far more weddings occur over the summer than winter months. The two summer peaks reflect a society heavily dependent on agriculture. June is preharvest and September/October is postharvest. The rate dropped in November, particularly in the number of weddings occurring in Quebec, which the authors attributed to lumbering drawing farmers away from villages in winter. Because of Lent, March was also a low point for weddings, although after 1965 this dip disappeared completely. Since 1965, the effects of the harvest have disappeared, and the summer months of July and August have became the most popular time of the year for weddings.

Marriage dates in Canada were also influenced by the *Income Tax Act*. Until 1985, a taxpayer who was married by December 31 could claim a spousal exemption for the calendar year. The 1985 amendment made the exemption proportional to the time married. That Canadians were cognizant of these tax concerns when deciding on a wedding day is evidenced by the increased number of December weddings before 1985 and the declining number after.

POWER IN CONJUGAL RELATIONSHIPS

One important aspect of the marital system is the power positions of husband and wife—both as individuals and in relation to each other. There is considerable agreement that *power* is the ability to influence others and affect their behaviour. *Conjugal power* is the ability of the husband and wife to influence each other. It is often measured by determining who makes certain decisions or who performs certain tasks.

Power involves the crucial dimensions of authority and influence. Social norms determine who has *authority* in that the culture designates the positions that have legitimate and prescribed power (authority). In some societies, authority is invested in the husband; in others, it rests with the oldest male in an extended family; and in others, authority goes to the mother-in-law. Other family members can *influence*—that is, exert pressure on—the person with authority. For example, the Prime Minister of Canada has the prescribed authority to make a wide range of decisions, but he or she can be influenced by the press, the public, and his or her own family, none of whom are given the authority to make political decisions. Similarly, while husbands have traditionally assumed authority over wives and children, they are also greatly influenced by them.

Throughout this text, frequent references are made to patriarchy, male dominance, male authoritarianism, and the like. Yet it is clear that, in spite of cultural norms reinforcing patriarchy and assumption of male dominance, females, in or out of marriage, influence other people, affect their behaviour, and get them to do what they want. (In other words, they have power.) The domestic arena is one in which women, wives, and mothers are probably not as passive and powerless as is often described or believed. Domestic power—the ability to impose one's will in decisions concerning sexual relations, household tasks, and the lives of children—is a complex dynamic. In a study of domestic power in southern Spain, an anthropologist showed that working-class women often united with their mothers to prevail in domestic decision-making, despite opposition from their husbands.[19]

How can this be explained or understood? Where and how do women get power in contexts of male dominance and patriarchal norms? The following section will examine some characteristics of conjugal power and key theories that explain it.

Characteristics of conjugal power

Several decades ago, Mary Rogers made several key points about power[20]:

1. Power is a capacity or an ability to influence others, *not* the exercise of that ability. Ability does not denote social action. The perceived or real ability to influence can affect outcomes even when the exercise of that ability is not undertaken.
2. An individual's power must be viewed relative to specific social systems and the positions (statuses) a person occupies within a given social system. Note that power is not inherent within a person. Power must be viewed in dynamic terms; the power of individuals to influence others is linked to their various social statuses and social roles.

3. If power is an ability to influence others, resources are the primary determinants of that ability. A *resource* is "any attribute, circumstance, or possession that increases the ability of its holder to influence a person or group."[21] Attributes might include age, sex, race, health, and level of energy; circumstances might include location, friendships or acquaintances, flexibility, and access to information; possessions might include money, land, property, goods, and so on.

The contention is that persons with greater resources have an advantage over those with fewer resources. In a social exchange perspective, they can bargain with others from a position of strength.

Rebecca Warner and others made a strong case for broadening the conceptualization of resources to include selected features of family and kinship structures (family organization).[22] For example, wives will have more power in marriages in societies with nuclear- rather than extended-family structures and in societies with matrilateral rather than patrilateral customs of residence and descent. Ethnographic data on over 100 nonindustrial societies provided support for these propositions, highlighting the fact that organizational resources may be as important as material and personal resources in understanding conjugal power.

Conjugal power and decision making in intimate relationships

One of the ways conjugal power has traditionally been measured is to determine which spouse makes the major decisions and how husband and wife decision-making patterns vary by area of concern. One of the most widely cited studies and one that served to stimulate many others was done in the late 1950s by Robert Blood and Donald Wolfe.[23] In an attempt to measure the balance of power between husbands and wives, they interviewed 731 city wives in metropolitan Detroit.

Blood and Wolfe selected eight situations that they felt would include both male and female decisions about the family as a whole:

1. What job the husband should take
2. What kind of car to get
3. Whether to buy life insurance
4. Where to go on vacation
5. What house or apartment to take
6. Whether the wife should go to work or quit work
7. What doctor to have when someone is sick
8. How much money the family can afford to spend per week on food

The wives' answers to the eight situations revealed that two decisions were primarily the husband's province (his job and car) and two were primarily the wife's province (her work and food, although many husbands were influential in decisions about wives' employment). All other decisions were joint.

Even though the results of this study were published more than 30 years ago, the responses of wives to these eight decision-making questions might not

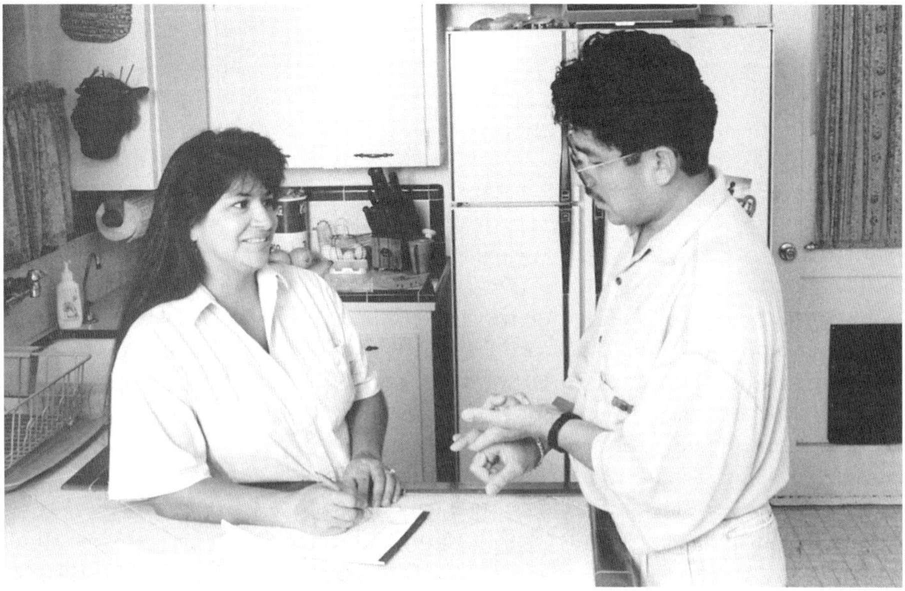

The issues of power, including decision-making processes and role assignments, are important in all relationships. Egalitarianism may be the norm or goal of many couples, but the reality is that male activities and control are pervasive in most societies. Patriarchal patterns decrease as women gain education and skills, jobs and incomes, and other resources that enable them to be more independent.

be very different today. In Canada, many families still assume that husbands will be primarily responsible for family economic support. Therefore his job and his work are his primary exertions in both time and energy. Culturally, we also make a stronger connection between men and cars than women and cars when it comes to repair and care.

Whether to buy life insurance, where to go on vacation, and what house or apartment to take are decisions that are more likely to be shared equally by husband and wife than made by either spouse separately. It could be assumed that the two spouses have equal competencies in these choices. Furthermore, these areas affect both partners more equally than do the other decision-making areas.

Blood and Wolfe's theoretical explanation of why husbands and wives make certain decisions individually versus together is based on *resource availability*—that is, the source of authority and power lies in the comparative resources each spouse has available. The balance of power is weighted toward the partner who has the greatest resources, as perceived by the other partner.

A number of writers have questioned the theoretical accuracy of explaining power on the basis of resources. The theory of resources (in reality, a proposition rather than a theory) contends that the more a partner controls resources of value to himself or herself and his or her mate, the greater his or her relative power. Data on this subject have shown some mixed and inconsistent results. To understand why requires examining the theory of resources issue more intensely.

Theory of resources issue

The **theory of resources** provides the conceptual core around which many later studies were built. Over the past several decades, a number of authors have stressed that power is based not only on an individual's resources but also on the comparative contributions (resources) and exchange processes of the husband and wife relative to each other. Hyman Rodman, for example, developed a theory of resources in a cultural context that takes into account the theory of resources, the theory of exchange, the comparative contributions of both husband and wife, and the cultural context in which the interaction occurs.[24] Rodman argued that one must not only be aware of resources in trying to explain conjugal power but consider as well the cultural context in which decision making takes place. Thus, in certain societies, it is the upper- and middle-status groups (the highest income, educational, and occupational groups) that first accept norms of marital egalitarianism. This in effect diminishes the impact of resources upon power in marital settings.

This differentiation of a basic resource theory from a **cultural resource theory** sheds some light on understanding variations in power between men and women, and between social classes, various groups, and even countries. One example that focused on this differentiation was a study of dual-career couples where half the wives earned at least one-third more than their husbands and half the husbands earned at least one-third more than their wives.[25] Consistently with *resource theory,* spouses who earned more viewed their careers as more important and had more say at home than spouses who earned less. Consistently with *cultural resource theory,* men overall had more say in financial matters, took less responsibility for the children and the household, and saw their own careers as more important than their wives' careers. Thus, even though resources had significant effects on the wives who had them (those who earned more than their husbands), these women were still more likely to say they would move on their husband's behalf.

Other studies have drawn similar conclusions. Mark Rank found that increments in wives' resources correlated positively with wives' influence, supporting the theory of resources argument.[26] But increments in husbands' resources correlated negatively with husbands' influence, thus not supporting the argument that greater resources lead to greater influence and power. The explanation is that as husbands gain higher levels of income, education, and occupational prestige, they come in contact with egalitarian norms regarding spousal relations. In brief, as both husbands and wives gain resources, women become less economically dependent on their spouses while men become socialized into an egalitarian ethic.

Another cautionary note on accepting the theory of resources per se or without qualifications comes from Karen Pyke.[27] It is her contention that women's market work (employment) is not considered a resource in some marriages and hence does not have a positive effect on marital power. Why? Consistently with a symbolic interaction perspective, it is necessary to examine the meanings couples give to the material and structural conditions of their lives. Thus a woman married to a man who views her employment as a threat rather than as a gift will derive less power from her employment. Likewise, the extent to which a woman views her own paid or unpaid labour as a gift or a burden will also affect her marital power.

Pyke's research gave support to these ideas in that men who were denied a sense of occupational success were less likely to view their wives' market work as a gift and some wives, sensitive to their husbands' feelings of failure, responded by not resisting their husbands' dominance to "balance" the husbands' low self-esteem. Pyke's research suggests that any explanation of marital power must reflect the gender of the actors and the gendered meanings these actors give to the powering process.

Egalitarian ethic

Joint decision making, sharing marital power, perceptions of both self and spouse doing a fair share of family work, and a feeling of equity appear to be positively related to marital and relationship satisfaction. This is particularly true of partners who hold less traditional gender attitudes.[28] Husbands who were more progressive (less traditional) were found to show increases in reported positive marital quality. Increases in egalitarianism were found to be associated with declines in reports of negative aspects of the marriage (problems, disagreements, divorce-proneness). The pattern was different, however, for women. Wives who held nontraditional gender-role attitudes reported increases in negative aspects of the marriage (less happiness, more disagreements, more problems). In contemporary marriages, stress is lessened when husbands, with their wives, have attitudes that support role sharing and gender equality.

Perhaps feminists lead the way in stressing an egalitarian ethic. Feminists have demonstrated the problematic nature of marital and family life for women and have provided an awareness of how traditionally structured marriage has an overwhelming cost to women in financial, emotional, and physical dimensions. Given the incongruence between the ideology and the practice of marital equality, a key question may be whether a feminist ideology of full equality is compatible with marriage.

A partial answer comes from a study of feminist heterosexual marriages.[29] Assessed was the possibility of establishing marital equality through a series of processes that involves the partners critiquing the gender injustices (an ongoing dialogue of gender expectations); engaging in public acts of equality (different names, common financial decisions); the husband's support of the wife's activity (her career, his children); reflective assessment (monitoring of the contributions of each); and emotional involvement (openness about feelings). Rather than rejecting marriage, these feminist couples considered revitalizing the relationship by promoting a vigilance to equality. The study suggests that feminist women need not forgo relationships with men but can expect men to assume feminist beliefs and, with women, strive to enact them.

Findings such as these have lent support to social exchange theories and equality models suggesting that personal happiness, the highest levels of marital satisfaction, and the lowest levels of depression occur when individuals, men and women, believe their partners contribute a fair share to housework and child care and perceive equality in the exchange. For many married persons, particularly wives, an inequitable balance of marital power is a serious problem. The perceived balance of costs and rewards in a marriage is relevant to success. In fact, the felt or perceived balance matters more than any objective reality.[30]

What conclusions can be drawn about an egalitarian ethic and partner's well-being? Steil,[31] in a summary of the empirical evidence, suggested the following:

- A wife's dominance in decision making, which is relatively rare, is associated with the lowest level of satisfaction for both partners.
- A husband's dominance in decision making may be more frequently associated with satisfaction for husbands than for wives.
- Equal sharing may be associated with the highest level of satisfaction for wives.
- When other measures than marital satisfaction are considered, relative equality is most beneficial for relationships.

Steil goes on to say that relatively equal relationships are characterized by more mutually supportive communication, less manipulative forms of influence, and greater sexual and marital satisfaction for both partners than are relationships in which either one or the partners is dominant.

MARITAL QUALITY

While the term **marital quality** is used throughout this section, *marital* is meant to incorporate the quality of any marriage-like relationship. What may be more significant than a legal status of being married is the degree of social attachment. Catherine Ross, for example, specified four levels of marital status on a continuum of social attachment: no partner, partner outside the household, living with partner in the household, and living with a married partner.[32] She discovered that the higher the level of social attachment, the lower the level of psychological distress. There were no significant differences in those living with a partner and those being married. Social attachments were stronger predictors of well-being than marital status.

The literature on marital quality and the quality of marriage-like relationships is extensive.[33] Many attempts have been made to assess the quality of marital and intimate relationships, using such concepts as *adjustment, success, satisfaction, stability, happiness, well-being, consensus, cohesion, adaptation, integration, role strain,* and the like. Sometimes these terms are used interchangeably; sometimes each denotes something different. Sometimes the terms are used in a psychological sense, referring to the state of one of the partners; sometimes they are used in a social/psychological sense, referring to the state of the relationship; and sometimes they are used in a sociological sense, referring to the state of the group or system. In addition, sometimes the terms are used to refer to the achievement of a goal, and sometimes they are used to refer to a dynamic process of making changes. All the concepts emphasize a dimension that contrasts with maladjustment, dissatisfaction, instability, and unhappiness.

Dimensions of marital or relationship quality

From the introductory statement, it should be clear that marital quality, marital adjustment, and marital well-being are varied concepts that lack a consensus of definition. *Marital quality* or *adjustment* is essentially a relative agreement by husband and wife on what issues are important, the sharing of similar tasks and activities, and the demonstration of affection for one another. *Marital success*, as distinguished from *marital quality*, generally refers to the achievement of one or more goals: permanence, companionship, fulfilling expectations of the community, and so forth. *Marital happiness*, distinguished from both *adjustment* and *success*, is an individual emotional response. Although marital happiness is an individual phenomenon, marital success and adjustment are dyadic achievements or states of the marriage or the relationship.

One study asked newlyweds to evaluate the quality (well-being) of their marriage.[34] Four dimensions of marital well-being emerged from a factor analysis of responses: happiness, equity, competence, and control. Happiness was more clearly associated with all aspects of well-being than any other, but feelings of equity in the relationship, feelings of competence in the marital role, and feelings of control over marital outcomes were important and separate dimensions of marital well-being.

Feelings of equity were addressed earlier. In regard to feelings of control, Catherine Ross suggested that, for women, marriage has a price and represents a tradeoff.[35] On the one hand, marriage functions to increase women's household incomes, thus increasing their sense of control over their lives. On the other hand, since women do most of the housework and child care, marriage functions to decrease their sense of control, independence, and autonomy. For men, marriage has little effect on their sense of control.

About 30 years ago, Jessie Bernard included the quality of the relationship as one of three major dimensions of marital adjustment. She said marital adjustment is determined by:

1. The degree or nature of the *differences* between or among the parties involved
2. The degree or nature of the *communication* between or among the parties
3. As just noted, the *quality of the relationship* between or among the parties (positive or negative, friendly or hostile)[36]

Differences may be a matter of degree, or they may be categorical (no flexibility, no leeway). Often, matters of principle are categorical and thus the most difficult to resolve. Thus, statements such as "We will never miss Mass" and beliefs such as "Oral sex is wrong," if taken categorically, do not permit flexibility in dealing with a mate or spouse who feels differently. On the other hand, differences of degree permit give and take, bargaining, and negotiation. The point is that differences as well as the nature and extent of those differences affect dyadic or interpersonal adjustment.

The second dimension, communication, necessitates interaction. Few people would doubt or question the importance of communication to successful relationships of any kind. Yet communication is an extremely complex factor in marital relationships: It may be verbal or nonverbal, it may be explicit or tacit, it may clarify or mislead, or it may draw relationships closer together or tear them apart. To not talk at all, to talk constantly, to order, to nag, to scold, to praise—each may convey a certain message.

A review of research over the past 20 years revealed strong support for the relationship between communication and marital satisfaction.[37] This relationship held true for both the content and the process of communication. Findings consistently replicated were that couples with higher rates of self-disclosure and expressions of love, support, and affection tended also to experience greater satisfaction. Research on process variables suggested that positive forms of nonverbal communication—such as laughter, voice tone, touching one's spouse, and body position—were found more frequently in happy couples. Nondistressed couples were more likely to show good listening skills and clarity of speech and to interpret their partners' behaviour positively.

The quality of the relationship was Bernard's third major dimension of adjustment. Spouses who are friendly and loving are not necessarily well adjusted to marriage, but such qualities make accommodation easier. Making sacrifices or changing plans is easier when spouses have love and genuine concern for one another. If the relationship is affectionate, results will be far different than if it is hateful or hostile.

The dynamics of marital quality were assessed in a recent American sample of married persons interviewed three times over an eight-year period.[38] It was found that marital quality, regardless of how it is measured, is a remarkably stable phenomenon, unaffected by gender and marital duration. Even among those couples who eventually divorced, the relationship, from formation to dissolution, did not fluctuate appreciably. Marital quality was said to be a dyadic property, not something that individuals carry from one marriage to another.

Evaluating marital quality

Assessing the quality of marriage and intimate relationships began in earnest in the late 1920s. In each decade since then, an extensive body of literature has been accumulated in an effort to predict marital success and determine factors, psychological and social, associated with marital quality or adjustment.

Probably the most widely used measurement of marital quality or interpersonal adjustment has been the Dyadic Adjustment Scale developed by Graham Spanier.[39] The scale consists of 32 items centring on four basic components: dyadic satisfaction, dyadic cohesion, dyadic consensus, and affectional expression.

- *Satisfaction* is measured by asking questions (such as, Do you confide in your mate? Do you regret that you married?) and inquiring into the degree of happiness in the relationship.
- *Cohesion* focuses on whether the couple does things together and exchanges ideas.

FAMILY DIVERSITY

Canadians say faithfulness is the most important factor for a successful marriage

As reported by *The Gallup Report*, when asked how important various factors were for a successful marriage, most Canadians ranked faithfulness as most important. Ninety-four percent of those sampled said that faithfulness was very important. Sixty-three percent said that a happy sexual relationship was very important, while 53 percent said sharing chores, and 46 percent indicated living away from in-laws.

When comparing responses across regions, there was some disagreement about the importance of a happy sexual relationship. More people in the Atlantic provinces (73 percent) thought it was very important than did people in British Columbia (45 percent). Respondents in Quebec felt more strongly about living apart from in-laws than did people in other regions.

Source: Gallup Canada Inc., *The Gallup Report*, February 13, 1992.

- *Consensus* measures the extent of agreement on issues such as finances, friends, religious matters, and household tasks.
- *Affectional expression* refers to the extent of agreement regarding demonstrations of affection, sexual relations, and showing love.

Other measures of marital quality or relationship adjustment, satisfaction, or well-being focus on related issues. Susan Hendrick developed a seven-item relationship assessment scale that asks each partner the following questions:

- How well does your partner meet your needs?
- What is your level of satisfaction with the relationship?
- How good is your relationship compared to most?
- How often do you wish you hadn't got into it?
- What is the extent to which the relationship meets your original expectations?
- How much do you love your partner?
- What are the problems in the relationship?[40]

Hendrick claimed that her seven-item scale is easily administered, is highly correlated with the longer Dyadic Adjustment Scale, and effectively discriminates between partners (married couples, cohabiters, gay couples, friends) who stay together versus those who split apart.

Jessie Bernard made a different point for evaluating marital relationships. She suggested that a criterion be set up in terms not of the best *imaginable* relationship but of the best *possible* one.[41] Thus, a marriage may be successful to the extent that it provides the highest satisfaction possible, not imaginable. However unsatisfactory the relationship may be in terms of happiness, it may still be judged better than the alternatives.

From this exchange and relativistic (viewed in context) point of view, a marital relationship is successful (1) if the satisfaction is positive (the rewards to both partners are greater than the costs) and (2) if the relationship is preferable to other alternatives. The following two examples illustrate exchange and relativistic perspectives:

> A and B do not like one another; they get on one another's nerves; the costs of remaining married are great in frustration and loneliness. But the rewards are great also; together they can afford a lovely home; they have high status in the community; the children are protected from scandal; the church approves of them; etc. This relationship is "successful" or "good," not because it is the best imaginable, but only because it is the best possible in the sense that the satisfactions are greater than the costs. ...
>
> An example in which a marital relationship is successful only because it is better than any alternative would be the marriage of a dependent woman to, let us say, an alcoholic, in which the costs in misery were much greater than the rewards in security or status; but the spread between costs and satisfactions would be much greater if she left him. She would then be alone; she would not have the protection of the status of marriage; she would not even have the occasional sober companionship of a husband, etc. Bad as it is, therefore, her marriage seems better to her than any alternative she has.[42]

Richard Udry suggested that the dimension of *marital alternatives* appears to be a better predictor of marital disruption than measures of satisfaction are.[43] Using longitudinal data of married couples from 16 U.S. urban areas, he measured the respondents' perceptions of marital alternatives: that is, how much better or worse they would be without their present spouse and how easily that spouse could be replaced with one of comparable quality. In the ensuing year or two after these resources were measured, couples in which spouses were rated high in marital alternatives had several times the disruption rate of those rated low in alternatives.

This observation perhaps gives a clearer idea of why many unhappy marriages remain intact: the spouses have no or few alternatives, or, as suggested by exchange theory, the existing alternatives have costs that exceed their benefits. Recent data have shown that about 7 percent of intact marriages are stable but unhappy. Age, lack of prior marital experience, commitment to marriage as an institution, low social activity, lack of control over one's life, and belief that divorce would detract from happiness are all factors that predict stability in unhappy marriages.[44]

What about marital conflict? Is it a sure sign of low marital quality?

Marital conflict

A social conflict frame of reference, as described in Chapter 1, is rooted in the basic assumption that conflict is natural and inevitable in all human interaction, including marital interaction.

As couples interact, as they define and redefine their relationship with one another, and as they perform daily activities and fulfill role expectations, conflict is inevitable: over work, over children, over criticism, over in-laws, over expenditures, over sex, and, as stressed in popular literature, even over matters such as how one should squeeze the toothpaste. The quality of a marriage, therefore, is not based on whether conflict exists but on how conflict is managed in a way mutually satisfactory to both partners.

In a chapter entitled "Marital Conflict as a Positive Force," John Scanzoni argued that, to understand the dynamics of husband/wife interaction, the first step is to throw out the notion that equilibrium or stability is a necessary ideal, and the second step is to throw out the idea that conflict is by nature bad or unhealthy within marriage.[45]

Conflict brings into the open issues that one or both partners consider unjust or inequitable. When such issues are presented, negotiated, and resolved in a way that is satisfactory to both partners, the outcome may be a new, more positive level of marital adjustment or solidarity. In contrast, failure to engage in conflict when injustice is perceived may result in a less beneficial, less rewarding situation for both partners and may actually increase the chances of dissolution of the marriage.

Conflict, when viewed from this perspective of injustice, should not be confused with difficulties and discord brought about by economic hardships or constraints. These, too, produce conflict and change in marital relations. Longitudinal data of couples who suffered income loss during the Depression (1929–39) showed marked decline in marital quality and an increase in marital discord.[46] Men who lacked adaptive resources became more difficult to live with and more tense, irritable, and explosive. More recently, economic distress induced by a downturn in agriculture was found to have clear effects on the marital quality of farm couples. Increased depression and contemplating divorce were two of the strongest effects of economic hardship.[47] These behaviours in themselves may produce conflict but seem related less to interpersonal inequities than to disrupted patterns of social interaction and adverse psychological changes brought about by economic loss.

Marital quality between generations

At the beginning of the chapter, it was noted that some scholars claim that marriage is in a state of decline and is an institution in decay. Given the popularity of marriage and marriage-like relationships, the institution of marriage, while exhibiting many changes, remains popular. It has been illustrated in previous chapters that marriage-like (cohabiting) relationships are far less stable than marriage relationships. But what about the quality of marital relationships? Has the quality of marriage declined over previous decades?

Rogers and Amato looked at two generations representing distinct marriage cohorts: married individuals from the original sample who were between 20 and 35 years of age in 1980 and married individuals from the offspring sample who were between 20 and 35 years of age in 1992.[48] Controlling for gender, race, duration of marriage, and marriage order, significant differences existed between the two cohorts in three of five dimensions of marital quality. The younger cohort reported lower levels of marital interaction and higher levels of marital conflict and marital problems. Declines were apparent for both husbands and wives. Interestingly, this younger cohort did not report lower levels of marital happiness or divorce proneness, in that commitment to the idea of a lifelong marriage appeared to be stronger in the younger cohort. These changes are accounted for by changes in economic resources, work and family demands, wives' gender role attitudes, and cohabitation prior to marriage. The writers conclude that such findings suggest

> that young married people may be committed to salvaging marriage, and that reports of increased marital tensions and difficulties reflect not the struggles of an outmoded social institution, but the inherent difficulties in adapting marriage to a rapidly changing social climate.

Marital quality over the life course

Developmental models and life-course models have been used effectively to study family change. These approaches, which deal with changes over time, have been used to test a number of issues, including satisfaction with the division of household labour (with wives' satisfaction starting high, decreasing dramatically, then increasing again, following a pronounced U-shaped curve across the life cycle)[49] and perceived marital quality (again, supporting a curvilinear, U-shaped trend).

What happens to marriages and marital quality over long periods of time? Most studies have sought answers to this question by comparing groups at different points in the life course or at different stages of the family life cycle. That is, newlyweds have been compared with families with preschool children, who have been compared with families with adolescents in the home, and so forth.

One unique exception to this approach took place at the Institute of Human Development at the University of California in Berkeley.[50] Seventeen couples, who had been married for 50 to 69 years, were the survivors of an original study of 250 couples who were first studied in 1928 and 1929 and then interviewed again from time to time over the following years. In all of the surviving marriages, partners had both shared and separate interests and had

News Item

Baby boomers celebrate parents' golden anniversaries

As the oldest baby boomers approach the half-century mark, their parents in turn celebrate golden wedding anniversaries. As Dorothy Lipovenko points out ("Postwar Marriages Good as Gold," *The Globe and Mail,* February 14, 1997), many young seniors have reached this stage because "they married early, are living longer and raised families when divorce was taboo." This kind of marital longevity may be an anomaly for future generations, given later marriage and increased divorce.

Couples celebrating their fiftieth anniversary may request congratulations from the Governor-General. "Last year, Government House mailed almost 13,800 letters, compared to about 7,700 in 1985."

The quality of marital relationships over time follows a curvilinear, or U-shaped, pattern. Marital satisfaction is high at the beginning of the marriage but declines sharply when children are born; the low point is during the years when children are adolescents. Marital satisfaction increases dramatically when children leave home and remains high or even increases through retirement.

both a commitment to the marriage and an acceptance of each other. Husbands tended to be more satisfied with their marriages than were wives. Of the authors' model of six types of very-long-term marriages,[51] the greatest number exhibited a U-shaped or a curvilinear pattern—that is, starting at a high level of affect and satisfaction, dipping during the years of having young children until the children left, and increasing in the later years to a point as high as at the beginning. All of the other couples were categorized as stable (positive, neutral, or negative), and no couples showed a continuous increase or a continuous decline in marital satisfaction. (Any such couples may have previously divorced.)

Numerous other studies have tried to discover how families manage their lives, what explains their relative successes and failures, and how their relationships change over time. One study asked 1140 families "What makes families work?" and analyzed results using a seven-stage, family life-cycle model.[52] This study confirmed the findings of other studies,[53] namely that satisfaction with marriage and family life tends to decrease over the early stages of the life cycle and then increase over later stages. The data, when plotted, form a U-shaped curve (see Figure 6.3). Specifically, from young couples without children (stage 1) to families with preschool-age children (stage 2) to families with school-age children (stage 3) to families with adolescents in the home (stage 4), there was a decline in family satisfaction for both husbands and wives. The decline continued for wives through the launching period (stage 5), but satisfaction increased slightly for husbands at this time. A sharp increase in family satisfaction occurred at the "empty nest" stage (stage 6), and satisfaction increased more or remained high through retirement (stage 7).

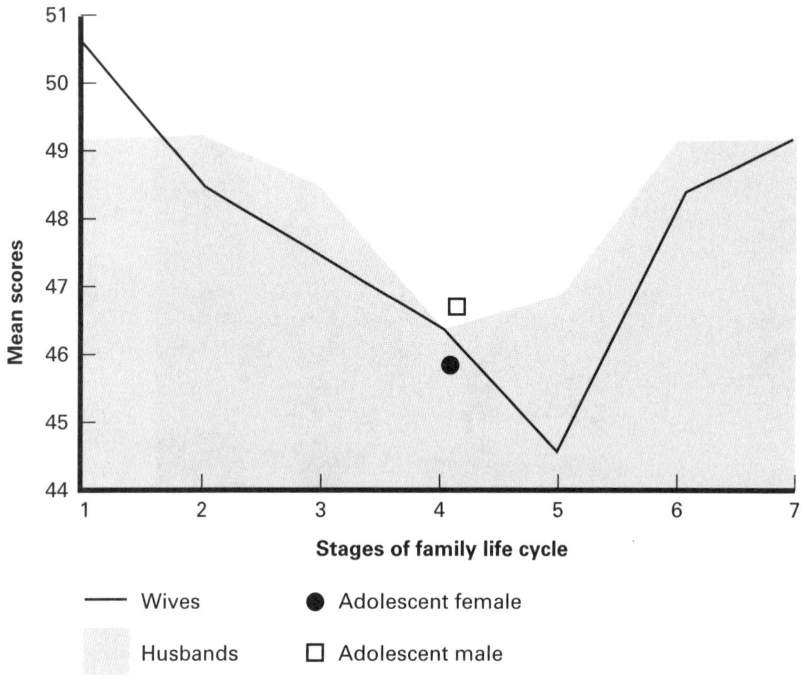

Figure 6.3
Family satisfaction by stage of family life cycle
Source: David H. Olson, Hamilton I. McCubbin, and associates, *Families: What Makes Them Work* (Beverly Hills: Sage, 1983), Figure 10.5, p. 181. Reprinted by permission of Sage Publications, Inc., and David H. Olson.

Some explanations for the dramatic increase in satisfaction found after the launching stage and into the later years may result from a shifting division of labour between spouses, the time couples have to spend together, and the sense of belonging. After the children leave home, couples may experience decreased financial responsibility. Russell Ward suggests that the quality of marital relationships in the later years is quite high and that time spent together and perceived fairness in the relationship is enhanced while arguments are relatively infrequent.[54] For both men and women, the quality of longer-term marriages is said to revolve around intimacy, interdependence, and a sense of companionship.

Results of studies showing the effects of having children on the marital happiness of parents are highly consistent. Overwhelming evidence has documented that, in North American society, the presence of children in the family lowers marital happiness for the parents. Glenn and McLanahan, in conducting their own national surveys and in reviewing many others, found no evidence for distinctly positive effects and strong evidence for negative effects of children on marital

Family Diversity

Long-term marriages—what keeps them going?

Marriage trends described in this chapter, indicating later marriage, increased single living, and increased cohabitation, and stable but high divorce rates described in Chapter 11 suggest a different commitment to long-term marriage than existed in the past. Will long-term marriages become increasingly rare in the future? What characterizes these long-lasting relationships?

Research done in the United States sheds some light on this issue. Data were gathered from 100 couples who had been married 45 years or more. What has kept them going? Why have their marriages lasted?

Men and women showed remarkable agreement on the keys to an enduring relationship. The top six perceived reasons for successful long-term marriages were:

- Mate is best friend
- Like mate as a person
- Marriage a long-term commitment
- Marriage a sacred institution
- Agree on aims and goals
- Laugh together frequently

Other reasons, which differed only slightly between men and women, including being proud of one's mate's achievements; agreeing on expression of affection, major decisions, and philosophy of life; and finding one's mate more interesting now than when first married.

The authors suggested that, even if it is true that men and women speak different languages and that it is appropriate to speak of "his" marriage and "her" marriage, it is also true that the men and women in this study perceived the same variables as critical for long-term marital success.

Source: Robert H. Lauer, Jeanette C. Lauer, and Sarah T. Kerr, "The Long-Term Marriage: Perceptions of Stability and Satisfaction," *International Journal of Aging and Human Development* 31 (1990): 189–195.

quality.[55] Given this highly consistent evidence, they suggested that it is ironic that most North Americans want to have and do have children. What's more, this phenomenon may serve as an example of the social function of ignorance; that is, people are motivated to perform the essential functions of reproduction and child care by the false belief that the psychological rewards of having children outweigh the costs or penalties. Perhaps there are perceptions of rewards, but research has not found them among the elements of marital satisfaction.

This negative effect of children on marital adjustment seems to appear early in parenthood. Immediately following the birth, there seems to be a happy, loving phase, but, within six months, a decline in marital adjustment occurs that is significantly lower than that during pregnancy.[56] The authors concluded that lowered marital adjustment during pregnancy would not be solved or improved by the birth of a child.

The Olson-McCubbin study *Families*,[57] as well as other research, has provided some precautionary notes to the life-cycle data presented. First, while consistent variation from stage to stage is found, the amount of change may be neither as great nor as significant as is often implied in textbooks such as this one. For example, adding data from those marriages that had dissolved would reduce the increase in satisfaction reported by most studies. Second, while male/female, husband/wife differences are found in most studies, these differences tend to be overplayed. Often, the sex differences were less pronounced than were differences across the life cycle. Third, reliance on cross-sectional data for the study of trends can be very misleading. That is, comparing groups who are at different stages in the life cycle (cross-sectional comparisons) rather than following the same group over time and through stages (longitudinal) does not adequately account for cohort effects, social desirability, or the tendency found in longitudinal studies to report as happy those marriages that have survived.

Summary

1. Marital systems fulfill many functions. For whatever reasons, married people are generally happier and experience fewer emotional and health problems than their unmarried counterparts. When the sexes are compared, men in particular benefit from marriage.
2. In Canada, marriage rates increased until the early 1970s and have declined significantly since. Typically marriage rates fluctuate under the influences of war, changing economic conditions, the sex ratio of the marriageable population, and the number of potential brides and grooms present in the general population. Marriage rates also vary by season, day of the week, and region of the country.
3. An important and widely researched area of marriage has addressed conjugal power, or the power positions of husband and wife as individuals and in relation to each other. *Power* is the ability to influence others and affect their behaviour. Power is often measured by determining who makes certain decisions, and includes the crucial dimensions of authority (legitimized power) and influence.
4. Studies of decision-making outcomes have indicated that certain decisions are made primarily by the husband, others primarily by the wife, and others jointly. Who makes which decision has been widely explained by a theory of resources: the person with the most resources—information, education, income, and so forth—makes the decision.
5. As with conjugal power, many attempts have been made to measure marital quality. Although no consensus exists as to what *quality* means, definitions generally include characteristics such as high levels of husband/wife agreement and sharing of activities, tasks, and affection.
6. A number of writers have suggested that marital alternatives may be a better predictor of marital disruption than are measures of adjustment or satisfaction. As suggested by exchange theory, when alternatives are perceived as having greater costs than benefits, many unhappy marriages will probably remain intact.
7. When marital quality, adjustment, and satisfaction are examined throughout the life cycle or life course, satisfaction appears to be highest at the beginning of marriage and lowest when the family has teenagers. Studies have indicated a curvilinear (U-shaped) relationship throughout the marital life course; the beginning and the end of marriage are the points of highest satisfaction.
8. This chapter examined selected aspects of the marital system, including trends, characteristics, power, and quality. Chapter 7 will return to an early stage of the marital life cycle, or life course, and investigate the parental system. The next two chapters will look at the transition to parenthood, family size, birth order, parent/child interaction, and socialization up to the launching stage.

KEY TERMS AND TOPICS

Marriage as a social institution p. 153
Marital status and well-being p. 153
Protection hypothesis p. 154
Marriage rates p. 155
Cohabitation rates p. 157
Variations in marriage rates p. 160
Power in conjugal relationships p. 161
Characteristics of conjugal power p. 161
Conjugal power and decision making p. 162
Theory of resources p. 164
Cultural resource theory p. 164
Egalitarian ethic p. 165
Marital quality p. 166
Dimensions of marital quality p. 167
Evaluating marital quality p. 168
Marital conflict p. 170
Marital quality over the life course p. 172

DISCUSSION QUESTIONS

1. Why do people marry? What explains the "happiness gap"—that the well-being of people who are married exceeds that of people who are unmarried? Why is it narrowing?
2. Compare provincial marriage rates. What may explain the differences?
3. Differentiate among the terms *power*, *authority*, and *influence*. How can women increase their relative marital power?
4. Make a list of 10 topics common in family decision-making. Take a brief survey among friends to determine which partner makes what decisions. Are certain decisions consistently made by one or the other? Give examples.
5. What is your theory of conjugal power? In what (if any) instances does the person with the greatest resources not have the most power? In what (if any) instances does the person with few resources still have a high degree of power?
6. Define the *egalitarian ethic*, and discuss its relationship to satisfaction in marriage. What might this suggest about the quality of relationships in highly patriarchal countries?
7. Discuss the concept of *marital quality*. What is it? Can it be measured or determined? Why or why not? Why do some couples who rate themselves low on marital quality stay together?
8. From the couples you know, select two or three who seem to have the best marriages. What factors tend to make these marriages so good? Do the same features exist in each marriage? Give examples.
9. What is the significance of conflict in a marriage or other relationship? Is conflict always destructive, or can it be beneficial? Explain.
10. What explains the curvilinear relationship between marital adjustment and the family life cycle or family life course?

FURTHER READINGS

Amato, Paul R., and Booth, Alan. *A Generation at Risk: Growing up in an Era of Family Upheaval*. Cambridge, MA: Harvard University Press, 1997. Data covering a 15-year period from two generations are used to determine how major changes in the American family have affected children.

Blumstein, Philip, and Schwartz, Pepper. *American Couples*. New York: Pocket Books, 1983. An intensive look at money, work, sex, and the lives of couples in the United States: married, cohabiters, gay men, and lesbians.

Cutrona, Carolyn E. *Social Support in Couples: Marriage as a Resource in Times of Stress*.

Thousand Oaks, CA: Sage, 1996. A book about social support with a focus on those who are closest: married couples.

Dumas, Jean, and Peron, Yves. *Marriage and Conjugal Life in Canada*. Ottawa: Minister of Supply and Services, 1992. Statistics Canada Catalogue 91-534E. A study of patterns of marriage, divorce, and remarriage in Canada, comparing age cohorts over time.

Fitzpatrick, Mary Anne. *Between Husbands and Wives: Communication in Marriage.* Newbury Park, CA: Sage, 1988. A book that establishes typologies of different types of marriage, styles of communication, and patterns of happiness.

Mackey, Richard A.; O'Brien, Bernard A.; and Mackey, Eileen F. *Gay and Lesbian Couples: Voices from Lasting Relationships.* An exploration of the development of relationships between couples of the same sex with a focus on the subjective experiences of partners as they live out lives together.

Olson, David H., McCubbin, Hamilton I. and associates. *Families: What Makes Them Work.* Beverly Hills: Sage, 1983. A study of more than 1100 couples, nearly 2700 individuals in intact marriages, and families from 31 states considered at seven stages of the family life cycle on five dimensions: family types, family resources, family stress and changes, family coping, and family satisfaction.

Scanzoni, John; Polonko, Karen; Teachman, Jay; and Thompson, Linda. *The Sexual Bond: Rethinking Families and Close Relationships*. Newbury Park, CA: Sage, 1989. A stimulating and innovative process approach to examining close, primary, sexually based relationships that extend beyond marriage and family to characterize the reality of relationships in the United States today.

Schwartz, Pepper. *Peer Marriage: How Love Between Equals Really Works.* New York: The Free Press, 1994. In-depth interviews with egalitarian marriages reveals how true equality is possible but only by a radical departure from traditional marriage patterns.

Ucko, Lenora Greenbaum. *Endangered Spouses: The Legacy of Marital Inequality.* Lanham, MD: University Press of America, 1995. Folk stories are used to focus graphically on the interaction of wives and husbands as they illustrate the central issues of family life.

Veroff, Joseph; Douvan, Elizabeth; and Hatchett, Shirley J. *Marital Instability: A Social and Behavioral Study of the Early Years.* Westport, CT: Praeger, 1995. A study of the major factors that make for commitment, stability, and happiness in married couples over the first four years.

WEBLINKS

http://www.ryerson.ca/family-soc/cas-coh1.htm

This link offers information concerning co-habitation by way of recent case studies.

http://www.utexas.edu/courses/pair/CaseStudy/ED.html

This web page contains good information on sex and marital satisfaction.

http://www.familydiscussions.com/books/illouz.htm

Eva Illouz discusses how love has been affected by the cultural contradictions of capitalism and how romantic love has become part of the large culture industry of "techno-capitalism," in which information and the media are central.

NOTES

1. Robert H. Coombs, "Marital Status and Personal Well-Being: A Literature Review," *Family Relations* 40 (January 1991): 97–102. See also Walter R. Gove, Carolyn Briggs Style, and Michael Hughes, "The Effect of Marriage on the Well-Being of Adults," *Journal of Family Issues* 11 (March 1990): 4–35.
2. Beth A. Hahn, "Marital Status and Women's Health: The Effect of Economic Marital Acquisitions," *Journal of Marriage and the Family* 55 (May 1993): 495–504.
3. Richard G. Rogers, "Marriage, Sex, and Mortality," *Journal of Marriage and the Family* 57 (May 1995): 515–526.
4. Floris W. Wood, ed., *An American Profile—Opinions and Behavior, 1972–1989* (Detroit: Gale Research, 1990): 239.
5. Norval D. Glenn, "The Recent Trend in Marital Success in the United States," *Journal of Marriage and the Family* 53 (May 1991): 261–270; and Norval D. Glenn and Charles N. Weaver, "The Changing Relationship of Marital Status to Reported Happiness," *Journal of Marriage and the Family* 50 (May 1988): 317–324.
6. Scott J. South, "Sex Ratios, Economic Power, and Women's Roles: A Theoretical Extension and Empirical Test," *Journal of Marriage and the Family* 50 (February 1988): 19–31.
7. Jillian Oderkirk, "Marriage in Canada: Changing Beliefs and Behaviours, 1600–1990," *Canadian Social Trends,* Statistics Canada Catalogue 11-008E (Summer 1994): 2–7.
8. Alain Bélanger, *Report on the Demographic Situation in Canada, 1998–1999,* Statistics Canada Catalogue 91-209-XPE, 1999: 31.
9. Ibid.
10. Statistics Canada, "1996 Census: Marital Status, Common-law Unions and Families," *The Daily* (October 14, 1997).
11. Oderkirk, 2–7.
12. Elizabeth Thompson and Ugo Colella, "Cohabitation and Marital Stability: Quality or Commitment?" *Journal of Marriage and the Family* 54 (May 1992): 259–267. Note also Alfred DeMaris and K. Vaninadha Rao, "Premarital Cohabitation and Subsequent Marital Stability in the United States: A Reassessment," *Journal of Marriage and the Family* 54 (February 1992): 178–190; and Jay D. Teachman, Jeffrey Thomas, and Kathleen Paasch, "Legal Status and the Stability of Coresidential Unions," *Demography* 28 (November 1991): 571–586.
13. Alan Booth and David Johnson, "Premarital Cohabitation and Marital Success," *Journal of Family Issues* 9 (June 1988): 255–272.
14. Neal G. Bennett, Ann Klimas Blanc, and David E. Bloom, "Commitment and the Modern Union: Assessing the Link Between Premarital Cohabitation and Subsequent Marital Stability," *American Sociological Review* 53 (February 1988): 127–138.
15. Robert Schoen, "First Unions and the Stability of First Marriages," *Journal of Marriage and the Family* 54 (May 1990): 281–284.
16. Thompson and Colella, "Cohabitation and Marital Stability," 259–260.
17. Statistics Canada, "1996 Census: Marital Status, Common-law Unions and Families," *The Daily* (October 14, 1997).
18. Jean Dumas and Yves Peron, *Marriage and Conjugal Life in Canada*, Statistics Canada Catalogue 91-534E (March 1992): 78–82.
19. David D. Gilmore, "Men and Women in Southern Spain: 'Domestic Power' Revisited," *American Anthropologist* 92 (December 1990): 953–970.
20. Mary F. Rogers, "Instrumental and Infra-Resources: The Base of Power," *American Journal of Sociology* 79 (May 1974): 1418–1433.
21. Ibid., 1425.
22. Rebecca L. Warner, Gary R. Lee, and Janet Lee,"Social Organization, Spousal Resources, and Marital Power: A Cross-Cultural Study," *Journal of Marriage and the Family* 48 (February 1986): 121–128.
23. Robert O. Blood, Jr., and Donald M. Wolfe, *Husbands and Wives: The Dynamics of Marital Living* (Glencoe, IL: Free Press, 1960).
24. Hyman Rodman, "Marital Power in France, Greece, Yugoslavia, and the United States: A Cross-National Discussion," *Journal of Marriage and the Family* 29 (May 1967): 320–324; Hyman Rodman, "Marital Power and the Theory of Resources in Cultural Context," *Journal of Comparative Family Studies* 3 (Spring 1972): 50–69.
25. Janice M. Steil and Karen Weltman, "Marital Inequality: The Importance of Resources, Personal Attributes, and Social Norms on Career Valuing and the Allocation of Domestic Responsibilities," *Sex Roles* 24 (1991): 161–179.
26. Mark R. Rank, "Determinants of Conjugal Influence in Wives' Employment Decision Making," *Journal of Marriage and the Family* 44 (August 1982): 591–604.
27. Karen D. Pyke, "Women's Employment as a Gift or Burden? Marital Power Across Marriage, Divorce, and Remarriage," *Gender and Society* 8 (March 1994): 73–91.
28. Paul R. Amato and Alan Booth, "Changes in Gender Role Attitudes and Perceived Marital Quality," *American Sociological Review* 60 (February 1995): 58–66.
29. Karen R. Blaisure and Katherine R. Allen, "Feminists and the Ideology and Practice of Marital Equality," *Journal of Marriage and the Family* 57 (February 1995): 5–19.

30. Dana Vannoy-Hiller and William W. Philliber, *Equal Partners: Successful Women in Marriage* (Newbury Park, CA: Sage, 1989): 143.

31. Steil and Weltman, 161–179.

32. Catherine E. Ross, "Reconceptualizing Marital Status as a Continuum of Social Attachment," *Journal of Marriage and the Family* 57 (February 1995): 129–140.

33. See Norval D. Glenn, "Quantitative Research on Marital Quality in the 1980s: A Critical Review," *Journal of Marriage and the Family* 52 (November 1990): 818–831.

34. Susan E. Crohan and Joseph Veroff, "Dimensions of Marital Well-Being Among White and Black Newlyweds," *Journal of Marriage and the Family* 51 (May 1989): 373–383.

35. Catherine E. Ross, "Marriage and the Sense of Control," *Journal of Marriage and the Family* 53 (November 1991): 831–838.

36. Jessie Bernard, "The Adjustment of Married Mates," in Harold T. Christensen, ed., *Handbook of Marriage and the Family* (Chicago: Rand McNally, 1964): 690.

37. Patricia Noller and Mary Anne Fitzpatrick, "Marital Communication in the Eighties," *Journal of Marriage and the Family* 52 (November 1990): 832–843; and W. Kim Halford, Kurt Hahlweg, and Michael Dunne, "The Cross-Cultural Consistency of Marital Communication Associated with Marital Distress," *Journal of Marriage and the Family* 52 (May 1990): 487–500.

38. David R. Johnson, Teodora O. Amoloza, and Alan Booth, "Stability and Development Change in Marital Quality: A Three-Wave Panel Analysis," *Journal of Marriage and the Family* 54 (August 1992): 582–594.

39. Graham B. Spanier, "Measuring Dyadic Adjustment: New Scales for Assessing the Quality of Marriage and Similar Dyads," *Journal of Marriage and the Family* 38 (February 1976): 15–28; and Graham B. Spanier and Linda Thompson, "A Confirmatory Analysis of the Dyadic Adjustment Scale," *Journal of Marriage and the Family* 44 (August 1982): 731–738.

40. Susan S. Hendrick, "A Generic Measure of Relationship Satisfaction," *Journal of Marriage and the Family* 50 (February 1988): 93–98.

41. Bernard, 732.

42. Ibid., 732–733.

43. J. Richard Udry, "Marital Alternatives and Marital Disruption," *Journal of Marriage and the Family* 43 (November 1981): 889–897.

44. Tim B. Heaton and Stan L. Albrecht, "Stable Unhappy Marriages," *Journal of Marriage and the Family* 53 (August 1991): 747–758.

45. John Scanzoni, *Sexual Bargaining: Power Politics in the American Marriage*, 2nd ed. (Chicago: University of Chicago Press, 1982): 61–102. Note also Suzanne M. Retzinger, *Violent Emotions: Shame and Rage in Marital Quarrels* (Newbury Park, CA: Sage, 1991).

46. Jeffrey K. Liker and Glen H. Elder, Jr., "Economic Hardship and Marital Relations in the 1930s," *American Sociological Review* 48 (June 1983): 343–359.

47. David R. Johnson and Alan Booth, "Rural Economic Decline and Marital Quality: A Panel Study of Farm Marriages," *Family Relations* 39 (April 1990): 159–165.

48. Stacy J. Rogers and Paul R. Amato, "Is Marital Quality Declining? The Evidence from Two Generations," *Social Forces* 75 (March 1997): 1089–1100.

49. J. Jill Suitor, "Marital Quality and Satisfaction with the Division of Household Labor Across the Life Cycle," *Journal of Marriage and the Family* 53 (February 1991): 221–230.

50. Sylvia Weishaus and Dorothy Field, "A Half Century of Marriage: Continuity or Change?" *Journal of Marriage and the Family* 50 (August 1988): 763–774.

51. These six types were classified as stable/positive (five couples), stable/neutral (three couples), stable/negative (two couples), curvilinear (seven couples), continuous decline (no couples), and continuous increase (no couples).

52. David H. Olson, Hamilton I. McCubbin, and associates, *Families: What Makes Them Work* (Beverly Hills: Sage, 1983).

53. David M. Lawson, "Love Attitude and Marital Adjustment in the Family Life Cycle," *Sociological Spectrum* 8 (1988): 391–406. Canadian data, as well, show a curvilinear relationship. See Eugene Lupri and James Frideres, "The Quality of Marriage and the Passage of Time: Marital Satisfaction over the Family Life Cycle," *Canadian Journal of Sociology* 6 (1981): 283–305.

54. Russell A. Ward, "Marital Happiness and Household Equity in Later Life," *Journal of Marriage and the Family* 55 (May 1993): 427–438.

55. Norval D. Glenn and Sara McLanahan, "Children and Marital Happiness: A Further Specification of the Relationship," *Journal of Marriage and the Family* 44 (February 1982): 63–72.

56. Pamela M. Wallace and Ian H. Gotlib, "Marital Adjustment During the Transition to Parenthood: Stability and Predictors of Change," *Journal of Marriage and the Family* 52 (February 1990): 21–29.

57. Olson, McCubbin, and associates, *Families: What Makes Them Work.*

CHAPTER

7 BECOMING PARENTS

The parental system centres on the relationships between parents and children. All societies have norms that frame this relationship. Some parent/child norms are nearly universal; others are unique to a particular society or subculture. For example, no society is known to place the primary responsibility for childrearing on men, and no society is known in which the young children are customarily dominant over the parents.

Wide variations occur from one society to another in family size, methods of childrearing, extended family sharing in child-related tasks, births to unmarried women, and the like. On the other hand, certain similarities exist across cultures in the norms and consequences of particular structural patterns within the parental system. Research in a number of Western countries has found consistent patterns in parenting related to class background. First-born children differ from other children in a wide variety of personal characteristics.

The parental system and selected structural patterns are the focus of description and analysis in this chapter. The next chapter, while dealing with some organizational characteristics, will focus more on interactional and social/psychological dimensions of the parent/child relationship.

NEWS ITEM

Traditional versus nontraditional family values

A Baptist church in Arkansas has closed its day-care centre, saying working mothers neglect their children, damage their marriages and set a bad example. A letter from the First Baptist Church of Berryville told parents that families could get by on one salary if they went without such luxuries as "big TVs, a microwave, new clothes, eating out and nice vacations." The closing—and the letter—infuriated parents left without a place to take their children in Berryville, a small town about 250 kilometres northwest of Little Rock.

Source: The Globe and Mail, April 5, 1997, A14.

PARENTHOOD AND SOCIAL CHANGE

Parenthood is influenced by social norms which are in turn formalized by public policy. Political perceptions of social values influence public policy, and it is policy which creates the framework for childrearing. In Canada, and perhaps more dramatically in the United States, some politicians, religious leaders, and journalists argue that the quality of parent/child relationships is at an all-time low. Divorce, single-parenthood, maternal employment, and a general erosion of parental support have been cited as *causes* for increases in children's delinquency, alcohol and drug use, sexual activity, and other negative outcomes.

This book, among others, has documented that many profound changes have taken place for both parents and children over the past 50 years. But David Demo, in assessing recent changes, has argued that the consequences of maternal employment, divorce, and single-parent family structure have been greatly exaggerated.[1] He has pointed to persuasive evidence that factors such as single-parenthood cannot be equated with lack of parental commitment or as *causes* of distress and maladjustment in children. In spite of widespread parent/child conflict, delinquency, unwed parenthood, drug use, and so forth, most parents are deeply concerned about their children's welfare. In addition, adolescents generally report close and satisfying relationships with parents to whom they routinely turn for advice and guidance on important decisions.

In most countries, married couples in general and women in particular face considerable social pressures to become parents. In industrialized countries, these cultural and social pressures seem to have decreased over recent years, as evidenced in the delay in first pregnancies, the increased ability to control conceptions and births, the decline in birth rates, the movement of increasing numbers of women into the paid labour force, and the emphasis on smaller families.

In spite of unplanned pregnancies, a decreasing birth rate, a decrease in the average family size, and an increase in childless marriages (all discussed later in this chapter), women continue to want and to have children voluntarily, and children are highly valued. Cross-culturally, the values of having children include attaining adult status and social identity, attaining immortality by "carrying on the family name," and satisfying a desire for love, primary-group ties, and feeling part of a family group. Children satisfy certain needs for individuals and couples and, as functionalists would have it, fulfill basic functions for society.

While children are significant to men and women around the world, the number of children and their value is changing. One explanation of these changes is based on an uncertainty reduction theory of parenthood.[2] The assumption of this theory states that throughout the world, people seek to reduce uncertainty. Children are of value in providing security (increasing certainty) when parents face divorce, widowhood, and financial insecurity. In many developing countries it is desirable to produce as many sons as possible to pass on the family name and provide assistance in old age. In more developed countries, fewer children (but some children) are needed to fulfill these uncertainties. The number of wanted children could continue to diminish but not to zero.

Most young Canadian men and women expect to become parents.[3] The 1995 General Social Survey asked the following question of Canadians: "What is the total number of children you intend to have, including those you have now and are currently expecting?" Nearly half of Canadians aged 20–39 expected to have two children, and one-quarter expected to have three or more. Canadians who were married or expected to marry expected more children, but men and women who expected to remain single also expected to have at least one child.[4]

Transition to parenthood

According to family development theorists, becoming a parent is one of the most significant family life-course transitions. Many would not consider a person or couple a *family* until they have children. Others consider parenthood to be the final recognition of reaching adulthood.

What must couples learn and what readjustments must they make to move smoothly from a childless state to parenthood? What is involved in the transition to parenthood? What is the effect of parenthood on the adult? What distinct roles and responsibilities do fathers and mothers have toward infants and young children?

There is little doubt that when a dyad (two persons, such as a couple) becomes a triad (parents and child) or when a single person becomes a parent, a major structural shift takes place. As noted in the last chapter, marital satisfaction tends to decrease after the birth of children through the preschool and school years until the children are getting ready to leave home.

Ralph LaRossa found that when parents were asked how their lives changed after their babies were born (rather than asked whether they were bothered or gratified), the one consistent response was *time*.[5] Both parents reported that sleep time, television time, communication time, sex time, and even bathroom time were in short supply as the result of having a child. Many of the difficulties in making the transition to parenthood may be resolved by adjusting to the additional time it takes to do all the tasks associated with children.

Changing motherhood; changing fatherhood

In every culture of the world, women are the primary caretakers of children. For many people, parenting and motherhood are synonymous. Indeed, parenting is often called *mothering* because of the assumption that the birth of, the nurturing of, and the primary responsibility for rearing children belongs to women. In the past in North America, fatherhood was synonymous with being the economic provider.

Were fathers in the past less involved in parenting than fathers today? What about fathers in non-Western countries? Data from 90 nonindustrialized societies indicated that, in many, men assumed substantial responsibility for childrearing, with a majority classified as having close father/child relationships. Societies with high levels of father/child proximity enhance the public status of women, giving them more participation in public decision-making and access to positions of authority.[6]

In earlier chapters, we documented important changes in women's lives that have had an impact on their roles as mothers. The most significant change has been the employment of mothers of young children. It is reasonable to assume that, as women take on increased responsibilities as paid workers, men will assume more domestic and child-care responsibilities. Indeed, we seem to have adopted a popular view of fathers as involved parents who are constrained by work schedules rather than traditional attitudes. Fathers are now present at the birth of their children and active in their care. However, as was clear in Chapter 3, while many men "help" with household chores and childcare, few families come close to an equitable division of labour. On the other hand, as you learned in Chapter 4, an increased number of fathers have sole or joint custody of their children. Over the last 30 years, as increased numbers of women have entered and remained in the paid labour force, maternal roles have changed dramatically. Paternal roles have changed too, but less significantly. Clearly there is a gap between cultural definitions of paternal nurturance and practice.

Studies of fathers indicate that fathers are important figures in the lives of children and young adults.[7] Closeness of children to fathers has been found to make a significant contribution to offspring happiness, life satisfaction, psychological well-being, intellectual development, and educational and occupational mobility. Likewise, the important role that fathers play in the lives of children is demonstrated in studies of father absence, showing lower levels of academic achievement, a heightened risk of delinquency and deviant behaviour, and a greater likelihood of dropping out of school.

Parents' roles

One report, using an international perspective, suggests that parenting is becoming more difficult around the world. Social changes such as high unemployment and poverty; high rates of divorce and single-parenting; parents and children sharing fewer activities and engaging in less face-to-face interaction; more emphasis on children's independence and autonomy accompanied by less tolerance of parental supervision; and the loss of traditional family structures and value conformity all contribute to difficulties in parenting.[8]

Nevertheless, a wealth of data exists showing that parenting patterns and disciplinary practices of parents continue to make a difference in children's behaviour. Take the use of tobacco by young adolescents, for example. Parents of seventh-graders were interviewed about parenting practices that were either harsh and inconsistent or nurturant and involved.[9]

Harsh/inconsistent parenting practices included interacting with the adolescent in an angry, irritable way; inconsistent discipline in response to rule violations; and punitive discipline, such as yelling, threatening, and physical punishment. Nurturant/involved parenting practices included interacting with the adolescent in an affectionate and responsive manner; using praise, approval, and special privileges when a good job was done; and setting standards and encouraging adolescent input regarding the reasons for rules and expectations.

As their model of social development predicted, harsh/inconsistent parenting behaviours were found to be directly related to adolescent tobacco use, while nurturant/involved parenting behaviours were related to a lower level of adolescent tobacco use. In addition, nurturant/involved parenting reduced the risk of children associating with peers who model or encourage substance use.

Other research shows that parental roles and the quality of parenting are influenced by many factors, including marital satisfaction, the emotional well-being of parents, parental satisfaction with children's behaviour, the parents' own exposure to harsh parenting during childhood, economic resources, social support from grandparents, and so forth.[10] Parenting roles and disciplinary practices, assumed under the topic of parent-child interaction and socialization, are addressed more comprehensively in the next chapter.

There are important differences in the impact of parenthood on the lives of mothers versus fathers. For example, it changes the employment patterns of women. The majority of ever-married women have jobs before pregnancy, but most experience job interruptions because of childrearing responsibilities. A recent analysis of Canadian employment patterns found that over half of women who have ever worked have experienced work stoppages for one year or more.[11] Women are three times more likely than men to experience lengthy work stoppages. For many women the consequences are long-term. Many reenter the labour force as part-time employees. Thus, one major social consequence of parenthood in Canada is the withdrawal of women from employment.

Another consequence of parenthood, at least in the short run, relates to marital stability. In Chapter 6, data were presented that showed how marital satisfaction drops with the presence of children; data will be presented later in this chapter that show how couples without children have higher levels of marital adjustment than couples with children. Nonetheless, studies from both New Zealand and the United States have shown strong, positive effects of the first birth and preschool children on the marital stability of young adults. It was estimated that, by the time the first child reached age two, more than 20 percent of the parents would have been divorced or separated if the child had not been born compared to actual disruption rates of 5 to 8 percent.[12] The presence of preschool children in the family acts as a protective factor that reduces risk of family breakdown.

Lynn White and Alan Booth referred to this factor as the **braking hypothesis.** They suggested that, although having children does not prevent divorce, doing so may cause couples to approach the divorce decision more slowly.[13] These researchers also found that new parents were significantly less likely to divorce over a three-year period than those who remained childless, again in contrast to the persistent negative correlation between the presence of children and marital happiness. The explanation for these seemingly inconsistent findings was not that persons in more stable marriages have children (a selectivity argument) and was only partially based on the argument that a new baby causes major negative changes in marital structure. Rather, White and Booth focused on a differential propensity to divorce. Childless couples, they suggested, give greater selectivity to marital happiness than parents. The result is a greater willingness of childless couples to divorce when unhappy.

Whatever the reason, fewer divorces seem to occur among couples with very young children. Studies reported in Chapter 11 will indicate how older children do not provide the same deterrent to divorce.

It is unlikely that prospective parents weigh all of these impacts into the decision to have a child. For a complex variety of reasons, both personal and social, most couples want, have, or expect to have children. But couples marry later than they did in the past and have fewer children later in marriage. More children are born to single women. In the following section we will look at these trends, and describe some implications of them.

FERTILITY

Birth rates and family size

In 1997 there were 348 598 babies born in Canada and the birth rate was 11.6.[14] The average number of children born per woman of childbearing age has been below two since the early 1970s. An average of two births per woman is referred to as the replacement value. When the average number of births per woman is below replacement, the size of the population cannot be maintained without immigration. Currently the average number of births per Canadian woman is 1.55.[15] Birth rates are one of the best documented series of descriptive social data available today. Census data show long-term declines in the birth rate beginning in the late nineteenth century, interrupted only by the baby boom of the 1950s and 1960s (see Figure 7.1). The late 1980s saw a "baby boomlet," in part due to births among older persons or couples who delayed childbearing. Figure 7.1 shows fertility by age of mother since 1951.

The long-term declines in fertility are due to smaller average family size and delayed births. Figures 7.1 and 7.2 both show the trend to delayed child-bearing. Figure 7.1 shows the fertility of women in their early thirties is *greater than* that of women in their early twenties.

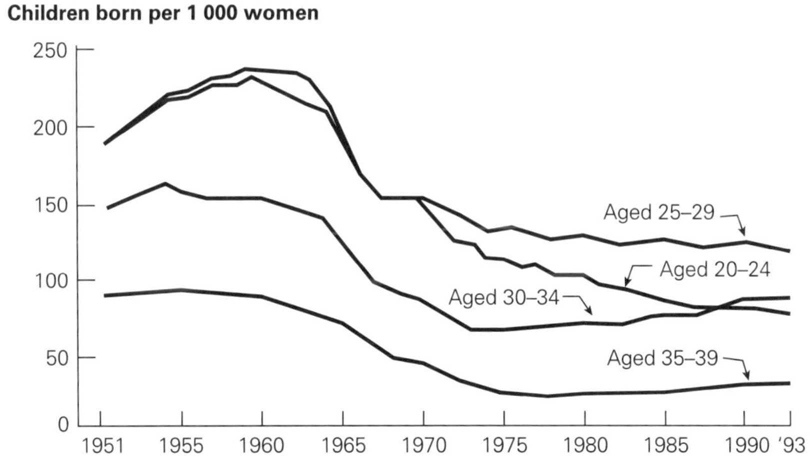

Figure 7.1
Fertility of women by age group, 1951–93
Sources: DATA: Statistics Canada Catalogues 82-553 and 84-210. GRAPH: Carl Grindstaff, "Canadian Fertility, 1951 to 1993," *Canadian Social Trends* (Winter 1995): 13.

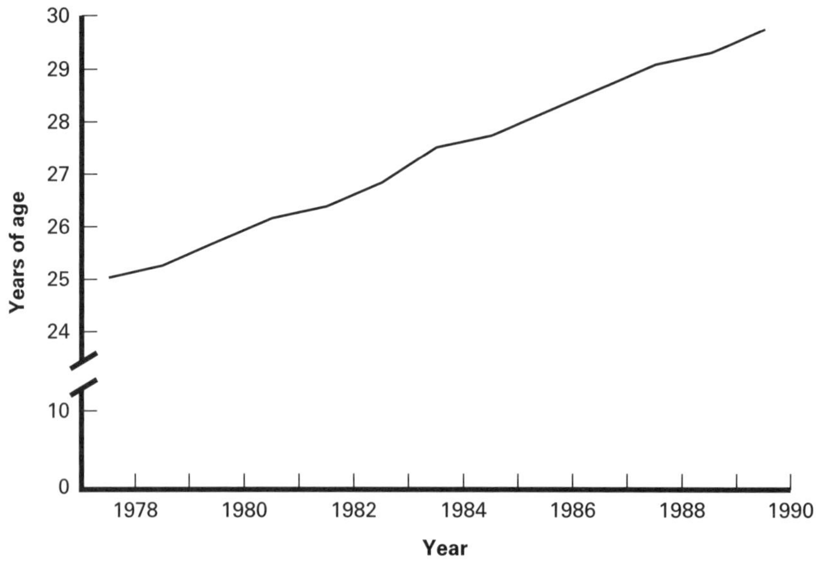

Figure 7.2
Average age of mothers at birth of first child, 1978–90
Source: A Portrait of Families in Canada, Statistics Canada Catalogue 89-523E (November 1993): 14.

Since the 1960s, improved methods of birth control, liberalized abortion laws, and increased acceptance of birth planning by Catholics have enabled women to delay first births. Women who delay childbearing have fewer children and are significantly better off economically than average-age childbearers. And by retirement age, the delayed childbearer with only one or two children appears better off than all other women.[16] The average age of first child in Canada has increased steadily over the last decade, reaching 27.1 years in 1996.[17]

Beginning in the mid-1960s, the number of large (three or more children) families declined sharply. In 1966, 28 percent of Canadian families had three or more children. By 1986, this figure had dropped to 10 percent. The average number of live births per woman in a lifetime was 1.71 in 1990 and 1.59 in 1999.[18] Some families may be smaller than they would wish to be under ideal circumstances. Canadian Gallup reports found that 59 percent of Canadians in 1991 thought the ideal number of children is two or less, while the other 41 percent say three or more. These figures represent a big change in attitude toward children since the 1950s when almost 80 percent of Canadians said the ideal number of children was three or more.[19]

What do demographers and journalists mean when they talk about the "baby boom"? Simply stated, the **baby boom** was a post–Second World War occurrence that upset what had been a century-long decline in fertility rate. The baby boom was an unanticipated, pronounced, and consequential rise in the

FAMILY DIVERSITY

Canadians would ban sale of sperm and eggs

As reproductive technologies increasingly bring the possibility of childbirth to an increased number of women, the need to regulate also increases. The *Report of the Federal Commission on Reproductive Technologies* recommended a ban on the sale of both sperm and eggs. Most Canadians agreed with this position.

An August 1996 Gallup poll asked Canadians the following two questions:

- Do you personally think that women should be legally able to sell their reproductive eggs for money?
- Do you personally think that men should be legally able to sell their sperm for money?

Sixty-six percent of Canadians said no to the first question and 65 percent said no to the second. Younger Canadians are more supportive of the right to sell eggs and sperm, as are Canadians with higher education. Females are more likely to oppose the sale of eggs or sperm.

These results are based on telephone interviews with a random sample of Canadians and are accurate within a 3.1 percentage point margin of error, 19 times out of 20.

Source: Canadian Gallup Poll, August 20, 1996.

birth rate. Theories as to its cause include increases in normative pressure on women to have children, the disruption and dislocation brought about by the war, the postwar economic prosperity, and the long-term psychological effects of growing up during the Depression.

This postwar spurt in annual births did not represent a return to the large families of the nineteenth century. Rather, the boom was a movement away from singlehood, childless marriage, and one-child families, and a bunching together of births. Only a minor part of the baby boom can be attributed to an increase in the number of families having three or more births.[20]

There are demographic consequences of delayed childbearing: fewer children but children who are better off economically, and a longer time between generations. The long-term consequence is a decrease in population growth; the short-term consequence is an upturn in growth. In North America, increases in birth rates have been substantial in the baby-boom cohort of women now aged 35 to 50 who have delayed having children. This trend offsets that of the cohort of older women who had their children when they were younger and were part of the high-fertility and earlier timing patterns of the 1950s and 1960s.

Related to the delay in first births is the spacing of births. Patterns of **child spacing** have not received the research attention given to number of births and family size, but this is an important issue for consideration. Particular child-spacing factors will probably influence the labour force participation and education of women as well as the health of the child. For example, low birth weight, a condition strongly associated with morbidity (sickness and disease) and mortality (death) among infants, is highest among children born very shortly after the end of their mothers' last pregnancies. In countries such as Bangladesh and the Philippines, for example, it was demonstrated that children who were born within 15 months of a preceding child were 60 to 80 percent more likely than other children to die in the first two years of life.[21]

Younger women experience longer birth intervals than older women.[22] While both groups of women are likely to have second births, the interval between births is longer for younger women. One study has found that group differences in spacing of births have decreased. That is, groups that in the past were most likely to have short intervals (those with less education, and those who married young and began childbearing early) are now much like others. Researchers suggested that these reductions in short birth intervals are the result of an increase in effective contraceptive use among women in these groups and a reduction in birth-timing failures. As fertility in Canada remains low, this pattern will likely become more uniform throughout the population.

A number of additional variables affect marital fertility including socio-economic status, multiple marriages, religion, race/ethnicity, education, urbanization, female income, child-care arrangements, age at marriage, age at first birth, interval since last birth, age of women, and others.[23] Even the size of the family of origin (number of brothers and sisters) appears to influence marital fertility. And, of course, many couples make a conscious choice to have no children or, for some reason, fail to have them. The next section will look at childless marriages and the final section will analyze patterns of unmarried childbirth.

Childless marriages

In the past, many people believed in a "maternal instinct" and assumed that all women wanted children and would instinctively love and care for their offspring. Thinking has changed and a great deal of evidence dispells these notions. All women do not want children, nor are all mothers compelled to care for the children they bear. Some women will choose to remain childless and some will be childless because of circumstances or an inability to conceive.

Among ever-married women in Canada, 13 percent of those 35 to 39 years old had never given birth. This figure was 7 percent in 1971 and 9 percent in 1981.[24] Some of these women may have children in their forties, however.

There is little doubt that children make enormous demands on parents in terms of emotional and financial costs. Yet most married couples want and have children, either voluntarily or involuntarily. As shown in Figure 7.3, few Canadians want to remain childless or expect to have only one child.

For whatever reason, actual childless rates are low. Among those people who can have children, temporary childlessness or delayed childbearing is more likely than permanent childlessness. In Western countries about 10 percent of women are expected to remain childless. The most important demographic predictors of childlessness were found to be:

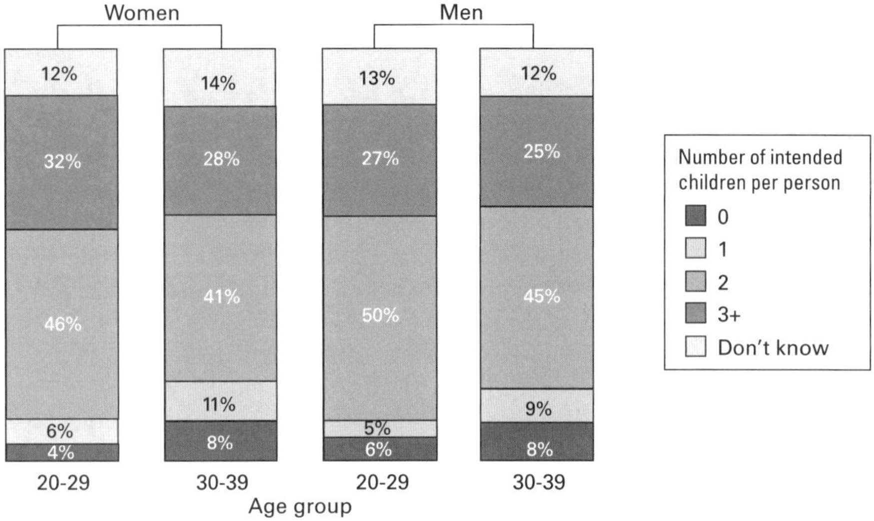

Figure 7.3
Childbearing intentions of Canadian men and women, 1995
Sources: Statistics Canada, 1995 General Social Survey; Dave Dupuis, "What Influences People's Plans to Have Children?" *Canadian Social Trends* (Spring 1998), Statistics Canada Catalogue 11-008-XPE: 2–5.

- *Fecundity*—Some people are unable to have children.
- *Marital status*—Never-married people are more likely to be childless than people who are or have been married.
- *Age*—As people grow older, they are less likely to have children.
- *Labour force participation*—People who are working or temporarily unemployed are less likely to have children.
- *Education*—The higher the level of education attained, the greater the likelihood of childlessness.

Voluntarily childless women, married or single, rate the costs of having a child higher and the satisfactions lower than other groups of women (such as mothers or those who desire to become mothers).[25] Victor Callan found that educated professional women, who had lived and enjoyed an adult-centred life, gave high ratings to the restrictions and disruptions of children and to general life-style costs, and low ratings to the emotional satisfaction and personal fulfillment a child might give them. These women also felt that their current life-style choices—especially their careers—did meet such needs.

If parenthood seems to interfere with personal happiness and freedoms, it seems to interfere with marriage and family life as well. As has been noted in several chapters, children impose a strain on marriage. Does this suggest that couples without children have higher levels of health and marital adjustment and satisfaction than do couples with children?

Apparently, it does. When voluntarily childless wives, undecided wives, and postponing wives were compared with mothers, the results from one study were that all three groups had higher mean levels of marital satisfaction than did the mothers.[26] Most available evidence shows that the consequences of voluntary childlessness to persons or marriages is more positive than negative.

Is this satisfaction true among **involuntarily childless women** too? In other words, what about women or couples who want children but can't have them? Infertility has been estimated to affect approximately 15 percent, or one in seven couples, in the United States and Canada. Studies of infertile couples with a desire for children have revealed high levels of stress.[27] Infertility is a major negative life event that has deleterious effects on both women's and men's well-being. Infertility would seem to be especially relevant for sexual and marriage issues, but its strongest impact may be on global well-being. That is, frustrations over infertility spill over into other domains, including work, finances, and social life, producing strained relationships with co-workers, friends, and family.

It would appear that, for couples of childbearing age, the choice to have or not to have children, and the ability to carry out that choice may be one of the most significant factors in the satisfaction or dissatisfaction that results from being childless. In other words, there is a big difference between being able to have children but choosing not to, and wanting to have children but not being able to. People who remain childless by choice are more likely to be satisfied with that result than are people who remain childless by fate.

What about older persons who, either by choice or necessity, have no children? One Canadian study of childless respondents aged 55 and over found the primary reason for childlessness among never-married individuals was the fact that they were single. The central reasons for childlessness among the ever-married were physiological factors, age and fate.[28] As might be expected, the reasons for childlessness varied within both never-married and ever-married, depending on whether this childlessness was a matter of choice or circumstance. Those childless by choice gave self-actualization (didn't have time, wanted to work or travel) and altruism or idealism (didn't want my children to be like me—gay; the world is too crowded; and the like as reasons).

The reproductive technologies available today can decrease the number of people who are involuntarily childless. Until recently, adoption was the only alternative for women and couples who were involuntarily childless and wanted to have a child. But the decline in the availability of infants for adoption has led many infertile women to seek alternative solutions, such as artificial insemination with the sperm of the husband (AIH); artificial insemination with the sperm of an anonymous donor (AID); in vitro fertilization, where an artificial environment outside the living organism is used; and surrogate motherhood, in which another woman is used to conceive, carry, and give birth to a child. These alternative methods of reproduction have led to heated debates over their social, legal, and moral implications.

Births outside marriage

Although birth rates in general are declining or levelling off, births to unmarried women have increased. In 1996, 30.9 percent[29] of Canadian babies were born to unmarried women. The figures were 9 percent in 1971 and 14 percent in 1981.[30] Indeed, the proportion of births to unmarried women has increased almost continuously since 1921, when it was only 2 percent. Figure 7.4 shows the increase in births to unmarried women in Canada since 1961, and Figure 7.5 shows the changes in the age of the mothers.

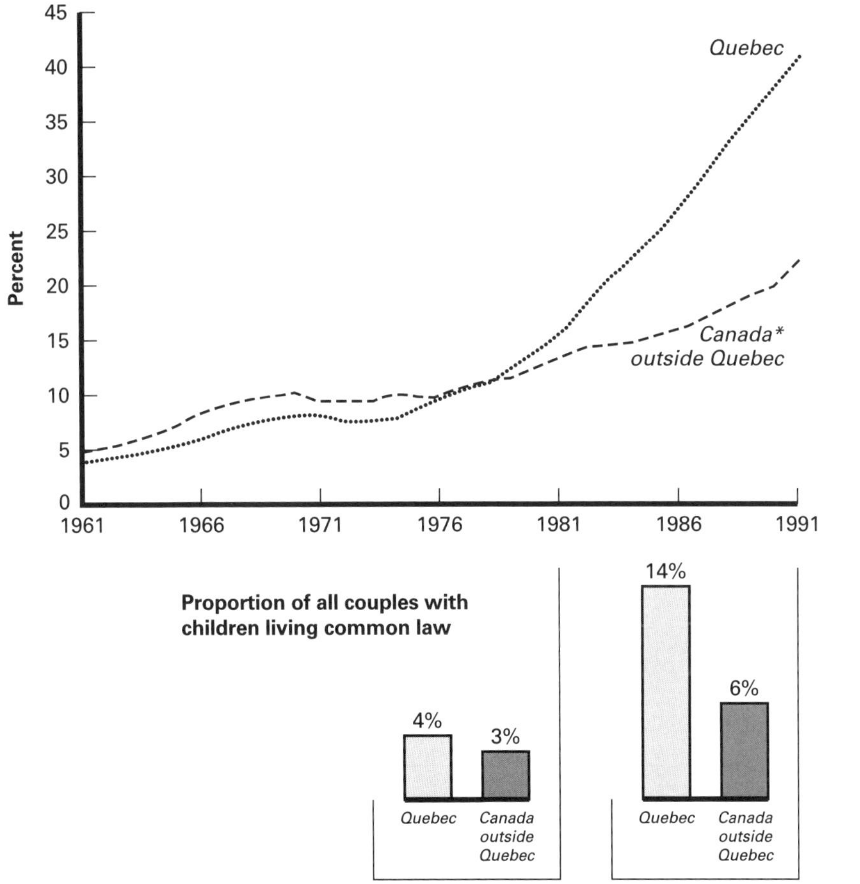

Figure 7.4
Proportion of births to unmarried women, 1961–91
*Excludes Newfoundland.
Source: Marilyn Belle and Kevin McQuillan, "Births Outside Marriage: A Growing Alternative," *Canadian Social Trends,* Statistics Canada Catalogue 11-008E (Spring 1994): 14–17.

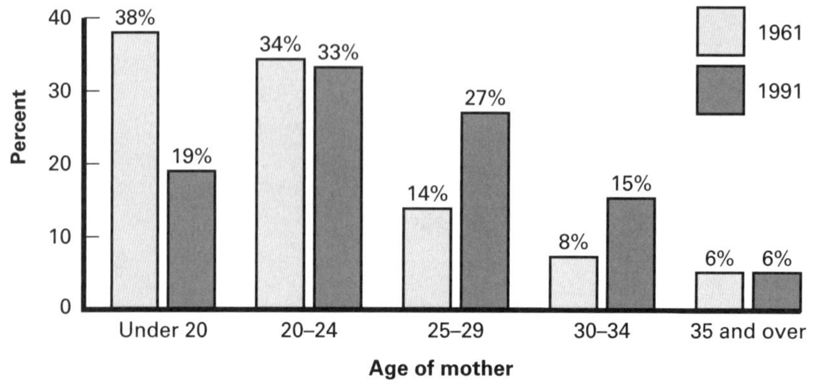

Figure 7.5
Proportion of births to unmarried women, by age of mother, 1961–91*
*Excludes Newfoundland.
Source: Marilyn Belle and Kevin McQuillan, "Births Outside Marriage: A Growing Alternative," *Canadian Social Trends,* Statistics Canada Catalogue 11-008E (Spring 1994): 14–17.

Unwed-parenthood is no longer most prevalent among teenagers. More than half of all unmarried mothers now are 25 or over, as against 30 percent in 1961.[31] The fact that unmarried childbirth is increasingly common among older women, rather than a primarily adolescent phenomenon, suggests that choice may play a stronger role. Furthermore, many unmarried mothers may be in cohabiting relationships. That unmarried births are highest in Quebec where cohabitation is far more common than in the rest of the country suggests that this is probably the case. Although adolescent premarital pregnancy is far less common in Canada than in the United States (see the discussion below), Canadians are concerned. A recent Gallup poll found that 90 percent of Canadians believe that unwanted teenage pregnancies is a serious problem for this country.[32]

News Item

Italy moves to outlaw the term "stepchild"

As reported in the *Toronto Star* (September 13, 1996, B3) it will soon be illegal to use the term "stepchild" for official purposes in Italy. Registry offices will instead list all children as sons or daughters, regardless of biological relationship. It was the feeling of the Italian government that the term was discriminatory and carried too many negative connotations.

Adolescent pregnancy in Canada and the United States

Both the number and rate of adolescent pregnancy in Canada were lower in 1994 than they were in 1974. However, both have increased since 1987.[33] There has also been a change in pregnancy outcomes since 1974. As Figure 7.6 shows, now, almost as many adolescent pregnancies end in abortion as in live births.

To some extent, the contrast in teenage pregnancy rates between Canada and countries with substantially lower rates may reflect differences in the availability of educational programs and the adoption of health practices by teenagers.[34]

American adolescents have far higher rates of premarital pregnancy than young women in other Western countries. Charles Westoff found that the teenage pregnancy rates in six other Western countries—Canada, England and Wales, Finland, the Netherlands, Norway, and Sweden—ranged from only 13 to 53 percent of the U.S. rate.[35] Teenagers in the United States appeared to be no more likely than their Canadian or European contemporaries to marry or engage in intercourse, but they seemed far less likely to practise contraception.

As Westoff explained, American teenagers do not have the same access to contraceptives as adolescents in other countries, face different costs in family-planning services compared to teens from countries with national health care systems, may be greater risk-takers (even teenage auto accident rates are two to eight times as high), and may have an ambivalence toward sexuality. That

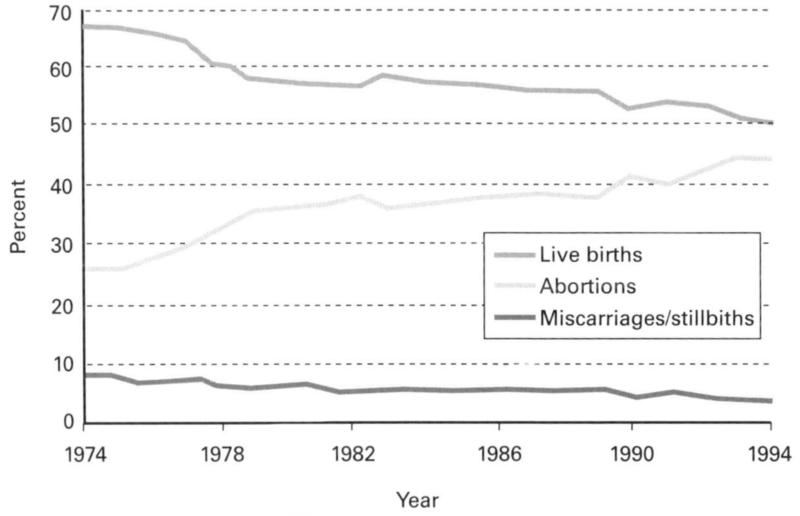

Figure 7.6
Percentage distribution of outcomes of teenage pregnancy, Canada, 1974 to 1994
Source: Health Reports (Winter 1997, Vol. 9, No. 3), Statistics Canada Catalogue 82-003-XPB: 12.

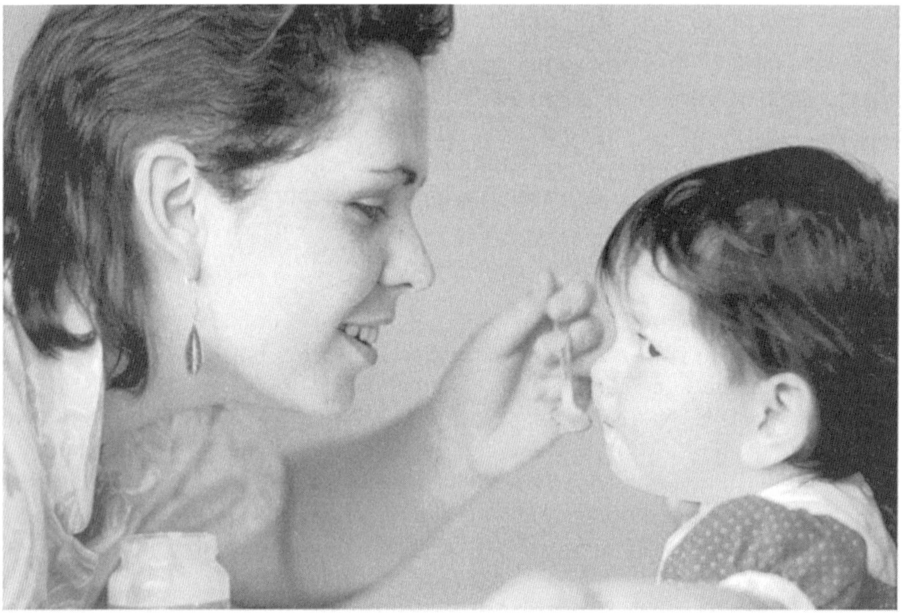

Young- and unwed-motherhood, often unplanned, presents a double-jeopardy situation. The lives of young mothers are disrupted, particularly in terms of educational and occupational/career opportunities. Many unwed mothers also face severe financial difficulties. These and other factors in the mothers' lives affect their children's lives, as well.

is, although sex saturates American television programs, movies, and advertisements, the media fail to communicate responsible attitudes about it; for the most part, birth control is a taboo subject.

Should Americans be concerned about this high incidence of adolescent pregnancy? The short answer is yes. High rates of teenage pregnancies and young-parenthood have tremendous educational, social, and economic consequences for the individuals involved and for society at large. When parenthood (and more specifically, motherhood) occurs at an early age, it is likely to have a negative effect on occupational and educational attainment, marital stability, income and asset accumulation, and the woman's health.[36] When compared to women in the 20- to 35-year age group, teenage mothers are most likely to postpone prenatal care, have children with low birth weights, and experience a higher rate of infant mortality.[37]

Now the questions "So what?" or "Who cares?" Does it really make a difference that so many births each year occur to single women? Do these children have more social, economic, and health problems than children born to married women? Is the presence of both male and female parents essential to the growth and development of a child? Does the unmarried mother face increased emotional and economic difficulties that seriously affect both her and her child?

Research evidence indicates that there are negative and long-lasting repercussions of teenage childbearing. From the moment they become aware of pregnancy, young parents have difficult decisions and adjustments to make.

What are the consequences of premarital fatherhood? Nock illustrated that never-married fathers seldom live with their children, are less likely to marry and more likely to cohabit.[38] Compared to their peers who did not father children before marriage, they were found to leave school earlier, have lower earnings, work fewer weeks per year, and be more likely to live in poverty. These factors clearly hamper young fathers' abilities to contribute financially to the support of their partners and children.

One of the consequences of increased contraceptive use, increased access to abortion, and increased numbers of single women raising their children is that the number of children available for adoption has decreased dramatically.

Adoption

Daly and Sobol have analyzed Canadian adoption statistics for the period from 1981 to 1990.[39] In 1981, 10.0 percent of infants born to unmarried women under

FAMILY DIVERSITY

Perinatal outcomes and marital status: results from Finland

Is marital status related in any way to perinatal death, low birth weight, and preterm infants? Apparently it is. The perinatal outcomes of more than 56 000 births were examined in Finland. After adjusting for the mother's age and education, the geographical area, and the degree of urbanization, it was found that perinatal death, low birth weight, and preterm infants were more common among single mothers than among married mothers.

Results for cohabiting mothers were more similar to those of married mothers than to those of single mothers. Cohabiting women gave birth to somewhat more infants with low birth weight than did married women, but there were hardly any differences in the numbers of preterm infants or deaths.

Why did infants of single mothers have poorer outcomes? The authors suggested that marital status may include causal factors such as social support and working conditions which have a direct impact on the outcome of the birth. Other causal factors, such as parity, social class, and smoking, may also be associated with marital status. Likewise, partner selection may be an issue, with healthier people marrying and those with more severe health problems having greater difficulty in finding and keeping marriage partners.

Reviews of other studies presented two basic explanations for the advantage of marriage on health: social support and economic well-being. Single mothers may have less support, and marriage and cohabitation may be associated with higher levels of economic well-being.

Source: Kristina Manderbacka, Jouni Merilainen, Elina Hemminki, Ossi Rahkonen, and Juha Teperi, "Marital Status as a Predictor of Perinatal Outcome in Finland," *Journal of Marriage and the Family* 54 (August 1992): 508–515.

25 were placed for adoption. This figure dropped to 3.6 percent in 1989. These authors found that the number of Canadian children placed in adoptive homes declined over the past decade from 5376 in 1980 to 2836 in 1990. A large part of this decline is due to the shrinking number of adoptions of children under one year, although the number of older or otherwise "difficult to place" children available for adoption has also declined. Proportionately more adoptions in recent years have been private adoptions.

What accounts for this decline? Interestingly, it is not due to an increase in the number of pregnancies terminated by abortion. In fact, the proportion of abortions to births has decreased over time. Daly and Sobol's research shows that the greatest change over the decade of the 1980s is in the increased numbers of birth mothers or nonadopting surrogate parents raising the child.[40] This may indicate increased childbearing in common-law unions. The findings indicate a clear pattern that adoption is less common as a means of family formation.

Why do some women decide that adoption is best? The majority (51 percent) feel they are too young to parent. Another 26 percent are financially unable to parent and 21 percent feel that parenting would interfere with education and career.[41] The reasons for wanting to adopt a child may seem obvious: a couple's inability to have their own child, and the desire to experience parenthood and complete a family. Figure 7.7 profiles birth mothers and adoptive parents in Canada.

The trend toward older unmarried childbirth might suggest fewer problems related to emotional immaturity, dropping out of school, and inexperience in child care, but whether it means fewer income and employment problems is unclear.

Mothers

- single
- aged 15–19
- Caucasian
- Protestant or Catholic
- completed junior high school
- no prior pregnancy
- not attending school or attending high school
- living with parents before pregnancy

Adoptive parents

- married
- aged 31–35
- Caucasian
- Protestant or Catholic
- fertility problem
- at least high school education
- no prior parenting experience

Figure 7.7

Profiles of mothers placing their child for adoption and adoptive parents*

*Adoption facilitators were asked to provide a typical profile of birth mothers and adoptive parents.

Source: Kerry Daly and Michael Sobol, "Adoption in Canada," *Canadian Social Trends*, Statistics Canada Catalogue 11-008E (Spring 1994): 2–5.

Family size

Little doubt exists that the number of people in a group influences the interaction and behaviour of the members of that group. For instance, when two roommates agree, a decision is unanimous. When there are three roommates, only two of whom agree, the third person has the unhappy choice of accepting their decision, trying to change the decision of at least one roommate, or going his or her own way.

Clearly, the number of interactions, the probability of dissensus, the attention given to any one person, and so on are influenced by the number of members in the group. The same factors hold true within a family system. One-child families are conducive to certain patterns of life that differ from two-, three-, and four-child families.

One-child families

In the past, a negative stereotype was associated with being an only child. In fact, one-child families have not been viewed positively for either parents or children. The only child has been described as spoiled, selfish, overly dependent, maladjusted, and lonely. Parents of an only child have been described as selfish, self-centred, immature, cold, and abnormal. National American surveys have consistently showed that a majority of respondents believe being an only child is a disadvantage. Very few people say they want to have just one child or that the ideal number of children for a family is one.

Research does not support the stereotype of the unhappy, maladjusted only child. Data from seven American surveys found that adults who were only children received high scores on measures of well-being.[42] Without exception, all the effects of being an only child were positive. Only children were more likely to say they were very happy, find life exciting, see their health as excellent, and get satisfaction from where they live, from their nonworking activities, from their family life, from their friendships, and from their physical condition.

Research on adult Canadian women who were only children indicated that, when compared with women who grew up with siblings, only children were less likely to have large families, more likely to marry and have their first children at older ages, more likely to attain high levels of education, and, among the younger cohort, more likely to cohabit at younger ages.[43] This study demonstrated clearly that being an only child has an important impact on life-course events and transitions.

Similar results came from Judith Blake, who concluded that research findings on the only child do not support the negative stereotypes that still persist about singletons.[44] She claimed that only children are intellectually superior, have no obvious personality defects, tend to count themselves happy, and are satisfied with important aspects of life, notably jobs and health. The single child has increased problems with health and achievement only when he or she comes from a broken family with its attendant loss of income, or when mothers were young enough at birth to continue childbearing but, due to difficulties of their own, were unable to do so. When parental background is controlled, only children do better than children from any other family size.[45]

Family size and achievement levels

Blake's research also showed clearly the overwhelming effect of family size on achievement.[46] In her study, an increased number of siblings had negative effects on both child and adult achievement outcomes. For example, the larger the family, the fewer the years of completed schooling. Even after controlling for major parental background differences, there was approximately a two-year difference in educational attainment of children between small and large families.

In a major study, Alice and Peter Rossi reported similar results.[47] They found that large-size families of origin had lower levels of financial well-being, which in turn restricted how far children went in their schooling. The effects of being part of a large family continued throughout the life course; members had less frequent social interaction and parents provided less extensive help to their adult children.

To explain these effects of family size on achievement, Blake proposed a **dilution hypothesis.** It in effect suggested a dilution of familial resources available to children in large families and a concentration of such resources in small ones.[48] These diluted resources include parents' time, emotional and physical energy (including that of a mother who is frequently pregnant), attention, and personal interaction, as well as material resources that enable personal living space and privacy, living in better neighbourhoods, specialized dental care, travel, and specialized instruction such as music lessons. According to Blake, the idea that the older children in large families function as parents to the younger ones assumes too much about sibling goodwill and maturity. Youngsters are not adults and are seldom the emotional and intellectual equivalent of parents.

Large families

To judge a family as large or small is relative. Today, the family with four or more children will likely be viewed as large. But in many other countries and perhaps in Canada 100 years ago, having four children would lead to a reaction such as "Only four?" Family size is certainly relative to cultural context.

A substantial body of evidence has been compiled concerning the relationships between family size or number of children and discipline, child abuse and neglect, and health. One review of family size effects showed that child-rearing in large families was more rule-ridden and less individualized, corporal punishment was more prevalent, and resources such as time and money were more limited.[49] Persons from small families tended to have higher IQs, and greater levels of academic achievement and occupational performance. Large families also produced more delinquents and alcoholics. In large families, perinatal (surrounding birth) morbidity and mortality rates were higher, and mothers were at greater risk of several physical diseases.

In the words of the authors:

> Women who have many children more frequently develop hypertension, stress symptoms, gall bladder disease, diabetes, and postpartum depression. Women with many children are at higher risk for cancer to the cervix, digestion organs, and peritoneum, but are at less risk for breast cancer. ... Fathers of large families are at greater risk of hypertension and peptic ulcers.[50]

Are there no positive effects of having many siblings or coming from a large family? For example, are not children from large families more sociable, personable, friendly, warm, affiliative, and less aloof?

Apparently not. Several American surveys found no relationship between sibling number and sociability or being affiliative as an adult (or perhaps at any age).[51] While a number of studies found no effects, positive or negative, associated with family size, very few studies substantiated positive effects associated with large families. The consequences of large family size, as with most social structural variables, will tend to vary by factors such as educational level, social class, and religious subculture.

Birth order and sibling relationships

Birth order (sibling position) has a major influence on a wide variety of behavioural and attitudinal phenomena. Research has suggested that, in general, first-borns tend to be intellectual achievers and have high levels of self-esteem. Female first-borns, in particular, tend to be more religious, more sexually conservative, more traditionally oriented toward feminine roles, and more likely to associate with adults. Last-born or youngest children, like only children, tend to be more sexually permissive, more likely to engage in social activities, more likely to visit with friends frequently, more likely to be high media consumers, and consistently less traditional. Explanations for these differences have often focused on the older child being a role model for the younger, having more responsibility for other children, and receiving less attention as siblings enter the scene.[52]

Even middle-born children appear to differ from first-borns and last-borns. An analysis of an American sample of several thousand adolescent males found middle-borns to have significantly lower levels of self-esteem than first- or last-borns.[53] A one- or three-year spacing between siblings was more positive for children's self-esteem than a two-year spacing, as was having female siblings as opposed to male or both male and female siblings. The explanation of a lower self-assessment of middle-born children may be based on a theory that first- and last-born children have a uniqueness that facilitates recognition and attention by parents and siblings. Middle children lack this inherent uniqueness.

Judith Blake found no birth-order effects for small families, but in large families middle-born children early in the sequence of offspring had their problems.[54] These children experience the full negative force of large *sibsize* (size of sibling group). Specifically, they have older siblings close in age with whom they have to compete for resources, and they also have to endure a long period during which younger siblings are born and are dependent.

Most people with siblings have probably considered the effects of having brothers and sisters, especially the impact of birth order and age differences. Factors such as these appear to influence a wide range of behaviours and attitudes, including levels of self-esteem, feelings of responsibility, intellectual achievement, and sexual conservatism.

The roles played by and significance of having siblings are often underrepresented in family textbooks. Yet it is clear that siblings have a major impact on one's socialization (described in the next chapter), on each other as friends and companions, and on parents. On the basis of a review of research, Ann Goetting illustrated how the sibling bond typically persists over the life cycle.[55] Some aspects of sibling relationships are relatively constant, such as companionship and emotional support, while others, such as specific types of caretaking and sibling rivalry, stand out as unique to specific stages in the life cycle. Sibling relationships are unique in their duration, their common social and/or genetic heritage, and their common early experiences with the family.

In an era of frequent remarriages and the formation of many stepsibling and half-sibling relationships, one might question if these relationships differ from full-sibling relationships in adulthood. Survey data have revealed that they do.[56] On the one hand, individuals define *stepsiblings* as real kin and maintain these relationships into adulthood. On the other hand, sibling relationships are prioritized, with full siblings reporting significantly more contact with one another than with stepsiblings. In one American study, contact with both full and stepsiblings was facilitated by factors such as geographical proximity and being young, black, and female. Having no full siblings also encouraged contact with step- and half-siblings.

Sex control

An interesting question to ponder at the end of a chapter dealing with the parental system is, what will be the consequences as parents can increasingly control whether to have a boy or a girl (sex control)?

The day is at hand when parents can choose the sex of their child using either of two basic procedures: (1) by controlling the type of sperm that fertilizes the egg or (2) by prenatally determining the sex of an embryo and then aborting it if it is of the undesired sex.[57] Amniocentesis and ultrasound photography are becoming low-risk, routine ways both to diagnose the health of fetuses already conceived and to confirm their sex months before birth occurs. It is no longer unrealistic to foresee the ability to guarantee the reproduction of offspring of the chosen sex.

Of course, there is more to this issue than technology. Debate surrounds the general issue of controlling life, as evidenced by the controversies over abortion and surrogate motherhood as well as various types of genetic research and engineering. Traditional views hold that life is God-given and should not be manipulated by humans for any purpose. Other views hold that knowledge about and abilities to control life should be used to improve and sustain the human condition. The controversy is likely to increase as techniques such as sex control become more prevalent. But the fact is, the technology exists.

Will techniques such as sex control result in an unbalanced sex ratio? It has been estimated that choosing the sex of the child will increase the proportion of male births by 7 to 10 percent. A series of research reports has indicated that boys are preferred over girls in much of Africa, Asia, and the Middle East; among the Swiss, Belgians, and Italians in Europe; and among Jews and Catholics in the United States, to mention a few. If this excess of males were to occur, would it increase the number of males who never marry due to a "marriage squeeze," delay their age at marriage, or encourage polyandry?

Would a consequence of choosing the sex of a child be a reduced birth rate? Parents would not have to bear additional children to have one or another of a particular sex. Studies have indicated that the desire for more children is closely correlated with the number of sons.

Finally, would a consequence of choosing a boy or a girl be improved family relationships by avoiding births of the undesired sex or by having fewer resented or rejected children? Irrespective of choice, having female children does seem to affect support for feminism and more egalitarian views. In studies in both the United States and Canada, women in both countries and men in Canada were more likely to recognize gender inequality, to support a more feminist ideology, and to hold more egalitarian views if they had female children.[58] Family structure, in terms of the sexes of children, affects attitudes and behaviours of parents and children.

People today are living in a biological revolution of which sex control is one aspect. Clearly, this and other biological advancements could have a far-reaching social impact on parental and family systems around the world.

SUMMARY

1. Chapter 6 examined various aspects of establishing commitment. Chapter 7 focused on structural factors relating to becoming parents: a system of interrelated statuses of parents and children.
2. The transition to parenthood and parenting requires a major reorganization of relationships. Shortage of time appears to be the major problem for most parents. Given that most married women in Canada now make a long-term commitment to paid employment, parenting behaviours have begun to change and fathers have begun to assume more responsibility for child care.
3. Fertility has declined dramatically in Canada. One reason is delayed first births. The average Canadian woman now has only 1.2 children. About 10 percent of Canadian marriages are childless.
4. Some couples have no children by choice, and these couples appear to have higher levels of health and marital satisfaction than do couples with children. However, involuntarily childless couples experience negative effects on their well-being. Many infertile couples turn to adoption or alternative means of conceiving and/or having children, such as surrogate motherhood and artificial insemination.
5. The number of births outside of marriage has been increasing. However, the greatest increases are not among teenagers but among women in their twenties. Adolescent pregnancy is a far more serious issue in the United States than in Canada or any other Western country. Young unmarried mothers are often at a disadvantage in terms of marriage, education, income, employment, and training in general.
6. Family size influences development of children. Research has supported the *dilution hypothesis*, which suggests a dilution of familial resources available to children in large families and a concentration of such resources in small families. Most of the negative stereotypes about small families and only children have little if any research support.
7. As with family size, order of birth also influences children's development. First-borns appear to be more traditionally oriented, less sexually permissive, and more achievement-oriented. Later-born children also differ in a variety of ways. Sibling and half-stepsibling relationships are unique in their duration and social heritage.
8. Some evidence has suggested that gender preferences exist within the population of many countries for male children. Perhaps within the near future, parents will be able to choose to have a child of one sex or the other. This ability to control sex could result in dramatic changes in the sex ratio, in birth rates, and in family relationships in general.
10. This chapter covered a range of topics dealing with parents and parenthood: its value, young- and unwed-parenthood, birth rates, family size, birth order, and so forth. The next chapter will continue with parenthood but focus more specifically on parent/child interaction, socialization patterns, and gender-role differences.

KEY TERMS AND TOPICS

Parenthood and social change p. 182
Transition to parenthood p. 183
Changes in parental roles p. 184
Braking hypothesis p. 186
Birth rates and family size p. 187
"Baby boom" p. 188
Child spacing p. 189
Childless marriages p. 190
Voluntary childlessness p. 191
Involuntary childlessness p. 192
Rates of birth outside marriage p. 193
Adolescent pregnancy p. 195
Adoption p. 197
Family size p. 199
One-child families p. 199
Dilution hypothesis p. 200
Birth order and sibling relationships p. 201
Sex control p. 203

DISCUSSION QUESTIONS

1. What is involved in the transition to parenthood? How does the presence of a child affect one's time, finances, marital adjustment, and household responsibilities?
2. To what extent are family changes—such as single-parenthood, divorce, and employment of mothers—responsible for teenage drug and alcohol use, juvenile delinquency, and adolescent sexual activity? Explain.
3. Do you believe that birth control clinics should be required to notify parents when their teenage children have requested contraceptive or abortion information?
4. Examine the birth rate data presented and explain the following: (a) why the birth rate dropped sharply in the 1930s; (b) how this drop was accomplished without birth control methods prevalent today, such as the pill, abortion, and sterilization; and (c) why the birth rate dropped again in the 1960s.
5. Why are childless marriages not likely to become the norm? Are there advantages to marriage without children? Explain.
6. Discuss the implications of the slogan "Stop at two" in regard to family size. Why two? What if everyone had two children? What means should be used to accomplish this goal if it is perceived as desirable?
7. Itemize advantages and disadvantages of growing up in large and small families. What are the consequences of being an only child? What types of factors are likely to influence the size of a family?
8. Discuss the implications of being an oldest, middle, or youngest child. Does child spacing affect the impact of birth order on an individual? How?
9. If the sex of the fetus could be determined accurately within a few weeks following pregnancy, what effect if any would this have on birth rates? Would most parents in Canada choose to have boys or girls or have no preference? What about in other countries, particularly outside the Western world?

FURTHER READINGS

Blake, Judith. *Family Size and Achievement.* Berkeley: University of California Press, 1989. An examination of what the author calls the "sibsize revolution," with a focus on the cognitive and educational consequences of coming from families of different sizes.

Blankenhorn, David. *Fatherless America: Confronting Our Most Urgent Social Problem.* New York: Basic Books, 1995. The founder and president of the Institute for Family Values argues for reinstituting marriage, which would in turn reestablish fathers as responsible husbands and providers.

Booth, Alan, and Crouter, Ann C., eds. *Men in Families: Why Do They get Involved? What Differences Does It Make?* Mahwah, NJ: Lawrence Erlbaum Associates, 1998. A series of essays based on presentations at a national symposium on men in families.

Boumil, Marcia Mobilia, and Friedman, Joel. *Deadbeat Dads: A National Child Support Scandal.* Westport, CT: Praeger, 1996. An examination of absent parents, usually fathers, who have absconded without fulfilling child support obligations.

Cicirelli, Victor G. *Sibling Relationships Across the Life Span.* New York: Plenum Press, 1995. A summary and integration of the various domains of sibling studies.

Dowd, Nancy E. *In Defense of Single-Parent Families.* New York: New York University Press, 1997. A look at single parents, what we know about them, how they can be positive role models, and how the law treats them.

Edin, Kathryn, and Lein, Laura. *Making Ends Meet: How Single Mothers Survive Welfare and Low-Wage Work.* New York: Russell Sage Foundation, 1997. A moving portrait of working mothers that shows the difficulties of making a transition from welfare to work, including the critical role of child-care costs, lack of access to health care, and supervision of their children.

Fenwick, Lynda Beck. *Private Choices, Public Consequences: Reproductive Technology and the New Ethics of Conception, Pregnancy, and Family.* New York: Dutton, 1998. Accounts are presented of persons faced with intimate decisions, public concerns, and the dilemmas resulting from genetic knowledge.

Hawkins, Alan J., and Dollahite, David C., eds. *Generative Fathering: Beyond Deficit Perspectives.* Thousand Oaks, CA: Sage, 1997. A fathering approach that examines the work fathers do for their children in terms of caring for and contributing to the life of the next generation.

LaRossa, Ralph. *The Modernization of Fatherhood: A Social and Political History.* Chicago: The University of Chicago Press, 1997. An explicit historical analysis of how American fatherhood was reshaped during the 1920s and 1930s into the modernized form that we see idealized today.

Ludtke, Melissa. *On Our Own: Unmarried Motherhood in America.* New York: Random House, 1997. Based on in-depth discussions, the author looks at two sets of unmarried mothers: teenagers among whom the incidence and costs are very high and older unwed mothers who seldom rely on public assistance.

Mackey, Wade C. *The American Father: Biocultural and Developmental Aspects.* New York: Plenum Press, 1996. The author examines fathering as a behavioural imperative and a biocultural phenomenon.

Marsiglio, William, ed. *Fatherhood: Contemporary Theory, Research and Social Policy.* Thousand Oaks, CA: Sage, 1995. A volume of empirical and theoretical research on fathers in families, examining differences in culture, class, nationality, and custodial status.

Ribbens, Jane. *Mothers and Their Children: A Feminist Sociology of Childrearing.* Thousand Oaks, CA: Sage Publications, 1995. The author considers the impact of social constraints on the development of mothers' approaches to childrearing.

WEBLINKS

http://www.todaysparent.com/

The online site for the Canadian magazine *Today's Parent* provides all sorts of useful information on parenting and tracks the problems faced today by parents.

http://www.dadscan.org/home.html

This homepage for the London-based national organization Dad's Can features information and resources for progressive and responsible fatherhood.

http://www.ccsd.ca/factsheets/fsrzch98.htm

The Canadian Council on Social Development estimates the financial costs of raising a child at each age until he or she reaches age 18. The costs are broken down into the categories food, clothing, health care, personal care, recreation/reading/gifts/school needs, transportation, child care, and shelter/furnishings.

NOTES

1. David H. Demo, "Parent-Child Relations: Assessing Recent Changes," *Journal of Marriage and the Family* 54 (February 1992): 104–117.
2. Debra Friedman, Michael Hechter, and Satoshi Kanazawa, "A Theory of the Value of Children," *Demography* 31 (August 1994): 375–401.
3. David Dupuis, "What Influences People's Plans to Have Children?" *Canadian Social Trends* (Spring 1998), Statistics Canada Catalogue 11-008-XPE: 2-5.
4. Ibid.
5. Ralph LaRossa, "The Transition to Parenthood and the Social Reality of Time," *Journal of Marriage and the Family* 45 (August 1983): 579–589.
6. Scott Coltrane, "Father-Child Relationships and the Status of Women: A Cross Cultural Study," *American Journal of Sociology* 93 (March 1988): 1060–1095.
7. Paul R. Amato, "Father-Child Relations, Mother-Child Relations, and Offspring Psychological Well-Being in Early Adulthood," *Journal of Marriage and the Family* 56 (November 1994): 1031–1042; and J. Snarey, *How Fathers Care for the Next Generation* (Cambridge, MA: Harvard University Press, 1993).
8. Anne-Marie Ambert, "An International Perspective on Parenting: Social Change and Social Constructs," *Journal of Marriage and the Family* 56 (August 1994): 529–543.
9. Janet N. Melby, Rand D. Conger, Katherine J. Conger, and Frederick O. Lorenz, "Effects of Parental Behavior on Tobacco Use by Young Male Adolescents," *Journal of Marriage and the Family* 55 (May 1993): 439–454. Note also Grace M. Barnes and Michael P. Farrell, "Parental Support and Control as Predictors of Adolescent Drinking, Delinquency, and Related Problem Behaviors," *Journal of Marriage and the Family* 54 (November 1992): 763–776.
10. Ronald L. Simons, Jay Beaman, Rand D. Conger, and Wei Chao, "Childhood Experience, Conceptions of Parenting, and Attitudes of Spouse as Determinants of Parental Behavior," *Journal of Marriage and the Family* 55 (February 1993): 91–106.
11. Peter S. Li and Dawn Currie, "Gender Differences in Work Interruptions as Unequal Effects of Marriage and Childrearing: Findings from a Canadian National Survey," *Journal of Comparative Family Studies* XXIII, 2 (Summer 1992): 217–229.
12. David M. Fergusson, L. John Horwood, and Michael Lloyd, "The Effect of Preschool Children on Family Stability," *Journal of Marriage and the Family* 52 (May 1990): 531–538; and Linda J. Waite, Gus Haggstrom, and David E. Kanouse, "The Consequences of Parenthood for the Marital Stability of Young Adults," *American Sociological Review* 50 (December 1985): 850–857.
13. Lynn K. White and Alan Booth, "The Transition to Parenthood and Marital Quality," *Journal of Family Issues* 6 (December 1985): 435–449.
14. Alain Bélanger, *Report on the Demographic Situation in Canada, 1998-1999*, Statistics Canada Catalogue 91-209-XPE: 2.
15. Ibid, 21.
16. Sandra L. Hofferth, "Long-Term Economic Consequences for Women of Delayed Childbearing and Reduced Family Size," *Demography* 21 (May 1984): 141–155; and Jane Riblett Wilkie, "The Trend Toward Delayed Parenthood," *Journal of Marriage and the Family* 43 (August 1981): 583–591.
17. *Vital Statistics Compendium, 1996*, Statistics Canada Catalogue 84-214-XPE: 28.
18. *A Portrait of Families in Canada*, Statistics Canada Catalogue 89-523E (November 1993): 18.
19. Canadian Gallup Poll, "Majority of Canadians Believe Two-Child Family Ideal" (April 22, 1991).
20. Leon F. Bouvier, "America's Baby Boom Generation: The Fateful Bulge," *Population Bulletin* 35 (1980): 4. Published by the Population Reference Bureau, Inc., Washington, DC.
21. Jane E. Miller, James Trussell, Anne R. Pebley, and Barbara Vaughan, "Birth Spacing and Child Mortality in Bangladesh and the Philippines," *Demography* 29 (May 1992): 305–318.
22. Howard Wineberg and James McCarthy, "Child Spacing in the United States: Recent Trends and Differentials," *Journal of Marriage and the Family* 51 (February 1989): 213–228.
23. For example, see Howard Wineberg, "Variations in Fertility by Marital Status and Marriage Order," *Family Planning Perspectives* 22 (November/December 1990): 256–260; and William D. Mosher, Linda B. Williams, and David P. Johnson, "Religion and Fertility in the United States: New Patterns," *Demography* 29 (May 1992): 199–214.
24. Carl F. Grindstaff, "Canadian Fertility 1951 to 1993: From Boom to Bust to Stability?" *Canadian Social Trends* 39 (Winter 1995), Statistics Canada Catalogue 11-008E.
25. Victor J. Callan, "The Impact of the First Birth: Married and Single Women Preferring Childlessness, One Child, or Two Children," *Journal of Marriage and the Family* 48 (May 1986): 261–269.
26. Karen A. Polenko, John Scanzoni, and Jay D. Teachman, "Childlessness and Marital Satisfaction," *Journal of Family Issues* 3 (December 1982): 545–573.
27. Margaret V. Pepe and T. Jean Byrne, "Women's Perceptions of Immediate and Long-Term Effects of Failed Infertility Treatment on Marital and Sexual Satisfaction," *Family Relations* 40 (July 1991): 303–309; and Antonia Abbey, Frank M. Andrews, and L. Jill Halman,

"Infertility and Subjective Well-Being: The Mediating Roles of Self-Esteem, Internal Control, and Interpersonal Conflict," *Journal of Marriage and the Family* 54 (May 1992): 408–417.

28. Ingrid Connidis and Julie McMullin, "Reasons for and Perceptions of Childlessness among Older Persons: Exploring the Impact of Marital Status and Gender," *Journal of Aging Studies* 10 (1996): 205-222.
29. *Vital Statistics Compendium, 1996*, Statistics Canada Catalogue 84-214-XPE.
30. Marilyn Belle and Kevin McQuillan, "Births Outside Marriage: A Growing Alternative," *Canadian Social Trends*, Statistics Canada Catalogue 11-008E (Spring 1994): 14–17.
31. Ibid.
32. Canadian Gallup Poll, "Canadians Worried About Unwanted Teenage Pregnancies," (September 21, 1992).
33. Surinder Wadhera and Wayne Millar, "Teenage Pregnancies, 1974-1994," *Health Reports* (Winter 1997), Vol. 9 No. 3, Statistics Canada Catalogue 82-003-XPB: 9–16.
34. Ibid., 15.
35. Charles F. Westoff, "Unintended Pregnancy in America and Abroad," *Family Planning Perspectives* 20 (November/December 1988): 254–661.
36. James Trussell, "Teenage Pregnancy in the United States," *Family Planning Perspectives* 20 (November/December 1988): 262–272. For determinants of *American* adolescent pregnancy, see Patricia Voydanoff and Brenda W. Donnelly, *Adolescent Sexuality and Pregnancy* (Newbury Park, CA: Sage, 1990), Chapter 3.
37. Saul Hoffman, E. Michael Foster and Frank Furstenberg, Jr., "Reevaluating the Costs of Teenage Childbearing," *Demography* 30 (February 1993): 1–13.
38. Steven Nock, "The Consequences of Premarital Fatherhood," *American Sociological Review* 63 (April 1998): 250–263.
39. Kerry Daly and Michael Sobol, "Adoption in Canada," *Canadian Social Trends*, Statistics Canada Catalogue 11-008E (Spring 1994): 2–5; and Michael Sobol and Kerry Daly, "Canadian Adoption Statistics: 1981–1990," *Journal of Marriage and the Family* 56 (May 1994): 493–499.
40. Michael Sobol and Kerry Daly, "Canadian Adoption Statistics: 1981–1990," 496.
41. Kerry Daly and Michael Sobol, "Adoption in Canada," 2–5.
42. Norval D. Glenn and Sue Keir Hoppe, "Only Children as Adults," *Journal of Family Issues* 5 (September 1984): 363–382.
43. Ellen M. Gee, "Only Children as Adult Women: Life Course Events and Timing," *Social Indicators Research* 26 (1992): 183–197.
44. Judith Blake, "The Only Child in America: Prejudice Versus Performance," *Population and Development Review* 7 (March 1981): 43–54; and Judith Blake, "Number of Siblings and Personality," *Family Planning Perspectives* 23 (November/December 1991): 272–274.
45. Judith Blake, *Family Size and Achievement* (Berkeley: University of California Press, 1989).
46. Ibid.
47. Alice S. Rossi and Peter H. Rossi, *Of Human Bonding: Parent-Child Relations Across the Life Course* (New York: Aldine, 1990), 493–494.
48. Blake, *Family Size and Achievement*, 10–12.
49. Mazie Earle Wagner, Herman J. P. Schubert, and Daniel S. P. Schubert, "Family Size Effects: A Review," *The Journal of Genetic Psychology* 146 (March 1985): 65–78.
50. Ibid., 72.
51. Judith Blake, Barbra Richardson, and Jennifer Bhattacharya, "Number of Siblings and Sociability," *Journal of Marriage and the Family* 53 (May 1991): 271–283.
52. Note, for example, Joseph Lee Rodgers, David C. Rowe, and David F. Harris, "Sibling Differences in Adolescent Sexual Behavior: Inferring Process Models from Family Composition Patterns," *Journal of Marriage and the Family* 54 (February 1992): 142–152.
53. Thomas Ewin Smith, "Sex and Sibling Structure: Interaction Effects upon the Accuracy of Adolescent Perceptions of Parental Orientations," *Journal of Marriage and the Family* 46 (November 1984): 901–907.
54. Blake, *Family Size and Achievement*, 300–301.
55. Ann Goetting, "The Developmental Tasks of Siblingship over the Life Cycle," *Journal of Marriage and the Family* 48 (November 1986): 703–714.
56. Lynn K. White and Agnes Riedmann, "When the Brady Bunch Grows Up: Step/Half- and Full-Sibling," *Journal of Marriage and the Family* 54 (February 1992): 197–208.
57. See Elizabeth Moen, "Sex Selective Eugenic Abortion: Prospects in China and India," *Issues in Reproductive and Genetic Engineering* 4 (1991): 231–249; and Alison Dundes Renteln, "Sex Selection and Reproductive Freedom," *Women's Studies International Forum* 15 (1992): 405–426.
58. Rebecca L. Warner, "Does the Sex of Your Child Matter? Support for Feminism Among Women and Men in the United States and Canada," *Journal of Marriage and the Family* 53 (November 1991): 1051–1056.

CHAPTER

8 PARENT/CHILD INTERACTION AND SOCIALIZATION

Chapter 7 examined selected structural arrangements of the family system: norms and values surrounding parenthood, young-parenthood, parenthood outside of marriage, birth rates and birth expectations, effects of large or small families, birth order, and the like. This chapter, as well, will look at selected social structural patterns such as gender, but it will focus on interactional and social psychological patterns in parent/child relationships. Of central concern are various theoretical frames of reference that explain the socialization process.

SOCIALIZATION OF PARENTS AND CHILDREN

The helplessness of human infants is perhaps unequalled among newborns. Human infants cannot walk, feed themselves, recognize danger, seek food or shelter, or even roll over. Infants may grow up to be criminals, teachers, or athletic stars, but, first, they must learn to care for basic needs, to interact with other humans, and what behaviour is expected and accepted. In short, they must learn to be human.

The process of acquiring the physical and social skills needed to become a social being and a member of society is called *socialization*. Socialization, the central concept of this chapter, is a never-ending process of developing the self and of learning the ways of a given society and culture. While the focus of socialization literature is generally on the newborn and the young child, people in their teens, middle years, and older are also in a continual process of learning skills, developing the self, and participating in the groups and social systems of society. Parents, too, need to be socialized to parenthood. Parents not only influence and shape the behaviour of children; children do the same to parents.

Socialization, particularly of young infants, appears to be one function of the family that is found in every society in the world. There may be other functions as well, such as social placement, but every society appears to link people by affinity (marriage) or consanguineous (blood) ties to the nurturant socialization of persons. This does not mean that families do not fulfill other functions, that socialization occurs only among infants, or that the family is the only socializing agent. Rather, the key implication is that a basic function of the family in all societies is nurturant socialization.

Preconditions for socialization

Frederick Elkin and Gerald Handel stated that there are two preconditions for adequate socialization:

1. Children must have the requisite biological inheritance.
2. There must be an ongoing society.[1]

FAMILY DIVERSITY

Parenting style and children's development

As explained in an earlier chapter, Canadians now have a wonderful resource to test theories of child development and the effects of family, schools, and neighbourhoods on their physical and emotional well-being. The National Longitudinal Survey of Children and Youth (NLSCY) is a panel study of Canadian children beginning in 1994. The same children are to be interviewed every two years. "In 1994 there were 4.7 million children under the age of 12 in Canada. They made up 16% of the total population."

Initial findings confirm that parenting style is a key factor in a child's development. A strong correlation was found between hostile parenting practices and children's low scores for ability to get along with others. The survey measured the proportion of children exposed to a variety of risk factors (see accompanying table). Importantly, positive parenting can have a big impact on the lives of at-risk children. "The NLSCY findings show that children in at-risk situations generally had lower development scores than children who were not at risk. But at-risk children who had positive parenting scored at least as high as children in more favourable circumstances but who had negative parenting."

Correlation between parenting practices and selected measures of child development

	Child Development Factors					
		Helping Behaviour		*Motor and Social Development*		
	Overall Social Relationships	*2–3 years*	*4–11 years*	*0–23 months*	*2–3 years*	*Receptive Vocabulary*
Parenting practices						
Positive interaction	0.240	0.165	0.179	0.228	0.175	0.069
Hostility	–0.487	–0.021	–0.235	–0.072	–0.073	–0.035
Consistency	0.132	0.114	0.163	n/a[1]	0.096	0.146
Aversive parenting	–0.320	–0.167	–0.238	n/a[1]	–0.176	–0.041

[1]Data not collected for children in this age group.

continued

Proportion of children aged 0 to 11 exposed to selected risk factors, 1994

	Age Group		
	0–23 months	*2–3 years*	*4–11 years*
Risk factor			
Lone-parent family	12.3	16.7	16.3
Teenage parent family[1]	3.3	3.8	4.4
Low-income family	27.3	27.0	23.4
Low social support	3.6	3.4	3.4
Low education of PMK[2]	7.0	6.7	7.8
Depression of PMK	9.2	10.1	9.5
Dysfunctional family	8.3	9.7	8.2
Recent immigrant[3]	5.1	2.7	2.7
Four or more children at home	6.9	8.1	12.8
Difficult temperament	4.4	5.9	n/a[4]
Prenatal problem	29.0	n/a[4]	n/a[4]
Four or more at-risk factors	5.5	4.4	3.4

[1]Person most knowledgeable about the child (PMK) was less than 20 years old when the child was born.
[2]Person most knowledgeable about the child (PMK) had no more than Grade 8 education.
[3]Child arrived in Canada less than 5 years before the survey was conducted.
[4]Data not collected for children in this age group.

Sources: Statistics Canada Catalogue 89-550-MPE; "Canadian Children in the 1990s: Selected Findings of the National Longitudinal Survey of Children and Youth," *Canadian Social Trends* (Spring 1997): 2–9.

The first precondition for socialization is a biological inheritance that is adequate to permit learning processes to occur. Thus, a brain, a digestive system, and a beating heart are clearly prerequisites for socialization. These prerequisites, however, while necessary, are not sufficient. A perfect biological system, while influencing the socialization process, will not be the determinant of what is internalized mentally. Factors such as brain damage, deafness, extreme tallness or shortness, shape of nose and chin, and a wide variety of other physical conditions may hinder or influence interaction and socializing processes.

But it should be made extremely clear that biological inheritance, while influencing learning processes and necessary for their occurrence, is never sufficient for socialization. Certain needs, such as food, drink, and sleep, are basic to survival, but they can be satisfied in a wide variety of ways. And even though temperaments and intelligence may be basically biological, the development or direction they take is influenced and modified by the society in which the infant exists. In brief, biological requisites are necessary for adequate socialization, but they are not alone determinants of socialization.

The second precondition for socialization is an existing society that has values, norms, statuses, roles, institutions, and a variety of social structures that are highly regular and patterned but in constant change. The unsocialized infant has no knowledge of these changes, structures, and processes. The patterns of thinking, feeling, and acting in that society are what the socializing agents must pass on to the newcomer. This is the task of socialization.

THEORIES OF SOCIALIZATION PROCESSES

As previously defined, *socialization* refers to the process by which infants and adults learn the ways of a given society and culture, and develop into participants capable of operating in that society. A number of relatively comprehensive theories have been developed to explain various aspects of this process.

Learning/behaviourist frame of reference

Learning theory—also recognized as reinforcement theory, stimulus/response theory, and behaviourism—assumes that the same concepts and principles that apply to other animals apply to humans. Thus, it is logical and rational to spend time in the laboratory experimenting with rats, cats, dogs, pigeons, monkeys, and other animals to learn more about humans. Although there are many variations of learning theory, as with the theories that follow, basic assumptions and common lines of agreement do exist.

Learning, or socialization, as applied to the newborn infant, involves changes in behaviour that result from experience (as opposed to changes in behaviour that result from physiological maturation or biological conditions). Learning involves conditioning that may include classical conditioning or instrumental (operant) conditioning.

Classical conditioning links a response to a known stimulus. Many people are familiar with Pavlov's dog experiment, which provides a good example of classical conditioning. The hungry dog, placed in a soundproof room, heard a tuning fork before receiving meat. When repeated on several occasions, the dog salivated upon hearing the tuning fork before receiving and even without receiving the meat. The tuning fork, a conditioned stimulus, produced the response, salivation. In the classical conditioning experiment, the focus of attention is largely on the stimulus. If conditioning works with dogs, the same principle should hold true with an infant upon hearing his or her mother's voice or approaching footsteps. The voice or footstep stimulus, with repeated occurrences, should elicit a response from the child.

Instrumental conditioning, or what Skinner called **operant conditioning,** places the focus of attention on the response. The response is not related to any known stimuli; rather, it functions in an instrumental fashion. One learns to make a certain response on the basis of the consequences that response produces. It is the response, rather than the stimulus, that correlates with reinforcement. Return to the example of the hungry dog. Under classical conditioning, the dog salivated upon hearing the tuning fork, the stimulus. Under operant conditioning, the hungry dog would sniff, paw, and chew whatever was around. If, upon pawing, the dog opened a door, behind which was food, the sniffing and chewing would soon decrease and the pawing on the door would occur whenever food were desired. Thus, instrumental conditioning is a response followed by a reward (reinforcement).

How does this apply to an infant? Suppose the infant utters sounds such as "da-da-da." The father, who is convinced the child is saying "Daddy," rewards him or her by picking up, feeding, or rocking the child. As a result, the infant uses the response ("da-da-da") all day long. The infant has learned to make a certain response on the basis of the consequence or result the response has produced; the response is correlated with reinforcement.

These same general principles—refined by behaviourists with reference to intermittent reinforcement, partial reinforcement, negative and positive reinforcement, discrimination of stimuli, differentiation of response, behaviour modification, and the like—apply in learning any kind of behaviour. Socialization results from stimulus/response conditioning and from positive and negative reinforcements. The conditioning stimuli (classical conditioning) and the consequences of responses (operant conditioning) are both *external* to the animal or human.

Many of these processes are most easily observed in early childhood, when parents use rewards and punishments as deliberate techniques for teaching the child approved forms of behaviour. As individuals mature, sanctioning becomes increasingly complex. Candy, weekly allowances, spanking, and other forms of rewards and punishments lose their ability either to eliminate undesirable behaviour or to increase desirable behaviour.

Within the learning theory/behaviourist framework, symbols, language, reasoning, internalized meanings, and other internal processes play a minimal role. This is in sharp contrast to the symbolic interaction framework (described in Chapter 1 and later in this section) in which the socialized being can create his or her own stimuli and responses, can define and categorize, can distinguish between self and oneself, can separate inner and outer sensations, and can take the role of the other. As a result, most sociologists, to whom the self, roles, reference groups, symbolic processes, and meanings *internal* to the individual are viewed as central to understanding human behaviour, reject the behaviouristic approach. Although learning theory has been extremely illuminating in research with animals and infants, it has been less successful in explaining social situations, group norms, and the learning of language itself.

From the biased perspective of these authors, it is largely a waste of time, effort, and expense to try to understand the behaviour of socialized humanity (capable as we are of dealing with symbolic processes, reasoning, shared meanings, and the like) by studying nonhuman forms. Behaviourism does, however, add greatly to understanding the human (1) who has not learned to share meanings (infants, people who are isolated or severely retarded) or (2) who once learned but no longer has the capacity to share meanings (people with severe cases of aphasia or schizophrenia in which words may exist but the meanings are not shared with others).

This brief, minimal treatment of learning theory may seem unfair to the disciples of behaviourism. The same can be said for the minimal treatment of psychoanalytic theory, which follows. Both discussions are intended to illustrate contrasting views on the nature of socialization.

Psychoanalytic frame of reference

Classic psychoanalytic theory, developed by Sigmund Freud and his followers, stresses the importance of biological drives and unconscious processes.[2] This theory is in sharp contrast to the behaviourist theory just described.

The process of socialization, according to this framework, consists of a number of precise though overlapping stages of development. What happens at these stages, from birth to age five or six, although unconscious, becomes relatively fixed and permanent. These stages are called the *oral*, *anal*, and *phallic* stages, followed later by a period of *latency* and then a *genital* phase. Attention is focussed on three principal erogenous zones—the mouth, the anus, and the genitals—which are the regions of the body in which excitatory processes tend to become focalized and from which tensions can be removed by some action such as stroking or sucking. These regions are of extreme importance in the socialization process because they are the first important sources of irritating excitations with which the baby has to contend and upon which the first pleasurable experiences occur.

The first stage of development, the **oral stage,** occurs during the first year of the child's life. The earliest erotic gratifications come from the mouth, and, as a result, the child forms a strong emotional attachment to the mother, who supplies the source of food, warmth, and sucking. During the first year, the child is narcissistic; self-gratification is derived via the oral source, namely, the mouth. The mouth's functions include taking in, holding on, biting, spitting out, and closing, all prototypes for ways of adjusting to painful or disturbing states. These functions serve as models for adaptations in later life.

The **anal stage** of development follows and overlaps with the oral stage. This phase is so called because the child experiences pleasure in excretion and because toilet training may become a major problem. At this point, two functions become central: retention and elimination. Since the mother is still the predominant figure in the child's life, her methods of training the child and her attitudes about such matters as defecation, cleanliness, and control are said to determine the impact that toilet training will have upon the development of the person. Carried to the extreme, the mother who praises the child for a large bowel movement may produce an adolescent or adult who will be motivated to produce or create things to please others or to please himself or herself, as he or she once made feces to please his or her mother. On the other hand, if the mother is strict and punitive, the child may intentionally soil himself or herself and, as an adolescent or adult, be messy, irresponsible, disorderly, wasteful, and extravagant.

The **phallic stage** is the period of growth during which the child is preoccupied with the genitals. Before this stage, the first love object of both the boy and girl is the mother. But in the phallic stage, the sexual urge increases, the boy's love for his mother becomes more intense, and the result is jealousy of the father, who is seen as the boy's rival. The boy's attachment to his mother is widely known as the *Oedipus complex*. Concurrently, the boy becomes fearful that his father will remove his genitals and develops a fear known as *castration anxiety*. This anxiety increases upon observing the female, who has, in his unconscious mind, already been castrated. A similar or reverse process operates for the female. She forms an attachment to her father, the *Electra complex*, but has mixed feelings for him because he possesses something that she does not have. The result is *penis envy*. According to traditional Freudian psychology, penis envy is the key to feminine psychology. Located in this phenomenon are the roots of male dominance and female submissiveness, and male superiority and female inferiority.

The oral, anal, and phallic stages taken together are called the *pregenital period* and occupy the first five or six years of a child's life. These are the important years, during which basic personality patterns are established and fixed. Following this time, for the next six or seven years until the onset of puberty, the male and female egos go through a **latency phase,** during which the erotic desires of the child are repressed and he or she forms attachments to the parent of the same sex.

Finally, with the arrival of puberty, the **genital phase** of development begins. This period is less a stage than the final working out of the previous stages, particularly the oral, anal, and phallic stages that occurred during the pregenital period. During the genital phase, group activities, marriage, establishing a home, developing vocational responsibilities, and adult interests become the focus of attention. Given the importance of the early years, one can readily understand why factors such as bottle or breastfeeding, nursing on an imposed regular or self-demand schedule, weaning abruptly or gradually, bowel training early or late, bladder training early or late, punishment or nonpunishment for toilet accidents, and sleeping alone or with one's parents serve as crucial developments to the psychoanalyst.

Freudian claims regarding the importance of infant training to personality adjustment have received mixed empirical support. What support exists has, in general, been derived from clinical studies of emotionally disturbed individuals. Other studies have shown different results.

For example, one attempt to test empirically the crucial role of infant discipline in character formation and personality adjustment was published more than 45 years ago and has since become a somewhat classic article on the subject.[3] That study set up a series of null hypotheses concerning the relationship of specific infant disciplines to subsequent personality adjustments. The general hypothesis was that the personality adjustment and traits of children who had undergone varying infant-training experiences would not differ significantly from each other. These infant-training experiences included a self-demand feeding schedule, gradual weaning, late bowel training, and similar factors. The results supported the *null hypothesis*; that is, no significant differences in the personality adjustments of children who had undergone varying infant-training experiences were found. Of 460 statistical tests, only 18 were significant at or beyond the 0.05 level.[4] Of these, 11 supported basic psychoanalytic writings, and 7 did not. Such practices as breastfeeding, gradual weaning, demand schedule, and bowel and bladder training, which have been so emphasized in the psychoanalytic literature, were almost completely insignificant in terms of their relationship to personality adjustment.

Child development frames of reference: Erikson and Piaget

The ideas of Erik Erikson and Jean Piaget are also of interest in dealing with the socialization issue. Like Freud, both theorists focussed primarily on stages of development. Unlike Freud, both extended their stages beyond the early years and placed more importance on social structure and reasoning.

Erik Erikson, one of Freud's students, was a psychoanalyst who saw socialization as a lifelong process that begins at birth and continues into old age. Erikson developed and is well known for his eight stages of human development.[5] Each stage constitutes a crisis brought on by physiological changes and the constantly changing social situation:

- In infancy (the first year), the crisis centres on *trust versus mistrust*.
- In early childhood (the first two to three years), the issue centres on *autonomy versus shame and doubt*.
- The play stage (age four or five) involves the issue of *initiative versus guilt*.
- From school age up to adolescence, the issue is *industry versus inferiority*.
- In adolescence, the issue is *identity versus role confusion*. *Identity*, the focal concern of Erikson, is defined as being able to achieve a sense of continuity about one's past, present, and future.
- Young adulthood, another major turning point in life, involves the issue of *intimacy versus isolation*.
- In young adulthood and middle age, the issue is *generativity versus stagnation*.
- Old age, the last stage of development, is a time of reflection and evaluation and focuses on the issue of *integrity versus despair*.

In sum, Erikson sees the social order as resulting from and being in harmony with these eight stages of development. As people work out solutions to these developmental concerns, those solutions become institutionalized in the culture.

Jean Piaget, a Swiss social psychologist, spent more than 30 years observing and studying the development of intellectual functions and logic in children.[6] His work has stimulated an interest in maturational stages of development and in the importance of cognition in human development. Differing dramatically from supporters of the learning and psychoanalytic frames of reference, Piaget characterized development as an ability to reason abstractly, to think about hypothetical situations logically, and to organize rules (which he calls *operations*) into complex, higher-order structures. For instance, children are able to invent ideas and behaviours that they have never witnessed or had reinforced.

Piaget asserted that there are four major stages of intellectual development:

1. *Sensorimotor*—0 to 18 months old
2. *Preoperational*—18 months to 7 years old
3. *Concrete operational*—7 to 12 years old
4. *Formal operational*—12 years old and up

The stages are continuous; each is built upon and is derived from the earlier one.

The *sensorimotor stage* is characterized by the child's physical understanding of him- or herself and the world. Unlearned responses, such as sucking and closing one's fist, become repetitive, but the child performs them with no intent, purpose, or interest in the effect this behaviour has on the environment. Later in this first stage, activities become more intentional.

The *preoperational stage* involves language and its acquisition. Objects are treated as symbolic of things other than themselves. For example, a doll may be treated as a baby, or a stick may be treated as a candle. At this stage, overt actions and the meanings of objects and events are manipulated, but the child has difficulty seeing the point of view of another child or adult.

During the *concrete operational stage*, the child acquires the abilities to have a mental representation of a series of actions (for example, a child may be able to draw the route to a store several blocks away) and grasp the notion of relational terms (*darker, larger*), reason simultaneously about part of the whole and the whole, and arrange objects according to some quantified dimension, such as weight or size. He or she learns to manipulate the tools of his or her culture and appreciate the fact that mass remains constant in spite of changes in form. The child learns to understand cause and effect, to classify objects, to consider the viewpoints of others, and to differentiate between dreams and reality. By approximately age 12, he or she enters the adult world and the stage of formal operations.

The *formal operational stage* is characterized by the ability to think in terms of abstract concepts, theories, and general principles. Alternate solutions to problems can be formulated, and hypothetical propositions can be formulated and answered. Preoccupation with thought is the principal component of this stage of development.

Piaget's insights into cognitive development are unsurpassed. His stages take into account both social and psychological phenomena. Like Freud, Piaget had a specific conception of the goals of maturity and adulthood. Also like Freud, Piaget believed that the child passes through stages. But whereas Freud emphasized emotional maturity and the unconscious, Piaget emphasized reasoning and consciousness. And whereas Freud focused on bodily zones, Piaget focused on the quality of reasoning.

The frames of reference covered up to this point can be summarized by suggesting that the learning theorists are concerned with overt behaviour, the

Freudians with motives and emotions (often unconscious and rooted early in childhood), and the child developmentalists with motor skills, thought, reasoning processes, and conflicts. The symbolic interaction frame of reference, discussed next, shares many assumptions of Erikson and Piaget in the importance given to language, reasoning, and societal influences.

Symbolic interaction frame of reference

Contrasting considerably with the learning and psychoanalytic frames of reference is the symbolic interaction frame of reference. Within this framework, the first five years of life are considered important, but it is not believed that personality becomes fixed; rather, socialization is a lifelong process. Although mothers are important figures, so, too, are fathers, siblings, grandparents, teachers, and many others whom the child or adult perceives as significant.

Internal needs and drives are important energy sources and motivating devices, but greater significance comes from interactions with others and the internalized definitions and meanings of the world in which one interacts. For instance, erogenous zones may be sources of pleasure and gratification, but the significance of these zones depends on the learned internalized meanings attached to them. Unconscious processes may be at the core of socialization (purely speculative), but conscious processes relating to perceptions of self and others have prime importance. Although rewards and punishments influence behaviour, even these can only be understood in the light of the meanings attached to them. Thus, while conditioning (classical or operant) is significant and basic to learning, internal processes cannot be ignored.

To understand socialization as explained within a symbolic interaction frame of reference (see Chapter 1), it is necessary to review in more detail the basic assumptions and meanings of key concepts such as *social self, significant others*, and *reference group*.

Basic assumptions

As summarized in Chapter 1, the interactionist frame of reference, when applied to the study of the family and to an understanding of socialization, is based on several basic assumptions. Sheldon Stryker delineated four of these.[7]

- *Humans must be studied on their own level.* Symbolic interactionism is antireductionistic. If one wants to understand socialization, infant development, and parent/child relationships among humans, then he or she must study humans and not infer their behaviour from the study of nonhuman or infrahuman forms of life.

The basic difference between *human* and *infrahuman* is not simply a matter of *degree* but one of *kind*. The evolutionary process involves quantitative differences among species, not merely qualitative ones. Human/nonhuman differences include language, symbols, meanings, gestures, and related processes. Thus, to understand a person's social development and behaviour, relatively little can be gained by observing chimpanzees, dogs, pigeons, or rats. Social life—unlike

Family Diversity

Gender differences in Sweden

In Sweden, the roles of males and females—and their interrelationships—is one of the most widely discussed and studied aspects of intimate relationships. Considerable evidence supports the claim that this country is one of the most, if not the most, egalitarian in the world.

Linda Haas, in a number of writings, revealed how Swedish couples engage in parenting and domestic role sharing to a greater extent than American couples. Yet Haas found that the *practice* of gender-role equality still lags considerably behind the official ideology. Swedish women's position in the labour market is still not equal to men's when it comes to pay, hours, type of job and power, although they seem better off in these areas than women in most other parts of the world. Two important obstacles to an egalitarian division of labour appear to be having children and attitudes toward the man's role as breadwinner. As in most countries of the world, even if the woman is gainfully employed, she is still primarily responsible for home and child care.

See Linda Haas, *Equal Parenthood and Social Policy: A Study of Parental Leave in Sweden* (Albany, NY: State University of New York Press, 1992); and Linda Haas, "Family Policy in Sweden," *Journal of Family and Economic Issues* 17 (Spring 1996): 47–92.

biological, physiological life, or any nonhuman form—involves sharing meanings and communicating symbolically. Using language and gestures, human beings can correspond with one another, relaying intentions and meanings.

This assumption is in direct contrast with the behaviourist assumption, which suggests that humans can best be understood by studying forms of life other than human. Psychologists who assume that the difference between humans and animals is one of degree have relatively good success in explaining and controlling those who do not share meanings or communicate with one another at a symbolic level: infants, isolated children, and people who are extremely psychotic, severely retarded, brain-damaged, or aphasic. To the interactionist, the possession of language enables humans alone to deal with events in terms of the past, present, or future, and to imagine objects or events that may be remote in space or entirely nonexistent.

The differences between socialized human beings and other animals (or between human families and nonhuman families) may be summarized by saying that the lower animals do not have culture. They have no system of beliefs, values, and ideas that is shared and symbolically transmitted among the group. Animals have no familial, educational, religious, political, or economic institutions. They have no sets of moral codes, norms, or ideologies.

Similarities between the animal and human worlds are often stressed, but equal emphasis should be given to understanding and focusing on the differences. Recognizing these differences, symbolic interactionists assume that one must study humans to understand humans. Little can be learned about socialization—of any people in any life-style or social class—by studying nonhuman forms.

▪ *The most fruitful approach to social behaviour is through analysis of society.* One can best understand the behaviour of a husband, wife, or child through a study and an analysis of the society and subculture of which he or she is a part. Personal behaviour is not exclusively or even primarily an individual phenomenon but is predominantly a social one. The assumption is not made that society is the ultimate reality, that society has some metaphysical priority over the individual, or that cultural determinism explains all behaviour. Neither biogenic nor psychogenic factors are excluded as important in explaining or understanding behaviour. However, these factors are not salient variables. They are viewed as constants in a social setting and as random variables in a personality system.

Being born into a given society means that the language one speaks, the definitions one gives to situations, and the appropriateness or inappropriateness one assigns to any activity are those learned within that social and cultural context. Thus, the behaviour of a couple from the rural Philippines, who would not be seen holding hands in public, versus the behaviour of a Canadian couple, kissing and caressing in a public park, can only be understood by analyzing the society in which each of these behaviours takes place.

▪ *The human infant at birth is asocial.* Original nature lacks organization. Thus, the infant is neither social nor antisocial (as with original sin in certain religious organizations or the id within the psychoanalytic scheme). The "equipment" with which the newborn enters life does, however, give him or her the potential for social development.

Society and the specific social context in which a behaviour occurs determine whether that behaviour is social or antisocial. A newborn infant does not cry all night to punish or displease parents nor does he or she sleep all night to please them. Only after these expectations become internalized do social and antisocial acts take on meaning. Although the newborn infant has impulses, as does any biological organism, these impulses are not channelled or directed toward any specific ends. But, having the potential for social development, the human infant can, with time and training, organize these impulses and channel them in specific directions. This process, by which the newborn infant becomes a social being, is the main concern of social psychologists, who are interested in the process of socialization, and of family sociologists, who are interested in childrearing.

▪ *A socialized human being (meaning one who can communicate symbolically and share meanings) is an actor as well as a reactor.* This does not simply mean that one person acts and another reacts. Socialized human beings do not simply respond to stimuli from the external environment. Rather, humans respond to a symbolic environment that involves responses to interpreted and anticipated stimuli. Humans can talk to themselves, think through alternative courses of action, feel guilty over past behaviours, and dream of future possibilities.

That humans are actors as well as reactors suggests that investigators cannot understand behaviour simply by studying the external environment and external forces; they must see the world from the viewpoint of the subject of their investigation. Humans not only respond to stimuli but select and interpret them. As a result, it becomes crucial and essential that this interpretation and meaning be known. It is this assumption that most precisely differentiates symbolic interactionists from positivists in sociology and behaviourists in psychology.

The assumption that humans are both actors and reactors suggests that humans alone can take the roles of others; that is, they can view the world from the perspectives of other people. Thus, one can put oneself "in someone else's shoes," feeling sad over the misfortune of a friend or sharing the joys of one's children. A professor can take the role of the student and anticipate his or her response to a three-hour lecture or a certain type of exam without giving either the lecture or the exam. One spouse can anticipate the response of the other spouse to an embrace or to inviting friends to dinner. The responses of the professor and the spouse may be inaccurate, but the perception and meaning or definition attached to the situation will influence and direct behaviour. In short, a person's behaviour is not simply a response to others but is a self-stimulating response: a response to internal symbolic productions.

Development of a social self

Self is the key concept in understanding socialization and personality. Self, although often defined in psychological and personal terms, is a social phenomenon. Self is developed in interaction with others. The process of socialization, a primary concern of childrearing and that which makes humans social beings, is the development of a social self: the organization of internalized roles.

A woman may occupy the statuses of wife, mother, sister, student, executive, and many others. Each status has expectations (roles) assigned to it. A person must know how each role is related to the others, and all these roles must be organized and integrated into some reasonable, consistent unity. This organization of internalized roles is the **social self.**

This organization and internalization of roles occurs in interaction with others; the social self is never fixed, static, or in a final state. George Herbert Mead used the term *self* to mean simply that a person is the object of his or her own activities; he or she can act toward himself or herself as he or she acts toward others.[8] Thus, one can talk to oneself or feel proud, ashamed, or guilty of oneself.

Who one is, how one feels, what one wants, and so on constitute one's social self. One's social self consists of self-concepts, self-perceptions, and definitions of self-worth and self-esteem. Personality, then, consists of these definitions of self with the predisposition to act and behave consistently. The person who is convinced that he or she is not capable of passing the exam, not attractive enough to meet that special person, or not able to fulfill the expectations of a job may position himself or herself for failure. A self-fulfilling prophecy may become operative. The person will fail at the very thing he or she knew would bring failure. The opposite is equally true. Knowing one can do something increases the probability that one will.

These self-concepts and senses of self-worth develop in interaction with others. Such feelings and values do not exist at birth but must be internalized;

that is, they must be learned. It does not take much imagination to assess the central role a spouse, sibling, parent, or grandparent—family members—may each play in the development of the social self. Research has shown that parent support and behaviour affect the self-esteem of children and adolescents, and, reciprocally, that the self-esteem of children affects how much support their parents give them.[9]

In another study, perceived parental rejection was found to be a potent cause of depressive symptoms and low self-esteem among young people.[10] Mothers with high self-esteem were more likely to provide their children with greater decision-making freedom, to communicate better with them, and to be less concerned about their children's behaviour. Fathers with high self-esteem were less likely to report using a physical form of punishment.[11]

An interactionist frame of reference cautions against assuming that specific parental acts will always produce identical outcomes or results. For example, spanking (corporal punishment) is deeply rooted in the legal and religious traditions of American culture. Although it varies by sex (boys more than girls), age of children (preschool more than older), marital status (unmarried mothers more than married ones), social class (higher among the lower classes), and region of the country (highest in the south), most parents (90–95 percent) claim to have spanked their children and most parents (75–85 percent) approve of spanking and believe it is necessary to discipline a child.[12]

But with what effects? Does it improve the mental health and well-being of children and adolescents or lead to aggression and psychological disorders? Does it lead to conformity and tolerance of others or result in adolescent delinquency and adult abusiveness? A literature review can perhaps find evidence for any or all of the above. Is it corporal punishment per se that produces (causes) specific outcomes or do parental intents and social contexts modify the results?

Family Diversity

Spanking illegal in Sweden

Sweden has outlawed the adage "Spare the rod and spoil the child." It is illegal for Swedish parents to spank their children or treat them in a humiliating way.

A 1979 law, passed in the Swedish parliament by an overwhelming majority of 259 to 6, says that "the parent or guardian should exercise the necessary supervision in accordance with the child's age and other circumstances. The child should not be subjected to corporal punishment or other injurious or humiliating treatment."

A member of the justice ministry in Stockholm said that this law is an attempt to change people's attitudes toward the physical punishment of their children and to show them that society does not approve of this sort of behaviour. It is based on the belief that the reaction of children when hit by parents is one of revenge, not one of respect, and that physical punishment of children stimulates fear instead of love.

Support for the latter position was revealed in a study that examined the impact of harsh corporal punishment and quality of parental involvement on adolescent aggressiveness, delinquency, and psychological well-being.[13] Basically the results indicated that it was not corporal punishment per se that predicted negative adolescent outcomes but the disregard, inconsistency, and uninvolvement of parents that increases a child's risk for problem behaviours. Spanking in a context of parental support and involvement did not have a detrimental impact. Spanking in different contexts, however, often results in physical injury to the child, feelings of anger, defiance, and rejection, psychological disturbances, aggressive action, and delinquent behaviours. In fact, given the high prevalence of spanking per se, much of which is outside a context of love and parental involvement, led Straus to recommend that spanking elimination should become a public health agenda because it presents a serious threat to the well-being of American children.[14]

In brief, the development of self-esteem, sound mental health or well-being, or any other aspect of internalizing definitions of the self must be viewed in a sociocultural context. Since everyone learns in interaction with others, attention must be paid to *culturally prescribed meanings* of socialization behaviours as well as to *social structural variations* in which the socialization occurs.[15]

Note again the futility of studying nonhumans in dealing with issues such as these. Animals and others (including newborn infants) who have neither language nor internalized role definitions (senses of self-worth) have no social selves. They cannot take the positions of others and view themselves as objects. Neither can they judge past, present, or prospective behaviour. Only humans, who have the potential to share meanings, can develop social selves.

Significant others and reference groups

Significant others and reference groups are of central importance in understanding the development of the child and modification of the social self. Not all persons or groups are of equal importance to individuals. Certain persons and groups—again, in processes of interaction—come to be perceived as more important, as more significant, and as sources of reference. These persons and groups with which one psychologically identifies are termed, respectively, **significant others** and **reference groups.**

To most infants and young children, Mother is a significant person—that is, an object of emotional involvement, especially in the child's development. Note that *Mother*, in terms of interaction and involvement, is a social, not a biological, concept. As a result, an adoptive parent, foster parent, grandparent, or other person—male or female—can fulfill the expectations (roles) of Mother. And Mother (socially or biologically is not the only significant other. Fathers, siblings, peers, teachers, athletes, and movie stars are all important people with whom one psychologically identifies. We want to please and receive approval from those others who are significant.

Significant others present themselves in two essential ways: (1) by what they do and (2) by what they say and how they say it. Doing and saying are organized

George Herbert Mead postulated that, in the process of socialization to adulthood, children go through a play stage, in which they imitate people whom they observe. Children are particularly likely to model behaviour after that of their parents.

in terms of roles. Mothers (traditionally, at least) change diapers, cook meals, clean house, offer tenderness, and the like. Fathers read newspapers, complain about bills, watch football games, and so on.

As a child or an adult interacts with other people, he or she will become interested in some and attached to others; it follows that he or she will share certain expectations and behaviours with those people. Significant others are role models. Personal behaviour and thinking are patterned on the conduct of these persons. A favourite relative, a particular television performer, a favourite teacher, as a significant other, may each play a part in the socialization and development of one's social self. A sister or brother, a boyfriend or girlfriend, or a television figure may become a role model, a significant other, and thus a person with whom one psychologically identifies.

In addition to persons who are viewed as significant, groups (real or imaginary) are used as frames of reference with which a person psychologically identifies. These groups, generally called *reference groups*, are any from which an individual seeks acceptance or that he or she uses as a source of comparison. A religious group, a club, or a company may serve as a point of reference in making comparisons or contrasts, especially in forming judgments about oneself. In some instances, a person may attempt to gain membership or acceptance in the group, although this is not always the case. These groups, like significant others, serve as standards for conduct, as bases for self-evaluation, and as sources of attitude formation.

To most adolescents, peers rather than parents are key reference groups. As such, peers cannot be ignored in theories of child development and socialization. Central themes in peer culture include:

1. The importance of sharing and social participation
2. An attempt to deal with confusions, concerns, fears, and conflicts in their daily lives
3. A resistance to and challenging of adult rules and authority[16]

Thus, peers—who understand the adolescent and share his or her world—become a reference point for sizing up problems, strivings, and ambitions. Including peers as a source of reference may help one understand why the values of adolescents appear to be more like those of similar-age youth than those of parents.

Peers as a source of reference may also help one understand that behaviour defined as deviant by parents may be given social approval by peers. Using drugs or alcohol, engaging in sexual intercourse, dating interracially, espousing certain political views, and the like may be conforming behaviour to peers. The antisocial behaviour of adolescents, as viewed by parents, may simply mean that the adolescent is "marching to a different drummer" (peers).

Socialization stages and interaction processes

The importance of the early years cannot be denied. Very early experiences provide the infant with his or her first senses of self, other persons, and social relationships. The mother usually becomes the first, primary, and most significant other. The significant dimensions in the socialization process become attention, love, and warmth or their absence, rather than specific priorities such as bottle- or breastfeeding or toilet training early or late.

More important, the nature of the social relationships with the mother and others influences the image that the infant or child has of himself or herself. Scolding, slapping, pampering, or praising may not be crucial per se, but their repetitive nature leads to internalization of a sense of self-worth and an image of oneself. Although the mother is crucial in the development of these images, so are the father, siblings, other kin, and friends. Although the mother may carry out most infant care, the socialization experiences of most infants include interaction with members of the nuclear family, extended family, and others. Each relationship provides a unique contribution to socialization.

In the development of the self, George Herbert Mead postulated that children go through three continuous **stages of observation:** preparatory, play, and game.[17] In the *preparatory stage*, children do not have the ability to view their own behaviour. Actions of others are imitated. As described under the learning frame of reference and also under the interaction frame of reference, certain sounds, such as "da-da-da," bring attention and response from others. This operant conditioning leads the child to repeat and learn the sounds.

The second stage, overlapping with and continuing the preparatory stage, is the *play stage*. At this point, children take roles of others; that is, they play at being whom they observe. A child may sweep the floor, put on a hat, or pretend to read a book. Elkin and Handel described a four-year-old "playing Daddy" who put on his hat and coat, said "goodbye," and walked out the front door, only to return a few minutes later because he did not know what to do next.[18]

Later, children enter the *game stage*. At this point, they do not merely play or take the roles of others; they now participate in games involving an organization of roles and the development of self. At this point, they have to recognize the expected behaviours of everyone else, which involves responding to the expectations of several other people at the same time. This is termed the **generalized other.** In Mead's famous example of the baseball game,

> the child must have the responses of each position involved in his own position. He must know what everyone else is going to do in order to carry out his own play. He has to take all of these roles. They do not all have to be present in consciousness at the same time, but at some moments he has to have three or four individuals present in his own attitude, such as the one who is going to throw the ball, the one who is going to catch it, and so on. These responses must be, in some degree, present in his own makeup.[19]

The concept of generalized other enables one to understand how given individuals may be consistent in their behaviour even though they move in varying social environments. People learn to see themselves from the standpoints of multiple others who are either physically or symbolically present.

In the light of this perspective of socialization, it should be recognized that any behaviour results less from drives and needs, unconscious processes, and biological characteristics than from interaction processes and internalized

NEWS ITEM

Godparents make a secular comeback

Traditionally, godparents were identified in the christening of infants. Their role may have been more symbolic than functional, but in either case, the obligation was to serve as a religious influence. It seems that godparents are increasingly involved with their godchildren, and religion may be incidental to the relationship. One of the goals of greater involvement by godparents, and greater expectations of that involvement on the part of parents, is the desire to create the support once found in extended families.

According to Robert Glossop of the Vanier Institute of the Family in Ottawa, the diversity in the responsibilities of a godparent "reinforces the notion that parents [today] can't do it all on their own."

Source: Dorothy Lipovenko, "Godparents Make a Secular Comeback," *The Globe and Mail*, March 17, 1997, A6.

meanings of self and others. As a result, the behaviour appropriate to whites or blacks, royalty or outcasts, Jews or Gentiles, or males or females is dependent less on skin colour, genital makeup, and other biological facts than upon the internalized meanings and definitions that result from interaction with others. These interactions, viewed in their broadest context, include schools, peers, the mass media, and all involvement of daily living.

Given this, the concern over latchkey children, neglected and abused children, foster children, and the extensive violence portrayed on television can be viewed in a different light and be more fully understood. Traditional norms continue to relegate child-care responsibilities and childrearing to women and mothers.[20] But with the changes taking place in society regarding the roles of men and women, the increasing proportion of mothers in the paid labour force, and so on, there seems to be a weakening link between marriage and the care of children.[21]

Perhaps research is more important now than at any time in history in assessing the impact of parental substitutes and nontraditional patterns of interaction on the development of children. These interactions and socializing influences, both within families and external to them, not only are important to infants and preschool children, but also continue beyond early childhood, through adolescence and middle age, into old age.

SOCIALIZATION IN ADOLESCENCE AND BEYOND

Most books on socialization, most chapters on childrearing, and the greatest public interest in both topics generally focus on the young child. This interest is readily understandable, since, to the newborn child, the entire world is new. Even the most common and routine events must be learned. But if socialization involves learning roles and the ways of a given society and culture, and ultimately develops members who are capable of operating in society, how can anyone argue that socialization is complete after five or six years of life? In a rapidly changing society, people face unfamiliar events almost daily. Without a doubt, early socialization experiences will have a major influence and impact on the types of events and experiences that are acceptable or unacceptable. But socialization is a continuous process. What's more, learning experiences after the early years not only mean incorporating the new but discarding much of the old.

Many studies and reviews have clearly indicated the significance of socialization during the adolescent years. During the teen years, the school and the peer group are powerful and pervading socializing forces. Learning processes similar to those in early childhood are in operation. The adolescent is actively engaging in sex-role identification, learning the norms and expectations of the opposite sex, participating in new and different types of social activities, gaining insights and skills for the future occupational world, attempting to become emancipated from parents, and developing a new sense of self-reliance.

A life course perspective on socialization emphasizes the interdependence of life histories and the potential for both continuity and change. For example, an examination of daughters' gender ideology provides support for childhood socialization theory but also points to the importance of the daughters' own status achievement.[22] That is, there is an intergenerational transmission of gender and work role identity as well as the daughter's own life experiences.

Even though socialization does not end at adolescence, research interest apparently does. In regard to persons ages 20 through 60, a mythical assumption seems to exist that socialization to new roles, tasks, and activities either does not exist or is unnecessary. The social self, it seems, is believed to be relatively stable or even fixed in these adult years; thus, adult socialization is not an exciting or vital area for research. The only exception is the topic of people at retirement; some literature has made reference to the need for resocialization to new life-styles associated with aging and people who are aged.

Socialization—of young children, adolescents, midlife adults, or people who are aged—is rooted in basic interaction processes. The same is true in terms of content: socialization to violence, socialization to parenthood, sexual socialization, and socialization to gender/sex roles. This issue of sex-role socialization will be addressed for the rest of this chapter.

GENDER IDENTITY AND SEX-ROLE SOCIALIZATION

Confusion often exists over concepts such as *sex*, *sex roles*, *gender roles*, and *gender identity*. One's **sex,** irrespective of behaviour, refers to the biological condition of being male or female. **Sex roles,** therefore, refer to the expectations associated with being biologically of one sex or the other. **Gender,** in contrast to sex, is the umbrella term that refers to the totality of being male or female, masculine or feminine. **Gender roles** are thus the expectations associated with being masculine or feminine, which may or may not correspond precisely with one's sex. "Doesn't *he* [biological male] act *feminine* [gender expectation]?" is one example of how sex and gender can be differentiated. **Gender identity** refers to the way one defines or perceives oneself in terms of his or her sex, as male or female, and as masculine or feminine, or as heterosexual, bisexual or homosexual.

Sexual or gender identity formation is a developmental process but one that does not always move through stages in an orderly sequence. For example, one study of more than 400 lebians and bisexual women noted that these women experienced periods of ambivalence during which they wondered about their sexual identities, as well as periods during which they had no particular sexual identity. Bisexual-identified women became aware of their homosexual feelings and questioned their heterosexual identities at older ages than lesbian-identified women. Identities changed as a result of available social constructs, the sociopolitical landscape, and their own positions on that landscape.[23]

Roles, differentiated by both sex and gender, are discussed frequently throughout this book, particularly those of male/female and husband/wife. Chapter 1 described various approaches to roles consistent with structural-functional and interactional theoretical orientations. Chapter 2 examined differential treatment given to male and female members of kin groups. The entire third chapter focused on family and work, particularly the employment of women and male/female roles in the home. Other chapters have looked at gender-role differences among families from other countries in mate selection, in sexual behaviour, in marriage, in childrearing, and throughout the life cycle, with a particular focus on sexual differences in midlife and old age, in crisis, and in remarriage.

Female/male differences

There is no denying that normatively, attitudinally, behaviourally, and physically, males and females differ. Anthropologists have provided clear evidence that, worldwide, certain activities—such as hunting, trapping, herding, and fishing—are predominantly the province of men. Other activities—such as care of infants and children, grinding grain, carrying water, gathering herbs, and preserving food—are predominantly the province of women.

These divisions are found in both nonindustrial and highly industrialized societies, in the most rigid as well as the most egalitarian societies. Even in Finland and Sweden, where sex roles are deemphasized and a parental leave policy has been designed to eliminate the traditional gender-based division of labour, wives and mothers in the majority of families feed the family, shop for and wash the clothes, and serve as primary caregivers for the children.[24] Likewise, on Israeli kibbutzim, which were founded on sex-egalitarian terms, most of the men are in agricultural and industrial roles, and most of the women are in service and educational roles.

Not only do females and males differ in behaviours, but gender differences exist as well in value orientations. A national representative sample of U.S. adolescents found support for females being (1) more likely than males to express concern and responsibility for the well-being of others, (2) less likely than males to accept materialism and competition, and (3) more likely than males to indicate that finding purpose and meaning in life is extremely important.[25] In spite of major changes in gender-role attitudes and young women's occupational aspirations between the mid-1970s and early 1990s, these value differences persisted.

Beyond these male/female task and value differences, who would deny that physical differences exist between males and females? Probably no one. But who would argue that differences in the behaviour of males and females are innate, biological, or anatomical? Probably some people would, others would not be so sure, and still others would deny it forcefully. Maybe all three groups are partially correct.

For centuries, it was assumed that male/female differences in behaviour were inborn or natural. Females had maternal instincts and were submissive; males were aggressive and dominant. More recently, certain social scientists—

particularly anthropologists, who have analyzed societies in which men are passive and women are domineering—have questioned any relevance of biological factors in behaviour. They have argued that all behaviour is learned. The most accurate answer probably lies between the two positions and is far more complex than suggested by a nature/nurture, biology/culture argument.

It had been argued (and tested) that, irrespective of the extent of actual inborn differences between the sexes, the *belief* that they are innate provides a major ideological justification for a system of stratification by sex. Since men/husbands are in the advantageous power position, it might be expected that they would believe in innate, inborn sex roles more than women/wives. Research has found this to be true. Within a marriage, however, disagreement about the origin of sex roles was reduced by the mutual influence that husband's and wife's beliefs had on each other, resulting in more similar beliefs.[26]

The biological argument is deeply rooted in a number of theories of socialization, including the psychoanalytic frame of reference discussed earlier in this chapter. This view is further enhanced by research into hormones (such as progesterone and estrogen secreted by the ovaries in females, and testosterone and the androgens secreted by the testes in males) that initiate sexual differentiation in the fetus and later, at puberty, activate the reproductive system and the development of secondary sex characteristics. Research has shown that if a female fetus is given testosterone, she will develop male-like genitalia. If a male is castrated (testes removed) before puberty, he will not develop secondary sex characteristics such as a beard. But do these chemical substances, known generally as *hormones*, determine or predict behaviour?

The strength of cultural factors is overwhelming in understanding gender identity and sex-role socialization. One prime example comes from cross-cultural data that have shown great diversity in the attitudes, values, and behaviour of both men and women. Margaret Mead's classic study of three tribes in New Guinea found both men and women among the Arapesh to be cooperative, mild-mannered, gentle, and unaggressive (sex-typed feminine behaviour). Among the Mundugumor, both men and women were hostile, aggressive, combative, individualistic, and unresponsive (sex-typed masculine behaviour). Among the Tchambuli, the stereotypical sex roles found in the Western cultures were reversed: women were dominant, powerful, and impersonal; men were emotionally more dependent and less responsible.[27]

If it can be assumed that the biological makeups and hormonal balances of men and women in these tribes and men and women in the Western world are similar, then how can these differences be explained? It is not necessary to go to New Guinea in the 1930s to note the strength of cultural factors in gender differences and sex-role socialization. Data from students in the 1990s, for example, showed that the attitudes toward appropriate roles for men and women were strongly affected by fraternity and sorority membership, by race and ethnicity, and by religious affiliation.[28]

One line of research comes from studies of *hermaphrodites* (persons who possess complete sets of both male and female genitalia and reproductive organs). Infants who were assigned one sex at birth and were later found to belong biologically to the opposite sex behaved as they were assigned and taught to behave. For instance, biological females, defined and reared as males, had fantasies typical of males, enjoyed sports assigned generally to males, and fell in love with girls. Biological males, defined and reared as females, had maternal instincts, preferred marriage over careers, and were oriented toward dolls and domestic tasks.[29] Thus, when socialization contradicts biological, hormonal, or genetic factors, learned and interactional experiences prove to be powerful determinants of current gender roles.

Sex-role socialization

Socialization to sex (female/male) and gender (masculine/feminine) roles follows the basic socialization processes described earlier in this chapter. Socialization to anything, including sex roles, begins at birth and continues throughout one's lifetime. Following the moment of sex determination in the hospital, girls and boys are treated differently. Gender socialization constitutes one of life's most important learning experiences. In interaction with others as well as in words, deeds, films, and books, the child is taught what behaviour is appropriate for each sex.

Even as adolescents, the home continues as a key source of sex-role socialization.[30] His and her tasks are evident in who does inside chores and who does outside chores. Daughters perform more labour than sons, and their greater labour contributions are disproportionately allocated to those tasks traditionally defined as "women's work." Intergenerational continuity of stereotypical gender roles are being perpetuated in North American home life.

Culturally specific gender expectations are taught so effectively that, by adulthood, even within the same occupation, employed men more than employed women (1) are concerned about income, job security, and advancement into administration; (2) want to avoid being supervised; (3) are more likely to seek self-employment and/or autonomy in the work setting; and (4) value the opportunity to exercise leadership. Women more than men (1) want to work with and help people; (2) prefer part-time and employee status; and (3) emphasize the use of special occupational skills.[31]

If it is assumed that the workplace, parents, and others are influential in the sex-role socialization of children, one can predict a continuation of sex-role stereotyping in this and future decades. For example, throughout the school years, the educational system continues to stereotype males and females. Textbooks, achievement tests, athletic emphases, vocational counselling, and parental and peer pressures all tend to reinforce stereotypical expectations and behaviours. Beyond school, the mass media, religious and work worlds, and most social institutions tend quite consistently to stress appropriate and clearly different behaviours for women and men.

In the socialization of males and females, empirical evidence has documented a continuation of sex-role stereotyping and gender segregation in spite of tremendous shifts in sex-role attitudes. Current conceptions of femaleness

Empirical evidence shows continued sex-role stereotyping and gender segregation despite great shifts in attitudes to sex roles.

and maleness have marked similarities to earlier conceptions. A contemporary view of men as aggressive, work-minded, and capable of leadership is remarkably similar to that presented in earlier research. Current conceptions of femaleness, stressing sensitivity, affection, and consciousness of appearance, are also similar to earlier stereotypes of women.[32] In spite of shifts in attitudes, socialization to sex/gender roles continues to emphasize differentiation between males and females, concentrating on the perpetuation of traditional expectations and behaviours for each sex.

SUMMARY

1. The central concept in dealing with parent/child relationships is socialization: the process by which the infant and adult learn the ways of a given society and culture and develop into participants capable of operating in that society. Socialization of the young infant, believed to be a function of the family, is found in every society in the world. Preconditions for socialization include biological inheritance and an ongoing society.
2. Several frames of reference were examined to explain various aspects of socialization: a learning/behaviourist theory, a psychoanalytic theory, two theories of child development, and a symbolic interaction theory.
3. Learning (reinforcement) theory assumes that the same concepts and principles that apply to animal forms apply to humans. The conditioning processes may be classical or operant; the former links a response to a

known stimulus, and the latter links a response of the consequence produced by the response. Childrearing and socialization processes result from conditioning and positive or negative reinforcements.

4. Classic psychoanalytic theory contrasts sharply with behaviourist theory. Internal drives and unconscious processes are of central importance. Socialization takes place according to precise though overlapping stages of development. These include the oral, anal, and phallic stages, followed later by a period of latency and a genital phase. What happens in these early stages, from birth to age five or six, although unconscious, becomes relatively fixed and permanent, serving as the basis for responses in later life.
5. Child development theories focus on the individual and the manner in which motor skills, thought, and reasoning develop. Erikson described eight stages of human development, each constituting a crisis brought on by changing social situations as the individual moves from infancy through old age. Piaget focused more on the cognitive development of the child and described four major stages of intellectual development.
6. Symbolic interaction theory contrasts considerably with the theories already described. Infants are not born social; they develop through interaction with other persons. As interaction occurs, meanings are internalized and organized and the self develops. The social self enables a person to consciously and purposively represent to himself or herself what he or she wishes to represent to others.
7. A social being can take the role of others, can interpret and define, and can have and use symbols. In interaction with others, children learn to define themselves and the world in certain ways. These definitions and meanings in turn predispose them to behave in ways consistent with these self-concepts. Interaction, the social self, significant others, reference groups, and the generalized other are concepts basic to the socialization process.
8. Socialization does not end at any given age; it is a lifelong process. For teens, school and peer groups serve as important sources of reference, interaction, and identity. Minimal research exists on adult socialization; some research has focused on resocialization for people who are elderly.
9. *Gender identity* and *gender roles* refer to one's identity and the expectations associated with being masculine or feminine. Male/female and masculine/feminine differences are universal. Debate continues over the extent to which sex and gender roles have their roots in biology, culture, or a combination of the two.
10. Sex-role socialization follows the principles of any type of socialization. In interaction with others, children learn about gender/sex roles very early in their lives. These roles are heavily reinforced in schools, including children's books. While some change in attitudes toward sex roles has taken place, current conceptions of femaleness and maleness fit earlier stereotypes and highly traditional expectations.
11. Chapter 7 on the parental system and this chapter on parent/child interaction follow a life-course sequence that generally but not always follows marriage. Chapter 9 will continue this time sequence by turning to families in the middle and later years.

KEY TERMS AND TOPICS

Socialization of parents and children p. 210
Preconditions for socialization p. 210
Learning/behaviourist frame of reference p. 213
Classical conditioning p. 213
Operant conditioning p. 213
Psychoanalytic frame of reference p. 215
Child development frames of reference p. 217
Symbolic interaction frame of reference p. 219
Four basic assumptions of symbolic interactionism p. 219
Social self p. 222
Significant others and reference groups p. 224

Mead's three stages of observation p. 226
Generalized other p. 227
Socialization in adolescence and beyond p. 228
Sex and sex roles p. 229
Gender identity p. 229
Female/male differences p. 230
Sex-role socialization p. 232

DISCUSSION QUESTIONS

1. Discuss ways in which parents need to be socialized. What role does the infant, young child, and adolescent play throughout this process?
2. Review the two preconditions for adequate socialization. What would happen if either of them were absent? Would socialization be possible? Why or why not?
3. What factors are most important in the development of stable, healthy adults? Why?
4. Contrast the learning/behaviourist, psychoanalytic, child development, and symbolic interaction frames of reference in regard to how each defines *socialization*. What contributions does each theory make? What drawbacks does each have?
5. Interview three parents of preschool children. Find out whether the arrival of the first child was a traumatic event; whether they toilet-trained their child early, breastfed or bottle-fed him or her, and whether they believe their choices made any difference; what means of punishment they have used; what role the father plays in childrearing; how other children assist or hinder the socialization process; and so forth. What similar ties link the parents' answers?
6. In what ways and areas are you being socialized? To what extent are you a victim of early childhood experiences, perhaps a father-absent family, poverty, or a home with marital conflict? When will you be fully socialized? Why?
7. What influence did early adolescence, dating, friendship relationships, siblings, and teenage experiences have on your personality? To what extent is your personality today a product of your early (as opposed to more recent) socialization experiences?
8. Is a marriage with no sex- or gender-role differentiation (androgyny) possible? Explain and give examples.
9. To what extent does one's biological sex determine one's behaviour? Could you be socialized to think and act like someone of the opposite sex? Why?
10. In spite of the women's movement, the increasing number of women entering the paid work force, decreasing family size, and so forth, why do school materials, the mass media, and the work world continue to differentiate and segregate people by sex?

FURTHER READINGS

Ambert, Anne-Marie. *The Effect of Children on Parents*. NY: Haworth Press, 1992. An interdisciplinary approach with a feminist orientation to various aspects of how children affect their parents.

Arendell, Terry, ed. *Contemporary Parenting: Challenges and Issues*. Thousand Oaks, CA: Sage, 1997. The use of a social constructionist and feminist lens to examine issues surrounding parenting.

Coltrane, Scott. *Gender and Families*. Thousand Oaks, CA: Sage, 1998. Using images from popular culture, the book explores how families and gender are inseparably linked.

Corsaro, William A. *The Sociology of Childhood*. Thousand Oaks, CA: Pine Forge Press, 1997. A synthesis of theoretical ideas and empirical research on children with a focus on children as social agents rather than in terms of their future as adults.

Elkin, Frederick, and Handel, Gerald. *The Child and Society: The Process of Socialization*. 5th ed. New York: Random House, 1989. A coherent treatment, from a sociological standpoint, of how children are socialized in modern society.

Elliot, Faith Robertson. *Gender, Family, and Society*. New York: St. Martin's Press, 1996. A book showing how ethnic differentiation, unsettled labour markets, population aging, violence, AIDS, and other factors are changing the face of family and social life in contemporary Western societies.

Ferree, Myra Marx; Lorber, Judith; and Hess, Beth B., eds. *Revisioning Gender*. Thousand Oaks, CA: Sage, 1998. A reflection on the advances of gender scholarship during the past decade.

Kostash, Myrna. *No Kidding: Inside the World of Teenage Girls*. Toronto: McClelland and Stewart, 1987. A Canadian study by journalist Myrna Kostash based on interviews with teenaged girls who talk candidly about boys, friends, and sex.

Lamb, Michael E., ed. *The Role of the Father in Child Development*. 3rd ed. New York: John Wiley & Sons, Inc., 1997. Sixteen chapters written for this volume about father–child relationships including preschoolers, school-age, adolescents, those with special needs, stepfamilies, and others.

Lorber, Judith. *Paradoxes of Gender*. New Haven, CT: Yale University Press, 1994. An extensive analysis of gender as a social institution that establishes patterns of expectations for individuals, orders the social processes of everyday life, and is built into the major social organizations of society.

Lupton, Deborah, and Barclay, Lesley. *Constructing Fatherhood: Discourses and Experiences*. Thousand Oaks, CA: Sage, 1997. An analysis of the social, cultural, and symbolic meanings of fatherhood in contemporary Western societies.

Mortimer, Jeylan T., and Finch, Michael D., eds. *Adolescents, Work, and Family: An Intergenerational Developmental Analysis*. Thousand Oaks, CA: Sage, 1996. Eight articles focusing on adolescents—their participation in the family economy and paid work, changes in a sense of competence, and shifts in parent–child relationships.

Roche, Jeremy, and Tucker, Stanley, eds. *Youth in Society: Contemporary Theory, Policy and Practice*. Thousand Oaks, CA: Sage, 1997. A series of 27 readings to encourage thinking about the changing and diverse lives and priorities of young people.

Rowe, David C. *The Limits of Family Influence: Genes, Experience, and Behavior*. New York: Guilford Press, 1994. A book on socialization proposing the radical theme that family environments may exert little influence on child outcomes such as intelligence, personality, and psychopathology.

Straus, Murray A., with Donnelly, Denise A. *Beating the Devil out of Them*. New York: Lexington Books, 1994. Straus makes the argument that corporal punishment is violence, that it is a major social problem, and that the ending of it is one of the most important steps to achieving a less violent world.

Weblinks

http://www.cfc-efc.ca//docs/00000899.htm

This website is entitled "Canada's Kid's: Thriving or Surviving" and provides an assessment of the relation between children and families in the 1990s.

http://members.aol.com/amsapage

The American Men's Studies Association is a not-for-profit professional organization of scholars, therapists, and others interested in the exploration of masculinity in modern society.

http:www.parentswithoutpartners.org/

Parents Without Partners is an organization devoted to single-parent families.

NOTES

1. Frederick Elkin and Gerald Handel, *The Child and Society: The Process of Socialization*, 5th ed. (New York: Random House, 1989), 8–25.
2. For a recent application of psychoanalytic theory with people who are chronically emotionally ill, see Alexander Grainick, "Psychoanalytic Principles and Long-Term Hospital Practice," *Psychoanalysis and Psychotherapy* 8 (Fall/Winter 1990): 169–179. For an excellent treatment of feminism, see Nancy J. Chodorow, *Feminism and Psychoanalytic Theory* (New Haven, CT: Yale University Press, 1989).
3. William H. Sewall, "Infant Training and the Personality of the Child," *The American Journal Sociology* 58 (September 1952): 150–159.
4. The 0.05 level means that these relationships would occur simply by chance less than 5 times in 100.
5. Erik K. Erikson, *Childhood and Society*, 2nd ed. (New York: W.W. Norton, 1963), Chapter 7.
6. See Jean Piaget and Barbara Inhelder, *The Psychology of the Child* (New York: Basic Books, 1969); and Jean Piaget, *The Construction of Reality in the Child* (New York: Basic Books, 1954).
7. Sheldon Stryker, "The International and Situational Approaches," in *Handbook of Marriage and the Family*, ed. Harold T. Christensen (Chicago: Rand McNally, 1964): 134–136; and Sheldon Stryker, "Symbolic Interaction Theory: A Review and Some Suggestions for Comparative Family Research," *Journal of Comparative Family Studies* 3 (Spring 1972): 17–32.
8. George Herbert Mead, *Mind, Self and Society* (Chicago: University of Chicago Press, 1934).
9. Viktor Gecas and Michael L. Schwalbe, "Parental Behavior and Adolescent Self-Esteem," *Journal of Marriage and the Family* 48 (February 1986): 37–46; and Richard B. Felson and Mary Z. Zielinski, "Children's Self-Esteem and Parental Support," *Journal of Marriage and the Family* 51 (August 1989): 727–735.
10. Joan F. Robertson and Ronald L. Simons, "Family Factors, Self-Esteem, and Adolescent Depression," *Journal of Marriage and the Family* 51 (February 1989): 125–138.
11. Stephen A. Small, "Parental Self-Esteem and Its Relationship to Childrearing Practices, Parent-Adolescent Interaction, and Adolescent Behavior," *Journal of Marriage and the Family* 50 (November 1988): 1063–1072; and Ronald P. Rohner, Kevin J. Kean, and David E. Cournoyer, "Effects of Corporal Punishment, Perceived Caretaker Warmth, and Cultural Beliefs on the Psychological Adjustment of Children in St. Kitts, West Indies," *Journal of Marriage and the Family* 53 (August 1991): 681–693.
12. Jean Giles-Sims, Murray A. Straus, and David B. Sugarman, "Child, Maternal, and Family Characteristics Associated with Spanking," *Family Relations* 44 (April 1995): 170–176; and Clifton P. Flynn, "Regional Differences in Attitudes Toward Corporal Punishment," *Journal of Marriage and the Family* 56 (May 1994): 314–324.
13. Ronald L. Simons, Christine Johnson, and Rand D. Conger, "Harsh Corporal Punishment Versus Quality of Parental Involvement as an Explanation of Adolescent Maladjustment," *Journal of Marriage and the Family* 56 (August 1994): 591–607.
14. Murray A. Straus with Denise Donnelly, *Beating the Devil out of Them* (New York: Lexington/Macmillan, 1994); and Murray A. Straus, "Discipline and Deviance: Physical Punishment of Children and Violence and Other Crime in Adulthood," *Social Problems* 38 (1991): 101–123.
15. Note, for example, Elizabeth Thomson, Sara S. McLanahan, and Roberta Braun Curtin, "Family Structure, Gender, and Parental Socialization," *Journal of Marriage and the Family* 54 (May 1992): 368–378.
16. William A. Corsaro and Donna Eder, "Children's Peer Cultures," *Annual Review of Sociology* 16 (1990): 197–220.
17. George Herbert Mead, *Mind, Self and Society*, 150. For a comparison of Piaget and Mead regarding play and games, see Norma K. Denzin, "Play, Games and Interaction: The Contexts of Childhood Socialization," *The Sociological Quarterly* 16 (Autumn 1975): 458–478.
18. Elkin and Handel, *The Child and Society*, 57.
19. Mead, *Mind, Self and Society*, 151.
20. For an overview of child care and children's development, see Jay Belsky, "Parental and Nonparental Child Care and Children's Socioemotional Development: A Decade in Review," *Journal of Marriage and the Family* 52 (November 1990): 885–903.
21. Andrew J. Cherlin, "The Weakening Link Between Marriage and the Care of Children," *Family Planning Perspectives* 20 (November/December 1988): 302–306.
22. Phyllis Moen, Mary Ann Erickson, and Donna Dempster-McClain, "Their Mother's Daughters? The

Intergenerational Transmission of Gender Attitudes in a World of Changing Roles," *Journal of Marriage and the Family* 59 (May 1997): 281–293.

23. Paula C. Rust, "'Coming Out' in the Age of Social Constructionism: Sexual Identity Formation Among Lesbian and Bisexual Women," *Gender and Society* 7 (March 1993): 50–77. Note also Frederick L. Whitam, Christopher Daskalos, Curt G. Sobolewski, and Peter Padilla, "The Emergence of Lesbian Sexuality and Identity Cross-Culturally: Brazil, Peru, the Philippines, and the United States," *Archives of Sexual Behavior* 27 (1998): 31–56.

24. Linda Haas, "Gender Equality and Social Policy," *Journal of Family Issues* 11 (December 1990): 401–423.

25. Ann M. Beutel and Margaret Mooney Marini, "Gender and Values," *American Sociological Review* 60 (June 1995): 436–448.

26. John Mirowsky and Catherine E. Ross, "Belief in Innate Sex Roles: Sex Stratification Versus Interpersonal Influence in Marriage," *Journal of Marriage and the Family* 49 (August 1987): 527–540.

27. Margaret Mead, *Sex and Temperament in Three Primitive Societies* (New York: Mentor, 1950) (originally published in 1935 by Morrow).

28. Ilsa L. Lottes and Peter J. Kuriloff, "Sexual Socialization Differences by Gender, Greek Membership, Ethnicity, and Religious Background," *Psychology of Women Quarterly* 18 (1994): 203–219.

29. John Money, *Sex Research: New Developments* (New York: Holt, Rinehart and Winston, 1965). See also John Money, "Sex Assignment in Anatomically Intersexed Infants," in *Readings in Sociology*, ed. by M. A. Watson (Dubuque, IA: Kendall/Hunt, 1984).

30. John F. Peters, "Gender Socialization of Adolescents in the Home: Research and Discussion," *Adolescence* 29 (Winter 1994): 913–934; and Sampson Lee Blair, "The Sex-Typing of Children's Household Labor: Parental Influences on Daughters' and Sons' Housework," *Youth and Society* 24 (December 1992): 178–203.

31. Michael Betz and Lenahan O'Connell, "Work Orientations of Males and Females: Exploring the Gender Socialization Approach," *Sociological Inquiry* 59 (August 1989): 318–329.

32. Barrie Thorne and Zella Luria, "Sexuality and Gender in Children's Daily Worlds," *Social Problems* 33 (February 1986): 176–190; and Raymond J. Adamek and Mike Miller, "Changes in Coeds' Sex Role Concepts: 1969 and 1980," *Sociological Spectrum* 4 (1984): 71–87.

CHAPTER

9 THE MIDDLE AND LATER YEARS

Chapters 7 and 8 examined selected aspects of families with children. But marriage and family life do not end when children enter adolescence or in later adolescence, when the children leave home for marriage, employment, school, or some other reason. Family structure, interactions, and life-styles change considerably at this period of the family life cycle: the second half. A prime example of this change was shown in Chapter 6, regarding marital satisfaction over the life cycle. Studies indicated increasing disenchantment and decreasing satisfaction throughout the years of parenting, followed by increasing satisfaction in the later years, after the children have left home.

This chapter will examine two major periods in the life course: the middle years, from approximately age 40 to retirement, and the later years, from approximately age 60 or 65. This examination will include general descriptions of families at these periods with specific consideration given to grandparents, retirement, socialization of people who are aged, and social conditions and problems faced by this group.

POSTPARENTAL PERIOD: THE MIDDLE YEARS

To describe the experience of the period after children leave home, a number of phrases have been used. Among these are the *"empty nest"* period, the *launching stage*, the period of *contracting family size*, and the term used here, the **postparental period.**

Technically, the term *postparental* is a misnomer; parents do not stop being parents or become ex-parents after their children leave home. The term suggests that, at this time, the children are now legally and socially recognized as adults and assume greater independence from their parents as well as greater personal autonomy and responsibility. They are, in effect, ready to be "launched" from the family. Aquilino notes that in young adulthood, leaving home acts as a signal to parents that their child is entering a new stage, and it appears to be the transition that has the greatest power to shake up earlier styles of relating.[1] As might be expected, parental control lessens and shared leisure time declines. What was not anticipated was the finding that parents do not feel as emotionally close to children who have left. The quality of the relationship with adult children improves when their children marry and establish themselves in the labour force. The postparental period may include episodes of child "reentry" into the parental home for many families. But essentially, this period is characterized by the return of the conjugal family to a two-person, married-couple household and of many nuclear one-parent families to a one-person household. The periods of family life from this point until the death of one or both parents can be classified as:

1. *Families launching their oldest children*—parents' ages 45 to 54
2. *Families of preretirement*—parents' ages 55 to 64
3. *"Young/old" retired families*—parents' ages 65 to 74
4. *"Old/old" families in the later years*—parents' ages 75 and older

Table 9.1
Marital status of men and women ages 45–54 and 55–64, Canada, 1991

	% of Men		*% of Women*	
Marital Status	***45–54***	***55–64***	***45–54***	***55–64***
Never married	7.0	6.8	6.0	5.6
Married	82.8	82.7	77.2	70.8
Separated	2.9	2.4	3.5	2.7
Widowed	0.8	2.8	4.0	13.9
Divorced	6.3	5.2	11.6	8.6

Source: Calculated from "Age, Sex, and Marital Status," *The Nation*, Statistics Canada Catalogue 93-310 (July 1992), Table 3.

The following section examines families in the middle years, as they launch their children and approach retirement, when the parents are approximately 45 to 65 years old.

Marital status and coresidence in the middle years

In 1991 in Canada, of those persons ages 45 to 64, about 82.7 percent of the men and 74.3 percent of the women were married with a spouse present (see Table 9.1). Compared with other age categories, the percentage of people married was high, and the percentages of people never married, separated, widowed, and divorced were relatively low. For women, the percentage who were widowed climbed sharply at 10-year intervals after age 50. The figures changed from 7.7 percent (ages 50 to 59) to 22.7 percent (ages 60 to 69) to 46.5 percent (ages 70 to 79) to 70.4 percent (ages 80 to 89) to 82.3 percent for women over 90.[2]

The period after the children leave home lasts longer than any other in the marital life cycle. Interestingly, this phenomenon is unique to families of the twenty-first century. In 1900, a man married at age 26, had his last child at age 36, saw his last child marry at age 59, and lost his spouse at age 57. A woman married at age 22, had her last child at 32, saw her last child married at 55, and lost her spouse at 53.[3] The result for both sexes was no postparental period, since the average couple died two years before their last child (which, on average, was their fifth) was expected to marry.

In contrast today, both sexes marry in their midtwenties, have their last child in their early thirties, see their last child launched in their mid- to late forties, but do not lose their spouse until their early or mid-seventies. The result is a postparental period of 20 to 25 years. Couples marry in their late twenties, but have fewer children. These factors, combined with longer life expectancies, give the average couple an extended period of postparenting. Nevertheless, some postparental households are changed by children returning; others change because an aging parent moves in.

Coresidence

Coresidence refers to adult children living in the same household as their parents. Demographic indicators show that more young adults reside with their parents now than they did a few years ago. It seems that the parental home is the primary residence for the transition to adulthood. Compared to the past, young people in both Canada and the United States are more likely to leave to achieve independent living and less likely to leave for marriage. In Canada, 48 percent of unmarried men and 36 percent of unmarried women aged 25–29 were living in their parents' home.[4] For unmarried children in the 30–34 age group, 32 percent of men and 19 percent of women still lived with one or both parents. The tendency to live in the parental home depends on the parents' marital status. Children are less likely to live at home if parents are divorced or one parent is widowed.[5] Adult children in blended families are particularly vulnerable to leaving home early. This is because relations between stepparents and stepchildren may lessen intergenerational closeness, weaken favourable attitudes toward the continued support of adult children and generate conflict over parental authority and discipline in children.

What about "boomerang kids," those who leave and return? One study done in Canada found that parents are willing to accept one or two returns home, but that a pattern of bouncing back and forth strains family relationships, thus diminishing the marital satisfaction of parents.[6] Those who leave and return do so for a variety of reasons: following a job loss or divorce or separation; unwed motherhood; or when other hardships, particularly economic, arise. Both nonfamily living and cohabitation lead to much higher return rates than does marriage. The parents' characteristics—such as health, marital and employment status—have little bearing on whether their children return in either middle or later life. Returning home, in direct contrast to leaving home, is not an event constrained by age. Rather, the child's needs and situations are more important predictors of coresidence.[7]

Significance of the middle years

What is the significance of being a *quadragenarian* (ages 40 through 49)? To many couples, the middle years are the "prime of life." Business and professional careers typically peak during this period, and for two-income couples total family income is at its peak.

Debate exists over whether the middle years are, in fact, the prime of life, as family income data suggest, or a period of great stress and even depression. The middle years bring many physical and emotional changes which may create confusion and anxiety. The man who saw himself as a "ladies' man" at 20 or 30 may, at 40, need to convince himself of his virility. The woman who loses her ability to "make men look twice" may have similar doubts about her attractiveness and sexuality. What's more, menopause brings on the loss of reproductive capacity and emotional changes, which may challenge the woman's self-perception. Children growing up, leaving home, and getting married will likely stir emotions of both parents, who see their families changing and themselves aging.

The middle years are also filled with pressures to be successful and get ahead. For many people, "it's now or never." During this time, the prestigious position a person wants to attain, the book he or she wants to write, the children he or she wants to have, or the stardom he or she yearns for may become a reality or simply remain a dream, never to be fulfilled. Supporting a comfortable life-style, paying for things such as university and college tuition and weddings, and planning for retirement add to economic pressures. Thus, the argument can be made that the middle years are rough—physically, socially, emotionally, and economically.

The opposite argument suggests that the middle years are the period of life when things are brightest. Income is highest, leisure time is greatest, child-bearing responsibility is past, and opportunities exist as never before. Which view is correct—or is it possible that both are?

Michael Farrell and Stanley Rosenberg addressed this issue, comparing 300 men entering middle age to men in their late twenties. Contrary to their expectations, they did not find evidence of a universal midlife crisis or signs of increased alienation or social disconnection[8] except among men in the lowest socioeconomic class. Men who worked as unskilled labourers gave evidence of personal disorganization and psychopathology as they approached middle age.

FAMILY DIVERSITY

The "sandwich generation"

Parents in these middle years have sometimes been referred to as the "sandwich generation," squeezed between the demands and needs of their children and those of their aging parents. As Smith and Dumas (1994) point out, this is a misleading metaphor. Indeed, the term cannot refer to a *generation*, for all parents with living parents and living children fit the definition, and this group is constantly being renewed. Nor are those in the middle generation typically "sandwiched" by demands. Smith and Dumas suggest that what we are really talking about is more a *phase in the life cycle* than a generation.

Their study included people aged 35 to 64 who had at least one child at home and at least one living parent aged 65 or over, and was based on data collected in the 1990 General Social Survey. According to this survey, over a third (37 percent) of Canadians in the 35–64 age group are part of the "sandwich generation," characterized as follows: "first, they are as well placed financially as they will probably ever be, but, second, they also have the least time to devote to supportive activities." However, as the authors explain, most children, and most parents over 65, do not present huge burdens to their parents or children. Few will be severely dependent. Only about 3 percent of the "sandwich generation" have parents living with them. Indeed, two-thirds of this group "do not have children or parents in the age group most associated with dependence: children under 5 and parents aged 85 or older."

Source: Gordon Smith and Jean Dumas, "The Sandwich Generation: Myths and Reality," in Jean Dumas and Alain Bélanger, *Report on the Demographic Situation in Canada 1994*, Statistics Canada Catalogue 91-209E (1994): 111–148.

Lower-middle-class men (skilled workers, clerical workers, small businessmen) showed a remarkable ability to ignore, distort, or deny information that challenged their world views. Professionals and middle-class executives exhibited neither denial patterns nor identity problems but reported satisfaction with work, family, and position in the community.

Some social scientists have referred to a **midlife transition** for men around age 40. This transition may go relatively smoothly or may involve considerable turmoil. The transition to an "empty nest" may or may not be an important factor for men. For example, the vast majority of fathers do not report distress or unhappiness when their children leave home. Some research, however, has suggested greater distress and unhappiness among fathers when the youngest child leaves home, particularly among farm families.[9] But most research has documented that the majority of families, farm or nonfarm, are not affected negatively when their children leave home. A greater stressor may be the unexpected return home of a young adult child.

What about women? Is the empty-nest (postparental) period of the family life course traumatic and unhappy? Not according to two psychologists who studied 700 women between young adulthood and old age.[10] Women in their early fifties rated their quality of life higher than did younger or older women. This was their prime of life, a time of good health combined with greater autonomy and relational security.

The notion of the **empty nest syndrome** as a period of depression, identity crisis, role loss, and lowered sense of well-being for females has little research support. The extent to which it occurs at all may vary by factors such as socioeconomic level and employment status. Dolores Borland hypothesized that, if an empty-nest syndrome does occur, it may occur to a greater degree in a particular cohort of white middle-class women because of the unique set of social circumstances in which they live and the unique set of family values and social norms concerning women's so-called proper roles.[11] Specifically, these women dedicate their lives selflessly to their families' needs and believe that to be feminine and happy is to be married and a mother. Lower- and upper-socioeconomic-status women, Borland argued, are less likely to experience this syndrome. The former have had to work throughout their lives to help support their families, and the latter have developed other community roles, have resources to find parental-role substitutes, and have smaller families, which leads them to the empty-nest stage at a younger age.

What about marital status and well-being in the middle years? Results from respondents 51 to 61 years old indicate that married women are less likely to report symptoms of depression that their unmarried counterparts.[12] As might be expected, unhappy married respondents are much more likely to be depressed than those who report higher levels of marital satisfaction. The health benefits of marriage are greater for men than women, for the married than the unmarried, for those more affluent and educated, and for those who are employed.

A study of American women over 13 years of midlife demonstrated a significant diversity in the occurrence of life events as well as in their sequencing and spacing.[13] A large portion of these women experienced no transitions, at least with respect to marriage and the presence of children in the home. Two events, however, had detectable and important effects on their employment patterns and economic well-being: the launching of the last child and marital dissolution.

These two events were found to have opposite effects. The empty-nest transition (launching the last child) increased both labour market involvement and economic well-being, while marital dissolution (divorce and widowhood) decreased well-being. The sequence of these events made a difference as well. If marital dissolution occurred first, the woman suffered a reduction in income while maintaining custody of the child. Recovery from this situation was difficult, even when benefits of an empty-nest transition were forthcoming. If the empty nest occurred first, the woman benefited economically as long as her marriage was intact.

The absence of children symbolizes the mother's new independence. Once the children are gone, many mothers form new, nonfamilial relationships to fill the void. Many women in this age category become more active in civic and religious affairs, and an increasing number of wives and mothers become employed (see Chapter 3). This is also the time period in which parents become grandparents.

As you will see later in the chapter, older women are better off financially than were seniors in the past. However, Canadian women in the 55–64 age bracket face some unique problems—especially those not living with family members.[14] Over the last two decades, the number of women in this age bracket living alone has increased. Some of these women are never married and some are widowed, but the increase is largely due to the increased number of divorced women living on their own. These women tend to have low incomes compared to other women. They are too old to increase their income earning potential and too young for old age security benefits.

GRANDPARENTHOOD

Grandparenting has become a middle-age as well as an old-age phenomenon, given the potential of being a grandparent for three or four decades of life. With the majority of men and women in Canada marrying in their late twenties, parents may become grandparents in their fifties. The rocking chair and cane-carrying images seem grossly inappropriate. The reduction in family size has made the transition to grandparenthood a distinct status of the middle years, separate from one's own parenting years.

Grandparenthood now receives greater attention in the literature on adulthood, family development, and intergenerational relations. Two key demographic changes have shaped modern grandparenthood: increased life expectancy and changed fertility patterns. Because more people reach old age, more people experience grandparenthood as well as great- and great-

great-grandparenthood. Consistent with grandparents, great-grandparents revealed in interviews that most found the role to be significant and emotionally fulfilling, providing a sense of personal and familial renewal, diversion to their lives, and a mark of longevity.[15]

It has been suggested that the grandparent role represents a double bind.[16] On the one hand, grandparents are helpful and supportive, act warmly toward their grandchildren, and serve as resources for knowledge of family heritage and affective bonds. On the other hand, grandparents often interfere in child-rearing and provide children and grandchildren with unwelcome advice.

Perhaps this double bind illustrates the "roleless role" idea and the confusion that surrounds the appropriate expectations for grandparents. The kinship status of the grandparent includes role expectations to provide nurturance, assistance, and support to children and grandchildren. At the same time, no clear normative expectations exist as to specific rights, duties, and obligations, or at what point assistance becomes interference. Perhaps grandparents, particularly middle-class ones, must construct roles for themselves as babysitters, surrogate parents, gift givers, crisis interveners, and the like. In contrast to middle-class grandparents, working-class grandparents appear to be far more integrated into daily family life. The working-class maternal grandmother frequently socializes and nurtures her grandchildren, engages in regular interaction, and feels a sense of obligation far more than simple contact between generations.

Grandparenthood appears to have different meanings for grandmothers and grandfathers. Sometimes, the grandparent role is depicted as maternal, with women feeling greater responsibility to their grandchildren. One American study, for example, concluded that the grandfather role was more affectionate than functional.

In contrast to grandfathers, grandmothers are likely to have high levels of interaction with and provide mutual assistance to grandchildren. Grandmothers are more likely than grandfathers to be regular providers of day care. National data of a youth cohort, for example, showed that over one-half of young mothers with children relied upon relatives for child care when they were employed, and the primary relative was the grandmother.[17] The number of hours of child care provided per week by grandmothers was substantial, even though one-third of these middle-aged grandmothers were also employed. Like employed husbands and wives, who juggled their work schedules to care for children, so also grandmothers and their children juggled their work schedules to provide child care.

One underlying assumption of these patterns is that a relative, particularly the grandmother, is more emotionally committed to the child and will provide more loving care than nonrelatives. This assumption continues to be made, even today, when the availability of grandmother care seems to be declining while the need for infant and toddler care is increasing.

Given the frequency of divorce and remarriage, **stepgrandparents** are taking on new significance. Grandparenthood has been described as a "roleless role," but that description is even more apt for the grandparent by marriage rather than birth. Unlike grandparents, stepgrandparents have no biological tie

Throughout most of the world, grandparents serve as a valuable family resource to their children and grandchildren. Grandparents can fulfill many roles: custodians of family history, mediators in family conflicts, friends, gift givers, child-care providers, and significant others.

and a shorter relationship time with newly acquired grandchildren. Thus, children have greater contact, more social involvement in personal and social roles, and stronger relationships with grandparents than with stepgrandparents.[18]

Divorce/remarriage patterns not only affect stepgrandparents; they also have a major impact on grandparents. Many grandparents experience frustration in being unable to have frequent interaction and even to maintain contact with their grandchildren. This is particularly true when the grandchildren reside with the son- or daughter-in-law rather than the son or daughter.

These frustrations have prompted a relatively new and increasingly frequent phenomenon, specifically, legal cases involving **grandparent/grandchild visitation rights.**[19] In the United States all 50 states now statutorily provide an avenue by which grandparents can petition the courts for visitation with their grandchildren over a parent's objections. Such visitation laws allow grandparents to petition for the opportunity to visit with a grandchild following the child's adoption by a stepparent, to visit with a grandchild who has been adopted by strangers, to visit with a child who has been surrendered to an agency for adoption, and to force visitation with a grandchild living with his married parents in an intact home over the objection of those parents.

With the changes that are taking place over the life course, great-grandparenthood rather than grandparenthood is emerging as the familial status associated with old age. Because there are so few precedents or role models, great-grandparents today must create their own models of interaction regarding their relationships with their great-grandchildren.

FAMILIES IN LATER LIFE AND PEOPLE WHO ARE AGED

Growth of the elderly population

Since the turn of the century, one of the more significant changes in family and marital relationships has been **life expectancy.** Because people live longer, the proportion of older Canadians has increased dramatically. In 1998 there were 3.7 million seniors (people 65 and older), 12 percent of the population.[20] Longevity combined with low fertility means that the older population is increasing faster than the total population. Figure 9.1 shows the relative growth of the senior population, including projections into this century. By 2031, over 20 percent of the population will be seniors. The continual increase in the over-65 age group is not due to an increase in the life span (the biological age limit) but rather to an increase in the number of people living. If birth rates decline or remain stable, people over 65 will constitute an even larger proportion of the population for decades to come.

Life expectancy is a common indicator of population aging. Between 1921 and 1997, life expectancy for Canadians increased from 58.8 years to 75.8 years for men and from 60.6 years to 81.4 years for women. In other words, Canadian males born in 1997 will live 17 years longer than males born in 1921 and females will live 21 years longer.[21]

Another way to measure population aging is with dependency ratios: the proportion of older and younger people supported by the working population. In 1965, 19 percent of the dependent population was aged 65 or older. By 1987, this proportion was 34 percent and it is expected to be over half by 2030.[22]

In cultures that value filial piety, older people, especially parents, are highly respected. Men, in particular, receive increased status, prestige, and deference with age. In North America, however, old age does not bring increased prestige and status; indeed, aging has a negative connotation.[23] Frequently, old age is defined as a time of dependency and declining productivity and vitality. The elderly person's socioeconomic status is generally determined by his or her achievements earlier in life; if the achievements were limited and provisions for these later years were inadequate, opportunities for a full, meaningful life will be limited.

It is not difficult to be sensitive to the aging process and the people experiencing it. Community newspapers are filled with pictures of couples celebrating their 50th wedding anniversaries, announcements of community and business leaders retiring, polls showing attitudinal differences between the old and the young, and of course, obituary notices. All these serve as reminders of the social dimension of aging and of the position of the older person in society.

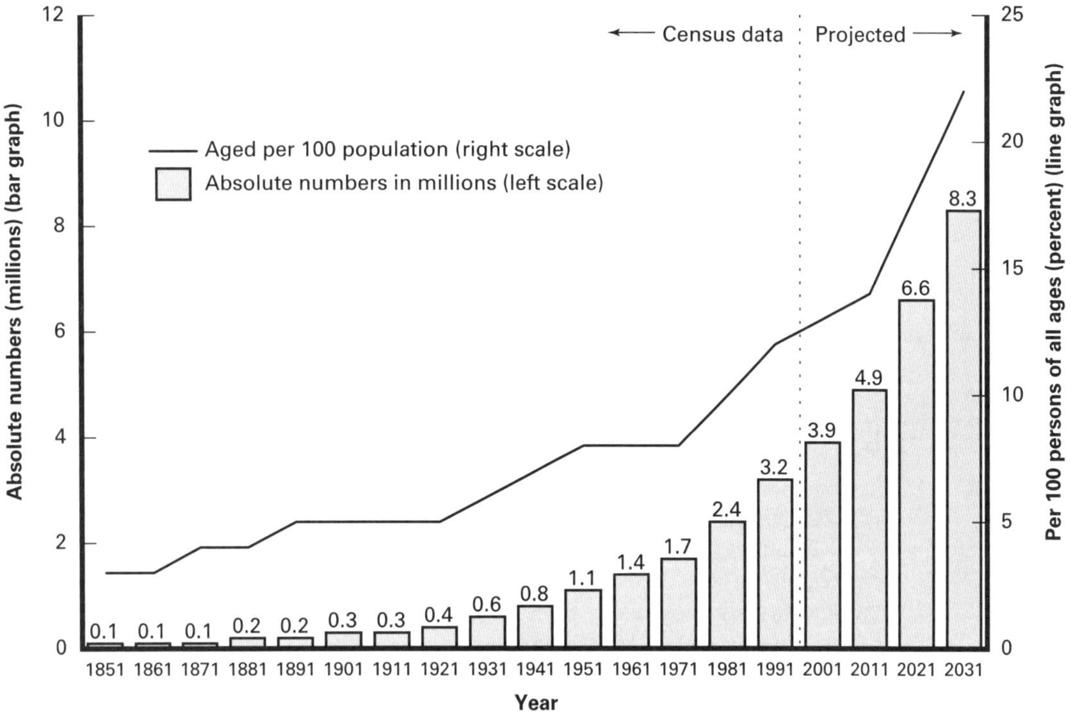

Figure 9.1
The aged population, Canada, 1851–2031 (absolute numbers and percentages)
Source: Profile of Canada's Seniors, Statistics Canada Catalogue 96-312E (1994): 6, and Prentice Hall Canada Inc.

News Item

Urban life expectancy longer

While we may have an image of life in rural Canada as stress-free, and dream of retiring away from the city, people living in Canadian cities with a population of 100 000 or more live longer. One of the reasons is that they have better access to health services; also, urbanites typically have higher incomes and higher education.

Across Canada there is a gender difference in longevity, and this holds true in urban centres as well. Canadian men live longest in British Columbia (75.8 years); Canadian women live longest in Saskatchewan (81.8 years).

Source: "Life Expectancy Longer on Average in Urban Centers," *The Globe and Mail*, January 9, 1997, A6.

Social gerontology, the study of older persons and the aging process, as well as the closely related field, the sociology of aging, have both been concerned with the social definition of who is thought to be old; their interaction patterns and behaviours; the expectations that are imposed upon them; their age, sex, place of residence, and other demographic factors; and the problems and needs that they have living in society. Within this framework, the family of later life has taken on particular significance in understanding these and other factors of concern to people who are aged.

Marriages and families in the later years

Later-life families are characterized by both continuity and change as they experience marriage, divorce, widowhood, remarriage, childlessness, grandparenthood, sibling relationships, and family caregiving.[24] The majority of Canadian seniors are married (see Table 9.2) but there are larger differences between men and women. Three-quarters of men but only half of women aged 65–74 live with their spouse. This difference persists into old age. For those seniors aged 85 and over, more than half of the men but only 10 percent of the women live with a spouse.

Relatively few men and women in these age categories were divorced, separated, or single. However, among these age groups, widowhood is common. Women are far more likely than men to be widowed. For all seniors, 12.7 percent of men compared to 46.1 percent of women are widows. For older seniors, the difference is as dramatic. Over the age of 85, 38.6 percent of men and 79.2 percent of women are widowed.[25] (Widows and widowers will be discussed later in this chapter.)

Married couples comprise a significant proportion of this over-65 group. Of those couples in first marriages, most had previously celebrated 25th wedding anniversaries, and many had celebrated or would soon celebrate 50th anniversaries. Over the years, these couples have shared many joys and weathered many crises. One rarely reads about divorce or incompatibility among these couples, but such problems do exist. Even when unhappy in their marriage, the experiences of their years, the lives and activities of their children, and perhaps the lack of realistic alternatives to the marriage keep the older couple together.

Marital and family relationships are often proclaimed to be the primary sources of social involvement, companionship, fulfillment, and happiness for people who are elderly. Existing studies have suggested that marriage has a positive effect on psychological well-being among people who are elderly (particularly when compared to people who are divorced and widowed)[26] and, as shown earlier, that marital satisfaction may be higher for married elderly people than for married people in the intermediate stages of the family life course.

What about elderly people who never married, or are divorced or widowed, groups that make up a sizeable proportion of the older population? How important are families to them? Studies have shown that geographic proximity to siblings, particularly same-sex siblings, exerts a positive influence on life satisfaction and well-being. The 1990 General Social Survey found that unmarried older men and women had frequent contact with siblings.[27]

Table 9.2
Family status of seniors, by age and sex, 1996

	Seniors aged								
	65–74			*75–84*			*85 and over*		
	Men	Women	Total	Men	Women	Total	Men	Women	Total
					%				
Living with family:									
With husband or wife	77.4	53.8	61.6	71.9	30.4	47.2	55.0	10.8	25.6
With common-law partner	2.3	1.1	1.7	1.2	0.5	0.8	0.8	0.2	0.4
Lone parent	1.6	5.9	3.9	1.9	5.7	4.2	3.3	7.3	6.0
Child living with parents	0.1	0.1	0.1	—	—	—	—	—	—
Living with extended family members	2.7	7.6	5.4	4.6	12.4	9.3	10.3	21.9	18.0
Total living with family	84.2	68.4	75.7	79.6	49.1	61.4	69.4	40.2	50.0
Not living with family:									
Living alone	13.8	29.8	22.4	18.6	49.2	36.9	28.6	57.8	48.0
Lving with non-relatives	2.0	1.8	1.9	1.7	1.7	1.7	20.0	2.0	2.0
Total not living with family	15.9	31.5	24.3	20.4	50.9	38.6	30.6	59.8	50.0
Total	100	100	100	100	100	100	100	100	100
Total population (000s)	923.9	1 088.3	2 012.2	411.0	609.6	1 020.6	73.6	145.8	219.4

Source: Statistics Canada, *1996 Census of Canada*, and *A Portrait of Seniors in Canada*, Statistics Canada Catalogue 89-519-XPE, 1999.

Of course, older Canadians typically have more siblings than younger Canadians. Given the long-term declines in family size, unmarried older Canadians in the future may come to depend on friends rather than siblings for support. Women are more likely than men to see relatives and maintain contact with them by phone.

A study of Canadian widows challenged the assumption that this is an isolated group. According to the 1995 General Social Survey, there were 661 000 widows aged 65 living alone. "Most of these widows had left home before age 25 to marry and have children. They remained married to the same man for an average of 39 years and were widowed at an average age of 63."[28] These women report strong social support networks and have close relations with adult children and friends.

Data from the Canadian National Population Health Survey supports the assumption that seniors are psychologically healthy and enjoy frequent social contacts.[29] Crompton and Kemeny found that most seniors reported that they were happy. Not surprisingly, health was strongly related to happiness. Over 90 percent of seniors who experienced good health said they were happy. Married seniors, even those in poor health, enjoy a high level of emotional support.

Intergenerational relationships

Intergenerational relationships encompass a wide variety of interaction patterns between family members of different generations. Chapters 7 and 8 focused primarily on the generations of young children and their parents. This chapter focuses on parents (adult children) and their parents. Parents in these middle years have sometimes been referred to as the "sandwich generation," squeezed between the demands and needs of their children and those of their aging parents. (See Family Diversity box on page 243.)

An overview of the dominant themes between these adult children and their parents concluded that, after years of investigation, there is no evidence that older people are alienated from their children.[30] Approximately half of all older Canadians lived within 10 kilometres of the child with whom they have most regular contact; 60 percent of this group were in weekly contact. Contact was more regular for women than men. Relationships between adult children and their older/aging parents are characterized by reciprocal support. These family members have frequent face-to-face contacts, keep in touch by phone and correspondence, exchange care during illnesses, give money and gifts, run errands, prepare meals, give emotional support and affection, and, in general, promote one another's well-being (happiness, satisfaction, morale). Again, note that the exchange patterns are mutually supportive. Contact, support, and so forth are seldom one-way but are instead reciprocal interactions.

In spite of older people not being alienated from their children and there being mutually supportive relationships between adult children and their parents, national data indicate that one-half of Americans do not *routinely* engage in giving or receiving relationships with their parents, and only one in ten are engaged in extensive exchange relationships.[31] This general pattern varied considerably, however, by demographic characteristics and the needs and resources of each generation. Aging parents are likely to be involved in giving and/or receiving aid with at least one of their adult children, and elderly parents are assisted more often in situations of poor health. Family support does provide an important security net for family members (old and young) during periods of high need (the presence of preschool children or when disability occurs).

Who is likely to provide a disproportionate amount of this support, particularly to older parents? As one might guess, significant differences exist by gender. Daughters, far more than daughters-in-law, not only provide more support but do so for different reasons than do sons.[32] Daughters are most motivated to provide support by intergenerational affection and altruism. Sons, on the other hand, are more motivated by principles of obligation, familiarity, and self-interest. They contribute to the support of their parents more out of an expectation of financial reward implicit in the endorsement of intergenerational inheritance than out of sentiment. Affection is a stronger predictor of support when mothers are the recipients, and inheritance is a more salient predictor when fathers are the recipients of care. Irrespective of motives, the notion that adult children abandon their elderly relatives or fail to meet their needs is basically a myth.

Another myth appears to be that high levels of conflict exist among generations who live together. Certain circumstances, such as financial dependency and unemployment, seem to increase parent/child conflict, but episodes of open disagreement and arguing occur much less often than episodes of enjoyable leisure time. Coresidency results in surprisingly low levels of conflict between parents and their resident adult children.[33] Even the parents' health and dependency are not related to parent/child conflict. Most parents and adult children, including those who live together, get along quite harmoniously.

What about people who are elderly and childless? The value of children to their elderly parents in providing emotional, material, financial, and other support has been widely asserted and empirically supported. However, one study of childless elderly people demonstrated levels of well-being that matched and sometimes exceeded those of elderly parents.[34] The childless group were more financially secure (see Chapter 7 on childless couples, as well) and in better health; the parents, however, tended to be surrounded by a greater number of friends and have more general satisfaction with life. By and large, this study and others showed that people who are elderly, whether parents or childless, are very satisfied with family, friendships, and life. They are less satisfied with health and income, two problems that will be discussed later in this chapter.

Living arrangements among the elderly

As persons reach and pass the age of 65, an increasing number retire, suffer decreases in income, and experience the loss by death of spouses and siblings. Where do people of this age category live? Are they institutionalized? Do they live with children? Do they live alone? Do living arrangements differ for men and women?

Knowing that the proportion of older Canadians has increased and that women typically live longer than men, we could predict that more older women will live alone and that more older people will live in institutions now than in the past. Nevertheless, the majority of seniors live with a spouse in their own homes.

Three-generation households are rare in Canada, representing only 3 percent of all family households. However, the number of three-generation households is rising.[35] One explanation for the increase is the rise in Asian immigrants to Canada. Nearly half of all three-generation households were headed by immigrants, and three-quarters of this group were Asian. A related reason for the increase is that 30 percent of immigrants from 1986 to 1996 were part of family reunification programs. We might expect more of these families to live in multi-generation households.

Filial piety, or the value of respect and care for older parents, has not been strong in Western cultures. In cultures in which three-generation households are common, caregiving between generations is reciprocal. The older generation may provide financial help and child care, and expect care and support as they age. In Asia, a strong tradition of filial piety reinforced by religious traditions exists. The fact that Canadians do not generally live in three-generation households does not mean that Canadians do not visit and support their older parents. Middle-aged children do have regular contact with their elderly parents. The closer parents live to their middle-aged children, the more frequent the contact. Five percent of men and 6 percent of women have daily contact with their parents (see Figure 9.2).[36]

According to the 1996 census, 29 percent of seniors lived alone. Few lived with extended family members, although the numbers increased with age of senior (see Table 9.2). When parents and children live together, the arrangement can work to the satisfaction of both. If a woman is employed, her mother or mother-in-law may assume much of the responsibility for running the household. Another arrangement that works for some families is for the parent and married children to have separate but geographically close residences. This arrangement allows for mutual support without constant physical presence. Only about 5 percent of Canadian men and 9 percent of women lived in senior residences, including special-care homes. The percentage of seniors living in institutions rises sharply with age. For those 75 to 84 years old, 6.7 percent of women and 10.3 percent of men live in special-care homes, in contrast to 24.3 percent of men and 37.7 percent of women over 85.

Contrary to some stereotypes of the elderly, (1) most people who are elderly are not in nursing homes or long-term care institutions, and (2) most elderly are not isolated from their families.

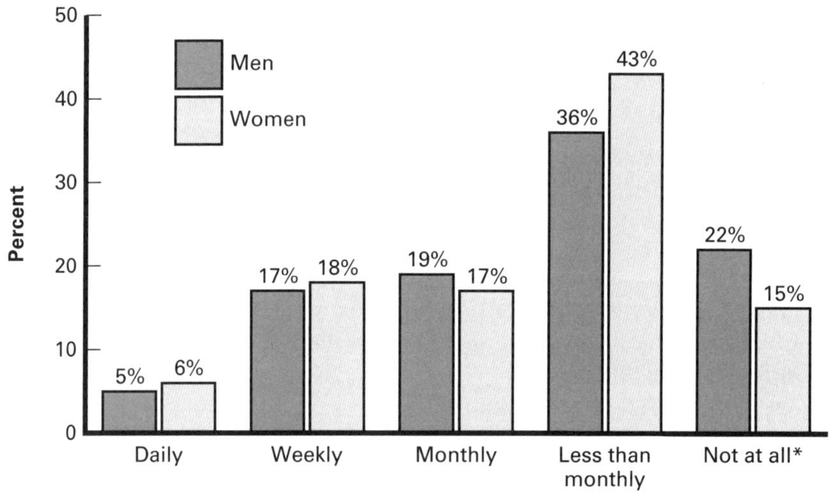

Figure 9.2
Personal contacts with siblings, by men and women aged 65 and over, 1990
*No personal contact in the past 12 months.
Source: Susan McDaniel, "Emotional Support and Family Contacts of Older Canadians," *Canadian Social Trends,* Statistics Canada Catalogue 11-008E (Spring 1993): 32.

CHALLENGES FACED BY OLDER ADULTS

Health and care

The longer one lives, the more likely one is to experience health problems. Daughters have played an important role as caregivers for noninstitutionalized elderly people. Daughters also serve as caregivers to both dependent and self-sufficient elderly mothers. One study found that caregiving was an intensification of a preexisting pattern of aid giving evident in female intergenerational relationships.[38]

It is a North American stereotype that we disregard (even discard) older family members—that instead of families today providing care for elderly and disabled members, we tend to institutionalize those who cannot care for themselves. Certainly, geographical mobility coupled with the fact that most married women are employed and dealing with the domestic requirements of their own households leave little time or energy to add care for older parents to the daily or weekly routine. Nevertheless, the stereotype is an exaggeration that gerontologists call the *myth of abandonment*.

Are caregiving tasks such as personal care (bathing, eating, toileting), mobility (from room to room or in and out of chairs or beds) and daily living tasks (shopping, cleaning, cooking) defined as a burden and does it produce stress? Common logic would suggest it is and does, and an abundance of literature documents the physical, emotional, financial, and interpersonal costs experienced by family members caring for parents with a disability. Exchange theory, too, suggests that if an elderly infirm parent requires much and can return little, stress will be high. Support was found to exist for this idea in that reciprocity by impaired mothers significantly reduced the stress and burden experienced by caregiving daughters.[39] The greater the number of reciprocal tasks the elder was able to perform, the lower the reported stress and burden of the primary caregiver. When tasks performed by the primary caregiver increased, both stress and burden were greater. Interestingly, reciprocity did not affect the satisfaction of the elderly parent. Explanations given were that the investments that elderly mothers made in their children over the life course may have been perceived as compensation and that mothers may feel they are reciprocating to the best of their abilities even though these abilities may be limited.

Family caregiving, however, does not seem to extend to multigenerational families. A study of four-generation families found that ties extended only to aging parents who cared for their now-adult children.[40] Consistent with other studies, the closest relationships were between mothers and daughters. In some families, such ties extended to three generations, but beyond two generations was a rarity. Ties weaken as the family line lengthens. Three- and four-generation families often have large numbers of members, but close ties among them are few. Divorce and disruption in the family leads to more fragmentation in family life and to enduring social distance, if not downright hostility. Although family members perform many caregiving services for their elders, this care frequently rests squarely on the shoulders of one female member of the family. Thus, in most cases, the arrangement could not be called an extended-family caregiving system.

Members of the so-called "sandwich generation" may find themselves caring for their young grandchildren as well as their elderly parents. Family members—particularly wives, mothers, and daughters—serve as caregivers and primary sources of support and affection for both the young and the old.

Children's problems

A second difficulty is a reversal of the common theme that elderly parents place stresses and burdens on their adult offspring. That is, do adult children's problems affect the well-being of their elderly parents?

Evidence has suggested that they do. A national survey of elderly people in Canada demonstrated that parents whose adult children have mental, physical, or stress-related problems experience greater depression than parents whose children do not have these problems.[41] While health status appears to be the most powerful predictor of distress in the elderly, their children's major problems have a direct and profound effect as well.

Income and standard of living

Many seniors in the past suffered financial crises with age. While too many seniors are poor today, the entrenched poverty has been alleviated and there has been an encouraging decline in poverty among seniors. Seniors today have income security from old age security pensions, guaranteed income supplements and, for some, the Canada and Quebec Pension Plans. In 1980, 27 percent of older men and 38 percent of older women in Canada were poor according to the definition used in Chapter 4. By 1992, these rates had dropped to 12 percent and 23 percent respectively. Table 9.3 shows the variation from province to province in the extent of poverty among older Canadians.

We can expect less disparity in the financial well-being of men and women over 65 as more women with labour force experience (and therefore pension earnings) retire. In the past, older women faced a high risk of poverty because they were likely to be widowed, and, with little labour force experience, had few sources of income in addition to old age security benefits. Few pension schemes provided survivor benefits.[42] However, marriage generally protects elderly people from the worst poverty; thus, elderly people who were widowed or divorced all had poverty rates significantly higher than those of married people. As we know from the earlier discussion of the unbalanced sex ratios among seniors, most unmarried seniors are women.

An American study by Madonna Mayer showed how the supposedly gender-neutral eligibility and benefit structures of Social Security, private pensions, and personal pensions such as individual retirement accounts—three major retirement income programs—are all structured around gender.[43] How? While the social security nets in Canada and the United States differ, her findings hold true in both countries.

1. Retirement income is linked to waged labour, which is itself gender-based.
2. Nonwaged reproductive labour, performed predominantly by women, is not recognized as labour.
3. Old-age pension schemes are grounded in a conceptualization of family status as permanent—having a male breadwinner—despite insurmountable evidence that family status is transient. With age, women are increasingly likely to become single.

Table 9.3
Poverty rates for men and women 65 and older, by province

	Men				*Women*			
	1980	***1995***	***1996***	***Percent change 1980–1996***	***1980***	***1995***	***1996***	***Percent change 1980–1996***
Newfoundland	27.6	6.6	11.4	–59%	36.9	13.7	14.5	–61%
Prince Edward Island	33.7	5.6	8.0	–76%	52.7	14.8	15.1	–71%
Nova Scotia	22.8	5.3	8.2	–64%	31.5	15.7	21.3	–32%
New Brunswick	22.1	8.8	6.5	–71%	34.2	14.0	16.6	–51%
Quebec	33.7	15.4	20.2	–40%	46.2	32.5	37.4	–19%
Ontario	24.0	8.9	10.7	–55%	34.3	19.7	18.5	–46%
Manitoba	23.8	10.3	14.4	–39%	41.2	22.2	28.1	–32%
Saskatchewan	28.1	3.3	6.1	–78%	49.0	12.6	16.0	–67%
Alberta	25.2	7.5	7.2	–71%	38.8	15.3	17.7	–54%
British Columbia	29.6	10.1	10.4	–65%	32.7	20.4	21.4	–35%
Canada	**27.3**	**10.2**	**12.4**	**–55%**	**38.4**	**22.1**	**23.9**	**–38%**

Source: National Council of Welfare, *Poverty Profile, 1996* (Ottawa: Minister of Supply and Services, Spring 1998): 89.

All three factors contribute to disproportionate impoverishment among older women.

David Cheal asserted that elderly Americans are overall not as deficient in economic resources as the image generally presented suggests,[44] and his conclusions hold true for Canadians as well. While average income declines sharply with age, so do average expenditures. The ownership of domestic assets, such as the family home, makes it possible for seniors to enjoy a certain standard of living with a lower income than would otherwise be required. In fact, Cheal suggested that young adults are major beneficiaries of familial transactions, that gift giving by elders is more significant than might be expected, and that financial aid is given by the elders to relatives more frequently than received.

Abuse and neglect

A fourth problem facing the elderly is abuse and neglect. Until the late 1970s there was little or no information published about domestic mistreatment of the elderly in their homes by relatives or other domestic caregivers. (This issue will be examined more thoroughly in the next chapter.)

Extreme caution must be taken in categorizing people who are aged as a homogeneous population. To be sure, dependency, sickness, isolation, and abuse occur frequently among elderly people. Nonetheless, a sizeable proportion of older people have few health problems, carry on active lives with families and friends, and continue to make major economic and social contributions to their communities and society.

SOCIALIZATION OF THE AGED

Tremendous emphasis has been given to children and youth in socialization literature, such that the resocialization needs of the aged have largely been ignored and overshadowed. In contrast to people who are aged, children receive much of their socialization within the family and from peers, schools, jobs, and the community. But what socializing agents direct the aged? Where is the training for retirement? Where is the training for widowhood? Where is the training to prepare for illness and death? Where is the training about narrowing of social relationships?

In many ways, our society overlooks the fact that persons over 65 are social beings, that their world is maintained and meaning is found through interaction with others. As should have become clear in the previous chapter, of primary importance to the socialization process and to defining and redefining the self is the extent and nature of friendship ties, association with significant others, involvement in groups of reference, and social interaction in general. Why should these factors be less important to persons over 65 than to those under 20? In fact, one could argue that social relationships take on increased importance as persons move outside of their occupational spheres and as they experience the deaths of their peers.

Intimacy and familiarity characterize the family system and make it highly suitable for fulfilling many of the needs, services, and interaction patterns of the individual members. Even when persons have no living kin, older people tend to substitute for missing relatives by converting close friends into quasi-kin.[45] *Fictive kin* for the elderly serve in much the same way as the fictive kin described in Chapter 4 among families in poverty. These nonrelatives serve as meaningful kin components of their social networks and as a valuable resource in meeting specific needs of elderly people.

It should be noted that family factors do not operate independently of the culture in which families operate. To avoid having people who are aged become "socially disabled," there must be congruence between the cultural goals and structural opportunities that society provides. The effectiveness of the family as a resource is largely contingent on the values and services of the larger society: job opportunities, leisure-time activities, health care, clarity of roles, perception of the aged as fulfilling valuable functions, and socializing and resocializing opportunities appropriate to the later stage of the life cycle.

RETIREMENT

The major problem of retirement involves resocializing men and women to life situations. Traditionally, men assumed the major economic responsibility for their families, and their lives revolved around work/employment roles. Thus, it followed that the literature on retirement focused heavily on men. Women's retirement was less studied because it was not perceived to constitute a salient social issue. With the dramatic increase in the labour force employment of women and the growing proportion of women retirees, studies of the preparation for and effects of retirement on both sexes are appearing with increasing frequency.

Robert Atchley viewed retirement as a process, an event, and a role.[46] As a *process*, it involves attitudes toward and preparation for retirement. As an *event*, it occurs at a specific time and may involve a ceremonial rite of passage. As a *role*, it involves the right to economic support without holding a job and duties associated with managing one's own life and living within one's income.

Most family-related studies of retirees have paralleled the findings of a study done in rural Iowa.[47] There, elderly people were well integrated into kinship networks. Satisfaction with family life was high for both sexes. Retired elderly people were neither abandoned nor neglected by their families; in fact, these elderly turned to family members rather than to formal support services. Children and siblings played a special role in support. Retired females had significantly more contact with siblings and children than did males. Overall, personal background characteristics of health, financial status, age, length of retirement, and marital status affected both the quantity and quality of kinship relations.

Irrespective of the reasons for retirement, it seems likely that this event will require major role readjustments for both sexes. Health, income, status, and feelings of self-worth often tend to decrease at the time of retirement, and the problems are compounded by the death of a spouse.

DYING AND DEATH

Death is an inescapable event, one that will occur within all family and kin networks. Certainly, the loss of those one loves most intensely—parent, spouse, child, or other family member—is likely to cause tremendous pain.

The death of a parent adversely affects marital relationships as well as the physical and psychological well-being of adult children.[48] Bereaved children suffer a decline in social support from their partners and an increase in the partner's negative behaviours. They and their partners may also experience a significant increase in psychological distress and/or alcohol consumption, and a decline in physical health status. Those individuals for whom relationships with parents were salient and positive prior to the parents' death were more adversely affected. The loss of a parental relationship characterized by negativity (a difficult family history) sometimes led to an improvement in an adult child's well-being. But for most, psychological distress was very apparent in the first few months following the death of a parent, with healing effects apparent later.

Terminal illness, dying, and death are separate but interrelated events and processes. The application of interaction theory to these events would suggest that definitions and meanings attached to illness and death greatly influence one's ability to accept, cope, or adjust to them. This theory may help explain why, from a life-course perspective, middle-aged adults seem to be the most adversely affected by the death of a spouse or sibling.[49] Recognizing significant others may help explain why many persons choose to endure illness and death at home rather than in a hospital or institutional setting. Understanding reference groups may help explain the relevance of religion, friends, and kin networks as support systems in facing these circumstances. While death may be a physical process, cultural, social, and interpersonal processes all influence and affect it. To mourn, to wear black, to commit suicide by burning following the death of a spouse, to build mausoleums, or to bury in airtight vaults are all responses dependent on cultural, class, and other social conditions.

The circumstances surrounding the death of a friend, child, or spouse frequently require major decisions by family members.

- Should a dying family member be assured the right to die with dignity and to determine the time, place, and manner of his or her death?
- Should euthanasia (the deliberate ending of a loved one's life to spare him or her from the suffering that goes with an incurable and agonizing disease) be permitted?
- If permitted, should euthanasia be **passive** (not preventing death through means of life support systems) or **active** (causing death by poisoning, strangling, shooting)?
- What about funeral and burial decisions—how, where, payment, and so forth?
- What about the disbursement of personal effects, the carrying out of a will, and the settlement of an estate?
- If a long-term illness preceded the death, is care and its cost the sole responsibility of the family?

Family Diversity

The "long-living" Abkhasians of southern Russia

The Abkhasians, who live in a rough, mountainous region in southern Russia, are said to have a disproportionate number of people who live to be over 100 years old and some who live to be 120. Many scientists have questioned the authenticity of these ages. Nevertheless, whether they are 70 or 107, how does one account for their good eyesight, having their own teeth, little loss of hearing, few, if any, cases of mental illness or cancer, rare hospitalization, and longevity?

Some accounts attribute these factors to their work habits and their physical daily labour as herders and farmers, to their taking walks of more than two miles a day, and to swimming in the mountain streams. Others claim they are due to their diet and the value they attach to staying slim, eating lots of fruits and vegetables, and consuming few fatty substances.

Explanations of longevity related to family life focus on (1) the family status accorded to them and (2) their sex practices. As to family status, Abkhasians are said to gain status throughout the life course with no self-devaluation and few abrupt changes in their lives. The old are granted certain rights and privileges not accorded the young. They feel needed by their children and grandchildren and enjoy secure roles and statuses in extended families.

As to their sexual practices, the norms of the culture call for sexual relations to be postponed until after 30, the traditional age at marriage. Writings suggest it was even considered unmanly for a new husband to exercise his sexual rights on his wedding night. Sex was a pleasure to be regulated for the sake of one's health, and like a good wine, to get better with age. Reports exist of Abkhasian men fathering children at the age of 100.

Source: Adapted from Harold G. Cox, *Later Life: The Realities of Aging*, 4th ed. (Saddle River, NJ: Prentice-Hall, 1996): 70–74.

- If the family cannot care for or pay, does the church, temple, mosque, or synagogue, community, state, or someone else bear the responsibility?

The list goes on and on.

In most cultures, the immediate family and the immediate kin network are the major sources of decision-making and social support. Among people who are elderly, the presence of relatives makes it possible for bedridden persons to live outside institutions. Elderly people turn first to their families for help, then to friends and neighbours, and, as a last resort, to bureaucratic organizations. Thus, it is not surprising that surveys have indicated most people say they would prefer to die at home.

A movement is under way in health care to make family/kin interaction with the terminally ill or dying patient more possible. One aspect of the movement, the **hospice,** is a therapeutic environment designed from the patient's point of view. Unlike a regular hospital, which stresses privacy, a hospice program emphasizes space for interaction with staff, family, and friends. Instead of subordinating the patient to the needs of the institution—leaving families waiting in the hall, for example—a hospice program is designed to provide as much care in the patient's home as possible; when medical facilities are needed, they involve a team of medical, nursing, psychiatric, and religious people plus social workers and family members, as appropriate. The concern in a hospice is on increasing the quality of the last days of life and on making humane care synonymous with good medical practice. The family of the institutionalized patient is encouraged to be involved, perhaps by bringing in home cooking, bathing the patient, supplying medication, or bringing along the family dog. Hours of visits are unlimited, and interaction is permitted with young children and grandchildren.

The significance of family ties takes on an added dimension when one looks at the relationship between marital status and mortality.[50] Mortality is lower for married persons than unmarried ones and lower for people with children than for those without children. These findings suggest that protection against early death may be afforded by different kinds of social ties, particularly marital, parental, and kin ties. Losing these ties is probably behind some of the difficulties of the widow or widower.

WIDOWS AND WIDOWERS

Some sociologists have called the life-cycle stage following the death of a spouse the *postmarital family*. Not all postmarital families will be older widows or widowers. However, given sex differences in longevity, women can expect to be widowed. In 1991, there were 1 344 700 widowed Canadians, 76.6 percent of whom were ages 65 and over. The majority of these were women.[51] Facing the loss of a spouse and making the shift from a married to widowed status often presents extreme emotional and financial difficulties.

Society compounds the difficulty of adjusting to widowed status by placing an unstated taboo on the discussion of death between husband and wife or parents and children while they are alive. As a result, the widow or widower is often unprepared for the decisions that need to be made following the death of a spouse.

Even if discussions preceded the death, the likelihood is great that loneliness, social isolation, and a need for major readjustments in living patterns will result. One study compared the adjustment process for women who lost a spouse through death and those who had experienced divorce.[52] Widowhood was more distressing and disruptive of identity than divorce. The loss of a spouse by death involved more positive evaluations of the deceased, and with time the husband became an "unusually good man." Divorce has quite the opposite effect. The adjustment process, however, was similar for both the widows and divorcees.

Readjustment may be less difficult if widowhood follows a major illness or some type of role change on the part of the spouse. Adjustment to widowhood is often best when a person has already established some personal autonomy, close continuing friendships, a realistic philosophy of life, economic security, and meaningful personal interests.

One problem, believed to be widespread among elderly persons in general but particularly among the widowed, is that of social isolation and loneliness.[53]

Social isolation is the objective condition of having few contacts with family, friends, or both. *Loneliness* is a subjective condition that includes feelings of emptiness, aimlessness, and lack of companionship. Life history data from a Dutch survey of nearly 3400 older adults showed that those currently not living with a partner are lonelier than those with a partner.[54] Furthermore, loneliness increased with the number of union dissolutions experienced and decreased with the time elapsed since the last dissolution. Time does not heal all wounds, as those who lost a partner felt more lonely that those who never had a partner. The loss of a partner was more detrimental for males than females.

The extreme outcome of such conditions is demonstrated by the frequency of suicide. Suicide rates of people who are widowed are consistently higher for all age groups than those of people who are married; the rate of completed suicides is significantly higher for males than for females.

Rosemary Blieszner, in viewing widowhood from a socialist-feminist perspective, writes that in some respects, women who have been in a traditional relationship have an edge over men in bereavement.[55] Widowed women are adept at housekeeping and kinkeeping, whereas widowed men are inexperienced at these tasks and are more susceptible to dependence on others. On the other hand, widows are less likely to have adequate financial resources since they have neither the savings, pension benefits, skills, nor work experience common to men.

Some widows and widowers remarry, but the chances of remarriage are, of course, higher for widowers than for widows. In one study, age was found to be the single most important factor in explaining the remarriage of widows; the younger the age, the greater the likelihood of remarriage. For widowers, age was not significant. Older widowers did not have higher remarriage rates than younger widowers, despite the greater availability of potential marriage partners.[56] In Canada, the sex ratio of males per 1,000 females drops from 816 for the 65-to-74 age group to 438 for seniors over 85. The sex ratio of unmarried men is even lower.

Programs to encourage remarriage among widows and widowers would not be successful given the unbalanced sex ratio, at least not in a monogamous system. The problem is further compounded by the norm that suggests that women should marry men of their own age or older. The remarriage problem for widowers is less severe, since there are both an excess of women their own age and social approval of marriage to women younger than themselves.

SUMMARY

1. This chapter examined two major periods of the life cycle: the middle years, from approximately age 40 to retirement, and the later years, from approximately age 60 or 65 until the end of the life span.
2. The postparental period—those middle years after the departure of children and before retirement—is one in which most men and women are married, with small percentages of single, widowed, and divorced people. This period is

one of the longest of the marital life cycle, covering a span of 20 to 25 years.

3. The significance of the middle years appears to differ for men and women. While family income approaches its peak, there is mixed evidence as to the extent to which this period of life is bright or difficult. Researchers talk of a midlife crisis or transition for men and an "empty nest" syndrome for women. The idea of a crisis in midlife seems to have little research support.
4. Grandparenting has become a middle-aged in addition to an old-age phenomenon. It may be an instrumental role for family systems in linking generations, in financial and service support functions, and in assisting the transition to other life-cycle stages. Grandparent appears to be a positive status for most respondents, although the roles are seldom clearly defined and tend to vary considerably by social class and cultural context.
5. Later life in Canada is often viewed as an undesirable period, characterized by dependent relationships and declining productivity. This perception contrasts with much of the world, where older persons receive increased status, prestige, and deference.
6. In Canada, over 80 percent of men but only about 56 percent of women aged 65 to 74 are married. After age 85, half of the men but only 10 percent of the women are married. Marriage in the later years is perceived as favourable when compared to marriage in preceding periods of the life course. Most of the men and women of this age are living in families or in geographical proximity to their children. Relatively few older people are in long-term-care institutions such as nursing homes.
7. The problems facing people who are aged are many, but this chapter focused briefly on four: the need for care, problems of children, income and standard of living, and abuse and neglect. Most health problems are handled in the home rather than in hospitals, with primary care coming from spouses or children. Adult children with mental, physical, and stress-related problems affect the well-being of their elderly parents. Income drops in old age, but most families cope quite well; elderly people often give more money to relatives than they receive. Little information is available on abuse and neglect, which is a recently identified social problem (see Chapter 10).
8. Retirement, widowhood, changing relationships, and the like create a need for resocialization of people who are elderly to new roles and definitions of self in relation to society.
9. Retirement has been described as a process, an event, and a role. For both sexes, retirement appears to be positive. Marital and household roles appear to change relatively little in retirement over the traditional patterns established during years of employment. The increased employment of women appears to be lessening the difference between the sexes in the significance of retirement.
10. Dying and death are processes and events of major importance and significance to family members. Family members are major supports both to the dying person and to one another following death. Recognition of this support seems to be encouraging movements in treating terminally ill and dying patients at home and in family-focused medical settings.
11. The postmarital family, particularly as represented by the widow or widower, is not unique to the aged family but is disproportionately represented among persons over age 65. More women occupy widow status than any other marital status. With the unbalanced sex ratio, remarriage is unlikely for a large number of women. For men, although the availability of a new spouse is less of a problem, the problems of widowhood may be equally severe.
12. Following old age and death, the family life course will end for a particular nuclear family, but it will continue for the multigenerational extended family. Each period of the life course is distinguished by circumstances that are unique to and different from those of earlier and later periods. This chapter examined selected factors relating to the postparental periods: middle years, retirement, and old age. Conflict, crisis, and marital disorganization, although present at these periods of the life cycles, are not confined to them. Chapter 10 will explore social patterns surrounding crisis and disorganization, with a particular focus on abuse and violence among intimates.

KEY TERMS AND TOPICS

Postparental period p. 240
Marital status and coresidence in the middle years p. 241
Significance of the middle years p. 242
Midlife transition p. 244
Empty-nest syndrome p. 244
Grandparenthood p. 245
Stepgrandparents p. 246
Families in later life and people who are aged p. 248
Growth of the elderly population p. 248
Life expectancy p. 248
Marriages and families in the later years p. 250
Intergenerational relationships p. 252
Living arrangements among the elderly p. 253
Challenges faced by older adults p. 255
Socialization of the aged p. 258
Retirement p. 259
Dying and death p. 260
Passive and active euthanasia p. 260
Hospice p. 261
Widows and widowers p. 262

DISCUSSION QUESTIONS

1. What is unique about the middle years, or the postparental period? How is the period of adjustment different for women and men?
2. Discuss the midlife transition and the empty-nest syndrome. Do they exist, and, if so, how serious are they? How might sex-role socialization patterns affect the middle years for men versus women?
3. Discuss changes in the grandparent role over the last 30 years. How might the grandparent status differ by class and subculture? What roles do stepgrandparents and great-grandparents play?
4. How true is the argument "You can't teach an old dog new tricks" when applied to the socialization or resocialization of the middle-aged or aged couple?
5. Health, children's problems, money, and abuse are problems facing people who are aged. What other problems exist? What types of social programs, tax structures, and social policies might lessen the negative impact of these problems?
6. Discuss changes in husband/wife roles that are likely to accompany illness, retirement, grandparenthood, remarriage, and so on. How can resocialization be facilitated?
7. What are the implications of retirement at age 70, 60, or 50? Note marital status and male/female differences in adjustment patterns after retirement.
8. Should dying family members be assured the right to die with dignity and to be allowed to determine the time, place, and manner of their death? Should active or passive euthanasia be supported? Why?
9. What advantages or disadvantages does the widow or widower have if living alone, if living with kin, if living in a private home with other than kin, or if living in an institution? What types of conditions make one situation more favourable than another?
10. Invite several persons over age 75 to your class or to a discussion group to address such topics as the empty-nest syndrome, grandparenthood, retirement, widowhood, and facing death. Examine the significance of having children and their importance as systems of support.

FURTHER READINGS

Anderson, Carol M.; Stewart, Susan; and Dimidjian, Sona. *Flying Solo: Single Women in Midlife*. New York: W. W. Norton, 1994. Stories are told of the lives of single women in midlife, stories based on interviews with about 90 women who were never married, were divorced, or were widowed.

Barusch, Amanda S. *Older Women in Poverty: Private Lives and Public Policies*. New York: Springer Publishing Co., 1994. On the basis of interviews with 62 low-income women, the book deals with a range of issues of older women in poverty, including chapters covering marriage, divorce, death, and remarriage.

Brown, Arnold S. *The Social Processes of Aging and Old Age*. 2nd ed. Upper Saddle River, NJ: Prentice-Hall, Inc., 1996. A paperback focusing on many aspects of aging covered in this chapter, including demographics, the elderly in the family, economic dependency, retirement, health, and death and dying.

Brubaker, Timothy H. *Families' Relationships in Later Life*. 2nd ed. Newbury Park, CA: Sage, 1990. An excellent collection of research-based articles on family relations and issues facing older persons in later life.

Cox, Harold G. *Later Life: The Realities of Aging*. 4th ed. Upper Saddle River, NJ: Prentice-Hall, Inc., 1996. A textbook on aging with specific chapters dealing with family patterns, minority groups, cross-cultural comparisons, and death and dying.

Dailey, Nancy. *When Baby Boom Women Retire.* Westport, CT: Praeger, 1998. An examination of three structural variables impacting future retirement of baby boom women: population aging, women's labour force participation, and retirement income sources.

Genovese, Rosalie G. *Americans at Midlife: Caught between Generations.* Westport, CT: Bergin & Garvey, 1997. A look at midlife parents and children—how they age together and how many nests aren't so empty.

Goldschneider, Frances K., and Goldschneider, Calvin. *Leaving Home Before Marriage: Ethnicity, Familism, and Generational Relationships.* Madison, WI: University of Wisconsin Press, 1993. Based on the responses of 60,000 young people and a subsample of their parents, nonfamily living in young adulthood is seen as a fragile life-course stage with parents serving as crucial influences in their children's decisions.

Hareven, Tamara K., ed. *Aging and Generational Relations: Life Course and Cross-Cultural Perspectives.* New York: Aldine de Gruyter, 1996. Focusing on contemporary Europe, the United States, and Asia, essays examine generational relations over the life course.

Kornhaber, Arthur. *Contemporary Grandparenting.* Thousand Oaks, CA: Sage, 1996. A synthesis of the current knowledge about grandparents and their role in families and society.

Logan, John R., and Spitze, Glenna D. *Family Ties: Enduring Relations between Parents and Their Grown Children.* Philadelphia: Temple University Press, 1996. Family ties deals with family relationships over the life cycle, revealing misconceptions about grown children caring for their aging parents.

Lopata, Helena Znaniecka. *Current Widowhood: Myths and Realities*. Thousand Oaks, CA: Sage Publications, 1995. An examination of two major themes of widowhood: how changes in society influence it and myths and assumptions surrounding it.

Nadeau, Janice Winchester. *Families Making Sense of Death.* Thousand Oaks, CA: Sage, 1998. Family grief is seen as a process of family meaning-making based on multigenerational grieving families.

Norris, Joan E., and Tindale, Joseph E. *Among Generations: The Cycle of Adult Relationships*. New York: W. H. Freeman, 1994. A successful attempt at answering questions of how couples become involved in intergenerational relationships, how parents parent their adult children, how interactions occur with grandparents, siblings, and friends, and the results.

Owen, Margaret, *A World of Widows*. Atlantic Highlands, NJ: Zed Books Ltd., 1996. A look at widows in the Third World, with illustrations of the kinds of constraints affecting them and their families.

Szinovacz, Maximiliane; Ekerdt, David J.; and Vinick, Barbara H., eds. *Families and Retirement*. Newbury Park, CA: Sage, 1992. Leading researchers in family studies and gerontology present information on retirement, marital, and extended-kin relationships and selected issues focusing on gender, ethnicity, and changes brought on by retirement.

Zal, H. Michael. *The Sandwich Generation*. New York: Plenum Press, 1992. An examination of the unique problem facing middle-age Americans who have to cope with maturing children as well as increasingly dependent parents.

WEBLINKS

http://www.trinity.edu/~mkearl/geron.html#in

This website provides a comprehensive index to issues relating to the aging and the institution of family. It is also a good resource for statistics on marriages based on age, sex and race.

http://www.cfc-efc.ca//docs/00000925.htm

This site discusses issues surrounding healthy relationships with older family members

http://www.acs.ohio-state.edu/units/research/archive/oldfight.htm

This link provides findings on research conducted at Ohio State University on the physical effects of stressful marriages for older couples.

NOTES

1. William S. Aquilino, "From Adolescent to Young Adult: A Prospective Study of Parent-child Relations during the Transition to Adulthood," *Journal of Marriage and the Family* 59 (August 1997): 670–686.
2. "Age, Sex, and Marital Status", *The Nation*, Statistics Canada Catalogue 93-310 (July 1992).
3. Figures are taken from Paul C. Glick, "The Life Cycle of the Family," *Marriage and Family Living* 17 (1955): 3–9.
4. Monica Boyd and Doug Norris, "The Crowded Nest: Young Adults at Home," *Canadian Social Trends* (Spring 1999), Statistics Canada Catalogue 11–800: 3.
5. Monica Boyd and Doug Norris, "Leaving the Nest? The Impact of Family Structure," *Canadian Social Trends* (Autumn 1995): 14–17.
6. Barbara A. Mitchell and Ellen M. Gee, "Boomerang Kids and Midlife Parental Marital Satisfaction," *Family Relations* 45 (October 1996): 442–448.
7. Russell Ward, John Logan, and Glenna Spitze, "The Influence of Parent and Child Needs on Coresidence in Middle and Later Life," *Journal of Marriage and the Family* 54 (February 1992): 209–221; and Richard A. Settersten, Jr., "A Time to Leave Home and a Time Never to Return? Age Constraints on the Living Arrangements of Young Adults," *Social Forces* 76 (June 1998): 1373–1400.
8. Michael P. Farrell and Stanley D. Rosenberg, *Men at Midlife* (Boston: Auburn House, 1981).
9. Robert A. Lewis, Robert J. Volk, and Stephen F. Duncan, "Stresses on Fathers and Family Relationships Related to Rural Youth Leaving and Returning Home," *Family Relations* 38 (April 1989): 174–181; and Pauline Boss, Debra Pearce-McCall, and Jan Greenberg, "Normative Loss in Mid-Life Families: Rural, Urban, and Gender Differences," *Family Relations* 36 (October 1987): 437–443.
10. Valory Mitchell and Ravenna Helson, "Woman's Prime of Life," *Psychology of Women Quarterly* 14 (1990): 451–470.
11. Dolores Cabic Borland, "A Cohort Analysis Approach to the Empty-Nest Syndrome Among Three Ethnic Groups of Women: A Theoretical Position," *Journal of Marriage and the Family* 44 (February 1982): 117–129.
12. John R. Earle, Mark H. Smith, Catherine T. Harris, and Charles F. Longino, Jr. "Women, Marital Status, and Symptoms of Depression in a Midlife National Sample," *Journal of Women and Aging* 10 (1998): 41–55.
13. Ken R. Smith and Phyllis Moen, "Passage Through Midlife: Women's Changing Family Roles and

Economic Well-Being," *The Sociological Quarterly* 29 (1988): 503–524. Note also Phyllis Moen, "Transition in Mid-Life: Women's Work and Family Roles in the 1970s," *Journal of Marriage and the Family* 53 (February 1991): 135–150.

14. Mary Anne Burke and Aron Spector, "Falling Through the Cracks: Women Aged 55–64 Living on Their Own," *Canadian Social Trends* (Winter 1991), Statistics Canada Catalogue 11-008E: 14–17.
15. Kenneth J. Doka and Mary Ellen Mertz, "The Meaning and Significance of Great-Grandparenthood," *The Gerontologist* 28 (1988): 192–197.
16. Jeanne L. Thomas, "The Grandparent Role: A Double Bind," *International Journal of Aging and Human Development* 31 (1990): 169–177.
17. Harriet B. Presser, "Some Economic Complexities of Child Care Provided by Grandmothers," *Journal of Marriage and the Family* 51 (August 1989): 581–591. Note also Margaret Platt Jendrik, "Grandparents Who Parent Their Grandchildren: Effects on Lifestyle," *Journal of Marriage and the Family* 55 (August 1993): 609–621.
18. Gregory F. Sanders and Debra W. Trygstad, "Step-grandparents and Grandparents: The View from Young Adults," *Family Relations* 38 (January 1989): 71–75. Note also Carolyn S. Henry, Cindi Penor Ceglian, and D. Wayne Matthews, "The Role Behaviors, Role Meanings, and Grandmothering Styles of Grandmothers and Step-grandmothers: Perceptions of the Middle Generation," *Journal of Divorce and Remarriage* 17 (1992): 1–22.
19. Edward M. Burns, "Grandparent Visitation Rights: Is It Time for the Pendulum to Fall?" *Family Law Quarterly* 25 (Spring 1991): 59–81.
20. *A Portrait of Seniors in Canada*, Statistics Canada Catalogue 89-519-XPE, 1999.
21. Alain Bélanger, *Report on the Demographic Situation in Canada, 1998-1999*, Statistics Canada Catalogue 91-209-XPE: 2.
22. Raj Chawla, "Dependency Ratios," *Canadian Social Trends*, Vol. 2 (Toronto: Thompson Educational Press, 1994), 13–16.
23. Donald O. Cowgill, "Aging in Comparative Cultural Perspective," *Mid-American Review of Sociology* 6 (1981): 1–28; and Carol Seefeldt, "Children's Attitudes Toward the Elderly: A Cross-Cultural Comparison," *International Journal of Aging and Human Development* 19 (1984): 319–328.
24. For an overview of these areas, see Timothy H. Brubaker, "Families in Later Life: A Burgeoning Research Area," *Journal of Marriage and the Family* 52 (November 1990): 959–981; and Vern L. Bengtson, Carolyn J. Rosenthal, and Linda M. Burton, "Families and Aging: Diversity and Heterogeneity," in *Handbook of Aging and the Social Sciences,* 3d ed., ed. Robert H. Binstock and Linda George (San Diego: Academic Press, 1990), 263–287.
25. *A Portrait of Seniors in Canada*, Statistics Canada Catalogue 89-519-XPE, 1999.
26. Walter R. Gove and Hee-Choon Shin, "The Psychological Well-Being of Divorced and Widowed Men and Women," *Journal of Family Issues* 10 (March 1989): 122–144.
27. Susan McDaniel, *Family and Friends*, General Social Survey Analysis Series, Statistics Canada Catalogue 11-612E, No. 9.
28. Irwin Bess, "Widows Living Alone," *Canadian Social Trends* (Summer 1999), Statistics Canada Catalogue 11-800: 2–5.
29. Susan Crompton and Anna Kemeny, "In Sickness and in Health: The Well-being of Married Seniors," *Canadian Social Trends* (Winter 1999), Statistics Canada Catalogue 11-800: 22–27.
30. Jay A. Mancini and Rosemary Blieszner, "Aging Parents and Adult Children: Research Themes in Intergenerational Relations," *Journal of Marriage and the Family* 51 (May 1989): 275–290. Note also Teresa M. Cooney and Peter Uhlenberg, "Support from Parents over the Life Course: The Adult Child's Perspective," *Social Forces* 71 (September 1992): 63–84; and Susan McDaniel, *Family and Friends*, General Social Survey Analysis Series, Statistics Canada Catalogue 11–612E, No. 9: 111.
31. Dennis P. Hogan, David J. Eggebeen, and Clifford C. Clogg, "The Structure of Intergenerational Exchanges in American Families," *American Journal of Sociology* 98 (May 1993): 1428–1458.
32. Merril Silverstein, Tonya M. Parrott, and Vern L. Bengston, "Factors That Predispose Middle-Aged Sons and Daughters to Provide Social Support to Older Persons," *Journal of Marriage and the Family* 57 (May 1995): 465–475; and Deborah M. Merrill, "Daughters-in-Law as Caregivers to the Elderly," *Research on Aging* 15 (March 1993): 70–91.
33. William S. Aquilino and Khalil R. Supple, "Parent-Child Relations and Parents' Satisfaction with Living Arrangements When Adult Children Live at Home," *Journal of Marriage and the Family* 53 (February 1991): 13–27; and J. Jill Suitor and Karl Pillemer, "Explaining Intergenerational Conflict When Adult Children and Elderly Parents Live Together," *Journal of Marriage and the Family* 50 (November 1988): 1037–1047.
34. Judith Rempel, "Childless Elderly: What Are They Missing," *Journal of Marriage and the Family* 47 (May 1985): 343–348.
35. Janet Che-Alford and Brian Hamon, "Under One Roof: Three Generations Living Together," *Canadian Social Trends* (Summer 1999), Statistics Canada Catalogue 11-800: 6–9.
36. Susan McDaniel, "Emotional Support and Family Contacts of Older Canadians," *Canadian Social Trends,* Statistics Canada Catalogue 11-008E (Spring 1993): 32.

37. *A Portrait of Seniors in Canada*, Statistics Canada Catalogue 89-519-XPE, 1999.

38. Alexis J. Walker and Clara C. Pratt, "Daughters' Help to Mothers: Intergenerational Aid versus Caregiving," *Journal of Marriage and the Family* 53 (February 1991): 3–12.

39. Jeffrey W. Dwyer, Gary R. Lee, and Thomas B. Jankowski, "Reciprocity, Elder Satisfaction, and Caregiver Stress and Burden: The Exchange of Aid in the Family Caregiving Relationship," *Journal of Marriage and the Family* 56 (February 1994): 35–43.

40. Martha Baum and Mary Page, "Caregiving and Multigenerational Families," *The Gerontologist* 31 (1991): 762–769.

41. Karl Pillemer and J. Jill Suitor, "Will I Ever Escape My Child's Problems? Effects of Adult Children's Problems on Elderly Parents," *Journal of Marriage and the Family* 53 (August 1991): 585–594.

42. National Council of Welfare, *Poverty Profile, 1992* (Ottawa: Minister of Supply and Services, 1994).

43. Madonna Harrington Meyer, "Family Status and Poverty Among Older Women: The Gender Distribution of Retirement Income in the United States," *Social Problems* 37 (November 1990): 551–563.

44. David J. Cheal, "Intergenerational Family Transfers," *Journal of Marriage and the Family* 45 (November 1983): 805–813.

45. Hazel MacRae, "Fictive Kin as a Component of the Social Networks of Older People," *Research on Aging* 14 (June 1992): 226–247.

46. Robert C. Atchley, *Social Forces and Aging*, 5th ed. (Belmont, CA: Wadsworth, 1988), Chapter 9.

47. Lorraine T. Dorfman and Carol E. Mertens, "Kinship Relations in Retired Rural Men and Women," *Family Relations* 39 (April 1990): 166–173.

48. Debra Umberson, "Marriage as Support or Strain? Marital Quality Following the Death of a Parent," *Journal of Marriage and the Family* 57 (August 1995): 709–723; and Debra Umberson and Meichu D. Chen, "Effects of a Parent's Death on Adult Children: Relationship Salience and Reaction to Loss," *American Sociological Review* 59 (February 1994): 152–168.

49. H. Wesley Perkins and Lynne B. Harris, "Family Bereavement and Health in Adult Life Course Perspective," *Journal of Marriage and the Family* 52 (February 1990): 233–241.

50. Cathleen D. Zick and Ken R. Smith, "Marital Transitions, Poverty, and Gender Differences in Mortality," *Journal of Marriage and the Family* 53 (May 1991): 327–336.

51. *Profile of Canada's Seniors*, Statistics Canada Catalogue 96-312E (1994): 23.

52. David S. DeGarmo and Gay C. Kitson, "Identity Relevance and Disruption as Predictors of Psychological Distress for Widowed and Divorced Women," *Journal of Marriage and the Family* 58 (November 1996): 983–997.

53. Philip G. Clark, Robert W. Siviski, and Ruth Weiner, "Coping Strategies of Widowers in the First Year," *Family Relations* 35 (July 1986): 425–430; and Marilyn J. Essex and Sunghee Nam, "Marital Status and Loneliness Among Older Women: The Differentiated Importance of Close Family and Friends," *Journal of Marriage and the Family* 49 (February 1987): 93–106.

54. Arnold Peters and Aart C. Liefbroer, "Beyond Marital Status: Partner History and Well-Being in Old Age," *Journal of Marriage and the Family* 59 (August 1997): 687–699.

55. Rosemary Blieszner, "A Socialist-Feminist Perspective on Widowhood," *Journal of Aging Studies* 7 (1993): 171–182.

56. Ken R. Smith, Cathleen D. Zick, and Greg J. Duncan, "Remarriage Patterns Among Recent Widows and Widowers," *Demography* 28 (August 1991): 361–374.

CHAPTER 10 *FAMILY VIOLENCE*

In the preceding chapters, we looked at marriages and families from a life course perspective. Each life transition carries the potential for **marital and interpersonal stress and crisis.** Earlier chapters addressed social conflict, lower levels of marital satisfaction 10 to 15 years into marriage, role conflicts, and the like. Each chapter referred to some event or process that produces strain, stress, various degrees of crisis, or the potential for violence.

We referred earlier to public concerns regarding Canadian family life. Such concerns are not unique to this century. Each generation has worried about issues of parental authority, nonmarital sexuality, alcohol or drugs, and so on. Regardless of when these concerns are expressed, they are usually contrasted to values and behaviours of the "old days," when authority was respected, when sexual taboos were observed, and when spouses were more understanding and tolerant.

That each generation refers to weakness and decline may indicate present dissatisfaction, sentimentality over the past, or that actual conditions are never equal to the ideal. Clearly, intimate relationships and family life are seldom perfect for couples or for other family members. Even anticipated life transitions such as parenthood or retirement are stressful. In addition, most families experience unanticipated crises—illness, unemployment or relocation, for example—that test their ability to adapt and reorganize. The following section examines social stresses on families.

SOCIAL STRESSES ON FAMILIES

In a widely quoted article, now more than 40 years old, Reuben Hill spoke of **stressor,** or crisis-provoking, **events.**[1] These are *sources* of stress and situations for which families have little or no preparation. Stressor events are never the same for different families; they vary in the power with which they strike and the hardships that accompany them. *Hardships* are those complications in a crisis-precipitating event that demand competencies from the family that the event itself may have temporarily paralyzed or made unavailable.

Pauline Boss used *stress* to mean "pressure or tension in the family system."[2] Stress is an *outcome*, or the degree of family disruption that results from particular events. With change comes disturbance and pressure—*stress*. It is normal, inevitable, and even desirable at times. The family's level of stress results from events or situations that have potential to cause change.

Why do different families respond so differently to particular events or circumstances? For example, why is a pregnancy a blessing to some and a curse to others? Why is a geographical move a positive experience for some family members and a severe disruption for others? Why do unemployment, divorce, or death severely cripple some persons while others seem to take them in stride? A key to answering questions such as these is to look at mediating factors between the *source* (event) and the *outcome* (level of stress).

ABCX model of stress

Hill provided a simple but powerful model in what today is widely called the **ABCX model of stress.** According to this model, A (the event) interacts with B (the family's crisis-meeting resources), which interacts with C (the appraisal or definition the family makes of the event) to produce X (the crisis).[3] This sequence can be stated as a formula:

$$A \rightarrow (B + C) = X$$

The two key dimensions in the formula are B and C. If both are adequate, the level of stress will be low or nonexistent. If one or both are inadequate, the level of stress will be high. Consider this ABCX formulation more closely.

Stressor events (factor A) may come from a wide variety of sources, both within and outside the family. The consequences of the events are likely to differ considerably depending on their source. For example, a general principle in sociology is that certain events outside a group, such as a war, flood, or depression, tend to solidify the group. Although stressful, certain external events may tend to unify the family into a more cohesive unit rather than contribute to its breakdown. Furthermore, the same events may not be defined as critically stressful when other persons are in the same situation or worse. For example, it is disappointing to professional researchers to have their writings rejected by editors of journals. The pain may be less severe if the researchers recognize that a given publication has a 90 percent rejection rate. To know that many others submitted articles and were rejected, did not get their research funded, lost their homes, had premature births, or were unemployed often makes events appear less critical. It helps to know that others share similar misfortunes.

Events within the family that are defined as stressful may be more disruptive because they arise from troubles that reflect poorly on the family's internal adequacy. These events may be nonsupport, mental breakdown, violence, suicide, or alcoholism, among others. The range of events, either within or outside the family, that disturb the family's role patterns is huge. These events involve losses of persons, jobs, or incomes as well as additions. The arrival of a child, grandparent, or parent-in-law may be as disruptive as the loss of any of the three. Gaining sudden fame or fortune may be as disruptive as losing either. Any sudden change in family status or conflict among family members in the conceptions of their roles may produce further family crisis.

The dimensions that characterize any given stressor or crisis-provoking event extend far beyond whether it occurs internally or externally to the family. A crisis-producing event may affect the entire system or only a limited part, may occur gradually or suddenly, may be intense or mild, may be a short- or long-term problem, may be expected and predicted or random, may arise from natural conditions or artificial and technological effects, may represent a shortage or an overabundance of vital commodities, may be perceived to be solvable or insolvable, and may vary in substantive content. The nature of the crisis event will influence the specific response of an individual or family system.

It should be noted that not all events or changes, irrespective of whether they come from within the family or outside it, are stressor events. For example, research has shown that major life changes and role transitions (job loss, divorce, retirement, widowhood, first marriage, first child, and so forth), often assumed to be stressor events, actually relieve stress when prior role stress is very high.[4] That is, life-transition events were found to be nonproblematic or even beneficial to mental health when preceded by chronic role problems—a case where more stress is actually a relief from existing stress.

Again, what factors make for crisis-proneness and freedom from crisis-proneness? The explanation lies in B and C in the formula presented earlier. To what extent do families have resources to meet the event (factor B) and to what extent do families define the event as a crisis (factor C)? Crisis-meeting resources (factor B) may include family adaptability, family roles, kin-support systems, income, insurance, friends, religious beliefs, education, good health, and the like. Problem families often do not have adequate resources with which to handle stressor events.

The extent to which the family defines the event as a crisis (factor C) reflects their value system and previous experience in meeting crises. This definition of the event refers to the meaning attached to it, the appraisal or the interpretation as to its seriousness, and the perception of the event as **enabling** (making other things possible) or **disabling** (weakening or destroying possibilities).

Crisis-proneness (X)—that is, the level or degree of stress—is therefore a function of both a deficiency in family organization resources (factor B) and the tendency to define hardships as crisis-producing (factor C). These two factors combine into one concept: family inadequacy or family adequacy.

Variations on the ABCX model

Hamilton McCubbin and others, in an attempt to build on Hill's ABCX model, proposed a **double-ABCX model** that differentiates the precrisis and postcrisis variables.[5] The model becomes a longitudinal one, and the factor of time differentiates the precrisis from the postcrisis situation. The initial stressor event becomes a double-A by separating the changes that occur irrespective of the initial stressor from those changes that are the consequences of the family's efforts to cope with the hardships of the situation. The resources become a double-B by differentiating those resources already available to the family from those coping resources strengthened or developed in response to the crisis situation. The perception and meaning become a double-C by differentiating the definition before the event of how stressful it may be from the postcrisis perceptions of the level of stress.

Many attempts have been made to test this double-ABCX model of family stress and adaptation, two of which will be mentioned here.[6] One model, dealing with relocation stress among clergy husbands and wives, found that wives reported significantly higher stress, more negative perceptions of their most recent relocation, lower coping resources, and lower well-being than did their clergy husbands. The other model, dealing with women who had severe physical disabilities, found that a perceived high level of stress and strain and a low level of individual resources contribute to a low level of personal and family adaptation.

Alexis Walker made a case for expanding the ABCX model of stress and crisis to incorporate new dimensions, recognizing the following:

1. All levels of the social system are interdependent.
2. Stress occurs in a unique and influential sociocultural context.[7]

The interdependence of levels incorporates individual factors with dyadic, family, nonfamily, and community ones. That is, levels more macro than individuals and families need to be incorporated into the model. Individual resources may differ from family, community, and societal resources. Definitions or perceptions may vary among members of a family. Whose definition or perception is most important? If members do not agree, will the crisis be unresolvable?

The sociohistorical context recognizes how perceptions of stressful circumstances and available resources vary considerably over time. Different contexts and the unique perspectives and resources related to a given context need to be recognized. In examining the process of adjustment to stress, it becomes necessary to focus, over time, on individual changes, dyadic changes, social network changes, and developments in the wider society that influence the ability of an individual, dyad, or family to respond effectively.

Another factor to consider is how stress in one area or from one source spills over into other areas. An article on the contagion of stress across multiple roles documented that home-to-work stress occurs more strongly among men than women and that both men and women reduce their involvement in stressful home situations following a stressful day at work.[8] Wives, in particular, modified their housework efforts to compensate for the work stresses of their husbands. Stresses in one area, such as work, affect stresses in other areas, such as home. What's more, stresses experienced by one spouse or partner affect stresses experienced by the other.

While the list of stressor events, family problems, and conflict situations in relationships and families may seem infinite, this chapter will focus on one: violence. A number of other potentially stressful events were discussed in earlier chapters, including AIDS, abortion, street children, commuter marriages, conflict between employment and family responsibilities, poverty, incest, conjugal decision-making, parenthood, father/mother absence, midlife crisis, widowhood, death, and aging. Other issues—including separation, divorce, and stepchildren—will be discussed in Chapter 11.

VIOLENCE IN FAMILIES AND AMONG INTIMATES

Since 1970, research on family violence has grown exponentially, despite the fact that evidence has not indicated an increase in levels of family violence.[9] The terms **family violence** and *violence among intimates* are used to refer to any act among legally related individuals or those in close primary relationships that is carried out with the intention of causing physical harm. This broad definition includes spanking a disobedient child, raping a lover, and murdering a spouse. Many people (readers included) are not aware that they are more likely to be physically assaulted, beaten, raped, or killed in their own homes at the hands of loved ones than any place else or by anyone else.[10]

Consider the following:

- Children are more likely to be kidnapped by their own parents than by strangers.
- More than half of all couples report physical violence by a partner.
- Sensational headlines report "Woman raped in public park," "Child beaten in day-care centre," and "Elderly person mugged in parking lot," but, in reality, these events occur most frequently in homes and are perpetrated by persons close to the victims.
- Nearly one out of every four murder victims in the United States, Great Britain and Denmark is killed by a member of his or her own family. In Canada, in 1991, one-third of all solved murders were committed by a family member or relative.[11]

Nevertheless, violence is not an inevitable consequence of family life. In studying violence cross-culturally, David Levinson found 16 societies of the 90 in his sample were relatively free of family violence.[12] Gatherer-hunters (Ona, Andamans, Siriono, !Kung), for example, rarely mistreated their children and were overrepresented among the societies without family violence.

According to Levinson:

> In general, in societies without family violence, husbands and wives share all domestic decision making, wives have some control over the fruits of family labor, wives can divorce their husbands as easily as their husbands can divorce them, marriage is monogamous, there is no pre-marital sex double standard, divorce is relatively infrequent, husbands and wives sleep together, men resolve disputes with other men peacefully, and intervention in wife beating incidents tends to be immediate.[13]

The central conclusion reached from these findings is that family violence does not occur in societies in which family life is characterized by cooperation, commitment, sharing, and equality. In contrast, family violence is more common in societies in which men control women's lives, violent resolution to conflicts is acceptable, and mothers bear the major responsibility for childrearing.

Precise data on conjugal and parental abuse and violence are difficult to obtain. Much violence and abuse goes unreported. Indeed, spouse shoving, child spanking, and sibling fighting may be defined in some families as appropriate and even necessary marital and family behaviours.

Given the lack of exact data, we can only infer how much intrafamily violence and abuse exist. One need not doubt, however, that violence is a pervasive and common feature between intimate partners or spouses and among family members in most societies in the world.

Myths of family violence

In a study of violence between intimates, Richard Gelles and Murray Straus identified a number of stereotypes about abusive partners and families.[14] Stereotypes or myths about the nature and causes of domestic violence serve a significant function: violence is attributed to "other people" (mentally disturbed, unbalanced people) rather than acknowledged as an outgrowth of the very structures of society and family.

Consider the following seven myths:

- *Myth 1—The family is nonviolent.* Because we do not know exactly how prevalent family violence is, it is easy to dismiss the problem as one that affects only a small and unique segment of the population.
- *Myth 2—Abusers are monsters.* The stereotype is that the abuser is mentally disturbed, psychologically unbalanced, or even psychotic. Gelles and Straus suggested that, in fact, only about 10 percent of abusive incidents are caused by persons with mental illness.
- *Myth 3—Abuse is confined to poor, minority or immigrant families.* Research has found that intimate violence is more likely to occur in lower-income and minority households, but it is not confined to them. Violence cuts across all classes and races; the poor have a greater likelihood of being violent and also run the risk of being overrepresented in official statistics. Attributing violence to poor or minority families is another way of seeing others as violent and one's own behaviour as "normal."
- *Myth 4—Alcohol and drugs are the real causes of violence in the home.* A strong association has been shown between violence and alcohol and drug use. But does it follow that violence will end when the drinking/drug problem is eliminated? Are alcohol or drugs actually the cause of the violence? Evidence has disputed the claim that alcohol causes violence and supported the claim that certain drugs are rarely associated with violence; in fact, some drugs produce a euphoric effect, reducing the level of violence. In short, curing or eliminating an alcohol or drug problem will not, by itself, eliminate domestic violence.
- *Myth 5—Children who are abused grow up to be abusers.* Again, this myth has some truth in that abused children *tend* to be abusive adults, but not *all* abused children grow up to be abusive. The claim that people who are abused are preprogrammed to be abusers has not been supported.
- *Myth 6—Battered women like being hit.* This myth is rooted in a misunderstanding as to why abused women stay in abusive situations and whether battered women provoke the abuse. The reality is that many abused women do not have the resources (including healthy self-esteem) to get out of abusive situations. And the longer they stay, the harder it is to leave.
- *Myth 7—Violence and love are incompatible.* Many battered spouses have strong loving feelings for their partners, and most battered and abused children continue to love their parents. Unlike violence in the streets, violence in the home includes bonds of love, attachment, and affection.

Gelles and Straus concluded the discussion of myths by stating:

> It is not only the myths that have to be abandoned, but the social function that they serve. The greatest function served by the seven myths we have discussed is that collectively they serve as a smoke screen that blinds us to our own potential for violence. Moreover, when our explanations focus on "kinds of people" (mentally disturbed, poor, alcoholics, drug abusers, etc.) we blind ourselves to the structural properties of the family as a social institution that makes it our most violent institution with the exception of the military in time of war.[15]

Causes of family violence

Why is there so much violence in the family? Many theories have been advanced to explain interpersonal violence in general and family violence more specifically. Some theories, as noted, place the cause within the individual, attributing violent behaviour to psychopathologies and alcohol and drug use. Other theories are social/psychological in nature and attribute violence to social learning, exchange, and interaction. A third group of theories is sociocultural and attributes violence to societal resources, conflict systems, and the larger culture.

Feminists argue that domestic violence is rooted in gender and power and represents men's active attempts to maintain dominance and control over women.[16] These theorists look at structurally induced economic problems (including unemployment and underemployment) as important variables affecting interpersonal relationships. Inequalities in income and education contribute to (or threaten) men's ability to control. Murray Straus and Christine Smith presented five social factors that converge to cause the high rates of intrafamily violence:

1. *Intrafamily conflict*—An irony of family life is that many of the same characteristics that contribute to intimacy and love among family members also contribute to conflict.
2. *Male dominance in family and society*—Given the concept of the man/husband as head of the family and the domination of men in North American society, force is a key resource in resolving conflict.
3. *Cultural norms permitting family violence*—Parents have a legal right and often a moral obligation to spank or slap their children.
4. *Family socialization in violence*—Children's early and continuing experience with violence between parents or by parents provides role models and a specific script in training for future violence.
5. *Pervasiveness of violence in society*—In Canadian society, socially legitimate violence includes physical punishment by parents, force by police, an active military presence, violent acts on television and in the movies, and so forth. Violence in one area of life spills over into other spheres of life.[17]

There are abundant data to support the factors listed, examples of which are incorporated throughout this chapter. In factor 4 above, family socialization in violence, the general processes of socialization described in Chapter 8 are equally applicable. It is clear that violence begets violence and that aggression is transmitted across generations. Parents who yell frequently are the ones most likely to hit frequently, and both verbal and physical violence appear to be transgenerational.[18] Fortunately most people are able to break out of this intergenerational cycle of abuse, but this does not negate the increased probability of yelling at children, spanking children, or hitting a partner if family violence was a pattern in one's childhood.

Forms of family abuse and violence

Child abuse and violence

Throughout the history of the Western world, children have been subject to a range of abuses and cruelties, including sexual abuse, beatings, and abandonment of infants left to die. Today, only isolated incidents of abandonment are reported, but cases of physical and sexual abuse are quite common.

In Sweden, a parent can be imprisoned for striking a child, whereas in North America many parents view **physical punishment** (striking and spanking) as an acceptable and appropriate means of discipline. Traditionally, this "privilege" of spanking was extended to schoolteachers and administrators as a means of punishment and maintaining discipline. The guideline commonly followed was "Spare the rod and spoil the child." Strauss found that over 90 percent of parents of children aged three and four in the United States used physical punishment to correct behaviour.[19]

In Sweden, Denmark, Norway, and Austria, physical punishment of children is banned. In Canada, parents, teachers, and caregivers are allowed to use "reasonable force" to correct children according to section 43 of the *Criminal Code of Canada*. Of course, we do not know how many adults actually use physical force (or the threat of force) in disciplining children. A telephone survey conducted by the *Toronto Star* in April 1994 suggests that the proportion may be high. Sixty-four percent of respondents agreed with spanking children as a form of punishment.[20]

What are the effects of physical punishment? Straus hypothesized that physical punishment by parents and teachers may produce conformity in the immediate situation but, in the long run, it increases the probability of deviance, including delinquency in adolescence and wife beating, child abuse, and crime outside the family (robbery, assault, and homicide) in adulthood.[21] Studies have not proven that physical punishment causes these problems but that there is a *spillover effect*.

A *cultural spillover theory* suggests that violence in one sphere of life tends to engender violence in other spheres. Thus, the more a society uses force to attain socially desired ends (maintaining order in schools, defending itself from foreign enemies), the greater the tendency for those engaged in illegitimate behaviour to also use force to attain their ends. Straus conceded that he could not prove the theory but that empirical findings were almost entirely consistent with it. There is a linkage between physical punishment of children and crime

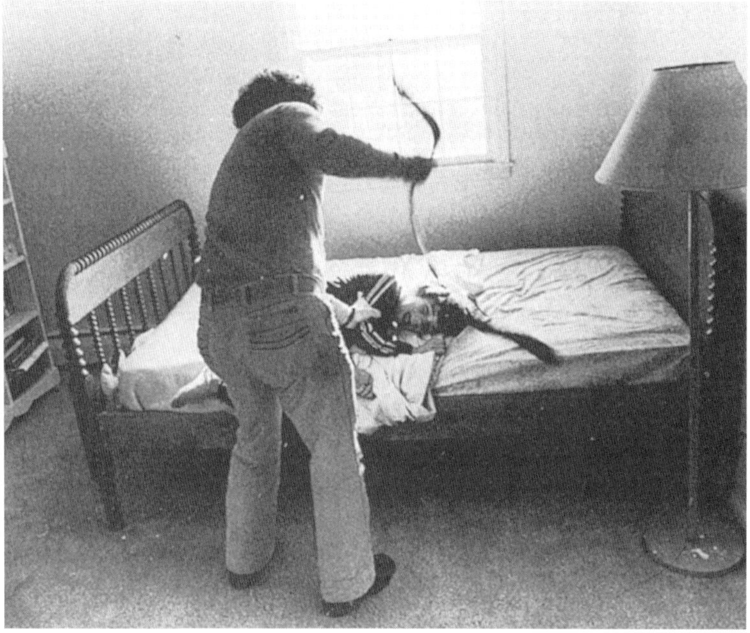

In contrast to Sweden, where it is illegal to spank children or treat them in a humiliating way, in Canada many parents view corporal punishment as an acceptable and appropriate means of discipline. Since physical punishment usually occurs "behind closed doors," most cases of child abuse are never discovered.

in society, and support for Straus' assertion that physical punishment may produce conformity in the short term but creates or exacerbates deviance in the long term.

An 18-year longitudinal study in New Zealand provides some additional support for Straus' assertions. The authors found that young people reporting exposure to harsh or abusive treatment during childhood had elevated roles of juvenile offending, alcohol abuse/dependence, and mental health problems.[22] While we need to be cautious in equating spanking or physical punishment used to correct behaviour with harsh or abusive treatment, the distance between the two is often unclear. The context of a loving-supportive parent and the meanings attached to it by both parents and child need to be considered.

Violence toward children is found in all social classes, although the incidence is higher among poor families. Examining an American probability sample of over 6000 households, Gelles reported that the incidence of overall violence was 4 percent higher among households with poverty-level incomes than among households with higher incomes. Severe violence (high probability of causing an injury) was 46 percent higher, and very severe violence (such as burning, threatening with or using a knife or gun) was 100 percent higher among poverty-level households.[23] Child abuse tends to increase as unemployment increases.[24] Factors such as poverty and unemployment are stressor events that influence family functioning, as exhibited in the greater abuse of children.

In Canada, almost half of all violent crimes against children are sexual assaults (see Table 10.1). Family members committed 32 percent of sexual

Table 10.1
Child victims of physical and sexual assault by accused-victim relationship, 1996[1]

Relationship of accused to victim		*Physical Assault*			*Sexual Assault*		
		Girls	Boys	Total	Girls	Boys	Total
Total	**No.**	**6160**	**10 199**	**16 359**	**5009**	**1465**	**6474**
	%	100	100	100	100	100	100
Family	%	30	14	20	33	30	32
Non-family	%	66	80	75	61	63	62
Unknown	%	4	5	5	6	7	6
Total family	**No.**	**1855**	**1473**	**3328**	**1662**	**440**	**2102**
	%	100	100	100	100	100	100
Parent	%	59	70	64	42	48	43
Sibling	%	21	21	21	29	24	28
Extended family[2]	%	6	8	7	27	28	27
Spouse	%	14	1	8	2	1	1

[1]Based on incidents reported to 154 police agencies which represent 47% of reported crime in Canada.
[2]Includes others related by blood or marriage, e.g. grandparents, aunts, uncles, cousins, in-laws.
Figures may not add to 100% due to rounding.

Source: Incident-based Uniform Crime Reporting Survey (UCR II), Canadian Centre for Justice Statistics, 1996; and *Family Violence in Canada*, Statistics Canada Catalogue 85-224 (1998): 22.

assaults against children and 20 percent of physical assaults. Girls are more likely than boys to be victimized by a family member for both sexual and physical assaults. Young adolescent girls seem to be more vulnerable to abuse by family members, whereas boys between 4 and 8 years are more likely to be physically abused.[25] **Child sexual abuse** generally includes elements of force, manipulation, or coercion. Children are assumed to be incapable of consenting to sex with an adult because they lack the power to decline involvement and do not understand what they are consenting to.

In Canada, records of child sexual abuse are compiled by the provinces, and data collection methods vary. There are no national estimates of the prevalence of child abuse. However, all provinces reported significant increases in the numbers of cases during the 1980s.[26] Presumably, part of this increase reflects increased vigilance and part increased public awareness of the issue of child sexual abuse.

In an American survey of adults and their history of childhood sexual abuse, 27 percent of the women and 16 percent of the men reported being abused.[27] The median age of abuse was slightly under 10. Boys were more likely to have been abused by strangers, whereas girls were more likely to have been abused by family members.

Another survey, representing several thousand cases of child sexual abuse, revealed that non-biologically-related caretakers (stepparents, adoptive parents, foster parents, babysitters, institutions) were substantially overrepresented and biologically-related caretakers (parents, siblings, grandparents) were substantially underrepresented in reports of child sexual abuse.[28] The numbers of male perpetrators greatly surpassed those of female perpetrators in all situations: three times as many biological fathers as mothers, nearly five times as many male babysitters as female, and more than twenty times as many males as females in other caretaker roles (stepparents, parents' paramours or lovers, institutional staff).

The consequences of child sexual abuse appear to be severe and long-lasting. In another study, both females and males who were sexually abused as children showed greater evidence than those not abused of sexual disturbance or dysfunction, depression, and even suicidal ideas.[29] Sexual maladjustment among abused females has been documented in several studies. American national data show that sexual contact with an adult during childhood increases the likelihood of engaging in an active and risky sexual career in adolescence and adulthood. Victims have sex at earlier ages, have more partners, are more likely to bear children before they turn 19, and are more likely to experience sexually transmitted infections and forced sex.[30] Research on over 500 young women from the state of Washington found that two-thirds of those who became pregnant as adolescents had been sexually abused.[31] Childhood sexual abuse was also found to be a precursor to prostitution and victimization among adolescent and adult homeless women.[32] The evidence showing both the severity and the long-term negative effects of child sexual abuse is clear and highly consistent among most studies.

Is there an epidemic of child abuse? Does the number of children who are abused increase each year? Apparently not. Straus and Gelles compared the rate of physical abuse of American children from a 1975 study with the rates from a 1985 replication.[33] Both studies showed extremely high incidences of severe physical violence against children; however, the 1985 rate of physical child abuse (as measured by the number of children who were kicked, punched, bitten, beaten up, or attacked with a knife or gun) was 47 percent lower than the 1975 rate.

How could this dramatic drop in violence toward children be explained? Critics argued that the change may have been due to methodological artifacts (differences resulting from gathering data by telephone rather than in home interviews). Straus and Gelles discounted that argument and even suggested that the anonymity provided by the telephone would have lead to more rather than less reporting of violence. A second explanation for the drop focused on people's greater reluctance to report severe violence following the massive amount of public and media attention paid to abuse over the decade. Again the authors discounted the argument, suggesting that, if anything, the increase in public attention should have made abused wives and children more likely to report their abuse. Despite the critics, Straus and Gelles remain convinced that a decline took place in violence toward children and (as will be discussed later) toward women, as well.

Lance Egley questioned these conclusions that child abuse (and wife abuse) were substantially lower in 1985 than in 1975. He demonstrated that changes in the age structure of the adult and child population explain most of the reported reduction.[34] That is, when adjustments were made for the aging population (age distribution) and for changes in respondents' reactions, the decline was *statistically* nonexistent. Egley also argued there was no reason to believe the reduction in domestic violence was substantial.

Whether the reduction was substantial or slight, these changes in levels of child abuse are consistent with other changes in the family and society over the past decade that most likely served to reduce violence in the home. Changes in family structure—such as increased ages at marriage and at first birth, the decline in the number of children per family, and the decreased number of unwanted children—are all related to lower rates of child abuse. Changes in the economy—for instance, lower rates of unemployment and inflation in 1985 than in 1975—also probably reduced the frequency of child abuse. The growth of new and innovative treatment programs, social services, and therapists and therapy approaches has probably helped to reduce intrafamily violence as well. And, finally, deterrence in the form of legal sanctions and the perceived high probability of getting caught and punished serve as reminders that abusive behaviour is inappropriate behaviour.

On the basis of their findings, Straus and Gelles suggested that, when a national effort is made to address some aspects of intrafamily violence (as with child abuse programs), national change can result. Nonetheless, slight reductions in rates of abuse should not cloud the seriousness of the issue. Too many Canadian children remain at risk.

The issue of child abuse and violence is complex. Concerns relate not only to the frequency and types of abuse but extend to child neglect, to the availability of services, and to the forms of legal intervention (custody and placement), decision-making, and program coordination. Case identification lags considerably behind the actual rates of abuse, and increased levels of reporting place strains on the limited services available.

Parent abuse and violence

Violence between parents and children is reciprocal. That is, children are not only victims of violence but are perpetrators as well. Many cases of parental abuse of children go unnoticed and unreported, but an assaulted parent, who is generally more powerful than the child, may go to great lengths to conceal being abused by him or her. Acts of severe violence, such as a child killing a parent, may get publicity, but cases of hitting and biting or making threats are likely to remain unnoticed by outsiders.

Parent assault exists but is rarely studied, and more attention has been focussed on adolescents who abuse parents than on younger children. Data from an American survey of adolescents showed that roughly 5 percent of the youth had hit one of their parents in the past year.[35] Both males and females assaulted parents; males were less likely to hit mothers and more likely to hit fathers as they got older, and females became more likely to hit either parent as they aged. The study reported that adolescents who assaulted parents were more likely (1) to have friends who assaulted parents; (2) to approve of delinquency, including violence; (3) to perceive the probability of official sanction as low; (4) to hold weak attachments to parents; and (5) to be white. More traditional violence factors, such as social isolation, drug use, stress, and power differentials, were largely unrelated to parent assault.

Wife and female partner abuse and violence

Violence against women is widespread in both Canada and the United States. In 1993, Statistics Canada conducted a national survey of male violence against women—the first study of this type done anywhere in the world.[36] The results were based on telephone interviews with a representative sample of over 12,000 Canadian women. Other studies based on police reports or women using shelters or counselling services probably underrepresent the problem. The study found a high incidence of violence against women. Over half of Canadian women have been victims of at least one incident of physical or sexual violence and, for 25 percent of Canadian women, their spouse or partner was the perpetrator. One in five violent incidents were serious enough to result in physical injury.

Much research on violence against women has focused on wives but, interestingly, findings have consistently shown that physical aggression is at least twice as common among cohabiting couples as among married couples. During a given year, about 35 out of every 100 cohabiting couples experience physical aggression. in contrast to 15 out of every 100 married couples.[37] And much of this physical aggression is directed at women, many of whom believe that their husbands or partners have the right to slap them or shove them under certain conditions. And as women learn that their male partners have this right, so do men learn that violence against their female partners is acceptable.

According to feminists, this acceptability is based on societal norms supporting patriarchy. Male dominance and superiority are viewed as the root causes of violence against women. Within relationships, men are generally observed to exercise more power than women. One way of expressing such power is through the roles in violent marriages, in which the man is usually the more powerful, violent person and the woman is the less powerful, abused person. Patriarchy reinforces the appropriateness of male dominance, power, aggression, and violence, whether they be exhibited in international conflicts or in interpersonal ones.

Michael Johnson argues that there are two distinct forms of violence against women.[38] One he calls **common couple violence.** This involves conflict between couples with an occasional outburst of violence from either husbands or wives. The other he calls **patriarchal terrorism.** As noted above, from a feminist perspective this is a product of patriarchal traditions of men's right to control "their" women (wives), not only by a systematic use of violence but also by economic subordination, threats, isolation, and other control factors. This pattern of violence is often referred to as wife beating, wife battery, and battered women. Johnson notes that patriarchal terrorism escalates (increases in frequency and intensity over time), whereas common couple violence does not. Common violence is an intermittent response to the occasional conflicts of everyday life, motivated by a need to control in the specific situation, but not a more general need to be in charge of the relationship.

The framework for such interpersonal acceptance is societal acceptance of dominance and aggression. Some researchers and theorists tie this acceptance to patriarchy because patriarchy sanctions male dominance, power, aggression, and violence, whether exhibited in international conflicts or in interpersonal ones. Historically, violence against wives has been perfectly acceptable behaviour. As recently as the late nineteenth century in Great Britain, Canada, and the United States, it was considered a part of a husband's marital obligation to control and chastise his wife through the use of physical force. Violence against wives and intimate partners, as suggested earlier, is a logical extension of the patriarchal family system, in which the husband uses whatever means necessary to obtain obedience and control.

Most physical abuse and violence toward wives and female partners does not take the form of beating; throwing things, shoving, pushing, grabbing, slapping, and hitting are more common. To be sure, many women are seriously hurt by their partners. Nursing research reported that at least 8 percent of women in prenatal and primary care settings and approximately 20 percent of women in emergency room settings were abused by male intimate partners.[39]

Female physical abuse is not uniformly distributed in all major social and demographic groups. Table 10.2 shows the number of Canadian women by age, income, and education who were victims of violence. Sociodemographic risk factors associated with wife abuse include low income and unemployment. A Canadian study based on male self-reports found that low-income males were far more likely (350 times) than high-income males to engage in *severe* abuse. Severe abuse was defined as both physical and chronic psychological (verbal or symbolic aggression) abuse. However, men who are university graduates show a high incidence of psychological violence. With age, the use of all kinds of abuse drops.[40] A Toronto study found that wife abuse is also more prevalent among people who are nonreligious, divorced or separated, and under age 30.[41] In addition, female abuse or battering appears to be influenced by and occurs more commonly at certain times, such as during a wife's pregnancy or following a husband's drinking. The Statistics Canada study referred to above found that 21 percent of women who were abused by a current or former partner were assaulted during pregnancy. Alcohol played a role in over 40 percent of violent incidents reported in this study. Rates of abuse are much higher for women who live with men who drink regularly.[42]

Too often family violence ends in death. Table 10.3 shows the number of family homicides and the accused-victim relationship. Between 1977 and 1996 there were 4193 known homicides where the accused and the victim were related. One-third of these were women killed by their partner.

Table 10.2
Number of family homicides by accused-victim relationship, 1977-1996

Accused was:	*Number*	*Percentage*
Husband	873	21
Common-law husband	532	13
Wife	216	5
Common-law wife	278	7
Ex-husband	120	3
Ex-wife	19	--
Father/Stepfather	539	13
Mother/Stepmother	368	9
Son/Stepson	385	9
Daughter/Stepdaughter	32	1
Brother/Stepbrother	245	6
Sister/Stepsister	26	1
Other family	560	13
Total family homicides	**4193**	**100**

-- amount too small to be expressed
Source: Homicide Survey, Canadian Centre for Justice Statistics, 1977-1996; and *Family Violence in Canada*, Statistics Canada Catalogue 85-224 (1998): 28.

NEWS ITEM

Femicide is increasing in Ontario

University of Toronto sociologist Rosemary Gartner, working with a group called the Women We Honour Action Committee, conducted a study of Ontario women killed by spouses or boyfriends. "At least 159 women were shot, stabbed, bludgeoned or choked to death by current or former partners in the four years from 1991 to 1994. ... Women killed by intimate partners constitute 70 percent of all female homicide victims."

The trigger in over half of the killings was the offender's anger or distress over the actual or impending estrangement from his partner. Another "cause" in 14 percent of cases was suspected or actual infidelity. Twelve percent of femicides were the culmination of a long history of violence.

In Ontario, as in other jurisdictions, women living in common-law relationships are at greater risk than married women, and separated women are at greater risk than women living with partners. Women in common-law relationships are *six times* more likely to be killed by their partners. Separated (not divorced) women are five times more likely to be killed.

Source: Jane Gadd, "Femicide Increasing, Study Shows," *The Globe and Mail*, April 29, 1997, A6.

Table 10.3
Number of women 18 years and over who have experienced violence in the past 12 months by age, household income, and education, Canada, 1993

	Total Female Population	***Total Women Victimized (past 12 months)***	
	Number (thousands)	***Number (thousands)***	***Percent***
Total	10 498	1,016	10%
Age group			
18–24	1 315	353	27
25–34	2 338	331	14
35–44	2 256	191	8
45–54	1 628	91	6
55 and over	2 961	49	2
Household income			
Less than $15,000	1 324	166	13
$15,000–$29,999	1 860	198	11
$30,000–$59,999	3 580	312	9
$60,000 or more	2 036	197	10
Not stated/don't know	1 698	142	8
Education			
Less than high school diploma	2 747	207	8
High school diploma	2 805	260	9
Some postsecondary education	3 299	401	12
University degree	1 628	148	9

Source: "The Violence Against Women Survey," *The Daily*, Statistics Canada Catalogue 11-001E (November 18, 1993): 4.

The nursing research cited previously found that approximately 8 percent of women were physically abused while pregnant and an additional 15 percent were beaten before the pregnancy. Richard Gelles also reported that pregnant women experience higher rates of minor, severe, and overall violence than nonpregnant women, particularly women under 25.[43] He suggested that these higher rates may be a methodological artifact in that women may be more outraged at violence when pregnant, may feel more vulnerable, or may keenly remember violent acts that occurred during pregnancy. It is possible, however, that husbands or partners may increase the frequency and severity of their violence toward women during pregnancy. They may also change the nature of the attacks, hitting the woman more on the abdomen instead of the face or other parts of the body.

What are the consequences of abuse to women? Studies suggest that both verbal and physical abuse have significant direct effects on both marital dissatisfaction and depression.[44] Victimized women's marital experience was characterized by less satisfaction and less stability but moderated by relationship efficacy and perceived intimacy and spousal support. That is, the negative consequences were less severe if wives attributed their husbands' negative behaviour to a cause other than the husband and did not see him as selfishly

Some violence against women is an intermittent response to the occasional conflicts of everyday life. However, patriarchal traditions of men's superiority over women lends support to men using any means to maintain their dominant position, including partner abuse and wife beating.

motivated or intentionally engaged in the negative behaviour. The occurrence of negative, humiliating events was a strong predictor of depression in women.

Marital rape is another form of violence sustained by women. The partner who forces sexual intercourse (technically, marital rape, although legally often not recognized as such) is seldom viewed as a rapist by his wife, who may blame herself for the incident. That women blame themselves or feel economically dependent may be why so little attention has been devoted to marital rape, although it may be a widespread occurrence.

The questions raised about changes in rates of child abuse must also be raised about wife or spouse abuse: Is there an epidemic of wife abuse? Are more women abused each year? And again, the answer, apparently, is no. The Straus/Gelles American studies mentioned earlier, which compared violence rates in 1975 and 1985, showed that wife beating (as measured by the number who were kicked, punched, hit with an object, bitten, beaten up, or attacked with a knife or gun) decreased by 27 percent over these 10 years.[45] Interestingly, similar severe assaults by wives on husbands (see next section) decreased only 4.3 percent. Even if these rates indicate actual reductions, the number of wives beaten each year in the United States is staggering: 1.5 million. In Canada, according to the Statistics Canada survey, one-quarter of all women have experienced violence at the hands of a current of past marital partner.

FAMILY DIVERSITY

Women in trouble

Feminist sociologist Elizabeth Comack recently published an insightful study of women jailed in Manitoba for a range of offences. In addition to their common experience of incarceration, the women shared experience of past physical and sexual abuse. In identifying this interconnection, Comack has raised important issues for all of us. As the "Violence Against Women survey" made clear, violence and abuse are endemic in Canadian society.

The 24 women in Comack's sample were young, with little education, and had childhoods marked by poverty, racism, and violence. "In some cases, law violations emerged as part of women's efforts to cope with the abuser. In others, law violations occurred in the context of resisting an abuser. For some of the women, both abuse and law violations were part and parcel of their ongoing struggle to survive the conditions of their endangerment."

Ironically, while in prison, the women had access to resources they were denied on the outside: jobs, educational upgrading, and counselling. Although resources were inadequate, in many cases they presented the first opportunity for women to begin to deal with their history of abuse. In her conclusion, Comack refers to the lessons she learned from the women in her study, who—despite histories of horrific abuse—remained strong and optimistic.

Source: Elizabeth Comack, *Women in Trouble* (Halifax: Fernwood Publishing, 1996).

Women respond to being abused in a number of ways (see "Treating and Preventing Family Violence" later in this chapter). Initially, most react with emotion, crying or yelling, hitting back, or leaving the room. After the incident has passed, some women withhold support and services from their husbands, from basic household and child-care tasks to sex. Some seek support and help from friends and relatives, but few contact the police or social services. Quite often, these women stay in their abusive situations. Why?

Some answers suggest that wives who are highly dependent economically on marriage are less able to discourage, avoid, leave, or put an end to abuse than women in marriages where the balance of resources between husband and wife is more nearly equal. Dependent wives lack both alternatives to marriage and resources within marriage to negotiate change. Other research considered the cognitive strategies women use to help them perceive their relationship positively. No matter the frequency of physical abuse experienced, some women are still able to focus on the positive features of the relationship. In sum, these two variables—no resources to leave and assessing the relationship positively—seem to fit the B and C in the ABCX model.

Husband and male partner abuse and violence

The abuse of husbands and male partners by women has received far less attention than the abuse of females. One writer noted the following:

1. Less empirical data exists on relationship violence committed by women.
2. Some feminists fear that drawing attention to battered husbands will impede attempts to battle the more serious problem of wife abuse.
3. Men are reluctant to acknowledge that they have been beaten by their wives, given traditional social values about male/female relationships.
4. Women's abuse is more visible, given the greater severity of physical damage that they suffer.[46]

Yet research has consistently shown that men and women engage in comparable amounts of violence. For example, Straus and Gelles found that "assaults by women on their male partners occur at about the same rate as assaults by men on their female partners, and women initiate such violence about as often as men."[47] They estimated that, in the United States, one out of six (about 16 percent), or 8.7 million, couples experienced an incident of physical assault in 1985, the year of their second national study. Most of these assaults were relatively minor—pushing, slapping, shoving, or throwing things—but a substantial number were serious—kicking, punching, biting, or choking.

That the rates for violence by wives were so similar to the rates for violence by husbands is quite surprising, given the extremely low rate of assault by women outside the family. The high rate within marriage may be explained by recognizing that many assaults by wives are acts of retaliation or self-defence, that implicit cultural norms tolerate or even accept marital violence, and that marriages involve a high degree of frustration.

Mutual marital abuse and violence

Wife abuse and husband abuse have been treated separately here, but it needs to be emphasized that *mutual* abuse is more common than either form alone. This is true not only for physical abuse but for verbal/symbolic aggression as well. Again, men and women engage in about equal amounts of verbal/symbolic aggression against their partners.[48]

Disparity between husbands and wives in recalling violence is evident. Women typically report more violence in intimate relationships than do men.[49] Spouses report more violence by their partners than they are willing to acknowledge by themselves. Also, each spouse is more likely to report his or her own victimization than his or her use of violence.

Disparity by gender exists as well in the effects of domestic violence. While men and women report similar rates of domestic violence as both victims and perpetrators, the violence is more frightening and undermining for women's sense of well-being than it is for men. Data from Canadian and American studies showed that women had higher depression and anxiety scores than men in cases of both physical and psychological violence.[50] In general, violence has greater adverse effects on a sense of personal control and is more detrimental to the self-perceptions and well-being of women than men.

The effects of family structure on both spouse and child abuse are evident from data on stepfamilies and remarriages. Findings have shown that spouse and child abuse are more likely in stepfamilies and in families in which one or both spouses have been divorced (remarried and reconstituted) than in never-divorced (intact) families.[51] Explanations for this occurrence may relate to carrying on previously learned behaviour patterns, to stepparents not having strong bonding and blood ties to children, to selecting spouses who dominate or can be dominated, and to higher levels of stress in remarried families. In any case, there is a continuity of abuse in reconstituted families.

Marital violence clearly affects persons other than those who are directly abused. Specifically, children who witness parents being abused may be vulnerable to a variety of behavioural and emotional difficulties. An American panel of married couples revealed that parents' marital violence was associated with divorce, reports of abusive behaviour, and alcohol/drug problems, and that these variables were, in turn, associated with several offspring problems.[52] These included poorer parent-child relationships, lower psychological well-being as seen in lower self-esteem, less satisfaction with life, and more violence in the offspring's own relationships. These findings are consistent with a *learned helplessness* model of wife abuse, which suggests that seeing one's mother in a helpless situation transmits the message that women are helpless to control their own lives. This message promotes depression in women, who are most likely to identify with the victim/mother. In contrast, men who witness parental violence tend to be more likely to identify with the aggressor/father and thus avoid depression. These men, in turn, are more likely to be abusive husbands themselves.

Sibling abuse and violence

The most frequent and acceptable form of violence within families occurs between siblings. Parent interviews from the Straus and Gelles studies revealed that 40 percent of children had hit a brother or sister with an object during the preceding year and 82 percent had engaged in some form of violence against a sibling.

Sibling violence is granted a high degree of tolerance. Identical acts between parent and child or husband and wife might well result in criminal charges and social service intervention. It appears that, while male sibling pairs outdo female sibling pairs in throwing things and pushing and hitting one another, the greatest amount of physical violence occurs between boy/girl pairs.

Sibling violence is usually explained in terms of sibling rivalry or jealousy. Supposedly, one sibling resents something the other has: parental attention, privileges, clothes, objects, and on. Differences may also centre on limited resources: use of the bathroom or telephone, what television show to watch, or who gets the remaining candy bar. These resentments and differences may become aggravated when parents intervene and insist that the children share or make a decision that favours one over the other. Reacting abusively toward a sibling, who is more one's equal in terms of size and age, is both more equitable and more acceptable than reacting abusively toward one's parents (although as noted earlier in this chapter, parent abuse occurs as well).

Sometimes sibling discord revolves around the division of labour in the family. Siblings normally compete in avoiding undesirable tasks or chores, such as doing dishes, cleaning rooms, sweeping walks, and so on. Age differences may aggravate the situation if younger children are assigned fewer chores. In short, exchange theory is operative, and perceived inequalities lead to conflict. Obviously, not all inequity leads to abuse or violence, but fighting or throwing objects are common reactions of many children. When one child is outmatched, parental intervention may be warranted in stopping the fight, protecting the younger sibling, and perhaps punishing the older sibling. Unfortunately, doing so may exacerbate the general problem of competition among siblings.

Factors such as these help to explain the common occurrence and perhaps cyclical nature of sibling abuse and violence. Recognizing the importance of socialization experiences and social contexts, one could expect that, even among siblings, differences in abuse would exist by sex, ethnicity, and social class.

Elder abuse and violence

The battered elderly parent is increasingly evident in the literature on aging, with a consensus among those writers that a substantial problem exists. With the aging of the population, the issue of elder abuse becomes more urgent. The variety and severity of mistreatment ranges from passive neglect (being unintentionally ignored, forgotten) to active neglect (financial exploitation; withholding medicine, food, assistance) and from verbal or emotional abuse (name calling, threatening, humiliating) to physical abuse (slapping, pushing, injuring). Abuse may take the form of tying the elderly person to a bed or chair, excessive use of medication or other drugs to keep the parent more manageable, battering with fists or objects to enforce particular behaviours, and nearly any conceivable activity.

Definitional problems have hampered research in the area of elder abuse. It is impossible to quantify behaviour when there is no accepted definition and no body responsible for collecting data. One available source is police reports, and this is the resource used by the 1998 Statistics Canada report on *Family Violence in Canada*.[53] The report recognizes that as with other forms of family abuse, only a small proportion of elder abuse comes to the attention of the justice system.

> Older adults may be reluctant to report abuse and maltreatment to police due to emotional, physical or financial dependence on the abuser or simply because of embarrassment that the abuse is taking place, especially if the abuser is an adult child. Fear may also contribute to the secrecy of the abuse if the older adult is being threatened with institutionalization.[54]

Family members were involved in 20 percent of all violent crimes against Canadians 65 and older. As Figure 10.1 shows, older women were most apt to be victimized by their spouse, older men by adult children.

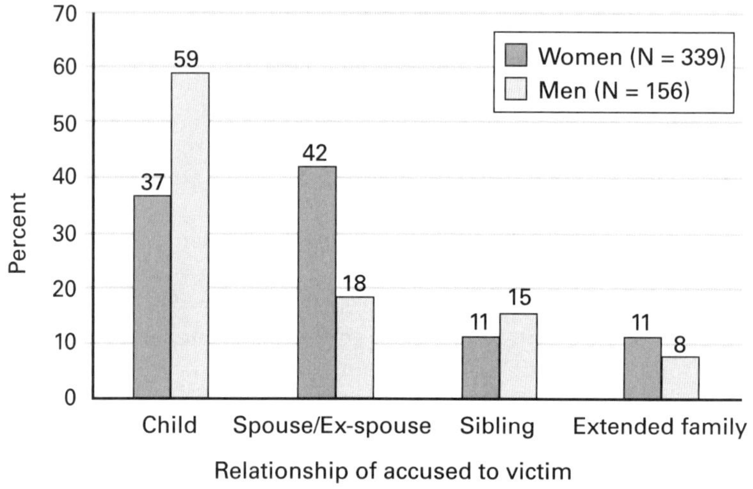

Figure 10.1
Older women victimized by spouse, older men by adult children, 1996
Source: Incident-based Uniform Crime Reporting Survey (UCR II), Canadian Centre for Justice Statistics, 1996; and *Family Violence in Canada,* Statistics Canada Catalogue 85-224 (1998): 27.

Elderly persons who are abused are generally frail, mentally or physically disabled, female, and living with the person responsible for mistreatment. A commonly cited cause of the abuse is that the caregiver has become overtaxed by the requirements of caring for the elderly adult, which often leads to despair, anger, resentment, or violence. In some instances, the abuse is clearly malicious and intentional; in other instances, caregivers have serious emotional and dependency problems. They do not deliberately intend to abuse but are unable to control their behaviour.

Violence among other intimates

Abuse and violence may be part of a relationship long before people marry and have children. Most studies of the courtship processes of dating, going steady, and becoming engaged have portrayed these events in a context of love, attraction, affection, mutual disclosure, and increasing closeness and commitment as the relationship moves toward exclusivity and marriage. Other recent studies, however, have suggested that violence and sexual exploitation are the dark side of courtship,[55] and that dating violence is prevalent. A study of Canadian university students found that at least one-third of women who dated had experienced physical aggression at some point in their dating history.[56]

As expected, the incidence of **courtship violence** that students know of greatly exceeds what had been directly experienced. Also as expected, extreme forms of violence, such as assault with an object or weapon, were less common than milder forms, such as pushing and slapping. Nearly two-fifths of the students knew of instances of threats, pushing, or slapping. Overall, males and females were about equal in initiating, committing, and sustaining violence. However, women were more often victims of serious forms of violence and more often reported sustaining sexual assault, physical injury, and emotional trauma. Males rarely reported that sexual assault was tried or occurred and did not perceive that females sustained greater physical or emotional harm. Attempts to explain these disparities were rooted in denial by the males, as shown by the nonrecognition or recall of details of experiences and the minimization of the frequency and intensity of the males' abuse.

Consistent with studies of college students, an American sample of never-married persons between the ages of 18 and 30 found that women were at least as likely to be physically aggressive as men.[57] This finding led the authors to note that, when developing a theory of dating aggression, the mechanisms that bring about both male and female aggression must be considered. Patriarchy may help explain dating aggression among men, but it does not explain why women are aggressive. The same source noted that people who are young, are from lower socioeconomic classes, and drink before a conflict are more prone to physical aggression. Once again, it seems that verbal aggression may be the seed of physical aggression, and that both verbal and physical aggressive behaviour are reciprocated in kind.

Date rape and sexual aggression and coercion constitute a particular kind of violence among intimates. A recent Canadawide study of college and university students provides a good indication of the extent of sexual aggression in the context of dating relationships in Canada. The sample included both men and women. The findings indicate that very serious forms of abuse are relatively common in campus dating; this finding reflects similar American findings. Almost 28 percent of women indicated that they had been victims of unwanted sexual contact, sexual coercion, attempted rape, or rape in the past year. Eleven percent of men reported victimizing a female in one of these ways in the past year. Almost half (45.1 percent) of the respondents said that they had been victimized since leaving high school and 19.5 percent of men said they had victimized a female since high school.[58] Another Canadian study of male students showed that those who were sexually aggressive also tended to be physically aggressive, traditional in sex role beliefs, accepting of interpersonal violence, and members of fraternities.[59]

The occurrence of violence during childhood or adolescence, whether exhibited toward parents or during courtship, seems to be a foundation for marital and parental violence. Unfortunately, the experience of violence between spouses and between parents and children is seldom the perpetrator's first experience.

Treating and preventing family violence

Application of the ABCX model (described at the beginning of this chapter) to violence in families suggests that the various types of violence that take place may or may not represent crisis events. A crisis event depends on the resources available to members (B) and the meanings or definitions attached to the acts (C).

The definition of what behaviours are *perceived* as violent may depend on the context, and the relationship between the individuals, as well as on gender. In an American Gallup poll in 1994 almost one person in four (23 percent) said they could imagine a situation in which they would approve of a wife slapping her husband.[60] People were more cautious about the opposite situation, however, as only 10 percent said they would ever approve of a husband slapping a wife.

The response of the abused persons—to endure, to fight back, or to escape—depends on the meanings and perceptions of the event as well as the resources available to those abused: strength, peer support, friends and kin, money or services, police and crisis intervention centres, and particularly self-esteem.

When Gelles and Straus asked women who had experienced violence how they reacted to the most recent incidence, more than half said they cried. Other responses, in order of frequency, were to run to another room, hit back, run out of the house, and call a friend or relative; the response in last place was to call the police.[61] The first few responses are all immediate and personal reactions to being hurt: crying, yelling, and running to get away. Longer-term responses are more closely related to personal and social resources, such as friends and relatives, as well as community services, such as the police.

Gelles and Straus suggested that an important and beneficial way to help battered women would be to empower them to negotiate with their husbands to end the violence. A particularly important intervention service (resource) would be education in mediation or conflict resolution techniques. Other important resources for battered women include sources of help such as police, social workers, shelters, medical services, and so forth.

Providing these resources is important, certainly, and a step in the right direction. But how can family violence be prevented in the first place? Specifically, how can assumptions that violence is a legitimate solution to conflict be modified?

Gelles and Straus argued that prevention policies and programs must be directed at the two factors that make it possible for people to abuse and maltreat those whom they love.[62] First is the need to eliminate cultural norms and values that accept violence as a means of resolving conflict and problems in families. Second is the need to develop programs and policies that support families and reduce internal and external stresses and inequalities. How can these goals be accomplished?

The first goal—to change cultural norms and values that support violence—necessitates establishing a moral code that loved ones are not to be hit. This means banning spanking and corporal punishment. Sweden and all other Scandinavian countries, for example, have taken the lead in this process by

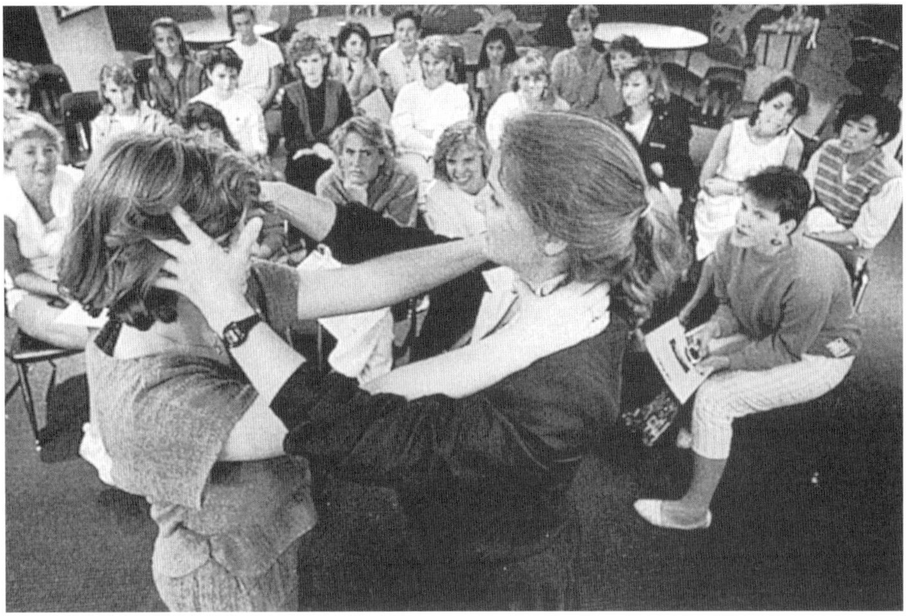

A number of community resources exist to assist women in coping with abusive situations, including medical services, shelters, support groups, conflict resolution training, and even self-defence training. In this session, women learn an eye-gouging technique for dealing with assailants.

banning capital punishment, outlawing corporal punishment of children in schools, and passing legislation prohibiting spanking. Firearm ownership is also rigorously controlled and violent programming on Swedish television is severely restricted. In contrast, most people in North America are aware of the controversies over capital punishment, corporal punishment, spanking, control over sale and registration of firearms, and violence on television, in movies, and in children's games. Violence, in general, including family, marital, parental, and sibling violence, will remain prevalent as long as the society in which it occurs glorifies killing, shooting, beating, hitting, and abusing.

The second goal of developing programs and policies that support families is closely related to the first goal of changing norms and values. Policies and programs have been enacted in many provinces and federally to address child abuse, spouse abuse, and marital rape. Additional efforts to eliminate poverty and unemployment; to provide adequate medical and hospital care to all families; to support effective planned parenthood; to reduce sexual, class, and racial inequality, both in the home and community; and to promote kin and community linkages and support networks would probably result in lowering levels of family violence.

SUMMARY

1. The central issues of this chapter—stress and violence—are not unique to any given point of the family life course or any particular family structure. A stressor, or crisis-provoking, event includes any situation that threatens the status quo and well-being of the system or its members. These events may come from sources both within and outside the family. Certain events may solidify the unit while others may be very disruptive.

2. The ABCX model refers to some event (A) interacting with the family's crisis-meeting resources (B) and the definition or meaning given to the event (C), resulting in the level or degree of crisis (X). When and if B and C are adequate, the levels of stress and crisis will be minimal. If they are inadequate, the levels of stress and crisis will be high.

3. Abuse and violence are common within many families. Unique characteristics of the family as a social group make it a violence-prone setting for spouses, for children, and for other interpersonal relationships. The prevalence of violence offers a persuasive counterargument to the myth of the family as nonviolent.

4. Considerable research attention has been focused on the abuse of children. Traditional modes of discipline grant legitimacy to spanking and other forms of physical punishment of children. Since most of such punishment occurs behind closed doors, most abuse never comes to the attention of the public.

5. Violence is sometimes directed by children, particularly adolescents, toward parents. Research has shown that parental assault is extensive, occurring among both males and females and directed at both mothers and fathers.

6. Wife and female partner abuse, like child abuse, is not always viewed as inappropriate, particularly in contexts of male authority and dominance. As with child abuse, abuse of female intimates may have actually decreased in recent years. Many female partners do not or cannot leave their violent male partners due to economic dependency and lack of alternatives and sometimes due to positive perceptions of the relationship.

7. Husband and male partner abuse is given far less attention than the abuse of children and wives; however, physical violence seems to be one aspect of intimate relationships that approaches equality between spouses.

8. Sibling abuse is the most frequent and acceptable form of violence within families. Explanations often centre on sibling rivalry and jealousy. Supposedly, one sibling resents something the other has, or tensions build over differences in availability of limited resources.

9. Abuse of people who are elderly frequently involves aging parents, particularly mothers. The mistreatment of elders ranges from positive or active neglect to verbal and physical abuse.

10. Other forms of violence among intimates include adolescents and young adults in the dating/courtship process. Such violence may take the form of threats or physical injury and may frequently involve sexual aggression, coercion, or date rape.

11. This chapter focused on marital and family stress and violence. Chapter 11 will turn to terminating marriages, particularly via divorce, and the subsequent pattern of remarriage.

KEY TERMS AND TOPICS

Marital and interpersonal stress and crisis p. 271
Social stresses on families p. 271
Stressor events p. 271
ABCX model of stress p. 272
Enabling and disabling events p. 273
Double-ABCX model p. 273
Family violence p. 274
Myths of family violence p. 276
Causes of family violence p. 277
Child abuse p. 278
Physical punishment p. 278
Child sexual abuse p. 280
Parent abuse p. 282
Wife and female partner abuse p. 283
Husband and male partner abuse p. 288
Mutual marital abuse p. 289
Sibling abuse p. 290
Elder abuse p. 291
Violence among other intimates p. 292
Courtship violence p. 293
Date rape and sexual aggression and coercion p. 293
Treating and preventing family violence p. 294

DISCUSSION QUESTIONS

1. List five stressor events for families. How can families prepare for events such as these? How is it possible that certain events strengthen families whereas others tear them apart?
2. What factors enhance crisis-proneness and crisis-preparedness? Using the ABCX formula given in the chapter, show how *resources* and *meanings* lead to family adequacy or inadequacy in facing potential crisis situations.
3. Select any personal or family problem. How could or does the availability of resources affect one's ability to address the problem? What types of resources are significant to families or individuals? How does one's definition of the problem affect the level of stress experienced?
4. Examine the seven myths of family violence. How many seem to be partially true? With which ones do you agree and disagree? Why?
5. What family and social circumstances put children at greater risk for abuse, both physical and sexual? What long-term effects does being abused have on individuals?
6. Consider the position that intimate relationships are private and personal matters. If so, should the community or state get involved in what lovers, couples, and families do to each other? Why or why not? Should any special protection be given to children and elderly people? What actions should outsiders take?
7. Why do many abused wives or female partners not leave abusive situations? What factors make a difference in women's decision-making?
8. Is it necessary to be concerned about or do research on violence toward husbands or between siblings? Can husbands take care of themselves? Are fights between children natural? Explain.
9. Think of personal childhood experiences of violence. What experiences do you recall? With whom? For what reasons?
10. Discuss various forms of abuse within families toward elderly parents. What types of action or programs might lessen the severity of or even resolve the problem?
11. Are you aware of abuse or violence in dating and nonmarital interactions? What forms does it take? Is sexual aggression or coercion actually violence? Why or why not?
12. What is the relationship of factors such as alcoholism, drug addiction, unemployment, and lack of money to violence and abuse? How might a pregnancy, birthday, or holiday affect the likelihood of violence?

Further Readings

Allison, Julie A., and Wrightsman, Lawrence S. *Rape, The Misunderstood Crime*. Newbury Park, CA: Sage, 1993. An extensive overview of available literature on the topic of rape, including information about the rapist, date rape, spousal rape, the law, as well as treatment of and preventive approaches to rape.

Barnett, Ola W.; Miller-Perrin, Cindy L.; and Perrin, Robin D. *Family Violence Across the Lifespan: An Introduction*. Thousand Oaks, CA: Sage, 1997. A book that covers the magnitude of family violence, how it is assessed, and its consequences.

Burr, Wesley R.; Klein, Shirley R.; and associates. *Reexamining Family Stress: New Theory and Research*. Thousand Oaks, CA: Sage, 1994. Building upon recent methodological developments, the writers introduce several systemic concepts into the family stress literature that contribute to theory, research, and practice.

Ewing, Charles Patrick. *Fatal Families: the Dynamics of Intrafamilial Homicide*. Thousand Oaks, CA: Sage, 1997. A case study approach that explores the social, cultural, and psychological forces that lead people to kill members of their own families.

Gelles, Richard J., and Loseke, Donileen R., eds. *Current Controversies on Family Violence*. Newbury Park, CA: Sage, 1993. Key professionals take varying perspectives on issues in conceptualization, definition and measurement, causes, and social intervention of family violence.

Hampton, Robert L.; Gullotta, Thomas P.; Adams, Gerald R.; Potter, Earl H.; and Weissberg, Roger, eds. *Family Violence: Prevention and Treatment*. Newbury Park, CA: Sage, 1993. A multidisciplinary focus on family violence from a variety of abusive contexts, including children, marriage, elderly, families of colour, and how it can be prevented and treated.

Jasinski, Jana L., and Williams, Linda M. *Partner Violence: A Comprehensive Review of 20 Years of Research*. Thousand Oaks, CA: Sage, 1998. Seven chapters that summarize the major findings on family violence.

Johnson, Holly. *Dangerous Domains: Violence Against Women in Canada*. Toronto: Nelson Canada, 1996. A comprehensive discussion based on the 1993 Violence Against Women Survey. This survey remains the most extensive investigation of its kind in the world.

Kantor, Glenda Kaufman, and Jasinski, Jana, eds. *Out of the Darkness: Contemporary Perspectives on Family Violence*. Thousand Oaks, CA: Sage, 1997. Using information from the international arena, the editors provide an interdisciplinary look at family violence.

McHenry, Patrick C., and Price, Sharon J., eds. *Families and Change: Coping with Stressful Events*. Thousand Oaks, CA: Sage, 1994. Eight chapters deal with stress and change over the family life cycle, such as gender issues, work/family, and aging. Five chapters deal with situational stressors such as divorce, drug and alcohol abuse, and violence.

Quinn, Mary Joy, and Tomita, Susan K. *Elder Abuse and Neglect: Causes, Diagnosis, and Intervention Strategies*. New York: Springer Publishing Co., 1997. An overview of elder mistreatment with an extensive section on the many forms of intervention.

Schwartz, Martin D., and DeKeseredy, Walter S. *Sexual Assault on the College Campus: The Role of Male Peer Support*. Thousand Oaks, CA: Sage, 1997. A story of sexual assault on the college campus and the peer support behind men committing these assaults.

Stacey, William A.; Hazlewood, Lonnie R.; and Shupe, Anson. *The Violent Couple*. Westport, CT: Praeger, 1994. A sample of violent partners is drawn from a counselling program to analyze the forms, pathways, and healing strategies for mutual abuse.

Straus, Murray A., and Gelles, Richard J. *Physical Violence in American Families*. New Brunswick, NJ: Transaction, 1990. An informative and extensive report of violence in American families, based on two national surveys conducted a decade apart.

Wolfe, David A.; Wekerle, Christine; and Scott, Katreena. *Alternatives to Violence: Empowering Youth to Develop Healthy Relationships*. Thousand Oaks, CA: Sage, 1997. An examination of how youth can seek and establish connections that will reduce not only the risk of violence against women and children but also the potential of men to become abusive.

WEBLINKS

http://www.cfc-efc.ca//docs/00000857.htm

The Centre for Social Welfare Studies at the Faculty of Social Work, Wilfrid Laurier University, reviews 20 years of research and literature on social support and other promising approaches to reduce child abuse and neglect and maintain families. Program characteristics and their relationships to outcome patterns are assessed.

http:www.bwss.org/

Founded in 1979 and based out of Vancouver, Battered Women's Support Services provides free support services to women who are or have been involved in abusive relationships or domestic situations. This website provides excellent educational resources including legal information and publications.

http://www.hc.sc.gc.ca/hppb/familyviolence/

The National Clearing House on Family Violence is an initiative of Health Canada. This homepage offers information, including current statistics and publications, on family violence in Canada.

NOTES

1. Reuben Hill, "Social Stresses on the Family," *Social Casework* 39 (February/March 1958): 139–150.
2. Pauline Boss, *Family Stress Management* (Newbury Park, CA: Sage, 1988).
3. Hill, "Social Stresses on the Family," 141.
4. Blair Wheaton, "Life Transitions, Role Histories, and Mental Health," *American Sociological Review* 55 (April 1990): 209–223.
5. Hamilton I. McCubbin and Joan M. Patterson, "Family Adaptation to Crisis," in *Family Stress, Coping, and Social Support*, ed. Hamilton I. McCubbin et al. (Springfield, IL: Charles C. Thomas, 1982), 44–46.
6. Marsha Wiggins Frame and Constance L. Shehan, "Relocation Stress and Coping Among Clergy Husbands and Wives," *Family Relations* 43 (April 1994): 196–205; and Victor Florian and Nira Dangoor, "Personal and Familial Adaptation of Women with Severe Physical Disabilities: A Further Validation of the Double ABCX Model," *Journal of Marriage and the Family* 56 (August 1994): 735–746.
7. Alexis J. Walker, "Reconceptualizing Family Stress," *Journal of Marriage and the Family* 47 (November 1985): 827–837.
8. Niall Bolger, Anita DeLongis, Ronald C. Kessler, and Elaine Wethington, "The Contagion of Stress Across Multiple Roles," *Journal of Marriage and the Family* 51 (February 1989): 175–183.
9. Murray A. Straus, "Sociological Research and Social Policy: The Case of Family Violence," *Sociological Forum* 7 (1992): 211–237.
10. Richard J. Gelles and Murray A. Straus, *Intimate Violence* (New York: Simon & Schuster, 1988), 18.
11. *Family Violence in Canada: A Statistical Profile*, Statistics Canada Catalogue 85-224, 1998.
12. David Levinson, *Family Violence in Cross-Cultural Perspective* (Newbury Park, CA: Sage, 1989), 102–107.
13. Ibid., 103.
14. Gelles and Straus, Chapter 2, 37–51.
15. Ibid., 51.
16. Kristin L Anderson, "Gender, Status and Domestic Violence: An Integration of Feminist and Family Violence Approaches," *Journal of Marriage and the Family* 59 (August 1997): 655-669.
17. Murray A. Straus and Christine Smith, "Family Patterns and Primary Prevention of Family Violence," in *Physical Violence in American Families*, ed. Murray A. Straus and Richard J. Gelles (New Brunswick, NJ: Transaction, 1990), 512–521.
18. David Hemenway, Sara Solnick, and Jennifer Carter, "Child-Rearing Violence," *Child Abuse and Neglect* 18 (1994): 1011–1020; and Diana Doumas, Gayla Margolin and Richard John, "The Intergenerational Transmission of Aggression Across Three Generations," *Journal of Family Violence* 9 (1994): 157–175.

19. Murray Straus, "Discipline and Deviance: Physical Punishment of Children and Violence and Other Crime in Adulthood," *Social Problems* 38 (May 1991): 136.

20. Lindsay Scotton, "To Spank or Not to Spank," *Toronto Star*, April 16, 1994, K9.

21. Murray A. Straus, "Discipline and Deviance: Physical Punishment of Children and Violence and Other Crime in Adulthood," *Social Problems* 38 (May 1991): 133–152.

22. David Fergusson and Michael Lynskey, "Physical Punishment/Maltreatment During Childhood and Adjustment in Young Adulthood," *Child Abuse and Neglect* 21 (1997): 617-636.

23. Richard J. Gelles, "Poverty and Violence Toward Children," *American Behavioral Scientist* 35 (January/February 1992): 258–274.

24. Loring Jones, "Unemployment and Child Abuse," *Families in Society: The Journal of Contemporary Human Services* (December 1990): 579–586.

25. *Family Violence in Canada: A Statistical Profile*, Statistics Canada Catalogue 85-224, 1998.

26. *Reaching for Solutions*, Report of the Special Advisor to the Minister of National Health and Welfare on Child Abuse in Canada (1990): 19.

27. David Finkelhor, Gerald Hotaling, I.A. Lewis and Christine Smith, "Sexual Abuse in a National Survey of Adult Men and Women: Prevalence, Characteristics and Risk Factors," *Child Abuse and Neglect* 14 (1990):19-28.

28. Leslie Margolin and John L. Craft, "Child Sexual Abuse by Caretakers," *Family Relations* 38 (October 1989): 450–455.

29. Joseph H. Beitchman, Kenneth J. Zucker, Jane E. Hood, Granville A. DaCosta, Donna Akman, and Erika Cassavia, "A Review of the Long-Term Effects of Child Sexual Abuse," *Child Abuse and Neglect* 16 (1992): 101–118.

30. Joseph Beitchman, Kenneth Zucker, Jane Hood, Granville DaCosta, Donna Akman and Erika Cassavia, "A Review of the Long-Term Effects of Child Sexual Abuse," *Child Abuse and Neglect* 16 (1992): 101–118; and Tom Luster and Stephen Small, "Sexual Abuse History and Problems in Adolescence: Exploring the Effects of Moderating Variables," *Journal of Marriage and the Family* 59 (February 1997): 131–142.

31. Debra Boyer and David Fine, "Sexual Abuse as a Factor in Adolescent Pregnancy and Child Maltreatment," *Family Planning Perspectives* 24 (January/February 1992): 4–11.

32. Ronald L. Simons and Les B. Whitbeck, "Sexual Abuse as a Precursor to Prostitution and Victimization Among Adolescent and Adult Homeless Women," *Journal of Family Issues* 12 (September 1991): 361–379.

33. Murray A. Straus and Richard J. Gelles, "Societal Change and Change in Family Violence from 1975 to 1985 as Revealed by Two National Surveys," *Journal of Marriage and the Family* 48 (August 1986): 465–479; and Gelles and Straus, *Intimate Violence*, 109–114.

34. Lance C. Egley, "What Changes the Societal Prevalence of Domestic Violence?" *Journal of Marriage and the Family* 53 (November 1991): 885–897.

35. Robert Agnew and Sandra Huguley, "Adolescent Violence Toward Parents," *Journal of Marriage and the Family* 51 (August 1989): 699–711.

36. "The Violence Against Women Survey," *The Daily*, Statistics Canada Catalogue 11-001E (November 18, 1993): 1–10.

37. Jan E. Stets, "Cohabiting and Marital Aggression: The Role of Social Isolation," *Journal of Marriage and the Family* 53 (August 1991): 669–680.

38. Michael P. Johnson, "Patriarchal Terrorism and Common Couple Violence: Two Forms of Violence Against Women," *Journal of Marriage and the Family* 57 (May 1995): 283–294.

39. Jacquelyn C. Campbell, "A Review of Nursing Research on Battering," in *Violence Against Women: Nursing Research, Education, and Practice Issues*, ed. Carolyn M. Sampselle (New York: Hemisphere, 1992), 69–81.

40. Eugene Lupri, Elaine Grandin, and Merlin Brinkerhoff, "Socioeconomic Status and Male Violence in the Canadian Home: A Reexamination," *Canadian Journal of Sociology* 19(1) (1994): 47–73.

41. Michael D. Smith, "Sociodemographic Risk Factors in Wife Abuse: Results from a Survey on Toronto Women," *Canadian Journal of Sociology* 15 (1990): 39–58.

42. "The Violence Against Women Survey," 4–5.

43. Richard J. Gelles, "Violence and Pregnancy: Are Pregnant Women at Greater Risk of Abuse?" *Journal of Marriage and the Family* 50 (August 1988): 841–847.

44. Ileana Arias, Carolyn M. Lyons and Amy Street, "Individual and Marital Consequences of Victimization: Moderating Effects of Relationship Efficacy and Spouse Support," *Journal of Family Violence* 12 (1997): 193–210.

45. Straus and Gelles, "Societal Change and Change in Family Violence," 465–479; and Gelles and Straus, 109.

46. Clifton P. Flynn, "Relationship Violence by Women: Issues and Implications," *Family Relations* 39 (April 1990): 194–198.

47. Murray A. Straus and Richard J. Gelles, *Physical Violence in American Families* (New Brunswick, NJ: Transaction, 1990), 110.

48. Murray A. Straus and Stephen Sweet, "Verbal/Symbolic Aggression in Couples: Incidence Rates and Relationships to Personal Characteristics," *Journal of Marriage and the Family* 54 (May 1992): 346–357.

49. Alfred DeMaris, Meredith D. Pugh, and Erika Harman, "Sex Differences in the Accuracy of Recall of Witnesses

of Portrayed Dyadic Violence," *Journal of Marriage and the Family* 54 (May 1992): 335–345.

50. Elaine Grandin, Eugene Lupri and Merlin Brinkerhoff, "Couple Violence and Psychological Distress," *Canadian Journal of Public Health*, 89 (January-February 1998): 43–47; and Debra Umberson, Kristin Anderson, Jennifer Glick and Adam Shapiro, "Domestic Violence, Personal Control and Gender," *Journal of Marriage and the Family* 60 (May 1998): 442–452.

51. Debra Kalmuss and Judith A. Seltzer, "Continuity of Marital Behavior in Remarriage: The Case of Spouse Abuse," *Journal of Marriage and the Family* 48 (February 1986): 113–120; and Jean Giles-Sims and David Finkelhor, "Child Abuse in Stepfamilies," *Family Relations* 33 (July 1984): 403–413.

52. Cosandra McNeal and Paul Amato, "Parents' Marital Violence: Long-Term Consequences for Children," *Journal of Family Issues* 19 (March 1998): 123–139.

53. *Family Violence in Canada: A Statistical Profile*, Statistics Canada Catalogue 85–224, 1998.

54. Ibid, 25.

55. Sally A. Lloyd, "The Darkside of Courtship: Violence and Sexual Exploitation," *Family Relations* 40 (January 1991): 14–20.

56. Gordon E. Barnes, Leonard Greenwood, and Reena Sommer, "Courtship Violence in a Canadian Sample of Male College Students," *Family Relations* 40 (January 1991): 37–44; and James M. Makepeace, "Gender Differences in Courtship Victimization," *Family Relations* 35 (July 1986): 383–388.

57. Jan E. Stets and Debra A. Henderson, "Contextual Factors Surrounding Conflict Resolution While Dating: Results from a National Study," *Family Relations* 40 (January 1991): 29–36; and Jan E. Stets, "Interactive Processes in Dating Aggression: A National Study," *Journal of Marriage and the Family* 54 (February 1992): 165–177.

58. Walter DeKeseredy and Katharine Kelly, "The Incidence and Prevalence of Woman Abuse in Canadian University and College Dating Relationships," *Canadian Journal of Sociology* 18(2) (1993): 137–159.

59. Leandra Lackie and Anton F. de Man, "Correlates of Sexual Aggression Among Male University Students," *Sex Roles* 37 (1997): 451–457.

60. David W. Moore, "Approval of Husband Slapping Wife Continues to Decline," *The Gallup Poll Monthly* 341 (February 1994): 2.

61. Gelles and Straus, Figure 10, 258.

62. Ibid., 194.

CHAPTER

11 DIVORCE AND REMARRIAGE

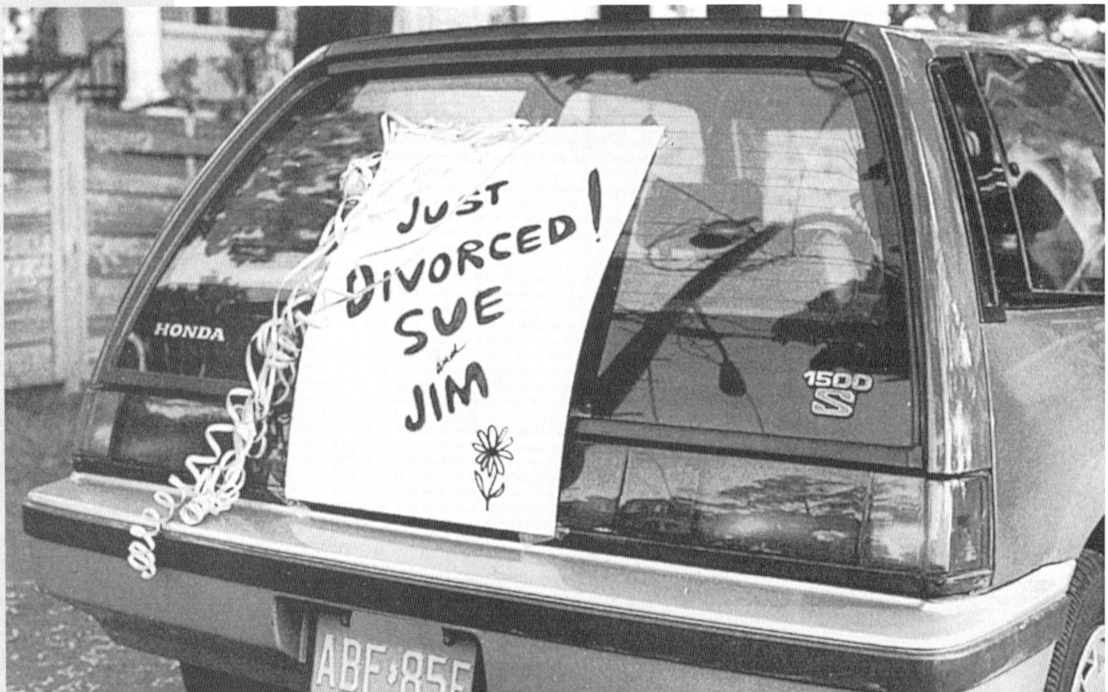

All societies provide one or more ways for husbands, wives, or both to deal with unsatisfactory marital relationships. Highly patriarchal, male-dominant societies are likely to permit men to have mistresses or concubines while they are married. In many societies, including Canada, marriage is regarded as a civil contract, in which the state specifies how old people have to be to get married, how many spouses they may have, and the conditions under which marriages can be dissolved.

In some countries, marriage was, until recently, indissoluble except by death or annulment. This was true in countries such as Argentina, Brazil, Chile, and Colombia in Latin America; the Philippines in Southeast Asia; and Italy, Ireland, and Spain in Europe. In some countries, such as Canada, the United States, France, Switzerland, Russia, Poland, and the Scandinavian countries, a divorce is granted if one or both parties have been guilty of a grave violation of marital obligations or if it is shown that the marriage has completely broken down. Finally, the official laws of Islam and of Judaism grant free power to the husband to terminate his marriage by repudiating his wife. In reality, this occurs infrequently, and movements exist to provide power to wives to dissolve their marriages as well.

In North America, divorce is the most common means of ending an unsatisfactory marital relationship, and most attention in this chapter will be devoted to divorce. Desertions, legal separations, informally-agreed-upon separations, and annulments are other means that people use to get out of a marriage, at least temporarily.

DESERTION, MARITAL SEPARATION, AND ANNULMENT

Desertion is the willful abandonment, without legal justification, of one's spouse, children, or both. Little is known about desertion, and few studies have considered this issue.

It has traditionally been assumed that desertion applied only to men. Today, there are reports of "runaway wives" as well. Unlike men, who may want out of a marriage, deserting women are more likely to seek escape from childrearing and home situations that have become unbearable. For both sexes, it appears that desertion is a response to one issue or many that seem unsolvable: children, marital conflicts, alcoholism, infidelity, inability to support a family, and so on.

Unlike divorce, desertion is not institutionalized. No registration takes place with the courts or any other official body, and neither the deserting nor nondeserting spouse can remarry. What constitutes desertion and the legal, economic, and social ramifications of marital desertion are not clear. For example, how many days' absence constitute desertion? What if a spouse leaves and returns several times? Is one spouse legally responsible for the expenses and activities of the other? Because of the lack of institutionalized norms and the ambiguity of events surrounding desertion, desertion may have far more negative effects than divorce.

What about **marital separation?** A widely held assumption is that marital separation is a stepping-stone to divorce, sometimes soon followed by another marriage. While divorce follows separation for many couples, others use separation as a time to work out a reconciliation, ending marital difficulties. Still other couples remain married but live in long-term, unresolved separations.

The Canadian census distinguishes people who are *married* from those who are *married but separated*—people who have been deserted or who have parted because they no longer want to live together but have not obtained a divorce. The *married but separated* category includes those people with legal separations, those living apart with intentions of obtaining a divorce, and other persons permanently or temporarily separated because of marital discord. In 1996, 700 000 Canadians indicated that they were married but separated.[1]

In cases of **legal separation,** the husband and wife are authorized to live apart, and formal agreements specify visiting patterns, support, and so forth. These separations are rare, and usually occur in cases where couples are opposed to divorce but do not choose to live together. Separations were more common when divorces were more difficult to obtain. Now, most legally separated couples subsequently divorce.

The majority of separations are not legalized. An **informal separation** is often an arrangement between a husband and wife where one or both decide to live separately. Unlike cases of desertion, each knows the whereabouts of the other, and, unlike cases of divorce, the couple is legally married and cannot remarry. Because these couples seem to be overrepresented among low-income families, informal separation has been called in the literature the "poor man's divorce."

One of the few studies of marital separations was done in the metropolitan Cleveland area with a random sample of over 1100 residents.[2] It found that one in six couples was likely to separate for at least 48 hours at some point in their relationship because of arguments or disagreements. Some separations were a step on the way to permanent separation or divorce. Other separations were used as a conflict-resolution technique or a dramatic gesture to force some action on the part of the spouse. Those most likely to separate were blacks, women, and those with low incomes and minor children. For most people, separations were associated with a high sense of emotional distress.

What about separations, temporary or permanent, for reasons other than marital discord? One source concluded that marital noncohabitation does not make the heart grow fonder.[3] Couples living in separate households—most often because of military service or incarceration (confined in prison)—were nearly twice as likely to divorce within three years as persons cohabiting with their spouses.

The word **annul,** legally defined, means to reduce to nothing, to obliterate, to make void and of no effect, to abolish, to do away with, to eradicate. When a marriage has been annulled, a court, acting under the law of the state, has found that causes existed *before* the marriage that render the marriage contract void. The court concludes that the marriage, when performed, was in fact no marriage at all. By annulling the marriage, the court in effect says that it never existed.

Generally, the distinction between divorce and annulment lies in when certain actions occurred. Divorce generally involves an action that occurred *after* the date of marriage—adultery, incompatibility, cruelty, desertion, nonsupport, alcoholism, and the like. Annulment generally involves an action that occurred *before* the date of marriage—being underage, already being married, insanity, incurable impotence, incestuous relationship, and the like.

It may seem odd that, while the marriage was a social and psychological reality, legally, it never existed. If there are children from the annulled marriage, the court may require the husband who "never existed" to support minor children. Socially, relatives and friends are well aware of the once-existing marriage. And psychologically, both the male and female involved are well aware of once being married and the mate-selection process that preceded it.

DIVORCE

Divorce around the world

The Western world has traditionally viewed divorce as an unfortunate event for the persons involved and as a clear index of failure of the family system. But over the past few decades, attitudes toward separation and divorce have changed. In Western countries, divorce has become increasingly easy to obtain, spousal support has become less common, efforts have been made to increase child-support awards and improve payment compliance, and shared parental decision-making authority has become increasingly encouraged.[4]

Currently, the United States may have the highest divorce rate in the world. According to the latest figures available from United Nations sources, the American rate of divorce per 1000 persons in the population was 4.4. It was 3.7 in Cuba, 2.7 in Australia and France, 2.6 in Canada, 2.5 in Sweden, 2.2 in Switzerland, 1.6 in Japan, 1.5 in Singapore, 1.4 in Israel, 1.0 in Poland, 0.8 in South Africa, 0.5 in Italy, and 0.4 in Mexico.[5]

How are variations in the rate or frequency of divorce explained? One study sampled 66 countries to investigate societal-level correlates of divorce.[6] Four variables were shown to bear a significant relationship to the likelihood of divorce. Associated with lower divorce rates were (1) a high sex ratio, indicating a relative undersupply of women, and (2) a late average age at marriage for women. Significantly but nonlinearly related to divorce were (3) level of socioeconomic development and (4) female labour force participation rate. Both of these variables exhibited U-shaped associations with divorce. This suggests that socioeconomic development and increased female labour force participation in the early stages of industrialization tend to reduce the rate of divorce, but at later stages of industrialization and modernization tend to increase the incidence of divorce.

Many societies in the Western world, including Canada, rate high in socioeconomic development and female labour force participation. Thus, with an erosion of traditional patriarchal patterns and a heavy emphasis on the

FAMILY DIVERSITY

Divorce in Japan

The Japanese divorce rate is about one-third that of the United States and about half that of Western Europe. Along with Italy, Japan is the only one among developed countries that has a low divorce rate. Suggested explanations for this include that the family is still powerful and that, for the sake of the children, many men and women do not divorce.

Yasuhiko Yuzawa described three common kinds of divorce in Japan:

1. *Divorce by consent* is effected simply by notifying the registration office of the divorce, so long as both husband and wife agree. This is recognized as the simplest mode of divorce procedure in the world, with no conditions or checks imposed. About 91 percent of Japanese divorces are of this kind.
2. *Divorce by conciliation* is for those who cannot reach an agreement. These couples go to family court and get a divorce through the mediation of a conciliation committee. About 8 percent of the divorces in Japan are of this type.
3. *Divorce by judgment* most closely parallels the common procedure for divorce in Western countries. When divorce cannot be settled by any of the above two methods, it is brought to the general court. Reasons for divorce must meet conditions of adultery, abandonment, an unknown fate of the spouse, a severe mental disorder with no hope of recovery, or other reasons that make continuation of the marriage impossible. Only about 1 percent of Japanese divorces are by judgment.

Source: Journal of Divorce 13 (1990): 129–141.

individual and small nuclear family in contrast to an emphasis on extended kin, one could expect high rates of divorce. The following sections will examine how divorce rates are determined and consider trends in Canada.

Divorce in Canada

Divorce rates[7]

Divorce rates are usually calculated in one of three ways:

1. By the number of divorces that take place per 1000 persons in the total population
2. By the number of divorces per 1000 marriages
3. By the ratio of divorces granted in a given year to the number of marriages contracted in the same year

Note the differences in rate depending on which figure is used. For instance, the number of divorces that took place *per 1000 persons in the total population* in Canada in 1995 was 2.6. That is, for every 1000 persons in the population (men, women, children, adults, married, single), 5.2 *persons* became divorced, or 2.6 *marriages* ended in divorce (or annulment). Or put another way, in a city with a population of 100 000, if 260 divorces were granted in 1995, the divorce rate was 2.6. Since the Canadian system is monogamous (two persons per divorce), 520 individuals in a city of 100 000 persons were divorced that year. Note how this divorce rate can be influenced by factors such as the age distribution or the proportion of the married to the single population. In a country or city with a large family size, a low life expectancy, a late age at marriage, a sizeable proportion of the population being children or single teenagers, or a disproportionate number of the population unmarried, a sizeable percentage of those married could get divorced, yet the country or city would have a seemingly low divorce rate.

The number of divorces that took place *per 1000 married* women in 1993 in Canada was approximately 12.4. This rate is probably the most accurate of the three measures. Unlike the first rate described, it is based on the number of legal marriages—the group susceptible to divorce. This figure can be used to compare divorce rates cross-culturally without being influenced by the number, age, or marital status of the total population.

The ratio of *divorces granted in a given year to the number of marriages in that year* is a less frequently used ratio, and we must be cautious about how to interpret it. Assume that a city with a population of 100 000 issued 1000 marriage licences in 1999. In the same year, 500 divorces were granted. This would result in a divorce/marriage ratio of 1 to 2, or 50 divorces per 100 marriages. There was one divorce for every two marriages in the community. Suppose, however, that the divorce law was modified that year, and instead of 500 divorces, 2000 divorces took place; the number of marriages remained constant at 1000. According to this rate, there are two divorces for every marriage, or a divorce rate of 200.

While it may be accurate to speak of twice as many divorces as marriages occurring in a given year, it is not accurate to say that, of those marriages that took place, one-half will end in divorce, because the marriages that occurred that year are not the ones that ended in divorce; those marriages began one, eight, or thirty years ago. There is no relevant link between the number of marriages begun and ended in a given year. Secondly, the percentage of all marriages that are remarriages for one or both spouses is not taken into account. Persons who divorce and remarry in the same year contribute to both the number of marriages and the number of divorces, producing a ratio of one to one: as many divorces as marriages.

Although the accuracy of divorce rates and statistics is improving, divorce data are not perfect. From 1921 until 1968, divorce statistics in Canada were limited. The only regularly published data were the number of divorces granted each year. Annual data on separations or annulments were not compiled, nor was it possible to know how many Canadians obtained divorces outside of Canada.[8] Since 1968, divorce statistics have included records of the age, marital status at marriage, and length of marriage of the divorcing pair.

Divorce rates around the world show a highly consistent pattern of increases over the past 50 years. A study of 27 nations based on United Nations data indicated that since 1950, divorce rates rose in 25 of the 27 nations (exceptions were Mexico and Yugoslavia).[9] At the same time, 22 of the 27 nations had a decreasing marriage rate and all 27 had a decreasing birth rate. Thus, while marriage and birth rates showed a decline, divorce rates showed an increase.

Canadian trends

Before 1900, divorce in Canada was extremely rare—less than 2 per million population.[10] By 1921, the rate had climbed to 6.4 per 100,000 population, rising only 0.4 to 3.8 by 1931. The corresponding rates for the next three decades were 21.4 in 1941, 37.6 in 1951, and 36.0 in 1961.

Is family life more unstable now than in the past? Beaujot and McQuillan[11] did an interesting analysis of the changing demographic basis of family life in Canada from 1851 to 1981. During this period life expectancy increased from 40.0 to 71.9 years for men and from 42.1 to 79.0 years for women. So, without divorce marriages in the twentieth century were twice as long as nineteenth-century marriages. In 1851 the typical couple married in their mid-twenties, raised seven children and died in their early forties, before their last child was independent. In 150 years, the average length of marriage has doubled, the number of children has dropped from seven to fewer than two, and the power imbalance between spouses has shifted. Greater gender equality is supported by women's labour force participation and protected by legislation. Increased gender equality has created a very different context for marital dynamics. Husbands and wives are less tied economically than in the past and expectations (for both men and women) regarding emotional satisfaction have increased dramatically. In short, the ties that held marriages together in the past have weakened considerably.

Divorce rates in Canada have been highly responsive to two amendments to the *Divorce Act* in 1968 and 1985. (These legal changes are described in more detail below.) Annual data from 1968 to 1990 are shown in Figure 11.1. The effect of the two legislative changes is evident, as is the effect of economic downturns. In 1968, there were 54.8 divorces per 100 000 population. The rate jumped to 124.2 in 1969 and continued to climb each year until 1982. The recessions of the early 1980s and the early 1990s created slight downward turns in divorce rates. Rates jumped again in 1986 and 1987 following the 1985 revisions to the *Divorce Act*. The number of divorces has decreased since 1987, when a record high number of divorces (96 200) were granted. In 1997, 67 408 couples divorced.[12]

The divorce rate for the United States is far higher than for Canada. There, the divorce rate per 1000 population increased from 2.0 in 1940 to 2.4 in 1954 to 3.5 in 1970 to 5.3 in 1981; the rate declined to 4.3 in 1996. (When comparing these figures, note that the base for Canadian figures is 100 000 and the base for American figures is 1000.) As in Canada, the increase was not as steady as it appears from the selected figures shown.

Many factors have been cited to explain changes in divorce rates over time. Many have focused on social characteristics such as social-structural variables rather than on individual characteristics. One structural explanation of the changing divorce rate included increasing industrialization, increasing urbanization, increasing female labour force participation, decreasing fertility rate, changing gender-role norms, religious diversity, and legal diversity.[13] Another explanation looked at the impact of wars—in particular, the Second World War.[14] And still another focused on economic conditions.

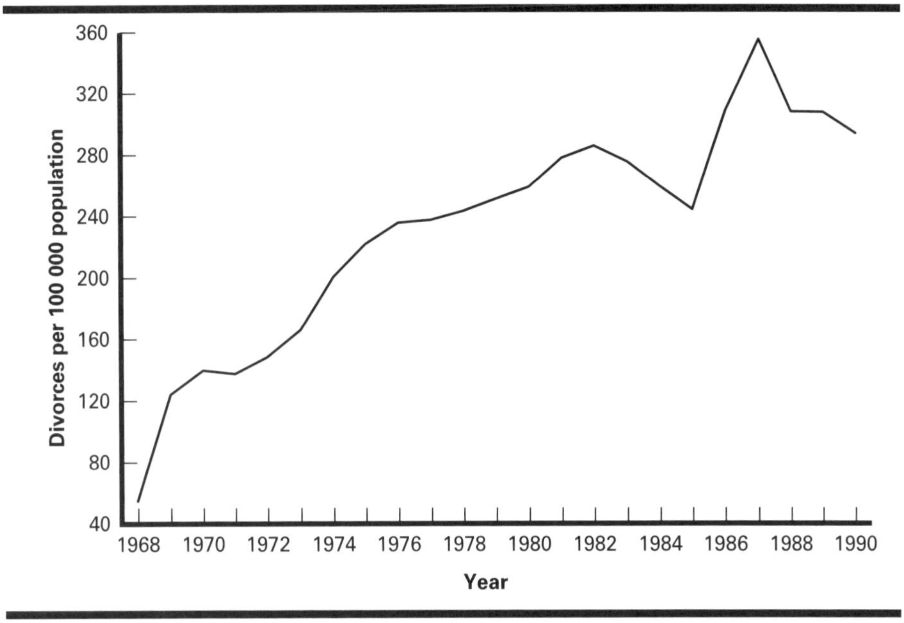

Figure 11.1
Divorces, 1971–91
Source: A Portrait of Families in Canada, Statistics Canada Catalogue 89-523E (November 1993): 17.

Variations in divorce

Divorce is permitted in every province in Canada. However, this was not always the case. Before Confederation, the existing provinces were free to adopt British divorce laws, although only New Brunswick and Nova Scotia did so. According to the *British North America Act, 1867,* jurisdiction over divorce is shared between the federal government, which enacts the law, and the provincial governments, which give provincial courts the authority to grant divorces. In fact, not all provinces gave this authority to their provincial courts. Citizens of these provinces had to apply to the federal government for a divorce. Ontario did not make this transition until 1930, Prince Edward Island until 1945, and Quebec until 1968.[15]

Geographic distribution

Since the nineteenth century in the United States, the geographic distribution of divorce has followed a general trend—it increases as one moves from east to west. The divorce rate is highest in the west, followed closely by the south, with a considerable drop in the midwest, followed by the northeast. In Canada, the Yukon, Alberta and British Columbia have had higher divorce rates than the other areas. The fact that divorce rates in Canada were so low for so long makes it difficult to determine if this trend is long-term.

How can these geographical variations be explained? Different factors probably operate in different areas, but, in general, the probability of divorce is believed to be lower in culturally homogeneous rather than heterogeneous communities and in communities with primary, face-to-face interactions in contrast to communities with anonymous relationships, segmented relationships, or both. In traditional Durkheimian social-structural terms, this pattern can be explained by a social integration hypothesis. There are fewer divorces in areas with a high consensus on rules of behaviour (norms) and effective social controls to ensure conformity. Communities or areas (regions, provinces, states) that are highly integrated socially tend to exert stronger social pressures against nontraditional behaviours (which divorce is generally perceived to be) and exert both formal and informal pressures for conformity to community norms.

The levels of social integration and pressure toward conformity are likely to be influenced by residential mobility as well. High levels of residential movement are related to both higher levels of divorce and lower levels of social integration. Norval Glenn and Beth Anne Shelton stated that the very high level of marital dissolution in the U.S. "divorce belt" (the West, South-Central, Mountain, and Pacific census divisions) can be accounted for by the very high level of residential mobility in that region.[16] Residential mobility and other variables associated with lower levels of social integration would not only affect variations in divorce rates by region and by state or province but would result in lower levels of divorce in rural than in urban areas as well.

Ages of husbands and wives

The average age of Canadian men who divorced in 1997 was 41.4. The corresponding age for women was 38.8. Both figures have increased slightly over time.[17]

Couples who marry early face a significantly higher risk of divorce. First marriages contracted before age 20 are far less stable than marriages among couples in their early twenties, and both are less stable that first marriages of people aged 25 or older. Explanations for these high rates may include emotional immaturity, inability to assume marital responsibilities, greater incidences of early marriage in lower socioeconomic statuses (where divorce is more likely), more premarital pregnancies (also related to higher incidences of divorce), and similar factors. Young marriages are not, however, responsible for changing divorce rates. Although young couples have higher rates of divorce, age at divorce has shifted upward over the past several decades, reflecting a steady rise in the age at first marriage. Very young marriages are increasingly rare in Canada.

Although divorce rates are highest in young marriages and occur most frequently in the first few years following a marriage, these factors should not obscure the reality that divorce may occur at any age or point in the life course, including the middle and later years. The increasing number of persons who are older, the changes in the perceptions of the roles of women, the shifting social acceptability of divorce, and so on present a realistic potential for dramatic increases in the number of divorced older persons.

Duration of marriage

In Canada, marriages that ended in divorce in 1997 had lasted an average of 12.7 years, and the average duration of marriage before divorce has been increasing since 1993.[18] This is likely explained by an increasing age of marriage and an increase in the number of couples living common-law. In the United States, the largest number of divorce decrees are granted one to four years after marriage, and that number declines relatively consistently with increased duration. The second, third, and fourth years of marriage appear to be the modal (most common) years for divorce.[19]

Divorce occurs irrespective of age or length of marriage; there is no evidence showing an increase in midlife divorce. A divorce that occurs late in the marriage may simply be the legal end of a marriage severely disrupted years earlier.

The duration of remarriages is influenced by many factors not at issue in first marriages: ex-spouses, ex-in-laws, stepchildren, and so on. For example, American data suggest that bringing stepchildren into a second marriage weakens the marital unit. Childbearing prior to remarriage increases the risk of marital dissolution, but having a child in the second marriage reduces the probability of dissolution.[20] In addition, perhaps remarriages are composed of people who see divorce as a viable solution to marital discontent.

Many marriages that never end in divorce are seriously disrupted all but legally. This observation leads to a point made at various times throughout the book: Length of marriage is not necessarily an index of marital success or adjustment, and divorce is not necessarily a good index of marital breakdown. Divorce may simply demonstrate a couple's willingness to provide a legal ending to their marital relationship.

Religion and socioeconomic status

What about religion and social class? Do divorce rates differ by religion and socioeconomic level? Is the probability of divorce different for Protestants and Catholics, and for people of lower and higher socioeconomic levels?

Data from seven U.S. surveys by Norval Glenn and Michael Supancic showed that marital dissolution is moderately higher for Protestants, considered as a whole, than for Catholics and lower for Jews than for Catholics.[21] The highest divorce rates are among persons with no religious affiliation. This finding is consistent with the data on frequency of attendance at religious services; religiosity is an important deterrent to divorce and separation.

Contrary to what one might expect, the Glenn and Supancic study, as well as others, showed that Protestant fundamentalists—the most conservative Protestant denominations (Nazarene, Pentecostal, Baptist)—have relatively high dissolution rates in spite of their strong disapproval of divorce. Factors associated with conversion and different degrees of commitment to these fundamentalist denominations were found to be important in producing the high dissolution rates.[22] Conversion may signify the cultural conflict that results from the radical transition from one context to another. It may also indicate a lack of normative integration in the antiseparation/divorce doctrine, on the one hand, while urging acceptance and tolerance of the converted "sinner" on the other. The higher divorce/separation rate may also reflect the lower-than-average socioeconomic status of persons in these denominations; the strong demands these groups make on the time, energy, and money of their adherents (which may negatively affect marriages); the inflexibility or rigidity of their theological position; or even the focus and emphasis on the next life rather than the current one.

What about socioeconomic level? The divorce rate has increased at all socioeconomic levels, yet the proportion of persons ever-divorced remains highest among relatively disadvantaged groups. Whether education, occupation, or income is used as an index of socioeconomic level, the divorce rate goes up as the socioeconomic level goes down. One exception to this relationship exists among professional women who have five or more years of college or university education. Compared to women in general of similar age groups, professional women were more likely never to have married, were more likely to divorce if they had married, and were less likely to remarry if they divorced. Female lawyers, in particular, were found to have a markedly higher rate of divorce and a lower rate of remarriage than women in other professions, such as teachers and doctors.[23] Marital disruption is high among professional women, in general, due perhaps to their lessened dependence on men, to the viable alternatives they have to marriage, and to the strain resulting from their efforts to balance work and family roles.

The alert reader may note what appears to be a contradiction in the data. For example, we mentioned in the text that divorce rates tend to decrease during times of economic depression and rise during times of prosperity. And it was just mentioned that the incidence of divorce increases as the socioeconomic level goes down. How is it possible that divorce rates decrease during recessions, when times are hard, and also increase among the lower strata, where times are also hard?

Several factors are involved. During economic depression, divorce rates drop at all class levels. During the Great Depression of the 1930s, people living with low incomes still had the highest divorce rate. Many of the marriages that survived the 1930s ended in divorce in the 1940s. As well, general life-style, sense of loyalty, links with kin, occupational and income security, and group support all affect rates of divorce. These factors were different in the 1930s for Depression families than they are now for lower-class families. Once again, the powerful influence of the social network is evident in something perceived to be as individualistic and personal as divorce.

Beyond geographic, demographic, and socioeconomic variations in the likelihood of divorce are other social factors. For example, couples who have siblings or friends who have divorced are themselves more likely to divorce.[24] Adult children of divorced parents are more likely to be exposed to poor models of dyadic behaviour and may not learn the skills and attitudes that facilitate successful functioning within marriage. Having divorced peers may reduce pressure to remain in an unhappy marriage.

Are there factors that help us to predict the likelihood of divorce? One longitudinal study found that marital problems at one point in time such as jealousy, drinking, spending money, moodiness, not communicating, and anger increased the odds of divorce 10 and 12 years later. And extramarital sex was a particularly powerful predictor of divorce.[25] Let us turn our attention to some of the grounds on which divorce occurs: legally and socially.

Legal and social grounds for divorce

In Canada, divorce legislation is a federal law, but divorce is regulated by the provinces. Before 1968, adultery, cruelty, and desertion of 10 years were the only grounds for obtaining a divorce, and rates were very low. After 1968, it became possible to obtain a divorce after a separation of three years. Couples already separated at the time of the change could divorce as soon as the time provision was met. This change led to a significant increase in divorce. The new act came into effect July 2, 1968. Canadians clearly anticipated and wanted the changes. The number of divorces increased from a rate of 54.8 per 100 000 in 1968 to 124.2 in 1969 to 139.8 in 1970.

The *Divorce Act* in 1985 made marriage breakdown the only ground for divorce. Marriage breakdown could occur for one of the following reasons: separation for not less than one year, adultery, physical cruelty, and mental cruelty. The requisite period of separation dropped to one year. Guilt or innocence was not considered in awarding custody or in the division of property.

The present **no-fault trend** began in California. Traditional fault grounds were abolished January 1, 1970, in favour of dissolution of marriage on the basis of "irreconcilable differences which have caused the irremediable breakdown of the marriage" and incurable insanity. **Irreconcilable differences** are defined as any grounds that the court determines to be substantial reasons for not continuing the marriage and that make it appear that the marriage should be dissolved. Since the first no-fault divorce law was instituted, most Western countries, including Canada, have replaced the traditional grounds for fault (adultery, desertion, cruelty) with the more subjective standards of irreconcilable differences. Have the no-fault law changes accomplished their intended goals?

Regrettably, studies of property settlements have suggested consistently that divorcing mothers are faring more poorly under the no-fault system than they did under the former adversary system. The no-fault system reduced the bargaining power of spouses who did not want to divorce, which led to substantial declines in the financial settlements received by women. One writer suggested that no-fault divorce probably reduced the quality of family life.[26] And a law review article expressed concern about the increased impoverishment of custodial mothers and their children and the extent to which no-fault statutes foster a casual commitment to marriage.[27]

Divorce proceedings under the no-fault system are relatively routine. Where cases are contested, they can become drawn-out affairs, resulting in much bitterness, fighting, and expense. Attempts to decrease such conflict have led to **divorce mediation.** Mediation is a conflict resolution process in which the divorcing couple meets with a neutral third-party intervener (mediator), who helps them negotiate an agreement about property distribution, support, and child custody. The emphasis is on direct communication, openness,

Divorce, or some means of terminating a marital or intimate relationship, exists in nearly all countries. The highest dissolution rates in the world are probably in the United States. Over the past few decades, divorce has changed considerably in Canada, from an adversarial system, in which fault or guilt had to be determined, to a no-fault system, in which irreconcilable differences are recognized.

attention to emotional issues and the underlying causes of the disputes, and avoidance of blame. Proponents of mediation stress that it relieves court dockets clogged with matrimonial actions, reduces the alienation couples experience in court, inspires durable consensual agreements, helps couples resume workable relationships to jointly rear their children, and translates into savings in time and money. The mediation process works on building and strengthening relationships, whereas the adversarial process tends to weaken and destroy them.

Most divorce settlements are the result of a negotiation process in which parents make decisions concerning child support, custody, visitation, and marital property without bringing any contested issue into court for adjudication (judicial settlement). The modal or standard divorce package is one in which the mother has custody of the children and is awarded child support, and the father pays child support and has visitation rights.[28]

Over 80 percent of divorces in Canada in 1997 were granted on the basis of "separation for not less than one year." Clearly, "separation" does not tell us very much about the reasons people decide to end a marriage. The reasons people might give to explain divorce to their friends and relatives differ from the legal reasons.[29] Goode suggests that most explanations involve some combination of the following:

Family Diversity

The probability of divorce in Alberta

Canadian sociologist Don Swenson tested the model shown here to determine the relative impact of structural, social-processional, and social-psychological factors on the probability of divorce. The numbers represent the predictive value of each component in the model; for example, a value of –0.458 for geographical location indicates that people in rural areas are less likely to divorce. The study was based on a sample of residents of Alberta based on telephone interviews conducted in 1989.

Swenson found the best predictors of divorce were geographical location, gender roles, and religious affiliation. In other words, married people who lived in an urban area, had traditional attitudes to gender roles, and were not affiliated with any religious denomination were most likely to divorce. In addition the likelihood of divorce increased for women who worked outside of the home, and for people with liberal views about divorce.

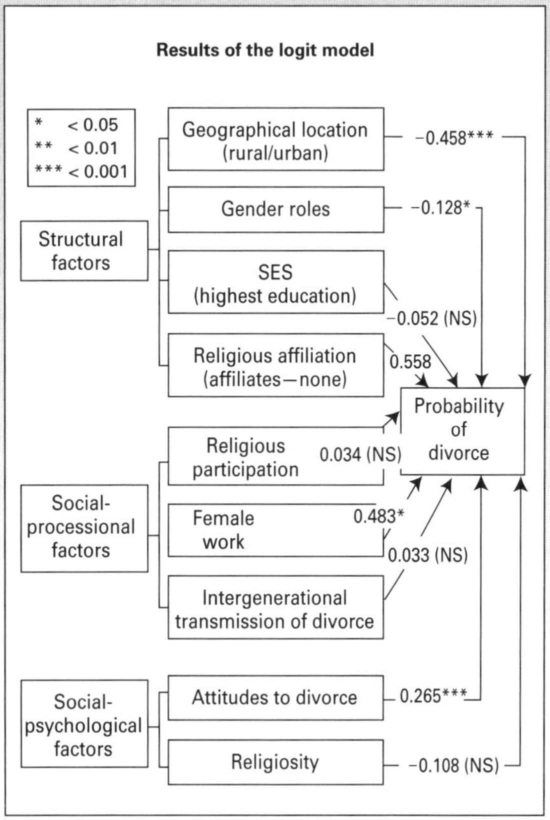

Source: Don Swenson, "A Logit Model of the Probability of Divorce," *Journal of Divorce and Remarriage* 25(1/2) (1996): 173–194.

1. Precipitating factors such as one spouse falling in love with someone else.
2. Predisposing factors such as feeling that the couple were never well suited.
3. The range of alternatives, which is likely a factor although people may not be candid about how much their decision was influenced by the alternatives available to them.
4. Social pressures from others.
5. The individuals' own norms and values.

In sum, the reasons for increased divorce are complex. Some variables operate on a societal level, others on an interpersonal level.

The accompanying box ("The Probability of Divorce in Alberta") shows that one of the best predictors of divorce is attitudes to divorce. Frederick and Hamel looked at sociodemographic characteristics that affect Canadian attitudes to divorce.[30] Most Canadians agree that an abusive or disrespectful partner is a ground for divorce, and over one-third think that constant arguments about money or an unsatisfactory sex life are also grounds. Fewer than half of Canadians would stay in an unhappy relationship because of their children. Age and experience are positively related to attitudes to divorce. Respondents were divided into three age categories: Elders (born before 1946), Boomers (born between 1946 and 1965) and Gen-Xers (born after 1965). Table 11.1 shows the percentage in each age category who agree that the issue indicated is grounds for divorce. All of the experiential issues listed in the table were more likely to be seen as grounds for divorce by elders and least likely by Gen-Xers. "It appears

Table 11.1
Canadian attitudes to divorce

	Gen-Xers 15–29	*Boomers 30–49*	*Elders 50 and over*	*Total*
	(% of population aged 15 and over)			
Fundamental issues				
Abusive behaviour from the partner	95	95	94	95
Unfaithful behaviour from the partner	89	95	89	88
Lack of love and respect from the partner	86	85	89	88
Partner drinks too much	68	73	80	74
Experiential issues				
Constant disagreement about how the family finances should be handled	28	40	49	40
Unsatisfactory sexual relationship with the partner	21	37	45	35
Unsatisfactory division of household tasks with the partner	12	16	21	17
Conflict about how the children are raised	14	17	21	17
Fertility issues				
Inability to have children with the partner	8	12	17	13
Disagreement about the number of children to have	3	6	11	7
Would stay for the children	44	39	52	43

Source: Statistics Canada, 1995 General Social Survey; and Judith Frederick and Jason Hamel, "Canadian Attitudes to Divorce," *Canadian Social Trends*, Statistics Canada Catalogue 11-008-XPE: 10.

that the more experience Canadians have dealing with these aspects of marital life, the less tolerant they become."[31] People in second marriages are more tolerant of divorce than those married for the first time.

Generally, the reasons why marriages dissolve focus on "push" factors that drive persons apart, such as adultery, abusiveness, drunkenness, or interpersonal conflict. However, a more open systems perspective on marital dissolution looks as well at "pull" factors: conditions in the environment that pull persons away from their current spouses or partners. These can be referred to as **marital alternatives.** Consciously or not, people compare their current relationships with alternative ones. If internal attractions and forces that keep a couple together become weaker than those from a viable alternative, the consequence is likely to be breakup.

Support for this idea comes from various sources. South and Lloyd, for example, found that the risk of dissolution is highest where either partner encounters alternatives to the existing relationship.[32] They note that a sizeable percentage of recently divorced persons had been romantically involved with someone other than their spouse prior to the divorce. This suggests that many married persons continue to be open to the possibility of an intimate (extramarital) relationship. Thus, a married man who works in an environment where a substantial percentage of unmarried women are employed is more likely to find an attractive alternative to his current wife or partner. Esterberg and others found that the increase in women's options outside of marriage, such as returning to school and consequent increased self-esteem, are more important than attitudinal factors in hastening the transition to divorce.[33]

The decision to divorce clearly contains important reward/cost considerations. The rewards (attractions) may include love, goods, services, security, joint possessions, children, sexual enjoyment, and so forth, and the costs (barriers) may include feelings of obligation or inadequacy, fears of family/friend reactions, religious prohibitions, financial costs, and the like. The probability for divorce increases as alternatives are perceived that provide greater rewards or lower costs than exist in marriage.

Consequences of divorce for adults

Consequences of divorce are evident at both the individual and interpersonal (micro) levels as well as at the organizational and societal (macro) levels.[34] Most research has focused on the micro levels. But one macro-level finding from several countries, including the United States, Finland, Norway, and Canada, supported the proposition of a direct relationship between divorce and suicide.[35] This proposition is consistent with the work on suicide originally published in 1897 by Emile Durkheim, who theorized that societies with low degrees of social integration typically share high rates of suicide.

Apart from suicide, one clearly defined consequence of divorce is its influence on adult well-being. Data from over 37 studies revealed that having one's parents divorce (or permanently separate) has broad negative consequences for that individual's quality of life in adulthood.[36] Outcomes associated with parental divorce included psychological well-being (depression, low life satisfaction), family well-being (low marital quality, divorce), socioeconomic well-being (low educational attainment, income, and occupational prestige), and physical health. These highly negative findings are somewhat tempered when community samples rather than clinical samples are used, when more recent studies rather than earlier studies are used, and when statistical controls (such as parental education and occupational status) are used rather than simple differences.

Divorce also has an impact on the separating spouses in several ways. For example, in one study, persons with a history of serial divorces reported less happiness and more frequent depression than persons with a history of one divorce, and persons with a history of one divorce reported more frequent depression than those with a history of no divorce. Divorced women reported more frequent depression than divorced men.[37] Newly divorced people, in particular, were significantly more depressed, reflecting greater economic problems, the perception that one's standard of living had deteriorated, and the lesser availability of close, confiding relationships.

Perhaps the most significant effect of divorce for women is economic. With divorce, the economic situation improves for men and declines for women. Lenore Weitzman did the classic study of the economic impacts of divorce for women. Her California data showed a radical change in the standard of living just one year after a legal divorce. Men experienced a 42 percent improvement in their postdivorce standard of living, while women experienced a 73 percent loss.[38] Even though more women are employed and having fewer children, Pamela Smock notes that the economic cost of marital disruption for women is as severe today as in the 1960s and 1970s.[39] Similarly, men continue to experience substantial increases in per capita income when they separate or divorce.

Studies in other countries find the same negative consequences for women. In Germany, women experienced an even bigger drop in economic status following divorce than their American counterparts. German men fared about as well as their American counterparts.[40] In both countries, men were more likely than women to work and to earn more in the labour market both before and after a divorce. In both countries, mothers were more likely than fathers to care for children after a divorce. These and other factors pose a greater economic hardship for divorced women than for divorced men.

Ross Finnie studied the economic consequences of divorce in Canada using tax data. As in the United States and Germany, Finnie found steep declines in income for women and moderate increases for men. For women, the effect is lasting. There was little income recovery three years following divorce. Finnie suggested that this economic imbalance gives men a small economic incentive to divorce, and forces a greater threshold of tolerance for women in marriage.[41]

American longitudinal surveys showed that 40 percent of widows and over 25 percent of divorced women fall into poverty for at least some time during the first five years after being single.[42] It is little wonder that more divorced women report that they are in constant financial crisis, are perpetually worried about not being able to pay their bills, have more stress, and feel less satisfied with their lives than any other group. In contrast, men who divorce or separate are immediately better off. They retain most of their labour income, typically do not pay large amounts of alimony and child support to their ex-wives, and no longer have to provide for their former families. While writers frequently refer to *his* and *her* marriages, those differences appear minor when comparing *his* and *her* divorces.

Children of divorced parents

Without question, divorce is difficult for a couple. It is also difficult for children, particularly preschoolers who are too young to understand its significance. In the United States, data from a national survey discovered that nearly one-third of all children have experienced family disruption by the time they reach the age of 15. When children of never-married parents and those not currently living with a biological parent are included in this group, the authors expect "that close to half of all children living in the United States today will reach age eighteen without having lived continuously with both biological parents."[43] Half of all divorces granted in 1997 in Canada involved dependent children.[44]

Are children a deterrent to divorce? The answer appears to be both yes and no. Table 11.1 shows that only 43 percent of Canadians *say* that they would stay married for the children. Data have shown that firstborn and other children increase the stability of marriage through their preschool years.[45] At least in the short run, young preschool children tend to keep couples together who would otherwise divorce. (Consider the braking hypothesis from Chapter 7.) However, older children and children born before marriage significantly increase chances of marital disruption. It is possible that the inhibiting effect of children on keeping couples together fades and that, as children get older, the strains of parenthood augment the strains of marriage, leading to increased risks of disruption.

Data from over 11,000 divorcing families in northern California clearly supported the relationship between the duration of marriage and the presence of children.[46] Explanations for children delaying (not preventing) divorce included the presence of children making divorce more costly than continuation in the marriage, the cost of having the wife in the home and less free to take paid employment, the articulation of older children about their feelings, the possibility that people who have children may be more secure in the marriage than their childless counterparts, the stigma couples may feel toward parents who divorce, and anticipated complications attending divorce action (child custody, co-parenting, single-parent problems). Note that all the couples in this study got divorced; thus, it provided no support for the myth that children prevent divorce. The study did support the notion of a longer duration of marriage before divorce with the presence of children.

Consequences of divorce for children

Given the numbers of children experiencing their parents' divorce, it is important to raise the question of consequences. Is divorce harder on children than living with parents who have a conflict-filled marriage? Should couples stay together for the sake of the children?

Laypeople assume that the psychological, economic, and social effects of divorce on children are predominantly negative, and these negative assumptions influence how people think about particular children. Research found that this negative prototype of children of divorce leads people to recall unfavourable information and fail to recall favourable information about such children.[47] This may lead to a self-fulfilling prophecy when teachers, counsellors, social workers, and parents expect children from divorced families to have more than their share of problems and treat them in ways that exacerbate or even generate these very problems.

Few people would quarrel with the notion that children are better off in happy, stable families than in divorced or unhappy, unstable families. Evidence has shown that divorce diminishes the economic and social resources available to children, which has negative consequences for educational attainment, marital timing, marital probability, and divorce probability.[48] That is, adolescent children of divorced parents are less likely to graduate from high school, tend to marry at an earlier age, have a lower probability of ever marrying, and have a higher probability of themselves getting divorced. Other evidence has shown that adolescents from divorced homes are more prone to commit delinquent acts, experience problems in peer relations, and are highly associated with family-related offences, such as running away and truancy.[49] These findings confirm the popular notion that divorce is bad for children.

But are the findings just presented the result of a divorce or separation as the central event in shaping the lives of children? Furstenberg and Teitler note that to focus on the impact of divorce itself makes it easy to overlook the circumstances leading up to the separation, some of which may begin even before the birth of the children.[50] These circumstances and processes that often end in divorce may be harmful to children whether the parents stay together or separate. High levels of marital conflict, poor parenting practices, or persistent economic stress may compromise children's economic, social, and psychological well-being in later life irrespective of a divorce or separation. Jekielek makes similar arguments.[51] Using national American data, she finds that both parental marital conflict and marital disruption increase the later anxiety/withdrawal of children aged 6 to 14. But she finds as well that children remaining in high-conflict environments exhibit lower levels of well-being than children who experienced high levels of parental conflict but whose parents divorced or separated. Given this, it may make little sense to argue that, for the sake of the children, partners in unhappy marriages should stay together. Unhappy families have two choices, neither of which are ideal or highly favourable for children. Both the intact home with persistent conflict and the divorced home are likely to cause varying degrees of stress, pain, and difficulty, but divorce may be the better choice.

Amato suggests focusing on two concepts: *resources* and *stressors*.[52] Children's development can be facilitated by resources such as parental emotional support, practical help, guidance, supervision, and role models, as well as economic resources. Stressors include interpersonal conflict that may follow

News Item

Children divorcing parents

When most people think of divorce, they think of adults terminating a marital relationship. But what about *children* divorcing their parents?

In September 1992, for the first time in the United States, family rights were ended on the basis of legal action brought by a Florida child. Gregory Kingsley, a 12-year-old boy, went to court for the right to divorce his parents. He realized his goal when a juvenile court judge ended the parental rights held by his natural mother and allowed the boy's foster parents to adopt him.

In making his decision in favour of Gregory, the judge said, "By clear and convincing evidence, almost beyond a reasonable doubt, the child has been abandoned and neglected by his mother" and that "it was in his best interest" that Gregory's mother's rights be terminated so that he could be adopted.

However, in August 1993, a Florida appeals court reviewed the original decision and, while agreeing with the basic outcome, decided the case on different legal grounds. Namely, the court ruled that, as a minor, Gregory could not take legal action to terminate his relationship with his parents; he could only do so upon turning 18. But because Gregory's foster parents (that is, adults) were also parties to the action, the decision stood to end Gregory's mother's parental rights. The appeals court also confirmed that Gregory could be adopted but overturned the original adoption on a technicality, requiring Gregory's foster parents to repeat the adoption process.

Additional legal action on this case may be pending, as the courts decide this and other issues involving children's versus parents' rights.

divorce and subsequent disruptive life changes. Amato argues that rather than looking at single factors such as parental conflict or economic hardships, one must look at the total configuration of resources and stressors. Thus economic hardship may be less problematic for children who have a close relationship with a warm and competent parent. Likewise, a severe stressor may negate a particular resource, such as contact with the noncustodial parent when there is continuing conflict between the parents. This type of perspective may highlight more clearly the variations that exist in children's reaction and adjustment to divorce.

The impact of divorce on children varies considerably according to the age of the children as well as age of the parents. If the children are adults, custody is not necessary but divorce still has an impact. As with young children, young adults had less contact with their fathers.[53] Even parental divorce in later life after the children are grown was shown to lower relationship quality and contact between adult children and parents.[54] The effects were stronger for father-child than for mother-child relations.

The impact of divorce on children will probably vary considerably according to the age of the children and many other factors. One of these factors is **child custody** and the level of economic support. An increasing number of custody arrangements in Canada are joint. Legal joint custody refers to joint or shared responsibility for decisions concerning the child or children. Physical joint custody, which is rare, refers to sharing physical custody. In essence, the child has two homes and moves between the two according to parental arrangement. Research found joint-custody fathers to be more involved in making parental decisions, sharing responsibilities, and making contact and participating in activities with their children than noncustodial fathers.[55] However, the most frequent custody arrangement, occurring in 61.2 percent of divorces in Canada in 1997, is that mothers have custody of children at divorce. Husbands received custody in 11 percent of cases. In the remaining 27.6 percent of divorces, husbands and wives were given joint custody.[56]

Divorced women with children are usually financially disadvantaged compared to divorced men—even men who have custody of their children. An obvious reason for this difference is the practical difficulty of combining paid work with child care. The gender discrepancy in earnings means that employed one-parent mothers pay proportionately more for child care. In the past, fathers' failure to pay child support may also have accounted for differences in economic well-being. Recently, legislation has made nonpayment more difficult. For example in Ontario, as of March 1992, employers must withhold child support payments from the wages of delinquent employees.[57]

Reasons for nonsupport or insufficient support include interpersonal reasons such as the level of attachment between former spouses, the quality of their relationship, and the frequency of visits by the noncustodial parents to their children.[58] Those fathers who do contribute to their children have more economic resources and enjoy better relationships with their custodial mother than do noncontributing fathers.[59]

In a study referred to earlier in the chapter, Finnie analyzed the economic disadvantage of divorce for Canadian women compared to the relative advantage for men. As he noted, this economic imbalance creates an emotional imbalance: men have less incentive to stay married than women do. Finnie therefore predicts that women will remain an unhappy marriages longer than men.[60]

REMARRIAGES AND STEPFAMILIES

Western countries practice monogamy. Yet it is likely that a greater number as well as a larger proportion of people in the West have more spouses than in many countries where polygamy is practised—albeit only one at a time.

Couples who remarry are likely to do so for reasons of love, to be monogamous, and to expect the marriage to last until death—just as they did the first time. Yet remarried couples differ from couples in first marriages, and have had different life experiences. People who remarry are older, on average, than those who marry for the first time, are presumably more mature, and are more likely to have children.

People who remarry

Earlier in Canada's history, when divorce was rare, remarriages typically involved widows or widowers. In Canada, until 1968 more than 90 percent of marriages were first marriages for both spouses. Now, with increased divorce, remarriages are far more common and typically involve younger people. Today in Canada, over 30 percent of marriages are remarriages for one or both spouses.[61] An estimated two-thirds of all divorced persons remarry (see Figure 11.2). However, remarriage is declining because of increased cohabitation.

Obviously, since widowhood increases with age, the median age of widows who do remarry is greater than the remarriage age of divorced women. Interestingly, the mean age at remarriage after widowhood for American women was 10 years less than the mean age at widowhood. This paradox suggests that, even though the probability of remarriage following widowhood is small for women, the youngest widows are most likely to remarry. Remarriage among older widows is compounded by the declining supply of potential husbands due to higher male mortality rates.

It is assumed that, in all countries in which remarriage occurs at all, the likelihood of remarriage varies, depending on social and demographic characteristics. In Western countries the likelihood of remarriage varies as follows:

- *By gender*—Remarriage is more likely for men than women.
- *By race and ethnicity*—Remarriage is both more likely and more timely for white than for black women.
- *By age*—Remarriage is more likely for those who married at a relatively young age and who are under age 30 at the time of divorce.

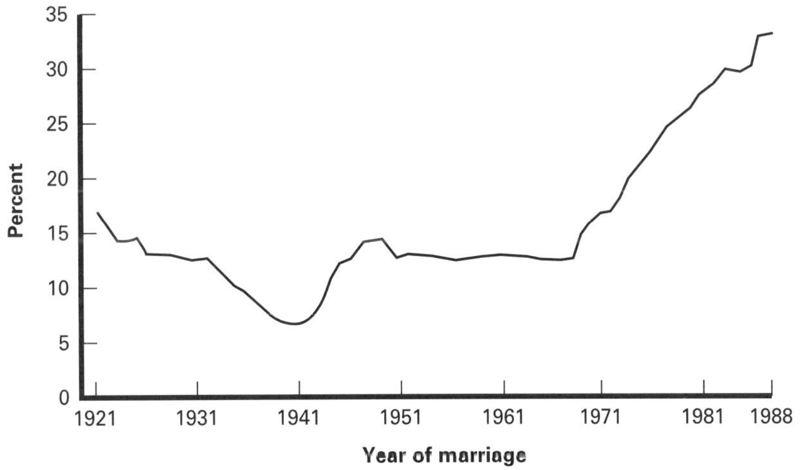

Figure 11.2
Proportion of marriages in which at least one spouse was previously married, 1921–88
Source: Jillian Oderkirk, "Marriage in Canada: Changing Beliefs and Behaviours, 1600–1990," *Canadian Social Trends,* Statistics Canada Catalogue 11-008E (Summer 1994): 5.

- *By children*—Remarriage is more likely for those who have no children or who have only a small number of children in their first marriage.
- *By education*—Remarriage is greater for those who have less than a college education.
- *By employment*—Remarriage is more likely if the woman is not in the labour force.
- *By income*—Remarriage is more likely for men with higher incomes and for women with lower incomes.

In analyzing remarriage according to the financial condition of women, Anne-Marie Ambert suggested that although financially secure women have more opportunities to meet men, have more dates, and have more steady relationships, they are also more likely to break up relationships that do not suit them, less likely to tolerate abusive male behaviour toward them, and less likely to flatter a man's ego.[62] In brief, consistent with an exchange theory model, high-status women have less to gain from remarriage than low-status women.

Similar patterns of remarriage were found in Japan but with some interesting differences. Japanese men were more likely to remarry than were women (although in far greater proportions), and the supply of available husbands decreased with age (a declining sex ratio). But the percentage of Japanese women who said they "do not want to remarry" was high, even among young women, and it increased with age. The result is that Japanese women are actually much less likely to remarry than are their North American peers.[63] This finding was explained by suggesting that, in a society with little divorce and where marriage is treated more as a practical relationship than as a romantic one, divorced women are more likely to be completely unenamoured with both their partners and the institution of marriage itself. When asked why they have not remarried, Japanese widows and divorcees both responded frequently, "I'm fed up with it."

Marriage among the remarried

Remarriage offers many benefits to those who experienced the ending of a previous marriage. It offers those involved a second or third chance. Remarriage is likely to involve older persons, which implies greater maturity, improved finances, and prior experience from which to benefit. Yet, earlier in this chapter it was stated that the length of the typical remarriage that ends in divorce is less than that of the average first marriage. Perhaps this is the case because remarriages include many persons who have already proved they will divorce rather than remain unhappily married. Perhaps second and third marriages are characterized by more ambiguous norms and more complex family structures. But among all married people, is there a difference in marital satisfaction for those in first marriages compared with those in remarriages? The answer from a review of 16 studies that addressed this question was yes.

Alan Booth and John Edwards addressed the issue of why remarriages are more unstable.[64] From a national American sample of married persons, they found that those in remarriages were more likely to be poorly integrated with parents and in-laws, more willing to leave the marriage, more likely to be poor marriage material, have lower socioeconomic status, and be in age-heterogamous marriages. All factors but socioeconomic status were found to explain a decline in marital quality and a higher probability of marital instability.

In Canada, a study comparing first-married and remarried couples demonstrated that the remarried group reported elevated levels of tension and disagreement.[65] The remarried group more frequently experienced financial difficulties that made the spousal relationship more difficult. They also more often reported disagreement over the rearing and discipline of children but less disagreement over relationships with in-laws. Marital adjustment scores were not significantly different for the first-married and remarried groups, but the remarried husbands gave in to their wives with greater frequency than first-married husbands, as reported by both husbands and wives. This might imply that wives have more leverage in remarried than in first-married situations, that husbands have greater needs in remarriages than in first marriages, or both.

Remarriages alone show tremendous variations as well. Considerable research over the past decade has noted the special problems of remarriage when adolescent children from prior marriages are present. These children appear to have a destabilizing effect on the husband/wife relationship. Remarried couples with adolescent stepchildren experience higher rates of divorce than other remarriages. These stepfamilies also move teenagers out of the home faster than first-married families.[66] Adolescents living in stepfamilies also report difficulties. Divided loyalty and discipline are particularly stressful problems for these youth. The nature and problems of remarried couples with stepchildren will be considered more closely in the following section.

Remarried couples with stepchildren: Reconstituted families

Most children who experience their parents' divorce also experience their custodial parent's remarriage and the creation of a *stepfamily*. Traditionally, remarriages and stepfamilies were formed primarily as a result of the death of a spouse; today, their formation results primarily from divorce. Terms including *remarried*, *reconstituted*, *binuclear*, *blended*, and *stepparent families* have been used to describe what constitutes significant nontraditional marital and family arrangements that present unique circumstances and relationships. A stepfamily may include a stepfather plus a mother and her children; a stepmother plus a father and his children; or a mother and father joining two sets of children.

Stepfamilies differ structurally from first families in a number of ways. First, one biological parent does not live in the household. Second, the parent-and-child relationship predates the new marriage. And third, even though a legal relationship binds the remarriage, none binds the stepchildren and stepparents. Clearly, stepfamilies are more complex structurally and interactionally than nuclear families. Added to the complexity are relationships with new extended family, stepsiblings, stepparents and so on. Visher and Visher liken remarriage to immigration. Family members acculturate at different rates, and children are like "dual citizens."[67]

The majority of people who divorce or end an intimate relationship eventually enter another marriage or exclusive relationship. Those people who have children create stepfamilies, in which multiple sets of parents interact with and assume responsibility for multiple sets of children. The step-, or binuclear, family may include the children of one or both partners.

These structural elements of stepfamilies have altered parenting practices in major ways. One American sample of children between the ages of 7 and 11 found that, in a majority of families, marital disruption effectively destroyed the relationship between the children and the biological parent living outside the home.[68] Nearly half of all children had not seen their nonresident fathers in the past year. Contrary to the picture painted by the media, children of divorce rarely have two homes, and only a minority ever sleep over at their fathers' houses. It was suggested that perhaps a majority have never set foot in the houses of their nonresident fathers.

When contact does exist with the outside parent, it tends to be a social rather than an instrumental exchange. That is, the nonresident parent may take the children to dinner or on trips but rarely helps with schoolwork and daily projects. Nonresident fathers are often characterized by similar circumstances: Some are still embroiled in conflicts with their former spouses, some have personal problems or barriers, some are long-distance fathers, and some have teenage children with busy lives.[69]

A puzzling finding in the literature on disrupted families is the absence of a remarriage benefit for children in stepfamily households. Although the remarriage of parents increases a family's economic security and brings an additional parental figure into the household, children in stepfamilies exhibit about the same number of adjustment problems as children in single-parent families and more problems than children in original, two-parent families. A large sample of nearly 14 000 adolescents in the Netherlands showed that those from one-parent and stepparent families reported lower self-esteem, more symptoms of anxiety and loneliness, and even more suicidal thoughts and attempts.[70]

Many structural variations of remarriage have the potential to create **boundary ambiguity:** the uncertainty of family members over who is part of the family and how family roles and relationships are to be defined. This uncertainty of boundaries is likely to increase both family stress and the risk of behaviour problems in children.[71] How will family members define the relationship between a stepmother and her nonresidential children or a grandparent with the children of his or her stepson?

Ambiguity and difficulty with children may be heightened when children visit rather than live with a stepparent. In her research, Ambert found the stepparenting experience, particularly for stepmothers, to be more positive with live-in stepchildren.[72] Most research has suggested that the role of stepmother is more difficult than that of stepfather, in large part because most stepmothers do not have live-in stepchildren. In contrast, most stepfathers do. When stepchildren visit, it is usually the stepmother and not the children's father who has to do the extra housecleaning, shopping for food, and cooking. Women often perceive this work as a burden because they receive little emotional benefit from the visits. Similarly, stepsiblings' relations were found to be more positive when the children lived together rather than just visited.

Research has also found that parents who cohabit before marriage have more positive parent/child relationships after marriage.[73] Cohabitation may provide a more gentle transition to remarriage, gradually incorporating the future stepfather into family routines. It was also found that the earlier the courtship for remarriage was introduced after divorce, the less the disruption of family and individual functioning. It seems that, with a more rapid transition to a new marriage, there is less time for children to adjust to living in a custodial mother household. In any case, these findings have called into question the idea that considerable time between divorce and remarriage is desirable or beneficial for the adjustment of children.

What happens to parent/child relationships when stepfamilies include children from both parents (**complex stepfamilies**) rather than from only one parent (**simple stepfamilies**)? A study of Australian couples discovered that the complex stepfamily had lower agreement scores on areas dealing with financial management, communication, personality scores, adjustments, and parenting.[74] In general, persons in complex stepfamilies experienced greater dissatisfaction and stress than did those in simple stepfamilies. Perhaps complex stepfamilies are well named in that they must deal with more complexities in discipline and external relationships than simple stepfamilies.

In general, the stepfamily has been classified as a high-risk setting for children.[75] In comparison to first families, stepfamilies are characterized by more pathological behaviours and higher rates of child sexual abuse. Sexual abuse, in particular, is probably more common because of issues of boundary ambiguity, as discussed earlier. Stepfathers, for instance, are not blood kin to their stepdaughters, which may weaken the taboo on incest. In addition, the simple fact that more people are around children in stepfamilies—including parents' boyfriends and girlfriends as well as *their* children, relatives, and friends—increases the potential for child sexual abuse.

The unique structural elements of stepfamilies clearly raise a variety of questions not relevant to the traditional nuclear unit: How does the ex-spouse affect the children's relationship with the new spouse? Which parent gets the child for birthdays, holidays, and special events? Do parents compete in giving the children expensive gifts? Do gifts come equally from parents and stepparents? Is discipline likely to be equal and consistent coming from a mother and stepfather or a father and stepmother? Are incestuous and other types of sexual abuse issues of concern, particularly between stepfathers and stepdaughters? Are children the messengers or communication links between the mother and father, who may or may not be on cordial terms? Are children living in homes with stepparents at risk for increased emotional and behaviour problems? What socialization difficulties occur in the process of stepparenting?

Given the predominance of stepfamilies today, these and other questions will probably be the subjects of future research.

SUMMARY

1. In Canada, divorce is the most common means of ending an unsatisfactory marital relationship. Desertion, marital separation, and annulment are other means of escaping a marriage, even if only temporarily.
2. When viewed cross-culturally, higher divorce rates are associated with a high sex ratio and a late average age at marriage. A curvilinear relationship exists between the level of socio-economic development and the rate of participation of females in the paid labour force.
3. The rate of divorce may be calculated in a number of ways such as (a) per 1000 persons in the total population, (b) per 1000 women ages 15 and over, or (c) the ratio of divorces to the number of marriages in a given year. Irrespective of how the divorce rate is calculated, the trend has been upward, levelling off or slightly decreasing in the last few years.
4. Divorce varies according to a wide range of geographic, demographic, and social characteristics. Rates vary both from province to province and within provinces. Divorce rates are higher for teenage couples than for those who marry when in their twenties. Persons who have been married more than once have a higher likelihood of divorce than those married only once. By religion, divorce rates are higher for Protestants than for Jews and Catholics; and by socioeconomic level, divorce rates tend to go up as educational level, income, and occupational position go down. One exception to this relationship exists among educated, professional women.
5. As the legal grounds for divorce have become more liberal over time, divorce rates have risen accordingly. The most widely used grounds are marital separation. This "no fault" divorce has alleviated the difficulties traditionally associated with proving "fault." Studies have suggested, however, that economically, women fare more poorly under no-fault than under the former adversary system.

6. Social grounds for divorce often differ considerably from legal grounds. Divorce mediation, as a conflict-resolution process, has grown rapidly as a means of diminishing the bitterness and divisiveness that usually accompany divorce. Reasons for staying in or ending a marriage constitute attractions (rewards) and barriers (costs). The decision whether to divorce is made in the light of the alternatives available.
7. The consequences of divorce for adults are evident at both macro levels and micro levels, as reflected by factors such as higher rates of suicide and depression. The economic consequences differ dramatically for males and females; men usually do much better and women much worse following divorce.
8. Children are a primary concern in considering divorce. Research does not support the idea that unhappy or unsuccessful marriages should remain intact for the sake of the children; however, research does acknowledge that children of divorced parents go through periods of stress and major readjustment. Neither alternative is without difficulty. Mothers tend to get custody of children; the underpayment or nonpayment of child support by fathers creates hardships for many women and children.
9. Most persons who end one marriage eventually enter another. The remarriage rate climbs with the divorce rate. Remarriage is, in general, more likely for men than for women, for divorcees than for widows, for younger persons than for older persons, for the childless than those with children, for those with less education and lower incomes than those with higher levels, and for women not in the paid labour force.
10. Remarriages appear to be less stable than first marriages. Compared to first-married people, remarried people have poorer integration with parents and in-laws, are more willing to leave the marriage, and report more difficult events, feelings of ill health, and greater use of alcohol and medicine.
11. The complexities of remarriage are compounded by the presence of children. Stepfamilies are structurally different from traditional nuclear families. Elements such as one biological parent not living in the home, the child predating the new marriage, and the lack of legal, binding relationships between stepchildren and stepparents alter parenting in dramatic ways. Consequences may even include destroying the relationship between the child and the biological parent living outside the parental home (usually the father).
12. This chapter focused on divorce and remarriage and addressed issues relevant to Canadian families. To offer programs and establish policies that support marriages and families is, at least in terms of rhetoric, the goal of government and community units. Chapter 12 will address this issue of the family and social policy.

KEY TERMS AND TOPICS

Desertion p. 303
Marital separation p. 304
Annulment p. 304
Divorce around the world p. 305
Divorce rates p. 306
Canadian trends p. 308
Variations in divorce p. 309
Geographic distribution p. 309
Ages of husbands and wives p. 310
Duration of marriage p. 311
Religion and socioeconomic status p. 311
Legal and social grounds for divorce p. 313
No-fault divorce p. 313
Irreconcilable differences p. 313
Divorce mediation p. 313
Consequences of divorce for adults p. 317
Children of divorced parents p. 319
Consequences of divorce for children p. 319
Child custody p. 321
Remarriages and stepfamilies p. 322
People who remarry p. 322
Marriage among the remarried p. 324
Remarried couples with stepchildren:
Reconstituted families p. 325
Boundary ambiguity p. 327
Complex and simple stepfamilies p. 327

Discussion Questions

1. What are some of the reasons for desertion, separation, and annulment versus divorce? How does each situation affect husbands, wives, and children?
2. Compare the divorce rates of different countries. Why are some much higher than others? What social factors might cause the likelihood of divorce to increase or decrease?
3. How are divorce rates determined? In this chapter, three different divorce rates were calculated for the same year. What does each mean? What factors influence each rate even when the number of divorces remains constant?
4. Divorce rates were found to differ by duration of marriage and by race, religion, socioeconomic status, and so on. What differences have been supported and how can these variations be explained?
5. Research has shown that, in the United States, conservative and fundamentalist Protestant religious groups that oppose divorce tend to have high divorce rates. Why?
6. Visit a local court that handles divorce cases. Arrange to meet with a judge to discuss the legal process, the legal grounds for divorce compared to the nonlegal reasons for divorce, and his or her views on divorce mediators, joint custody, grandparents' rights, and other legal issues. What legal changes does he or she view as necessary? Why?
7. Discuss the implications and consequences of no-fault divorce. What are its pros and cons? What effect is it likely to have on divorce rates, long-term trends, and the like?
8. What do you believe are the primary reasons that marriages end? Could any of these factors be discovered and perhaps influenced before marriage? If so, how? Why do many poor marriages not end?
9. Examine some of the consequences of divorce for adults. Why are the consequences so different for males and females?
10. What are the consequences of divorce for children? What are the consequences for children who live in unbroken but unhappy homes?
11. How do remarriages differ from first marriages? Address duration of marriage, likelihood of divorce, roles and boundaries, and common problems.
12. How do stepchildren affect a marriage? Discuss some of the advantages and problems that characterize reconstituted families or stepfamilies.

Further Readings

Ambert, Anne-Marie. *Ex-spouses and New Spouses: A Study of Relationships*. Greenwich: JAI Press, 1989. A Canadian study of postdivorce and remarried relationships.

Arendell, Terry. *Fathers & Divorce*. Thousand Oaks, CA: Sage Publications, 1995. On the basis of interviews with 75 divorced fathers, the author examines the masculine discourse of divorce, relationships with former wives, and parenting behaviours.

Booth, Alan, and Dunn, Judy. *Stepfamilies: Who Benefits? Who Does Not?* Hillsdale, NJ: Lawrence Erlbaum Associates, 1994. Seventeen chapters cover marriages that create stepfamilies, and how they function as childrearing organizations and as sources of support; they also detail needed research and policy agendas.

Cherlin, Andrew J. *Marriage, Divorce, Remarriage*. Rev. ed. Cambridge, MA: Harvard University Press, 1992. A brief paperback that the author suggests should be titled *Cohabitation, Marriage, Divorce, More Cohabitation, and Probably Remarriage*.

Emery, Robert E. *Renegotiating Family Relationships: Divorce, Child Custody, and Mediation*. New York: The Guilford Press, 1994. A discussion of how families renegotiate their relationships as a result of divorce and the conflicts that accompany divorce.

Funder, Kathleen; Harrison, Margaret; and Weston, Ruth. *Settling Down: Pathways of Parents After Divorce*. Melbourne: Australian Institute of Family Studies, 1993. A follow-up to an earlier study, *Settling Up*, tracing how 500 parents in Australia fared five to eight years after separation and divorce.

Ganong, Lawrence, and Coleman, Marilyn. *Remarried Family Relationships*. Thousand Oaks, CA: Sage Publications, 1994. A comprehensive look at remarried families, including pathways from divorce to remarriage and key relationships in remarried families, including stepparent/stepchild relationships.

Gottman, John Mordechai. *What Predicts Divorce?: The Relationship Between Marital Processes and Marital Outcomes*. Hillsdale, NJ: Lawrence Erlbaum Associates, 1994. A clinical psychologist examines marital processes that predict dissolution with a heavy focus on observing physiological arousal and its association with patterns of marital interaction.

Kitson, Gay C. *Portrait of Divorce*. New York: Guilford Press, 1992. Data are presented from four studies of marital instability and divorce; an excellent comprehensive portrait of the divorce process.

Kurtz, Demie. *For Richer, for Poorer: Mothers Confront Divorce*. New York: Routledge, 1995. Based on interviews with a random sample of 129 divorced women, the author examines the problems they face.

Pasley, Kay, and Ihinger-Tallman, Marilyn, eds. *Stepparenting: Issues in Theory, Research, and Practice*. New York: Praeger, 1994. An analysis of the current literature on stepparenting and a summary of the progress made in research, theory, and practice related to stepfamilies.

Stewart, Abigail J.; Copeland, Anne P.; Chester, Nia Lane; Malley, Janet E.; and Barenbaum, Nicole B. *Separating Together: How Divorce Transforms Families*. New York: The Guilford Press, 1997. A study of 160 "divorcing families," looking at how all members adapt to parental separation and how divorce represents a family transformation.

Twaite, James A.; Silitsky, Daniel; and Luchow, Anya K. *Children of Divorce: Adjustment, Parental Conflict, Custody, Remarriage, and Recommendations for Clinicians*. Northvale, NJ: Jason Aronson Inc., 1998. Two research studies that look at the effects of divorce on children, including custodial arrangements, remarriage of the parents, children's age and gender, and recommendations for clinicians.

WEBLINKS

http://www.divorceinfo.com

An excellent information source on divorce and related topics. This site has advice on helping children cope, coping with the pain of divorce, life after divorce and the costs involved.

http://www.ag.ohio-state.edu/~ohioline/hyg-fact/5000/5292.html

Stepfamilies face issues different from other family arrangements because there are at least two sets of parents working (or not working) to share parental authority and economic and emotional support of the children. This article explains strengths, vulnerabilities, and problem-solving situations peculiar to stepfamilies.

http://www.nignl/congress/3rdeuropeancongress1995/abstract/063-1114/html

This links to a case study on the effects of family changes on the elderly, focusing on the stepfamily.

NOTES

1. *Age, Sex and Marital Status*, Statistics Canada, *The Daily* (May 18, 1999).
2. Gay C. Kitson, "Marital Discord and Marital Separation: A County Survey," *Journal of Marriage and the Family* 47 (August 1985): 693–700.
3. Ronald R. Rindfuss and Elizabeth Hervey Stephen, "Marital Noncohabitation: Separation Does Not Make the Heart Grow Fonder," *Journal of Marriage and the Family* 52 (February 1990): 259–270.
4. Mark A. Fine and David R. Fine, "An Examination and Evaluation of Recent Changes in Divorce Laws in Five Western Countries: The Critical Role of Values," *Journal of Marriage and the Family* 56 (May 1994): 249–263.
5. United Nations, *Demographic Yearbook, 1996* (New York: United Nations, 1998), Table 14, 383–385.
6. Katherine Trent and Scott J. South, "Structural Determinants of the Divorce Rate: A Cross-Societal Analysis," *Journal of Marriage and the Family* 51 (May 1989): 391–404.
7. Data in this section are from the following sources: *Age, Sex and Marital Status: A Portrait of Families in Canada*, Statistics Canada Catalogue 89-523E (November 1993): 17; Jean Dumas and Yves Peron, *Marriage and Conjugal Life in Canada*, Statistics Canada Catalogue 91-534E (March 1992): 35–62; *Women in Canada: A Statistical Report*, Statistics Canada Catalogue 89-503E (August 1995); and "Marriages and Divorces, 1995," *Health Reports* 8(3) (Winter 1996): 47.
8. Jean Dumas and Yves Peron, *Marriage and Conjugal Life in Canada*, 52.
9. David Lester, "Trends in Divorce and Marriage Around the World," *Journal of Divorce and Remarriage* 25 (1996): 169–171.
10. Anne-Marie Ambert, *Divorce in Canada* (Don Mills, Ontario: Academic Press, 1980).
11. R.P. Beaujot and Kevin McQuillan, "The Social Effects of Demographic Change: Canada 1851-1981," *Journal of Canadian Studies*, Vol. 21, No. 1 (Spring 1986): 57–69.
12. Statistics Canada, *The Daily* (May 18, 1999).
13. Leonard Beeghley and Jeffrey W. Dwyer, "Social Structure and the Divorce Rate," *Perspectives on Social Problems* 1 (1989): 147–170.
14. Eliza K. Pavalko and Glen H. Elder, Jr., "World War II and Divorce: A Life-Course Perspective," *American Journal of Sociology* 5 (March 1990): 1213–1234.
15. R. Pike, "Legal Access and the Incidence of Divorce in Canada: A Sociohistorical Analysis," *Canadian Review of Sociology and Anthropology* 12 (1985): 115–133.
16. Norval D. Glenn and Beth Anne Shelton, "Regional Differences in Divorce in the United States," *Journal of Marriage and the Family* 47 (August 1985): 641–652; and Beth Anne Shelton, "Variations in Divorce Rates by Community Size: A Test of the Social Integration Explanation," *Journal of Marriage and the Family* 49 (November 1987): 827–832.
17. Statistics Canada, *The Daily* (May 18, 1999).
18. Ibid.
19. National Center for Health Statistics, *Monthly Vital Statistics Report* 43(9) (March 22, 1995): Table 11, 20.
20. Howard Weinberg, "Childbearing and Dissolution of the Second Marriage," *Journal of Marriage and the Family* 54 (November 1992): 879–887.
21. Norval D. Glenn and Michael Supancic, "The Social and Demographic Correlates of Divorce and Separation in the United States: An Update and Reconsideration," *Journal of Marriage and the Family* 46 (August 1984): 563–575.
22. S. Kenneth Chi and Sharon K. Houseknecht, "Protestant Fundamentalism and Marital Success: A Comparative Approach," *Sociology and Social Research* 69 (April 1985): 351–375.
23. Teresa M. Cooney and Peter Uhlenberg, "Family-Building Patterns of Professional Women: A Comparison of Lawyers, Physicians, and Postsecondary Teachers," *Journal of Marriage and the Family* 51 (August 1989): 749–758; and Sharon K. Houseknecht, Suzanne Vaughn, and Anne S. Macke, "Marital Disruption Among Professional Women: The Timing of Career and Family Events," *Social Problems* 31 (February 1984): 273–284.
24. Alan Booth, John N. Edwards, and David R. Johnson, "Social Integration and Divorce," *Social Forces* 70 (September 1991): 207–224.
25. Paul R. Amato and Stacy J. Rogers, "A Longitudinal Study of Marital Problems and Subsequent Divorce," *Journal of Marriage and the Family* 59 (August 1997): 612–624.
26. Allen M. Parkman, *No-Fault Divorce: What Went Wrong?* (Boulder, CO: Westview Press, 1992), Chapter 5, 71–109.
27. Lynn D. Wardle, "No-Fault Divorce and the Divorce Conundrum," *Brigham Young University Law Review* 1 (1991): 79–142.
28. Jay D. Teachman and Karen Polonko, "Negotiating Divorce Outcomes: Can We Identify Patterns in Divorce Settlements?" *Journal of Marriage and the Family* 52 (February 1990): 129–139.
29. William Goode, *World Changes in Divorce Patterns* (New Haven, CT: Yale University Press, 1993).
30. Judith Frederick and Jason Hamel, "Canadian Attitudes to Divorce," *Canadian Social Trends*, Statistics Canada Catalogue 11-008-XPE (Spring 1998): 6–11.
31. Ibid, 10.

32. Scott J. South and Kim M. Lloyd, "Spousal Alternatives and Marital Dissolution," *American Sociological Review* 60 (February 1995): 21–35.

33. Kristin G. Esterberg, Phyllis Moen, and Donna Dempster-McCain, "Transition to Divorce: A Life Course Approach to Women's Marital Duration and Dissolution," *The Sociological Quarterly* 35 (1994): 289–307.

34. See Gay C. Kitson and Leslie A. Morgan, "The Multiple Consequences of Divorce: A Decade Review," *Journal of Marriage and the Family* 52 (November 1990): 913–924; and Frank F. Furstenberg, Jr., "Divorce and the American Family," *Annual Review of Sociology* 16 (1990): 379–403.

35. Steve Stack, "The Effect of Divorce on Suicide in Finland: A Time Series Analysis," *Journal of Marriage and the Family* 54 (August 1992): 636–642; Steven Stack, "The Impact of Divorce on Suicide in Norway, 1951–1980," *Journal of Marriage and the Family* 51 (February 1989): 229–238; and Frank Trovato, "The Relationship Between Marital Dissolution and Suicide: The Canadian Case," *Journal of Marriage and the Family* 48 (May 1986): 341–348.

36. Paul R. Amato and Bruce Keith, "Parental Divorce and Adult Well-Being: A Meta-Analysis," *Journal of Marriage and the Family* 53 (February 1991): 43–58.

37. Lawrence A. Kurdek, "The Relations Between Reported Well-Being and Divorce History, Availability of a Proximate Adult, and Gender," *Journal of Marriage and the Family* 53 (February 1991): 71–78.

38. Lenore J. Weitzman, "The Economics of Divorce: Social and Economic Consequences of Property, Alimony, and Child Support Awards," *UCLA Law Review* 28 (August 1981): 1251.

39. Pamela J. Smock, "The Economic Costs of Marital Disruption for Young Women over the Past Two Decades," *Demography* 30 (August 1993): 353–371; and Pamela Smock, "Gender and the Short-Run Economic Consequences of Marital Disruption," *Social Forces* 73 (September 1994): 243–262.

40. Richard V. Burkhauser, Greg J. Duncan, Richard Hauser, and Roland Berntsen, "Wife or Frau, Women Do Worse: A Comparison of Men and Women in the United States and Germany After Marital Dissolution," *Demography* 28 (August 1991): 353–360.

41. Ross Finnie, "Women, Men, and the Economic Consequences of Divorce: Evidence from Canadian Longitudinal Data," *Canadian Review of Sociology and Anthropology* 30(2) (1993): 205-240.

42. Leslie A. Morgan, "Economic Well-Being Following Marital Termination," *Journal of Family Issues* 10 (March 1989): 86–101.

43. Frank F. Furstenberg, Jr., Christine Winquist Nord, James L. Peterson, and Nicholas Zill, "The Life Course of Children of Divorce: Marital Disruption and Parental Contact," *American Sociological Review* 48 (October 1983): 667.

44. Statistics Canada, *The Daily* (May 18, 1999).

45. Linda J. Waite and Lee A. Lillard, "Children and Marital Disruption," *American Journal of Sociology* 96 (January 1991): 930–953.

46. Robert M. Rankin and Jerry S. Maneker, "The Duration of Marriage in a Divorcing Population: The Impact of Children," *Journal of Marriage and the Family* 47 (February 1985): 43–52.

47. Paul R. Amato, "The 'Child of Divorce' as a Person Prototype: Bias in the Recall of Information About Children in Divorced Families," *Journal of Marriage and the Family* 53 (February 1991): 59–69.

48. Gary D. Sandefur, Sara McLanahan, and Roger A. Wojtkiewicz, "The Effects of Parental Marital Status During Adolescence on High School Graduation," *Social Forces* 71 (September 1992): 103–121; Norval D. Glenn and Kathryn B. Kramer, "The Marriages and Divorces of the Children of Divorce," *Journal of Marriage and the Family* 49 (November 1987): 811–825; and William R. Catton, Jr., "Family Divorce Heritage and Its Intergenerational Transmission," *Sociological Perspectives* 31 (October 1988): 398–419.

49. L. Edward Wells and Joseph H. Ranken, "Families and Delinquency: A Meta-Analysis of the Impact of Broken Homes," *Social Problems* 38 (February 1991): 71–93; and David H. Demo and Alan C. Acock, "The Impact of Divorce on Children," *Journal of Marriage and the Family* 50 (August 1988): 619–648.

50. Frank F. Furstenberg, Jr. and Julien O. Teitler, "Reconsidering the Effects of Martial Disruption: What Happens to Children of Divorce in Early Adulthood," *Journal of Family Issues* 15 (June 1994): 173–190.

51. Susan M. Jekielek, "Parental Conflict, Marital Disruption and Children's Emotional Well-Being," *Social Forces* 76 (March 1998): 905-935.

52. Paul R. Amato, "Children's Adjustment to Divorce: Theories, Hypotheses, and Empirical Support," *Journal of Marriage and the Family* 55 (February 1993): 23–38.

53. Teresa Cooney, "Young Adults' Relations with Parents: The Influence of Recent Parental Divorce," *Journal of Marriage and the Family* 56 (February 1994): 45–56; and Teresa M. Cooney, M. Katherine Hutchinson, and Diane M. Leather, "Surviving the Breakup? Predictors of Parent-Adult Child Relations After Parental Divorce," *Family Relations* 44 (April 1995): 153–161.

54. William S. Aquilino, "Later Life Parental Divorce and Widowhood: Impact on Young Adults' Assessment of Parent-Child Relations," *Journal of Marriage and the Family* 56 (November 1994): 908–922.

55. Judith A. Seltzer, "Legal Custody Arrangements and Children's Economic Welfare," *American Journal of Sociology* 96 (January 1991): 895–929; and Judith A.

Seltzer, "Relationships Between Fathers and Children Who Live Apart: The Father's Role After Separation," *Journal of Marriage and the Family* 53 (February 1991): 79–101.

56. Statistics Canada, *The Daily* (May 18, 1999).

57. Diane Galarneau, "Alimony and Child Support," *Canadian Social Trends*, Statistics Canada Catalogue 11-008E (Spring 1993): 8–11.

58. Judith A. Seltzer, Nora Cate Schaeffer, and Hong-Wen Charng, "Family Ties After Divorce: The Relationship Between Visiting and Paying Child Support," *Journal of Marriage and the Family* 51 (November 1989): 1013–1032.

59. Jay D. Teachman, "Contributions to Children by Divorced Fathers," *Social Problems* 38 (August 1991): 358–371.

60. Finnie, "Women, Men and the Economic Consequences of Divorce."

61. Jillian Oderkirk, "Marriage in Canada: Changing Beliefs and Behaviours, 1600–1990," *Canadian Social Trends*, Statistics Canada Catalogue 11-008E (Summer 1994): 2–7. For a review of this topic, see Larry Bumpass, James Sweet, and Teresa Castro Martin, "Changing Patterns of Remarriage," *Journal of Marriage and the Family* 52 (August 1990): 747–756; and Marilyn Coleman and Lawrence H. Ganong, "Remarriage and Stepfamily Research in the 1980s: Increased Interest in an Old Family Form," *Journal of Marriage and the Family* 52 (November 1990): 925–940.

62. Anne-Marie Ambert, "Separated Women and Remarriage Behavior: A Comparison of Financially Secure Women and Financially Insecure Women," *Journal of Divorce* 6 (Spring 1983): 43–54.

63. Laurel L. Cornell, "Gender Differences in Remarriage After Divorce in Japan and the United States," *Journal of Marriage and the Family* 51 (May 1989): 457–463.

64. Alan Booth and John N. Edwards, "Starting Over: Why Remarriages Are More Unstable," *Journal of Family Issues* 13 (June 1992): 179–194.

65. Charles Hobart, "Conflict in Remarriages," *Journal of Divorce and Remarriage* 15 (1991): 69–86.

66. Lynn K. White and Alan Booth, "The Quality and Stability of Remarriages: The Role of Stepchildren," *American Sociological Review* 50 (October 1985): 689–698.

67. Emily B. Visher and John S. Visher, "Remarriage, Families and Step-Parenting," in *Normal Family Processes*, 2nd ed., ed. Froma Walsh (New York: The Guilford Press, 1993): 235–253.

68. Frank F. Furstenberg, Jr., and Christine Winquist Nord, "Parenting Apart: Patterns of Childrearing After Marital Disruption," *Journal of Marriage and the Family* 47 (November 1985): 893–904.

69. James R. Dudley, "Increasing Our Understanding of Divorced Fathers Who Have Infrequent Contact with Their Children," *Family Relations* 40 (July 1991): 279–285.

70. Nadia Garnefski and Rene F.W. Diekstra, "Adolescents from One Parent, Stepparent and Intact Families: Emotional Problems and Suicide Attempts," *Journal of Adolescence* 20 (1997): 201–208.

71. B. Kay Pasley and Marilyn Ihinger-Tallman, "Boundary Ambiguity in Remarriage: Does Ambiguity Differentiate Degree of Marital Adjustment and Integration?" *Family Relations* 38 (January 1989): 46–52. See also Pauline Boss, *Family Stress Management* (Newbury Park, CA: Sage, 1989), Chapter 4.

72. Anne-Marie Ambert, "Being a Stepparent: Live-In and Visiting Stepchildren," *Journal of Marriage and the Family* 48 (November 1986): 795–804.

73. Marilyn J. Montgomery, Edward R. Anderson, E. Mavis Hetherington, and W. Glenn Clingempeel, "Patterns of Courtship for Remarriage: Implications for Child Adjustment and Parent-Child Relationships," *Journal of Marriage and the Family* 54 (August 1992): 686–698.

74. Noel C. Schultz, Cynthia L. Schultz, and David H. Olson, "Couple Strengths and Stressors in Complex and Simple Stepfamilies in Australia," *Journal of Marriage and the Family* 53 (August 1991): 555–564.

75. For a good overview of research on stepfamilies, see Marilyn Ihinger-Tallman, "Research on Stepfamilies," *Annual Review of Sociology* 14 (1988): 25–48.

CHAPTER

12 *Family and Social Policy*

Most persons, married and single, recognize that the family is significant and important in their own lives and in the lives of others. In fact, one could argue that, across cultures and throughout history, no single institution has had greater influence in shaping the lives of persons and in affecting interpersonal relationships.

Why then, one must ask, doesn't Canada have an explicit national policy (or policies) for families? Among all the agencies overseeing education, health, commerce, labour, energy, transportation, defence, agriculture, and the like, no agency is devoted specifically to the family.

Perhaps a national family policy is both unnecessary and unwanted. Perhaps establishing a family policy is an unrealistic goal, since no single policy could meet the needs of all Canadian families. Moreover, no single policy would be able to deal with the range of nonmarital and marital interactions, from partner selection to sexual relationships. Nor could one policy be made equally relevant to families at all stages of the marital and family life cycle. Thus, no one policy could answer questions that affect everything from violence to divorce and stepparenting. To address these issues, this chapter will begin by examining what is meant by *family policy*.

MEANING AND USE OF FAMILY POLICY

Many illustrations of family policy—from grounds for divorce to policies establishing a legal age for marriage—have been presented throughout the text. But what is meant by **family policy?**

It is clear that *family policy* can mean different things to different people. It can be defined broadly enough to incorporate everything that touches the lives of family members, or it can be defined so narrowly that it includes little or nothing because specific policies can be subsumed under policy headings such as health, taxation, employment, and education. In terms of government action, *explicit* family policy is minimal.

Phyllis Moen and Alvin Schorr, two leading family policy scholars, used the term *family policy* to mean a widely-agreed-upon set of objectives for families, which the state and other major social institutions try to realize through deliberately structured programs and policies.[1] Note the difference between policy and programs. *Policies* are objectives and goals that are more or less deliberate, intended and desirable. *Programs* are the practical applications that are used to achieve or fulfill the goals. As a result, it is possible and often likely that policies exist without any specific program to carry them out. Similarly, many programs continue year after year without any coherent or specifically designed policy. Like a governmental bureaucracy that has outlived its purpose but is ongoing, so, too, do many programs continue that fail to fulfill any specific policy goals or have outlived their original intent or purpose.

Shirley Zimmerman noted that *family policy* constitutes a collection of separate but interrelated policy choices that aim to address problems that families are perceived as experiencing in society.[2] These problems are likely to include many of the topics covered in this text: intimate violence, family breakup, AIDS, abortion, child care, poverty, homelessness, home/work demands, later-life families, and the like.

Zimmerman's goal of family policy is to maximize the well-being of families.[3] She defines family well-being as a value that includes the state of being healthy, happy, and free from want as well as achieving satisfaction with marriage, work, leisure, housing, and so forth. The goal of her family policy is to assist families in attaining these values.

One immediate difficulty in family policy is determining who and what constitutes a *family*. Should members be related economically, morally, or socially/psychologically rather than by birth or law? Moen and Schorr suggested that, rather than settling for one particular definition, it is more appropriate to define families according to the particular issues involved. For example, if the issue is the socialization of children, define the family to include households with children. If the issue involves a property settlement with cohabiting adults, define the family to include intimate primary relationships. The definition should not become so rigid and sacred that it defeats the program or action.

The range of programs and policies affecting families is broad. Some support a *nurturance* function: child care, health care, and services to people who are elderly or disabled. Other programs support the *economic* functions of the family by providing welfare benefits or stimulating employment. *Social* functions are served by programs that promote helping arrangements, social networks, and the exchange of services.

The approach in this book is to deal with family policy in general terms, particularly in defining both *family* and *policy*. Families will refer both to traditional forms and to intimately bonded relationships and life-styles that may not conform to traditional norms. Policies will refer to any laws, programs, or activities that affect families and influence their activities.

RESEARCH ON FAMILY POLICY

An issue social scientists frequently contest is the extent to which social research can or should be value-free. This issue becomes particularly acute when dealing with **family policy research.** One side of the issue argues for value-neutrality, objectivity, and basic research apart from any policy objective. The opposite side of the issue argues that value-free research is impossible, even if desired, and that trained social researchers need to apply their expertise to constructive ends.

One solution to this debate is to acknowledge both positions by "wearing two hats": one of researcher and one of advocate/citizen. The researcher provides empirical evidence of what exists, and the advocate/citizen works for goals he or she deems important. The *researcher* attempts to maintain objectivity throughout the research endeavour and ideally is open to all sides of an issue. This includes a willingness to accept findings that may contradict one's personal positions. The **advocate/citizen** endorses and actively works for a course of action that improves family life and hopefully enhances the well-being of its members. The advocate takes one side of an issue, usually consistent with his or her own value system, with the intent of influencing an action or decision viewed as beneficial to families and their members.

John Scanzoni made a case for both positions.[4] His research and theory in *Shaping Tomorrow's Family* was basically positivistic because it described and analyzed *what is*, yet it was stimulated by policy and normative considerations of *what should be*. According to Scanzoni, research itself should be conducted under the strictest positivist procedural canons possible. However, researchers should not be deluded into thinking they have no vested interest in the outcome of the investigation any less than a medical researcher has an interest in finding some cure or solution to a sickness or disease. Scanzoni recognized the difficulty in ensuring that empirical research was simultaneously distinct from, yet connected to, practical applications. This sort of "balancing act" is required because family *research* has often been devoid of practical application and family *policy* has often been devoid of basic research and organizing principles.

Research with a policy focus can take a number of directions: (1) to establish family policy, (2) to do family evaluation, and (3) to analyze family impact. Bogenschneider includes these three research positions (described later in this chapter) as models of professional roles for building family policy. In addition, she views family policy advocacy as an appropriate professional role when considered within the context of a new role of family policy: **alternative education.**[5]

Unlike the advocacy approach, alternative education does not lobby for a particular policy but rather clarifies the potential consequences of various policy alternatives. This position is based on the premise that when individuals have sufficient knowledge, they can make judgments for themselves better than others can make judgments for them. This knowledge of the consequences of policy alternatives is based on an objective integration and dissemination of research findings.

Research to establish family policy

Typically, research to establish policy starts with a general hypothesis that some kind of social action may be desirable. Such research does not necessarily assume a problem exists, does not evaluate an existing policy or program, and does not assess the consequences of a policy or program. Rather, given a nontraditional life-style (cohabitation, gay or lesbian marriage, chosen single-parenthood, and so forth), research for family policy examines that life-style and seeks to discover its outcome for the individuals involved as well as for society as a whole. The research may find that all is well and nothing needs to be done, or it may recommend that laws need to be changed, programs developed, or action taken to fulfill specific needs.

An example of research to establish family policy is a study aimed at discovering the socioeconomic processes that determine the use of welfare and its accompanying dependency, and the impact of labour market conditions on the

News Item

Punishment policy justice?

The *Detroit Free Press* (September 10, 1995) published a series of examples of "News of the Weird." Three of these examples included the case of:

... a man in California who was charged with beating his girlfriend and strangling her pet rabbit. As reported, for beating his girlfriend, the maximum fine in California is $1000 but for strangling the rabbit the maximum fine is $20 000.

... two Oklahoma police officers. One officer abused his girlfriend so badly she suffered a ruptured eardrum. The other officer kicked a cat at the airport in Oklahoma City. The first officer faced the possibility of a maximum jail time of 90 days. The second officer faced the possibility of a maximum prison time of five years.

... a dead woman in Florida. Sheriff's deputies charged a man with killing his mother and were set to charge his friend with having sex with her corpse. The latter charge failed when they discovered there is no law in Florida against having sex with a corpse.

What do you think?

determinants of dependency.[6] The issue was American low-income female-headed households dependent on welfare. Data were gathered from more than 300 women in New Jersey at three different time periods.

One of the hypotheses of the study was that the most immediate economic tradeoff low-income single female parents faced was between the expected monetary return from labour supplied to the formal labour market and the need for the parent at home. Findings provided basic support for the idea that welfare could be reduced by making the expected value of work outside the home greater than that of home-related work. The policy implication is not merely to expand jobs or to provide work of any kind (known as "workfare") but to provide jobs that maximize the potential for financial independence. In other words, producing fewer but relatively better jobs may be a more useful strategy than producing poor jobs for a broad cross-section of the low-income population.

The research suggested that welfare dependency among low-income women could be reduced by providing jobs with internal job ladders, the possibility of advancement, on-the-job training, and the job protection afforded by unionization. Unfortunately, support from the U.S. government has been largely withdrawn from these types of training and job experiences. And as this research found, workfare is unlikely to have a long-term positive impact if it is only an administrative requirement that some job be found, regardless of quality.

Research on family evaluation

A second type of policy research is done to evaluate existing policy. Family-evaluation research examines programs to determine the degree to which social programs have achieved or are achieving the stated goals of a public policy or resultant program.

Shirley Zimmerman, using a family perspective, examined research findings and other data dealing with government policies and programs to determine their effectiveness or lack thereof.[7] *Effectiveness* was defined as a fit between the goals or objectives of a program and their actual outcomes. Drawing upon other studies as the source of her evaluations, she assessed the effectiveness of income guarantee experiments, Aid to Families with Dependent Children (AFDC), Supplementary Security Income (SSI) and Social Security, deinstitutionalization of family members who are mentally ill or retarded, compensatory preschool education, and abortion services. Zimmerman claimed that, from a family perspective, government programs seem to have promoted family well-being under conditions that take family variables into account. When programs do run counter to family interests, the negative effects of such policies and programs on affected families tend to reflect the absence rather than the presence of supportive service policies and programs.

Research to analyze family impact

A third type of policy research is family-impact analysis. Here, the attempt is to assess the intended and unintended consequences of public policy and social programs. For example, what is the impact of capital gains taxes on those who invest? What are the effects of new reproductive technologies on mothers and children? What are the employment and income consequences of a policy that prohibits a woman from terminating a pregnancy?

Unlike evaluation research, which focuses on whether the goals or objectives are being met, family-impact analysis looks at how families are affected beyond the explicit intentions or goals of the policy or program. As a result, evaluation research may show that the intended goals are being met, but impact analysis may show the goals are counterproductive, producing unintended but negative consequences for families.

For example, in the last chapter, it was mentioned that two key determinants of economic well-being for divorced mothers are remarriage and child support. Evaluation research of child support showed that those mothers who get support are better off economically than those who do not. This result is obvious. But what other consequences (impact analysis) does child support have? For one, child support was shown to negatively affect the remarriage of divorced mothers, the other key determinant of economic well-being.[8]

Another example that assessed the impact of an existing policy—in this case, American welfare—came from Zimmerman. Drawing on Durkheim's theory of social integration, she analyzed states' spending on public welfare and their divorce rates.[9] Zimmerman wanted to test the assumption that state welfare services destabilizes family life, thus contributing to family breakup. She found that states that spent more on public welfare had lower rates of divorce as well as lower rates of population change and unemployment. She concluded that the connection critics have drawn between the welfare state and family breakup is mythical at best. In other words, irrespective of whether welfare accomplishes its intended goals (as would be determined in evaluation research), it does not increase the likelihood of divorce.

Overview of research

Effective family policy is highly dependent on all three types of research: research to determine what type of policy is needed, research to evaluate on existing program or policy, and research to assess the impact or consequences of a program or policy beyond its specific intent. The formulation and enforcement of policies affecting families is addressed in the next section, where some key issues are presented, again, in ideal-type terms.

ISSUES SURROUNDING FAMILY POLICY

Policy matters are usually characterized by divergent ideas, conflicts over positions, and opposing recommendations. When policy is made, it seldom satisfies all interest groups or gets the endorsement of all social and political organizations. At times, policy differences relate to basic philosophies of life, perceptions of the role of government, and images of what the family is or should be.

In the following sections, several of these differences are examined. While each is presented in dichotomous terms, remember that the two views exist simultaneously. Rarely can an issue be resolved into an "either/or" position.

Goals and objectives of family policy

The first issue addresses questions of function: namely, the type of family or families desired and the goals or objectives of family policy. Should policy be directed toward the traditional family or toward a diversity of life-styles, relationships, and families? Furthermore, should policy be directed at preventing the family from changing and maintaining the status quo, or at supporting change, flexibility, and creativity? This issue is at the heart of Scanzoni's differentiation of conventionals from progressives.[10]

Conventionals are those who believe the normal family is conjugal. A male, as husband and father, is head of the household and the sole economic provider. A female, as wife and mother, is a helpmate to her husband and a homemaker responsible for household duties, domestic care, and the socialization of the children. Children are helpless and dependent.

Conventionals, represented by political and religious conservatives, want to preserve this traditional image of what families should be. Groups representing this perspective view family change as a breakdown of morality and disintegration of *the* family. The function of policy, from the perspective of conventionals, is to maintain the status quo or return to some idealized image of what the family once was and should be.

FAMILY DIVERSITY

Parental leave in Sweden

Calls for equal parenthood in Sweden began in the early 1960s. In 1974, Sweden became the first country to institute parental leave for both mothers and fathers. What are some of the features of the contemporary parental-leave policy in Sweden?

A married or unmarried Swedish father has 15 months of paid leave; return to his original job is guaranteed. He can share this with his partner so that one parent can stay home with a newborn or adopted child. An additional six months' leave is available for parents of twins. As of 1990, the first 12 months of the leave are paid at the level of 90 to 100 percent of regular pay. The last 3 months are paid at a minimum level (about $10 a day).

Even maternal care practices have changed to encourage participation of fathers in prenatal care, parental education, and delivery. In employment, fathers get two weeks off with pay at the time of childbirth, sixty days off per year with pay (shared with mothers) to care for sick children, two days off to visit day-care centres and schools (again, with pay), and the right to reduce the workday to six hours for child-care purposes.

Benefits are paid out directly from social insurance offices rather than from employers. The leave program, however, is paid for mainly by employers, through payroll taxes on all employees.

The Swedish parental-leave policy developed in response to three social concerns. One was a concern over the low birth rate. Swedes have a high regard for children and view having children as something that should be encouraged. Parental leave is believed to improve a couple's chance of having children by helping them combine parental and employment roles. A second concern was the need for women's labour power. A low birth rate and a booming economy led to the employment of women in numbers that today make the female labour force participation rate among the highest in the world. Third was a concern over changing both men's and women's traditional roles. Extending maternity leave to fathers was intended to liberate men from traditional gender stereotypes. Today, while men are not fully liberated, they do share more in child care than fathers elsewhere in the world.

What do you think?

Source: Linda Haas, *Equal Parenthood and Social Policy: A Study of Parental Leave in Sweden* (Albany: State University of New York Press, 1992).

Progressives are those who believe a normal family can take many forms. The view is not of *the* family but of a *variety* of families and close relationships. A progressive model is pluralistic and allows many options. At the core of this model is the notion that involved adults should strive to become equal partners and to achieve equity among family members. Scanzoni stated that, given their pluralistic view of society, progressives accept the notion that alternative views of family should be allowed to compete in the marketplace, allowing nonaligned persons to gravitate toward those patterns suiting them best. Conservatives cannot accept this notion.[11]

Theoretically, Scanzoni linked functionalism with conventionals. The emphasis is on structure and stability. Thus, couples who stay together are successful and represent stability, and those who divorce are failures and represent breakdown. Out-of-wedlock births and female-headed households represent disorganization. Progressives are linked more closely with the conflict approach, where the emphasis is on process and change. A wide variety of goals are legitimate and result from complex negotiations between interest groups, each with preferred patterns and relationships. From this view, any number of life-styles or choices are acceptable: childless marriages; egalitarian relationships; divorce; marriage in middle or old age; diverse family forms among people who are minorities or poor; cohabitation without marriage; homosexual relationships; abortion; women, wives, and mothers in the employed labour force; and males as homemakers and childrearers.

Scanzoni noted that, in spite of the unified and influential efforts of conventionals, the major weakness of their model is that it is out of sync with the times. Their theory does not conform to reality—to what is actually happening. Society is not static, families are not uniform, and goals are not unanimous.

From the progressive perspective, the purpose of intimate relationships, including marriage, is not to carry out predictable, predetermined duties, where males do certain things and females do others; instead, such relationships are to provide a context for the facilitation of interests held by both persons. For instance, children are not helpless and dependent but can be effectively trained

Family Diversity

How about a tax-free family lunch?

Those familiar with basic Canadian social institutions are well aware of the tax breaks afforded them. All religious property and holdings, worth millions of dollars, are free of federal and provincial taxation. Educational expenses relating to employment—such as books, supplies, professional meetings, and additional training to improve skills in a current position—are also tax-deductible. Gifts to politicians, their travel expenses, postage costs, office space and supplies, and entertainment costs are at the taxpayers' expense. Business expenses—such as food, lodging, travel, supplies, labour, gifts, and entertainment done on behalf of a business—become legitimate preprofit expenses and are not subject to taxation when they exceed a certain percentage of one's income.

Should marriage and the family be of lesser social importance? Shouldn't dinner with a spouse be considered as worthwhile as dinner with a business associate? Shouldn't taking a son or daughter to one baseball game be as valid for society as the block of season tickets the company writes off as an expense? Shouldn't the home and shelter provided for families be as important to society as the churches, synagogues, and cathedrals of religious groups? Shouldn't a family vacation be equal in importance to the political junkets of a local official or a member of the legislature? Should the husband pay taxes at a higher rate because his wife takes a part-time job to supplement the family income? How about a tax-free family lunch?

What do you think?

Family policy and formal legislation take place at local, provincial and national levels. In Canada, laws governing marriage and divorce are federal, but administered by the provinces.

in the dynamics of equitable decision-making. An individual may choose not to marry, to cohabit, not to have children, and to find employment that was traditionally defined as inconsistent with his or her gender.

Policy should be aimed not at maintaining past traditions of the status quo that the majority of citizens have already discarded but at looking ahead and coming up with fresh ideas molded around an equal-partner framework. The functions of policy are (1) to recognize and accept the reality of changes already apparent in Western society[12] and (2) to implement further change in a way that is responsive both to the question of social order and to the preferences of the persons involved. Other, related issues surround this task.

Levels of policy control

A second issue is at what level—federal, provincial, or local—family policy should be formulated and enforced. As described in Chapter 11, laws governing marriage and divorce are federal but are administered by the provinces. Until 1968, Quebeckers who wanted a divorce could not obtain one through the provincial court system.

In Canada, income tax legislation makes implicit assumptions about various family structures even though the individual is the basic tax unit. Ironically, unmarried couples fare better under the tax system, particularly if there are children, than do married couples. This is largely because married couples cannot take advantage of the Equivalent to Married Credit and because the *Income Tax Act* stipulates which spouse must claim child-related deductions. Married couples also receive less benefit from transfer programs than do cohabiting couples. When two lone-parent families or two elderly people live together without being married, their combined transfer payment benefits will be greater than those received by comparable married-couple families.[13]

There are both advantages and disadvantages to establishing family policies either nationally or provincially. Some advantages of federal family policies include:

- Making the family and family-related issues visible nationally, not simply in a given province or community
- Giving family issues a national priority, as is done with defence, labour, and agriculture, for example
- Setting uniform national standards that minimize local prejudices and indifference
- Providing large-scale funding of programs and research that local or provincial governments cannot fund

In contrast to the distinct advantages of a federal family policy, there are inherent problems as well. One problem is national-level policies that have a negative impact on select groups of the population. For example, one writer assessed the impact of the "supply side" economics of the Reagan administration on family-support services, food-related programs, employment, education, and housing.[14] The policies of this administration were shown to have affected people who are poor (many of whom are African-American) more negatively than people in a better economic position. The philosophy stressing hard work, independence, thrift, minimum government intervention in the lives of citizens, tax cuts, and the like proved to hurt people who are poor.

A second problem centres on how policies can be best adapted to the special needs of racial, ethnic, regional, and cultural groups. And yet another problem centres on assessing the adequacy of monitoring services provided, which requires local control. According to this view of more local policy and control, neither money alone nor one level of government can do the job.

Public versus private positions

A third issue of family policy revolves around the extent to which intimate relationships and families are *public* or *private* institutions. Often, the family is seen as a private institution, separate from and closed to public scrutiny. Family policy, in contrast, demands that the family be open to public view and subject to public scrutiny.

The privacy position argues that the family or an intimate relationship is a matter of personal concern, a haven for privacy, a place of unconditional affection and love, a network for sharing fears, anxieties, and joys, and a source of protection and security free from "Big Brother" and public dominance. Cannot wives and husbands decide for themselves when, where, and how they desire to make love, the number of children they want or do not want to have, the manner in which they control that number, and how they discipline, educate, clothe, and feed these children?

The public position argues that the state and community have the right (and even the obligation) to establish boundaries on what happens in private. If children are hungry, wives are raped, or families are homeless, should not public agencies intervene? If so, when and to what extent? What about issues such as minimum income, child care, discipline and corporal punishment, abortion, alcohol and drug dependency, health care, and housing?

Advocates of the privacy position argue for minimal state intervention into family and intimacy matters. Advocates of the public position argue that laws must be written and enforced to protect all group members and enhance equal rights and opportunities for all citizens. Interestingly, on certain issues, such as child care and minimum family income, advocates of the privacy position often take a public position in favour of government intervention. For example, right-wing religious and political groups have led organized efforts against the inclusion of sexual orientation in provincial human rights legislation but for the passage of antiabortion laws.

The fact that no explicit national family policy exists should not lead one to believe that the government is totally uninvolved in or is neutral to issues pertaining to families. A wide range of public policies deal with the Canada Pension Plan and Old Age Security, health and medical care, child welfare, education, day care, and most areas of interest to family members. The lack of a coherent plan, set of services, or national policy is testimony to the fact that families have no organized or powerful lobby groups to influence legislation and oversee the impact of legislative matters on marriages and families. In contrast, business, religious, and medical groups have made strong, organized efforts to protect their vested interests.

Preventive or ameliorative policy

Assuming certain policies are necessary, a fourth issue is whether these policies should be directed toward all families and intimate relationships or only toward those with problems—that is, toward all intimate life-styles or toward marriages, families, or groups with pathologies.

A policy for *all* families or intimate relationships focuses on issues that affect everyone: employment, health, minimum wages, housing, sexual and racial/ethnic equality, tax equity, and the like. The *need* position focuses on select groups or behaviours that are defined as problems: unwed-parenthood, abortion, child and spouse abuse, single-parenthood, divorce, and so on.

Perhaps a medical analogy is relevant. Traditionally, medical care was directed toward people who were sick. Doctors were seen only when colds, diseases, or broken bones created the need for medical care. An emerging view is directed at prevention, at a holistic orientation to care, and toward maintaining a high level of health for everyone.

The problem, or need, position includes an added dimension of *deserving* and *undeserving*. Poor children and elderly persons who are ill have special needs. But, in addition, they deserve help. Why? Because their condition or circumstances exist through no fault of their own. Thus, child support and prescription drug coverage are legitimate programs because there is a need for them and the recipients deserve help. Likewise, Old Age Security is felt to be a worthwhile income-support program because it gives older Canadians, regardless of employment history, a measure of economic security. That many people have other income and do not really need Old Age Security is irrelevant, according to this view. Certainly, Old Age Security is not labelled or stigmatized as welfare because people deserve and are entitled to it. In contrast, welfare carries negative connotations. Why? In the eyes of many, welfare recipients are the undeserving poor.

It is interesting to note that labelling specific types of relationships or structures as *problematic*, *pathological*, or *ill* may in itself affect the types of policies directed toward them. Consider single-parenthood. If this form of structure—one parent with children—is pathological, then policy will probably focus on preventing the formation of single-parent family structures and on providing services designed to facilitate reconstitution of these "less than complete" families. On the other hand, if single-parent families are simply considered one of many accepted family life-styles, the policy will likely focus on what is necessary for all families: minimum incomes, adequate housing, inexpensive child care, employment opportunities, support services, and the like.

Micro-level versus macro-level policy

A fifth issue is whether policy should operate primarily at the *micro level* or the *macro level*. Micro-level policy focuses on persons and patterns of personal interactions that characterize everyday life. Macro-level policy focusses on the social patterns and forms of social organization that shape an entire society. These forms are beyond the control of any individual yet play a powerful role in affecting families and influencing personal lives.

At the micro level, the individual or set of individuals in interaction is the unit of analysis and focus of attention. To deal with a marital problem, counsel the spouses. To deal with delinquent youth, abused children, or people who are elderly, physically or mentally ill, provide housing (or institutionalization), personal counselling, and individual attention. This micro-level position is well understood and highly emphasized in terms of social policy and specific courses of action. The single mother or the person who is sick or mentally retarded has a problem and is in need of treatment or attention.

In contrast, at the macro level, the organization, system, or society is the unit of analysis and focus of attention. At this level, individuals or relationships are affected by how society is structured and by the nature of social systems within that society. Policies related to taxation, health care, employment, housing, education, and leisure all affect persons and families, but the focus of such policies is not on a given person or family with a specific problem.

For instance, if poverty status is characterized by lower levels of commitment to marriage and if high rates of marital dissolution are related to child abuse and low levels of mental and marital health, then it seems imperative that social policy be directed not merely at counselling the mother or the abused child but at the conditions maintaining poverty. If welfare policies force men to live separately from their spouses and children or if federal tax laws impose penalties on marriage, then these policies, operating at a macro level, need to be reexamined. If sexual or racial inequality in society prevents wives from establishing credit or owning property and prevents minority business owners from obtaining bank credit, then these practices and conditions need to be addressed at a level beyond any given individual or family.

One example of this distinction was provided by a paper dealing with the consequences of unemployment for families in the 1980s.[15] Phyllis Moen, using data from several depression periods, noted the following:

1. Most families of unemployed people who suffered financial hardship received no government income support.
2. Unemployment benefits were an important coping mechanism for families of the long-term unemployed.
3. Limiting the duration of unemployment appeared to be as important a strategy for preventing financial hardship as the availability of income support.
4. Families with more than a single wage-earner were much more able to avoid economic privation.

The differential distribution and unequal sharing of the costs of unemployment across families highlights the plight of single parents and of parents of young children, as well as how unemployment and its financial repercussions are shaped by broad social, economic, and political forces operating at the macro level. Even with a healthy economy with "full employment," some portion of the labour force remains jobless. Given major cutbacks in social programs plus the lag in government response, the financial toll on families experiencing unemployment can be traumatic. Note how events at the macro level increase or decrease the level of unemployment and how macro-level policies lessen or heighten the negative impact of being unemployed.

Moen suggested as well that public policies facilitating the employment of women (flexible work time, day care, nondiscriminatory hiring and wage practices) could help both two-earner families and single-parent women make ends meet.[16] Policies, however, are being developed and implemented slowly.

Scanzoni presented the argument that macro-level family-related objectives have rarely addressed fundamental issues, since it is impossible to define a family in concrete terms and not exclude many of the nontraditional forms, as described throughout this text.[17] Similarly, he suggested that micro-level responses have been inadequate because a gap often exists between the demands of contemporary society and the capabilities of conventional families and individuals to grapple with those demands. He argued for policy at a **meso level,** an alternative between the macro and the micro level.

The meso level involves *mediating structures*—that is, groups and organizations that extend beyond the person or family but do not encompass an entire province or country. These include community groups and agencies, religious organizations, local chapters of national organizations, unions and political action groups, and so on. These groups could mediate, train, and support the diverse range of family structures and concerns found in Canadian society.

FUTURE OF THE FAMILY SYSTEM

The underlying issue in this chapter on family policy–related issues is that of the future of the family system. Will it survive? What types of sexually bonded relationships, families, and societies will exist in the next 10, 50, or 100 years? How can people prepare for them? What types of training do people need to provide for their children and grandchildren (assuming they will be "their" children)? What types of structures will exist in the family realm? What functions will be expected of this institution? Will families be necessary? Will marriages exist? Will women have equal status with men? Will homosexual families have the same rights as heterosexual partners?

This is a sampling of the questions that might be raised. The answers will depend on who gives them, the basis or theory on which the projection is based, the length of time projected, the types of family and social policies instituted, and, perhaps, the personal wishes of the projector.

That families and intimate relationships are changing and will continue to change is perhaps, although not necessarily, a definitive statement, one on which there is widespread agreement. But comments on decay and breakdown and on progress and advancement must be approached cautiously. The following observations are made in relation to predicting the future:

- Changes that take place (and will take place) in society at large or among people in intimate relationships are not necessarily pleasing or regrettable, good or bad, or constructive or destructive per se. Changes are likely to be welcomed or rejected depending largely on one's own frame of reference, the groups with which one identifies, and the value orientations to which one adheres. For example, rising divorce rates may be viewed either as a problem or as a solution to other problems. Homosexuality may be viewed as deviance or as a right to love whomever one chooses. War may be viewed as vital to national defence

What does the future hold for marriage and the family? Clearly, what form they take and what functions they serve will be greatly affected by developments in other systems of the larger society. For example, given advances in computer technology, the home may increasingly become the centre for employment, shopping, communication, and entertainment.

or as an immoral destruction of life and property. This is not meant to imply that changes are never disruptive to the social order; rather, the point is that social matters must be seen in the context in which they occur.

- Although many people see the family as the core of society and as the most basic of all institutions, it must be clear that (as has been stated time and again) the family cannot be understood as an isolated phenomenon. The family must be viewed in relation to economic, educational, religious, and political institutions. In addition, factors such as population density, mobility patterns, and stratification divisions must be taken into account. It is not by chance that agricultural societies tend to emphasize extended families, parental involvement in partner selection, and, often, plural marriage. Neither is it by chance that our society places an emphasis on romantic love, separate households, and monogamous marriages. The central point is that, if accurate predictions are to be made, it is essential to understand what is going to take place in other social systems. A change in any element of a social system will lead to changes in other elements, including the family.
- The family is not a uniform entity. Change will occur, almost without question. But to speak of the changing family as if it were a uniform entity or that only

one particular form or structure is appropriate is both misleading and unrelated to the real world. From the beginning, Canadian society has been culturally diverse. There have always been variations in intimate relationships and family patterns along such factors as rural/urban residence, region of the country, religious affiliation, racial and ethnic identity, social-class background, and age. In the past, as today, one could expect to find variations by number of spouses, number of children, and size of the kinship network. In the past, as today, one could expect to find variations in employment patterns of both men and women, in the household tasks they performed, and in how they reared and disciplined their children. One must recognize the tremendous differences that exist in family structures and interpersonal relationships. At the same time, one must recognize that, within this diversity, strands of unity belie heterogeneous origins.

Undoubtedly, as long as society exists, some form of family system will exist. It is hard to dispute the opinion of DaVanzo et al.[18] that over the next few decades, certain demographic trends will continue, including:

- Women, including those who are mothers of young children, will continue to work outside their homes. Policies that would increase the compatibility of working and caring for children, or reduce the costs of child care, are likely to lead to even higher rates of labour force participation by mothers of young children.
- Economic opportunities for women will reduce the incentive to marry and have children, or at least delay marriage and childbearing, and may keep divorce rates fairly high. It is unlikely we will see important reversals in the trend toward cohabitation.
- There will be continued shifts in the proportions of children and older people in the population, with fewer of the former and more of the latter.

The passing of the traditional family has caused a great deal of trauma and left a number of loose ends. But the rebuilt family will include many variations on sexually bonded, primary, intimate, close relationships that will fulfill family-type functions. Most Canadians will continue to find marriage and family interactions as basic sources of emotional and psychic stability. Families will continue to be primary sources of socialization, security and affection, and meaning. Families are likely to remain the largest collective social service agency in the nation and world—responsible for the care of children and people who are sick, disabled, and elderly, responsible for the economic welfare of their members, and so forth. The nature of partners that constitute a relationship or marriage may change, the expectations of men and women may change, sexual codes and practices may change, and general family living may become vastly different.

But change by itself does not necessarily bring the deterioration of families. Rather, destruction of society and the family are more likely to result because of an inability to change.

SUMMARY

1. All areas of marriage and family life are affected by certain economic, political, and social policies. It seems safe to assume that, while most social policies have an effect on families, few were developed or formulated with families in mind.
2. As used in this chapter, *family policy* refers to objectives concerning family well-being that are met through specific courses of action. The intent of social policy is to guide, influence, or determine the structure, functions, behaviour, ideas, and values of Canadians.
3. Three types of family policy research were discussed in this chapter. Research to establish family policy examines some particular family structure or life-style to determine if certain policies or programs are necessary and to make recommendations as to what they should be. Family-evaluation research determines the degree to which social programs achieve their stated goals. Family-impact analysis assesses the intended and unintended consequences of public policy and social programs.
4. Policy matters are usually characterized by divergent ideas, conflicts over positions, and opposing recommendations. At a general level of analysis, five of these issues or differences were examined in this chapter:
   a. *Goals and objectives*—the extent to which policies are aimed at maintaining the status quo or serve as forces for change. Conventionals seek the status quo, as idealized in the traditional conjugal family, whereas progressives seek change and acceptance of multiple family forms more consistent with a pluralistic society.
   b. *Levels of control*—the extent to which policies should be established and enforced at the federal, provincial, or local level.
   c. *Public versus private positions*—the extent to which families and intimate relationships are public or private institutions, meaning basically the extent to which there should be a separation of family and government or legal intervention.
   d. *Preventive or ameliorative policy*—the extent to which policies should be directed toward all close relationships or toward families with problems.
   e. *Micro level versus macro level*—the extent to which policies should operate at primarily the micro or the macro level—that is, focusing on small-group or interpersonal relationships or on social patterns or forms of social organization that shape entire societies.
5. What is the future of the family? Social policies will, without doubt, affect the future patterns of intimate and family relationships. The family is changing and will continue to change. In sum:
   a. These changes are not good or bad per se.
   b. The future of the family cannot be understood separate from other institutions and systems.
   c. The family of the future will not be a uniform entity.
   d. Any type of social projection must be made cautiously.
6. Given qualifications such as these, it is predicted, unequivocally, that as long as a society exists, some form of family system will survive. It will include many differing structural arrangements, perform a variety of functions, and fulfill a range of personal and social needs. Whether our interest in the family is at a professional level of teaching, research, or social action or at a personal level of dating, childrearing, or caring for aged parents, it will be impossible for us not to be affected by the family.

KEY TERMS AND TOPICS

Family policy p. 336
Family policy research p. 337
Advocate/citizen p. 337
Alternative education p. 338
Research to establish family policy p. 338
Research on family evaluation p. 339
Research to analyze family impact p. 340
Issues surrounding family policy p. 341
Goals and objectives of family policy p. 341
Conventionals p. 341
Progressives p. 342
Levels of policy control p. 344
Public versus private positions p. 345
Preventive or ameliorative policy p. 346
Micro-level versus macro-level policy p. 347
Meso-level policy p. 349
Future of the family system p. 349

DISCUSSION QUESTIONS

1. Differentiate among the terms *policy*, *social policy*, and *family policy*. Can social policy exist independently of and have no impact on families? Why or why not?
2. Can or should family policy research be value-free? Can or should policy *research* be separated from policy *advocacy?* How can family policy researchers integrate knowledge of *what is* with concern over *what should be?*
3. Describe the different goals of (a) research to establish family policy, (b) family-evaluation research, and (c) family-impact analysis.
4. What arguments can be made for establishing policy to maintain the status quo as opposed to policy that permits or forces change and diversity? Is it possible to talk about *the* family in the Western world? Why or why not?
5. Contrast the stances taken by conventionals and progressives. How do these stances translate into policies on issues such as teenage sexual behaviour and contraceptive use, sex education, abortion, day-care facilities, cohabitation, divorce, remarriage, the employment of mothers of young children, and so on? (Select three issues.)
6. What arguments can be made for establishing family policy at a federal as opposed to a provincial or local level? What arguments can be made against this idea? Is a national family policy possible or realistic? Why or why not?
7. What arguments can be made for and against the separation of family and state? In which areas does the government clearly have no right to get involved? In which areas is government involvement mandatory?
8. What arguments can be made for directing policy at all intimate relationships versus only at families with problems? What are some effects of labelling certain living arrangements "problems"?
9. How might policies for children, single mothers, and people who are terminally ill or elderly differ, depending on whether the policies are directed at individuals or systems? Give an example.
10. Is effective family change more likely to occur within society by directing programs and policies at individuals and interpersonal relationships (at a micro level) or at social patterns and organizations (at a macro level)? Explain your answer.
11. All of the panels in this chapter end with the question, "What do you think?" Choose one of the panels and answer the question.
12. What predictions can be made about families and marriages in this century? Describe their structures and functions, the impact made on them by new technologies, changing parent/child relationships, the division of marital roles and tasks, the status of women, and sexual norms. Are any areas likely to remain static, stable, and relatively unchanged? Why or why not?

FURTHER READINGS

Anderson, Elaine A., and Hula, Richard C., eds. *The Reconstruction of Family Policy*. New York: Greenwood Press, 1991. Sixteen essays examine three major subject areas: the normative context of family policy, the link between theory and action, and the impact of specific policies.

Baker, Maureen. *Canada's Changing Families: Challenges to Public Policy*. Ottawa: The Vanier Institute of the Family, 1993. Ten chapters look at various aspects of family policy in Canada. Includes an analysis of Quebec's proactive policies.

Haveman, Robert H., and Wolfe, Barbara. *Succeeding Generations: On the Effects of Investments in Children*. New York: Russell Sage Foundation, 1994. On the basis of an ongoing longitudinal national survey, the authors present evidence on numerous fronts showing that American children do not fare well. The final chapter focuses on some policy implications.

Jacobs, Francine H., and Davies, Margery W., eds. *More Than Kissing Babies: Current and Family Policy in the United States*. Westport, CT: Auburn House, 1994. A case study approach is used to illustrate basic issues and themes of child and family policy in the United States.

Kagan, Sharon L., and Weissbourd, Bernice, eds. *Putting Families First: America's Family Support Movement and the Challenge of Change*. San Francisco: Jossey-Bass, 1994. Twenty chapters deal with family support in terms of change, social institutions, programs, and policies.

Kamerman, Sheila B., and Kahn, Alfred J. *Family Change and Family Policies in Great Britain, Canada, New Zealand and the United States*. Oxford: Clarendon Press, 1997. The first volume of a series reporting on the evolution of family policies in Western welfare states.

Lechner, Viola, and Creedon, Michael A. *Managing Work and Family Life*. New York: Springer, 1994. Two doctorates of social work provide a review of work and family dilemmas and recommend ways/policies to improve them.

Mason, Mary Ann; Skolnick, Arlene; and Sugarman, Stephen. *All Our Families: New Policies for a New Century*. New York: Oxford University Press, 1998. An interdisciplinary exploration of selected topics including teen pregnancy, divorce, child abuse, stepfamilies, and others—with a focus on policy reform.

Zigler, Edward F.; Kagan, Sharon Lynn; and Hall, Nancy W., eds. *Children, Families, and Government: Preparing for the Twenty-First Century*. New York: Press Syndicate of the University of Cambridge, 1996. Twenty-five chapters that focus on children and policy issues.

Zimmerman, Shirley L. *Understanding Family Policy: Theories and Applications*. 2nd ed. Thousand Oaks, CA: Sage Publications, 1995. An examination of what family policy is and the putting together of policy frameworks to enhance family well-being.

WEBLINKS

http://www.vifamily.ca

This homepage for the Vanier Institute of the Family is an excellent resource for information relating to programs dedicated to promoting the well-being of Canadian families.

http://www.uoguelph.ca/cfww/

The University of Guelph's Centre for Families, Work and Well-Being provides findings on current research and analysis of family policy in Canada.

http://www.cprn.com/cprn.html

This is a direct link to The Canadian Policy Research Network's information concerning contemporary family dynamics. It offers comments on policy development related to Canadian families.

NOTES

1. Phyllis Moen and Alvin L. Schorr, "Families and Social Policy," in *Handbook of Marriage and the Family*, ed. Marvin B. Sussman and Suzanne K. Steinmetz (New York: Plenum Press, 1987), Chapter 28, 795.
2. Shirley L. Zimmerman, *Understanding Family Policy: Theories and Applications*, 2nd ed. (Thousand Oaks, CA: Sage Publications, 1995), 3.
3. Ibid., 8.
4. John Scanzoni, *Shaping Tomorrow's Family: Theory and Policy for the 21st Century* (Beverly Hills, CA: Sage, 1983).
5. Karen Bogenschneider, "Roles for Professionals in Building Family Policy," *Family Relations* 44 (January 1995): 5–12.
6. Robert F. Kelly, "Welfare Dependency Under Depressed Labor Market Conditions: Lessons from the 1970s for the 1980s," *Journal of Urban Affairs* 5 (Fall 1983): 331–348.
7. Shirley L. Zimmerman, "Public Policies and Family Outcomes: Empirical Evidence or Ideology?" *Social Casework* 64 (March 1983): 138–146.
8. Karen Fox Folk, John W. Graham, and Andrea H. Beller, "Child Support and Remarriage," *Journal of Family Issues* 13 (June 1992): 142–157.
9. Shirley L. Zimmerman, "The Welfare State and Family Breakup: The Mythical Connection," *Family Relations* 40 (April 1991): 139–147.
10. Scanzoni, *Shaping Tomorrow's Family*; and John Scanzoni, "Reconsidering Family Policy: Status Quo or Force for Change?" *Journal of Family Issues* 3 (September 1982): 277–300.
11. Scanzoni, *Shaping Tomorrow's Family*, 153.
12 See Sanford M. Dornbusch and Myra H. Strober, eds., *Feminism, Children and the New Families* (New York: The Guilford Press, 1988). Note particularly Chapter 14, "Public Policy Alternatives," 327–355.
13. Richard Morrison and Jillian Oderkirk, "Married and Unmarried Couples: The Tax Question," *Canadian Social Trends*, Vol. 2 (Toronto: Thompson Educational Publishing Inc., 1994), 183–188.
14. Maurice A. St. Pierre, "Reaganomics and Its Implications for African-American Family Life," *Journal of Black Studies* 21 (March 1991): 325–340.
15. Phyllis Moen, "Unemployment, Public Policy, and Families: Forecasts for the 1980s," *Journal of Marriage and the Family* 45 (November 1983): 751–760.
16. Ibid., 758.
17. Scanzoni, *Shaping Tomorrow's Family*, 97–118 and 225–227. Note also Frances G. Pestello and Patricia Voydanoff, "In Search of Mesostructure in the Family: An Interactionist Approach to Division of Labor," *Symbolic Interaction* 14 (1991): 105–128.
18. Julie DaVanzo, M. Omar Rahman, and Kul T. Wadhwa, "Current Items: American Families: Policy Issues," *Population Index* 59 (Winter 1993): 547–566.

GLOSSARY

ABCX model A model of family crisis in which A (an event or situation) interacts with B (the resources available) and C (the definition or meaning of the event) to produce X (the level or degree of crisis).

Abortion The termination of a pregnancy, either spontaneously (miscarriage) or by induced means.

Achieved status A social position obtained through one's own efforts, such as husband or teacher.

Adoption The process of legally becoming the parent of a child not biologically one's own.

Affiliated families A variation of an extended family in which a nonrelative (often an older person) becomes recognized as a part of the nuclear-family network.

Affinity A relationship by marriage or a very close relationship.

AIDS (acquired immune deficiency syndrome) A sexually transmitted disease in which white blood cells, which hinder resistance to viruses and bacteria, are broken down.

Androgyny The condition of no sex-role differentiation; androgynous individuals are those who are capable of expressing both or either masculine or feminine behaviour.

Annulment The process of ending a marriage because of conditions that existed before it, in effect, making the marriage nonexistent.

Arranged marriage The pattern in which marital partners are selected by persons other than the couple themselves (parents, matchmakers, etc.).

Ascribed status A social position that is assigned to persons by society or by birth, such as age, race, or sex.

Assortive marrying The idea that people marry those like themselves more often than could be due to chance.

Authority Legitimate power.

"Baby boom" The dramatic rise in the number of births following the Second World War until about 1960.

Behaviourism A theory of learning that focuses on actual behaviour believed to be the result of conditioning through rewards and punishments.

Bigamy The marriage of one person to two persons of the opposite sex; similar to polygamy but restricted to two spouses.

Bilateral system A family system that traces descent and inheritance through both the male and female lines.

Bilocal residence A family system in which a newly married couple lives near the parents of either spouse.

Birth order Sibling position based on order of birth.

Birth rate The number of births per one thousand population in a given year.

Blue-collar families The working class, or the upper-lower class, of semiskilled, service, and other workers with various types of manual skills.

Boundary ambiguity The uncertainty of family members about who is part of the family and who performs or is responsible for certain roles and responsibilities within the family system; a common issue in stepfamilies.

Bourgeoisie The class or social group of people who control the means of production and use capital, natural resources, and labour to generate profit.

Braking hypothesis The idea that spouses may delay getting divorced or approach the decision to divorce more cautiously when they have children.

Bride price The goods, services, or money a family receives in exchange for giving their daughter in marriage.

Child abuse Overt acts of physical, sexual, or verbal aggression against a child.

Child custody The legal arrangement (usually following divorce) that provides parental responsibility for the care of a child. Under *sole custody*, one parent has this responsibility; under *joint custody*, both parents share this responsibility; and under *split custody*, each parent assumes responsibility for certain children.

Childless marriage A marriage in which the couple has no children, either voluntarily or involuntarily.

Child neglect The failure to provide for adequate physical and/or emotional care of a child.

Child snatching Stealing one's own child in a custody dispute.

Cohabitation An arrangement in which an unmarried male and female share a common dwelling.

Cohort A category of people who are born within a specific time period, such as five or ten years.

Coitus Sexual intercourse.

Common-law marriage A marriage in which cohabiting couples are recognized as legally married if they meet certain requirements (such as time living together or recognition of each other as husband and wife), as specified by the province in which they reside.

Commune A group of people sharing collective ownership and use of property.

Commuter marriage A marriage in which the couple desire to live together but maintain separate residences to enhance pursuit of their own goals.

Complementary marriage A traditional marriage in which the husband and wife perform interdependent but different tasks; for instance, he is employed outside the home and she does the domestic tasks.

Complementary needs A theory of mate selection based on the idea that people marry those who provide maximum need gratification; needs tend to be complementary rather than similar.

Concept A miniature system of meaning; a symbol that enables a meaning to be shared and a phenomenon to be perceived in a certain way.

Conceptual framework A cluster of interrelated concepts used to describe and classify phenomena.

Conjugal family A nuclear family that always has a husband and wife (the conjugal unit) and may or may not include children (*see* Nuclear family).

Conjugal power The ability of husbands and wives to control or influence the behaviour of one another.

Consanguine families Extended families based on blood relationships, or descent from the same ancestors.

Conventional Denoting groups and persons who want to maintain the status quo and adhere to a traditional image of what the family should be.

Courtship The process that couples go through in developing a close relationship or commitment to marriage.

Crisis A disturbance in the state of the family that leads to tension or pressure (*see* ABCX model).

Dependent variable A variable that is changed or influenced by the effect of another variable (called the *independent variable*).

Developmental frame of reference A perspective that emphasizes the life cycle and various stages of transition, with specific tasks to be accomplished at each stage.

Dilution hypothesis The notion that less resources (material, physical, and emotional) are available to children in large families than to children in small families.

Displaced homemaker A full-time homemaker who, through widowhood or divorce, loses her means of economic support.

Divorce The legal dissolution of a marriage.

Double standard The use of one set of norms and values for females and a different set for males.

Dowry The sum of money, property, and possessions brought to marriage by the wife.

Dual-career marriage A marriage in which both husband and wife have careers requiring high levels of commitment and offering continuous developmental sequences.

Dual-earner marriage A marriage in which both the husband and wife are in the paid labour force.

Ecology The relationship between the physical environment and the human population that lives in that environment.

Egalitarian family One in which the husband and wife have equal authority in family matters.

Electra complex According to Freudians, the unconscious desire of the female to marry her father.

"Empty nest" syndrome A postparental stage of family life when children leave the "nest" and the family household contracts in size to the couple or individual member.

Endogamy A marriage pattern in which persons marry others within their own social groups.

Ethnic group A group distinguished by its national origin or distinctive cultural patterns, such as religion, language, or region of the country.

Evaluation research As applied to families and family policy, research conducted at a pragmatic level to determine the extent to which stated goals are being achieved.

Exogamy A marriage pattern in which individuals marry outside their own group.

Extended family A family in which two or more generations of the same kin group live together; extension beyond the nuclear family.

Familism A philosophy under which the needs or interests of the family take precedence over those of the individual.

Family A kinship/structural group of persons related by blood, marriage, or adoption; usually related to the marital unit and including the rights and duties of parenthood.

Family life cycle The social sequence of events (such as marriage, children, "empty nest," retirement, and death) that are repeated by successive generations of families.

Family of orientation The nuclear family into which one was born and reared; consists of self, siblings, and parents.

Family of procreation The nuclear family formed by marriage; consists of self, spouse, and children.

Family policy A definite course or method of action with the intent of influencing or determining present and future forms of family organization, behaviours, and decisions; may be implemented and enforced at local, provincial, and federal levels.

Fecundity The biological potential of a woman to bear children (in contrast to *fertility*, the actual number of births).

Fertility The actual number of births to women of childbearing age.

Fertility rate The number of live births per thousand women ages 15 to 44.

Fictive kinship Exchange patterns resembling those of kin in which nonrelated friends offer services, support, and goods.

Fraternal polyandry The marriage of one woman to two or more men, all of whom are brothers.

Function As related to a structural-functional frame of reference, what a system does (the functions it performs) or the consequences of a given form of structure.

Gender The umbrella term that refers to the totality of being male or female, which may or may not correspond precisely to one's sex.

Gender identity The way one defines or perceives oneself in terms of one's sex, male or female; sexual identity.

Gender role The expected behaviours appropriate to one's gender that are assigned by a given culture.

Group marriage The marriage of two or more women to two or more men at the same time.

Hermeneutics The art or theory of interpretation.

Heterogamy A marriage pattern in which individuals marry outside their own group. **Exogamy** is the *requirement* that individuals marry outside their group.

Heterosexuality Sexual preference for members of the opposite sex.

Homelessness The condition of individuals and families who do not have dwellings in which to live and thus no stable place of residence within a community.

Homogamy A marriage pattern in which people marry others with similar social characteristics.

Homosexuality Sexual preference for members of the same sex.

Homosexual marriage A couple of the same sex who share a common residence, who have made a sexual and emotional commitment, and who recognize one another as united in marriage.

Horizontal mobility A change from one social status to another that is roughly equivalent.

Household The group of persons who occupy a housing unit.

Househusband A husband who stays at home and performs the domestic tasks and care of the children while his wife is engaged in full-time paid employment.

Hypergamy A marriage pattern in which the female marries upward into a higher social stratum (the male marries downward).

Hypogamy A marriage pattern in which the female marries downward into a lower social stratum (the male marries upward).

Hypothesis A statement of a relationship between variables that can be put to an empirical test.

Ideal-type constructs Hypothetical models of opposite extremes that provide contrasting (polar) qualities with which to characterize any social phenomenon.

Impact analysis Research aimed at assessing the intended and unintended consequences of family policy and programs.

Incest Socially forbidden sexual relationships or marriage with certain close relatives.

Independent variable A variable that causes a change or variation in another variable (termed the *dependent variable*).

Infertility The inability to conceive or give birth to a child.

Institution A stable cluster of values, norms, statuses, and roles that develop around a basic social need.

Intergenerational mobility A change in the social status of family members from one generation to the next.

Internalization The process by which one makes society's values part of one's personality.

In vitro fertilization The conception of a baby outside a woman's body (as in a laboratory dish); the fertilized egg is then placed within the woman's uterus for it to develop.

Joint family One type of extended family in which brothers share property but do not always live in a single household.

Kin A network of persons who are related by common ancestry (birth), adoption, or marriage.

Latchkey children Children who are unsupervised for part of the day, often the time between the end of the school day and the time a parent gets home from work.

Legal separation The state in which legally married couples maintain separate residences and have established legal responsibilities of support, rights of visitation, and so on.

Lesbian A female who is sexually oriented toward other females.

Levirate The marriage of a widow to the brother of her deceased husband.

Life course A developmental perspective of change that focuses on an individual's own life span, social time and transitions, or the historical time in which a person lives.

Life expectancy The average number of years that a person in a given population cohort can expect to live.

Lifespan The maximum length of life possible in a given society.

Macho or Machismo As used popularly in North America, *macho* means to be very masculine; as used in traditional Spanish or Latin America, *machismo* is an ideal of manliness, characterized by strength, daring, virility, and authoritarianism.

Macrolevel policy A policy that focuses on large-scale units, such as social categories, systems, and forms of social organization that affect families (taxation, medical care, employment, housing, education, laws, and so on).

Marital separation The state in which individuals are legally married but do not share a common household or residence.

Marriage A socially approved sexual union of some permanence between two or more persons.

"Marriage squeeze" The effects of an imbalance between the number of males and females in the prime marriage ages due to rising or falling birth rates and the median age difference at marriage.

Mating gradient The tendency for women to seek men of similar or higher status and of men to seek women of similar or lower status; the result is that high-status women and low-status men are less likely to date and marry.

Matriarchal family A family in which the wife rules or has dominance over the husband.

Matrilineal system A family system that traces descent and inheritance through the mother's line.

Matrilocal residence A family system in which a newly married couple is expected to live with the wife's family.

Mediation A conflict resolution process where a divorcing couple meets with a third party who helps them negotiate an agreement on property settlement, child support and custody, and other important matters.

Mésalliance Marriage with a person of a lower social position.

Mesolevel policy A policy that focuses on groups and organizations as mediating structures between the large-scale macro units and the small-scale micro units.

Microlevel policy A policy that focuses on small-scale units, such as individuals and small-group interaction.

Midlife transition The changes that take place in men and women at about age 40 or 45 as they reassess where they have been and what lies ahead; traditionally referred to as *midlife crisis*.

Minority group Any group that is subordinate to another group.

Modified-nuclear and modified-extended families Nuclear families that retain considerable autonomy yet maintain a coalition with other nuclear families with whom they exchange goods and services.

Monogamy A marriage pattern in which one male is married to one female at a time.

Neolocal residence A family system in which a newly married couple is expected to establish a new place of residence, separate from their parents.

"No-fault" divorce The legal dissolution of marriage based on irreconcilable differences where neither party is at fault.

Norm A rule that tells members of a society how to behave in a particular situation.

Nuclear family Any two or more persons of the same or adjoining generation, related by blood, marriage, or adoption, and sharing a common residence.

Oedipus complex According to Freudians, the unconscious desire of the male to marry his mother.

Opportunity cost A way of measuring the societal value of household work by estimating what homemakers would earn if they were employed for money.

Orderly replacement The notion that successive generations are duplicates of or similar to preceding generations.

Ordinal position in birth order One's position of birth among siblings, such as being the oldest or youngest child.

Parallel marriage A marriage in which the husband and wife perform similar tasks on an equitable basis; both are employed and both share child care and domestic tasks.

Patriarchal family A family in which the husband rules or has dominance over the wife.

Patrilineal system A family system that traces descent and inheritance through the father's line.

Patrilocal residence A family system in which a newly married couple is expected to live with the husband's family.

Peer group A group of people with similar or equal status and usually of similar age.

Perinatal Occurring near the time of birth.

Pluralism Many and varied forms of family and marital organization.

Polyandry The marriage of one woman to more than one man at the same time.

Polygamy The marriage of one man or one woman to more than one wife or more than one husband at the same time.

Polygyny The marriage of one man to more than one woman at the same time.

Postparental period The stage of the family life cycle in which children typically leave home and are legally and socially recognized as adults; the conjugal family returns to a two-person, married-couple household and the single parent to a one-person household.

Poverty level A classification of families below a specified income, based on a sliding scale of money income that is adjusted for factors such as family size, composition, and farm/nonfarm residence.

Power The ability to control or influence the behaviour of others, even without their consent.

Primary group A small group of people who interact in personal, direct, and intimate ways.

Principle of least interest The notion that the partner with the least interest in a relationship is in a position to exploit the other.

Progressive Denoting groups and persons who view families as pluralistic and accept change and nontraditional life-styles as legitimate.

Proletariat The class, or social group, of people who labour and serve as the instrument of production for the bourgeoisie.

Propinquity Proximity; with regard to marriage, the notion that persons who live close to one another are more likely to marry.

Proposition A statement of the relationship between two or more concepts.

Random sample A group of persons selected in a way such that every member of the population had an equal chance of being chosen.

Rape Sexual intercourse by force or threat of force without the consent of the victim; it can involve vaginal, anal, or oral penetration. *Marital rape* refers to the same conditions occurring between spouses. *Acquaintance rape* is where the assailant is personally known to the victim.

Reciprocity The two-way exchange of goods or services; basic to a social exchange frame of reference.

Reconstituted family A family including a man and a woman, at least one of whom has been previously married, and the children from one or both prior marriages; a stepfamily.

Reference group A group with which persons psychologically identify and to whom people refer when making evaluations of themselves and their behaviour.

Remarriage Marriage by anyone who has previously been married.

Replacement cost A way of measuring the societal value of household work by estimating the earnings of someone who does similar work (babysitting, cleaning, cooking, etc.) in the labour market.

Role The social expectations or behaviours that accompany a particular status.

Role conflict The situation in which incompatible expectations or behaviours accompany a given status or set of statuses.

Role taking The ability to assume the status of persons with whom one interacts and to see the world from their perspective.

Secondary group A group whose members interact in an impersonal manner, have few emotional ties, and come together for a specific, practical purpose.

Sequential or serial monogamy Marriage to a succession of partners but only one at a time.

Sex The biological condition of being male or female.

Sex control The ability to control the sex of an unborn offspring.

Sex ratio The number of males per hundred females in a population.

Sex roles Learned and expected patterns of behaviour associated with being biologically of one sex or the other.

Sexual harassment Deliberate and unwanted sexual behaviour, such as propositioning, abusive or suggestive language, physical attacks, or gestures such as body language, whistles, and stares; serves to annoy, intimidate, or threaten the person at whom it is directed.

Sexualization Sexual socialization; the process by which individuals acquire their sexual self-concepts, values, attitudes, and behaviours.

Sexual script The learned designation of the who, what, when, where, and why of one's sexuality.

Sibling One's brother or sister.

Significant other A person with whom one psychologically identifies and whose opinions are important.

Single parent Generally, used in reference to a mother/child or father/child nuclear family unit.

Social class An aggregate of individuals who occupy a broadly similar position on a scale of wealth, prestige, and power.

Social conflict frame of reference A perspective of society that views conflict as natural, permanent, and inevitable, and as a significant source of social change.

Social exchange frame of reference A perspective that seeks to explain personal and social behaviours based on reciprocity of rewards and costs.

Social mobility The extent to which it is possible for an individual or family to move from one social class to another.

Social self The organization of internalized roles developed in interaction with others.

Social stratification The ranking of people into positions of equality and inequality; the arrangement of social classes.

Social structure The parts or components of a social system and the way it is organized; the network of interrelated statuses.

Social system A set of interrelated social statuses (positions) and the accompanying expectations (roles) that accompany them.

Socialization The process of learning the rules of and expectations for behaviour for a given society.

Society A group of interacting individuals sharing the same territory and participating in a common culture.

Sociology The study of human society and social behaviour.

Sororal polygamy The marriage of one man to two or more women, all of whom are sisters.

Sororate The marriage of a widower to the sister of his deceased wife.

Status A socially defined position occupied by a person; may be ascribed (age, race, sex, and so forth) or achieved (husband, father, teacher, and so forth).

Stem family An extended-family type consisting of two families in adjacent generations joined by economic and blood ties.

Stepchildren The children by a former marriage of one's husband or wife (stepmother, wife of one's father by remarriage; stepbrother, son of one's stepparent by a former marriage; etc.).

Stepfamily A family including a man and a woman, at least one of whom has been previously married, and often including children from that previous marriage. *Simple stepfamilies* include children from just one remarried parent; *complex stepfamilies* include children from both remarried parents.

Stressor events Crisis-provoking events and situations for which families have little or no preparation.

Structural-functional frame of reference A perspective that emphasizes the units of organization plus the consequences of that particular structural arrangement.

Subculture A group of persons that shares in the overall culture of a society but also has its own distinctive values, norms, and life-styles.

Surrogate mother A woman who conceives, carries, and bears a child for another couple.

"Swinging" A type of extramarital coitus in which the couple openly and willingly engage in sexual relationships with other married persons; sometimes referred to as *co-marital sexual mate sharing* or *consensual adultery*.

Symbolic interaction frame of reference A perspective that stresses interaction among people as well as the social processes that occur within individuals made possible by language and internalized meanings.

Symmetrical family A family as a consumption unit rather than a production unit in which marital roles based on gender are eliminated.

Theory A set of logically and systematically interrelated propositions that explain some particular process.

Traditional family The pattern of family organization, customs, life-styles, and behaviours passed down from prior generations and maintained or valued because of an idealized image of how things once were and should be today.

Unilineal system A family system that traces descent and inheritance through either the male line or the female line.

Universal permanent availability The notion that any individual is a potential mate, available for marriage, with any other individual at any time.

Values Ideas and beliefs about what is worthwhile and important; a value theory of mate selection suggests that people select partners who share similar values.

Variable A concept that represents degree or value; a characteristic such as age, class, or income that can vary from one person or context to another.

Vertical mobility Social mobility that involves movement toward a higher or lower social status.

Violence Any act carried out with the intention of physically hurting someone else; family violence focuses on behaviours among parents, spouses, children, siblings, and people who are elderly.

Virginity The state of not having ever engaged in sexual intercourse.

White-collar families The middle-class category of professionals, clerical workers, salespeople, and other employees who have traditionally worn white shirts in their work; often differentiated from blue-collar, or working-class, families.

Widowhood The state of having lost one's spouse through death.

NAME INDEX

SUBJECT INDEX

P

PHOTO CREDITS

Chapter 1: p. 1, R.P. Kingston Collection/The Picture Cube; p. 12, Kathleen Belleisles; p. 18, Gail Kenney/Prentice Hall Archives.

Chapter 2: p. 32, Emily Meetsma; p. 39, Mahoney/The Image Works, Inc.; p. 43, Blue C/Liaison Agency; p. 49, Bob Daemmrich/The Image Works, Inc.

Chapter 3: p. 59, Michael Siluk/The Image Works, Inc.; p. 79, Jim Whitmer/Stock, Boston, Inc.; p. 82, Katherine McGlynn/The Image Works, Inc.

Chapter 4: p. 90, Smith/Monkmeyer Press; p. 99, David M. Grossman/Photo Researchers, Inc.; p. 106, Ian Macdonald/Canapress.

Chapter 5: p. 118, Spencer Grant/The Picture Cube; p. 121, Deborah Kahn-Kalas/Stock, Boston Inc.; p. 129, Harvey Finkle/Impact Visuals; p. 136, Ed Carlin/The Picture Cube.

Chapter 6: p. 152, Jean Higgins/Aristock, Inc.; p. 163, Laima Druskis/Stock Boston; p. 173, Chester Higgins Jr./ Photo Researchers, Inc.

Chapter 7: p. 181, Elizabeth Crews/The Image Works, Inc.; p. 196, CanadaWide/ Toronto Sun; p. 202, Judy Gelles/Stock, Boston, Inc.

Chapter 8: p. 209, Elizabeth Crews/The Image Works; p. 225, Prentice Hall Archives; p. 233, David S. Strickler/The Picture Cube.

Chapter 9: p. 239, Rhoda Sidney/The Image Works, Inc.; p. 247, Mary Ellen Lepionka; p. 256, Dick Hemingway.

Chapter 10: p. 270, CanadaWide; p. 279, Robert Kalman/The Image Works, Inc.; p. 287, George Cohen/Impact Visuals; p. 295, Spencer Grant III/Stock, Boston, Inc.

Chapter 11: p. 302, Rhoda Sidney/Leo de Wys, Inc.; p. 314, H. Armstrong Roberts; p. 326, Anna Kaufman Moon/Stock, Boston, Inc.

Chapter 12: p. 335, CanadaWide, p. 344, CanadaWide; p. 350, Sarah Putnam/The Picture Cube, Inc.